Modern Art

A Critical Introduction

This exciting Introduction, now in its second edition, provides a comprehensive introduction to modern and contemporary art. Pam Meecham and Julie Sheldon bring together theory, history and the art works themselves to help students understand how and why meanings are formed in relation to art practices in the modern period.

Modern Art: A Critical Introduction traces the historical and contemporary contexts for understanding modern art movements and the theories which influenced and attempted to explain them. This approach forgoes the chronological march of art movements and '-isms' in favour of looking at the ways in which art has been understood. It investigates the main developments in art interpretation from the same period, from Kant to post-structuralism, and draws examples from a wide range of art genres including painting, sculpture, photography, installation and performance art. The book includes detailed discussions of visual art practices both inside and outside the museum.

This new edition has been restructured to make the key themes as accessible as possible and updated to include many more recent examples of art practice. An expanded glossary and notes section and a list of key figures and events provide definitions of the range of terms used within theoretical discussion and critical reference. Individual chapters explore key themes of the modern era, such as the relationship between artists and galleries, the politics of representation, the changing nature of self-expression, the public monument, nature and the urban, the 'machine aesthetic', performance art and the changing construction of the body. Illustrated with a wide range of visual examples, *Modern Art: A Critical Introduction* is a lively and accessible account of modern art and its histories.

Pam Meecham is Senior Lecturer in Museum and Gallery Studies at the Institute of Education, University of London. **Julie Sheldon** is Programme Leader for BA (Hons) Art History in the Department of Contextual Studies at Liverpool School of Art and Design, Liverpool John Moores University.

Modern Art
A Critical Introduction

Second edition

Pam Meecham
and
Julie Sheldon

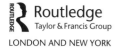
Routledge
Taylor & Francis Group

LONDON AND NEW YORK

First edition published 2000;
second edition published 2005
by Routledge
2 Park Square, Milton Park, Abingdon, Oxon OX14 4RN

Simultaneously published in the USA and Canada
by Routledge
270 Madison Ave, New York, NY 10016

Routledge is an imprint of the Taylor & Francis Group

© 2000, 2005 Pam Meecham and Julie Sheldon

Typeset in Janson
by Florence Production Ltd, Stoodleigh Court, Stoodleigh, Devon
Printed and bound in Great Britain
by TJ International Ltd, Padstow, Cornwall

British Library Cataloguing in Publication Data
A catalogue record for this book is available from the British Library

Library of Congress Cataloging in Publication Data
Meecham, Pam.
  Modern art: a critical introduction/Pam Meecham and Julie
  Sheldon. – 2nd ed.
      p. cm.
    1. Modernism (Art). 2. Postmodernism. 3. Art, Modern – 20th
  century. 4. Art – Study and teaching. I. Sheldon, Julie, 1963–.
  II. Title.
  N6494.M64M44 2004
  709'.04–dc22   2004010473

ISBN 0–415–28193–8 (hbk)
ISBN 0–415–28194–6 (pbk)

For Doris and Barbara

Contents

Illustrations

Colour plates

Acknowledgements

The following extracts are reproduced courtesy of the copyright holders:
Chapter 1, p. 13 Epigraph from *Batman: the killing joke*, courtesy of DC Comics.
Chapter 2, p. 60 *Transcendence* by Richard Pousette-Dart, courtesy of the Estate of Richard Pousette-Dart.
Chapter 8, p. 258 *Piss Posy* by Helen Chadwick, courtesy of the Zelda Cheatle Gallery.

The authors would like to thank the School of Education and Community Studies and Liverpool School of Art and Design at Liverpool John Moores University for supporting this project. In addition our thanks to colleagues for their practical support and encouragement, in particular to Colin Fallows, Neil Hall, Sean Halligan, Elaine Prisk and Ken Travis. Other thanks should go to Jindra Hubena of National Museums and Galleries in Prague, Nicola Taschevski, who acted as translator and photographic adviser and David Ollerton. We are grateful to our commissioning editor Rebecca Barden at Routledge for her patience and confidence in the project. The authors would also like to thank the administrative and technical staff, Josephine Borradaile, Kelvin Gwilliam and Peter Thomas in the School of Arts and Humanities at the Institute of Education, University of London for their unfailing practical support for this project. Finally our personal thanks to family and friends who have been forced to live with 'the book', especially to Joseph Ollerton and Colin Fallows.

Pam Meecham and Julie Sheldon, June 2004

Introduction

They come out of a tradition which has been very *talky*. The theory has bound itself into the work so tightly that it in fact generates another form.

(Laurie Anderson)

Even a cursory glance at the processes by which two art works are made, one at the beginning of the twentieth century – Adolph A. Weinman sculpting a cow in 1903 (see Figure A) – and the other at the end – Damien Hirst in a field with a cow in 1997 (Figure B) – demonstrates shifts in our understanding of what it is that constitutes, first, the *artist* and, second, *art* itself. Weinman and Hirst stand in a field, each with his bovine subject: Weinman fashions a small clay cow model, probably to be later cast in bronze, demonstrating the requisite manual skills to accomplish the task and achieve a convincing likeness of the real thing. Hirst, ninety or so years later, seems implicated in a related set of concerns. In *Some Comfort Gained from the Acceptance of the Inherent Lies in Everything* (1996) (Figure C) Hirst's now-familiar dead-animal motif is the focus. Unlike Weinman's art work, however, Hirst's requires the skills of the taxidermist and the aquarium builder. Each work is a 'ready-made' of sorts (in the sense that Marcel Duchamp had first coined the term to describe existing objects that he would redesignate as art objects). Apart from its title, Figure C would not, at first sight, look out of place in a Natural History Museum. Closer scrutiny of Hirst's piece reveals not randomness but a strictly ordered, if unscientific, pattern: twelve glass tanks contain the bodies of two cows (A and B), each divided into six segments, those of cow A alternating with those of cow B. The title of the piece, moreover, underscores Hirst's philosophical (as opposed to zoological) ruminations.

The juxtaposing of Weinman's and Hirst's work demonstrates something of both the continuity and the ruptures within twentieth-century art. The way we make art, as well as write and talk about it, has shifted. What we attempt in this book is to show how changing ways of making art and changing ways of writing about art belong to a broader climate of change. Theoretical discourses – such as poststructuralism, feminism, Marxism, postcolonialism – often drive contemporary art practice. Of course, this is not to say that Weinman's work is not theoretically driven, it is, but its theoretical

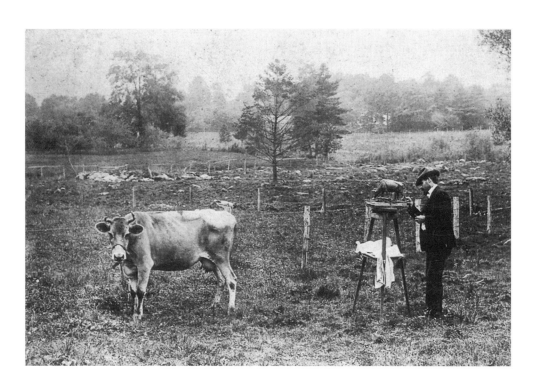

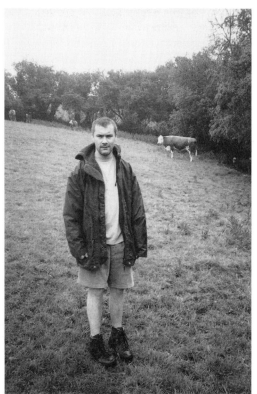

Figure A (above)   Adolph A. Weinman sculpting a cow, 1903.

Figure B (left)   Johnny Shand Kydd, *Damien Hirst***, 1997.** Courtesy of the artist and Jay Jopling/White Cube, London.

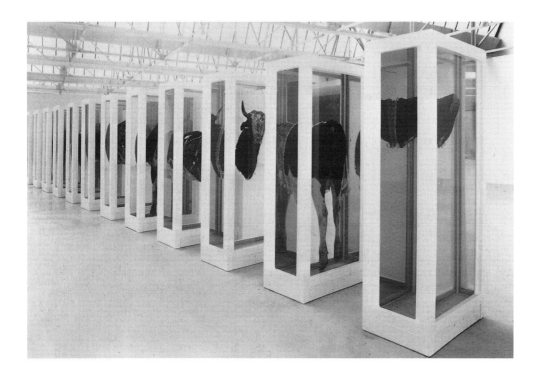

Figure C   Damien Hirst, *Some Comfort Gained from the Acceptance of the Inherent Lies in Everything*, 1996. Courtesy of the artist and Jay Jopling/White Cube, London.

co-ordinates map a different terrain. We will see how theory and art practice are linked, even in cases in which no link is evident or acknowledged.

For the student of modern art and art history, an inspection of the literature reveals 'disciplines' torn between theory and practice. There are numerous anthologies of art which bring together the received authorities of the twentieth century. And there are other overviews of modern art which chart the 'story of art' (linear histories which divide modern art into a chronology of the dominant historical '-isms' – impressionism, expressionism, cubism, surrealism, etc.). But these illustrate our point: literature on the subject of modern art often founders either because it surveys the art of the period in terms which serve to isolate that art from the contextual factors that contribute so vitally to its intelligibility, or because it presents historical accounts of the period which have little or no connection to the works of art that readers may encounter. Although the genealogy of art can afford important structural lessons, this book has little concern with the chronological ordering of the art of the modern period. We prefer that the history of art should be thematically driven: we try to uncover 'significant' moments in the critical analysis of art and to consider art works as responses to the changing contexts of their production, consumption and evaluation.

The main aims of this book, then, are to locate modern art in its varied contexts, to look critically at recent developments in theoretical inquiry, and to indicate how art practice and theory may be usefully integrated.

Art history as a discipline has undergone considerable revisions since the 1960s and has been compelled to re-evaluate the status of what it calls 'knowledge' – partly fuelled by massive social upheavals. As Figures A and C illustrate, what we think of as being art has changed over the course of the past century. Similarly art history (the way in which we classify and evaluate these works) has changed: there has been a drift within the discipline towards a broader understanding of visual culture, and art history's importation of literary and linguistic theories over the past thirty or so years has changed many of the basic premises on which the discipline has rested. We do not after all, it seems, actually *know* art history. By this statement we use the word *know* in the sense that the eighteenth-century philosopher Immanuel Kant thought of knowing – that is, as having an a-priori cognitive structure. To return to our illustrations, the grounds upon which we *know* Figure A are not the same as the knowledge required to understand Figure C. We no longer *know* art history, we suggest, because our conceptual frameworks for creating and solving problems appear to have multiplied.

Since the 1960s the human sciences have turned to language as a model for understanding culture in all its forms. One characteristic of contemporary art history has been its extensive use of non-art-historical texts. This assimilation permits connections between diverse and apparently unconnected material – drawing upon sociology, anthropology, linguistics, film and popular culture. It may be difficult to accept the relevance of theories which address subjects other than the agenda of art history, but the fact remains that such theories have gained credence in the discipline in recent years. On the whole, visual-art theorists have found it more difficult than their peers specialising in literature and film, for instance, to accommodate poststructuralist ideas. That is to say, poststructuralist concepts apparently are more readily applicable to written 'texts', as they are encoded in the same textual practices, than they are to works of art, which in relation to language present a different set of problems. The encroachment of text, for example from its incorporation in cubist collage early in the twentieth century to the entirely text-based images of artists such as Jenny Holzer in the 1990s, is matched, as Laurie Anderson has observed, by the increasingly 'talky' nature of modern art practice, exemplified in the observation 'minimal art, maximum explanation'. Jenny Holzer's work, such as the words *Protect Me From What I Want*, emblazoned in LED underneath Caesar's Palace in Las Vegas, is just one example of the use of text in contemporary art. As well as the increasing presence of text in art, it is important to grasp the sheer scale of the convergence of art with what is called 'textuality' over the past thirty years, a symptom of just how far contemporary thought is linguistically oriented. Hence the often-quoted poststructuralist maxim that unless you can articulate something it does not exist and therefore that we are all constructed 'in and by language', or, to put it simply, 'you are what you communicate'.

Meanwhile, the assimilation by art-historical studies of literary theory and sociology has introduced a whole new vocabulary into the art historian's lexicon. A comparison of the entries to be found in a dictionary of art from the 1970s with those in a more contemporary dictionary reveals just how many terms have been imported from discourses such as race, gender, semiotics and psychoanalysis and how even familiar words ('intention', 'representation', 'materialism') have acquired a layer of specific art-historical/cultural studies' meaning that is quite distinct from everyday usage. Even the style of writing about art has changed. A relentless ticker tape of theoretical exposition

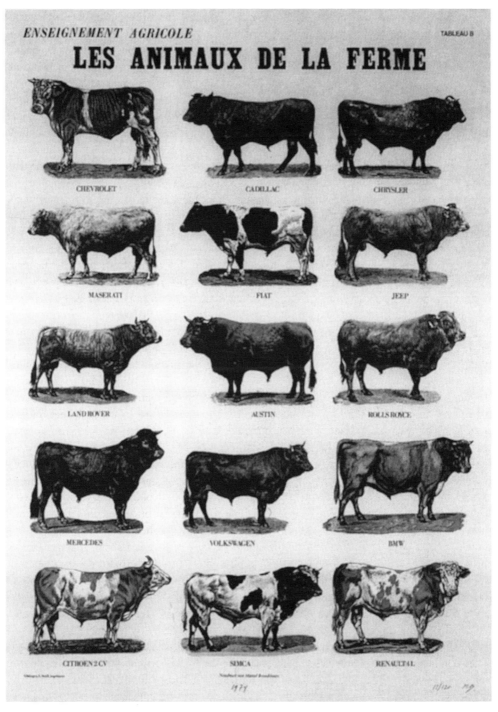

Figure D   Marcel Broodthaers, *Les Animaux de la ferme*, 1974. © DACS, 2004. Courtesy of Kenewig Galerie, Cologne. In *Les Animaux de la ferme* Broodthaers explores the arbitrary nature of language and continues the project of looking at the way classification systems function and so produces what could be termed a second order of classification.

is poured out featuring phrases such as 'offering a reading', 'mapping the trajectory' and 'interrogating the image' to describe a methodology far removed from the apparent simplicity of nineteenth-century doctrines of 'truth to nature' and 'beauty is truth'.

One hundred years ago the relationship between art and language was very different. Art critics used colourful language (poetic equivalence) in their attempt to recreate in words the thrill they felt when looking at works of art they held in high regard. These were not, by and large, professional art historians but interested amateurs and 'men of letters'. 'Connoisseurship' required art historians to use language which either investigated the art object (usually through archival research) or made philosophical points about art in general (often in terms of quality, beauty and morality). Underlying the central tenets of 'art appreciation' lay a sincere belief in the power of art to enhance, uplift and improve human life. In the democratic revolutions of the early twentieth century, connoisseurial art appreciation came to be seen as both reactionary and elitist, a powerful representative of class values. Presented independently of socio-political, economic or historical context, connoisseurship was supported by notions about aesthetics which acted as criteria about what did and did not constitute good taste.

The formulation of principles of taste and beauty in art implied that 'beauty' (in itself a loaded concept) resides in the art object and that 'taste' is the viewer's capacity for appreciating the beautiful. Increasingly with modern art, where beauty is often redefined or irrelevant, the services of an art critic are required to intercede with and to define the work's quality and to establish parameters of taste. Ironically, the early twentieth-century insistence on the capacity of art to 'speak for itself' did not undermine the presumption that in certain viewers (usually white, male and middle class) the capacity to appreciate artistic beauty was innate. This notion of a timeless faculty for the recognition and appreciation of 'great' art pervaded the diverse discourses that passed for art history, which, as in most of the humanities, were fixed upon Western culture and the output of male artists. So art history became the history of individual men whose genius was determined by their unique 'essence', which was capable of transcending conditions of time and place and 'spoke' to those possessed of the proper aesthetic sensibility – or 'taste'. However, the radical shift in understanding of personal identity as somehow immanent to, but also differentiated from, the body to something that is reconstituted in and by language ('you are what you communicate') has undermined many such 'common-sense' givens. This is not to suggest that there are no continuities or that, as Weinman and Hirst jointly demonstrate, we have altogether dispensed with the values of the past. However, as a general view, modern art and its histories have been, and still are, subject to quite substantial revisions.

In recent years art history has dispensed with the kind of overt connoisseurship we have just described, and to such an extent that we are often shy of using words like 'quality' and 'beauty' in case our professional authority is mistaken for amateurish enthusiasm or, worse, elitism. Instead of appreciating art in terms of its quality and beauty, we will talk about 'reading' works of art (although what we actually mean by 'reading' is an endeavour altogether different from the conventional sense of the word). We do not necessarily read a narrative or interpret the story of a work of art, even though this might still play a supporting role in our analysis. Often narrative elements are missing or are subordinate to what we call 'modern' in art works, or the claim, made on behalf of the modernist art work, that it is 'a thing in itself' and not an adjunct to narrative, inhibits such reading. So if 'reading' works of art is not solely a matter of uncovering content, then 'reading' has to be understood in a climate of contingency. By and large, we 'read' art works by putting them in one or other context or measuring them against one or other theory of art. This inevitably means that theory – as, for example, it is assimilated by Hirst – comes out into the open, even to the extent that, occasionally, it seems as if art works have to be, from the outset, theoretically accountable.

This growing tendency towards declaring the theory under which you labour, a practice that grew largely out of Marxism, has spawned a new set of cultural gurus who lend their names to diverse theoretical positions. We have seen how the history of '-isms' has been superseded. Somewhat perversely, we have to acknowledge that there has been a trend simultaneously towards '-ians' – Freudian, Greenbergian, Lacanian, etc. – which foreground a particular methodology or act as a working example of how theory is applied. These theories, individually and collectively, tend to confound rather than confirm the grounds on which much of the confidence of the past was based. These theories have radically altered our understanding of the staple of art history – its roll of great artists and its canon of 'masterpieces'. At best, this has resulted in a broadening of the canon to include works by previously marginalised artists and art forms – in part the outcome of a collapse of divisions between 'high art' and popular culture. At worst, it has resulted in 'indifferencism' – a sense that anything goes and an academic inability to define quality.

So why should we pay attention to theory? What we have been calling 'theory' is actually a summation of all kinds of shifts in thinking about art that have taken place since the Enlightenment, although there is a growing tendency to ground theory in 1960s and 1970s poststructuralism. Theory can take different forms, positions, methods and practices – some of which do not naturally combine, some of which confusingly overlap, while others again are simply irreconcilable. All the same, theory has become something of a dogma in all arts and humanities disciplines in recent years. There is, however, a good argument to say that theory has, and always has had, its place; it is simply because it has never before been incumbent upon us to acknowledge that we are all, knowingly or unknowingly, in thrall to one or other theory.

It would probably be fair to say that for art history, as an academic discipline, the acknowledgement of the importance of theory, from the 1960s onwards, has been part and parcel of a general receptiveness to poststructuralist and postcolonial theories. This in itself was a reaction to the particular kind of art history (connoisseurial liberal humanist) we have already discussed. Art history was almost the last of the disciplines to re-evaluate its procedures. Art historians remained blinkered to the pivotal changes of the 1960s – such as the civil rights and women's movements, gay rights and the declarations by the former colonies of their independence. Ironically, perhaps, even historians in thrall to varying degrees of theoretical Marxism resolutely failed to acknowledge the artistic contribution of groups identified as 'other'. As the Guerrilla Girls, an anonymous feminist collective, have pointed out, even Pliny the Elder, Boccaccio and Vasari acknowledged more women artists than ever did Meyer Schapiro or T.J. Clark, two of the major twentieth-century Marxist art historians. As late as 1983, Norman Bryson wrote:

> It is a sad fact: art history lags behind the study of the other arts . . . while the last three decades or so have witnessed extraordinary and fertile change in the study of

> literature, of history, of anthropology, in the discipline of art history there has reigned a stagnant peace . . . at an increasingly remote margin of the humanities . . . little can change without a radical re-examination of the methods art history uses – the tacit assumptions that guide the normal activity of the art historian.
>
> (Bryson 1983: xi)

It is very revealing that in the partial shake-up which followed the 1960s it is phrases such as 'untheorised' and 'unreconstructed' that came to describe the old art history – even in relation to the formidable scholarship of Erwin Panofsky and Ernst Gombrich. Of course, to claim enlightenment at the beginning of the twenty-first century at the expense of the 'naive' art history of a former age would be undeniably smug. At the same time, it would be reductive to dismiss the all-singing, all-dancing new art history as just a wink in the direction of 'political correctness'. Even though theory has injected the new art history with a suspicion of such 'totalising' ideas as 'great art' and 'old masters', as a discipline art history is more fragmented than ever before. Any notion that the old art history has been swept aside by a torrent of radicalism needs to be tempered by the acknowledgement that blockbuster exhibitions of Picasso and Monet and monographs on 'geniuses' of art remained buoyed up because of the support they received from institutional practices.

All the same, the new art historian, just as likely to be sited in the cultural studies department as in the art history faculty, considers art in significantly disparate terms from those of his or her forebears. The new art historian will, for instance, probably be sceptical of the ideological construction of 'the artist' and will openly acknowledge that trying to uncover the artist's intention (as a received formula for uncovering the meaning of an art work) is a fruitless and *passé* enterprise. He or she is unlikely to hold original art works in any great esteem – in fact the 'aura' of the original art work has been replaced by self-reflexive debates about authenticity per se. The new art history argues that 'man' is a construct of social and historical circumstances, that 'he' is not an autonomous agent of historical change. Feminism, lesbian and gay criticism and postcolonial art history have cumulatively shown how the claims to universality that used to be made on behalf of literature, music, art and culture are bogus. There is no such thing as human nature through which the human 'essence' is expressed, only a process of 'subjectification' which, as we will see, is part of the push and pull of the art of the modern period.

In a nutshell, then, what has come to operate under the aegis of postmodern theory, in all its shapes and forms, has issued us with several warnings: at its most extreme, that everything is contingent and nothing is absolute; that truth is always provisional and partial; and that 'reading' a work of art is a local, relative and unstable endeavour which will inevitably be revised by other 'readers'. The plurality of theoretical approaches in which all positions are 'open and equal' has given us a plurality of conceptual frameworks – histories for history, truths for truth. What goes, then, is the quest for the definitive, abiding, universal interpretation of the unique work of art – once the foundation for art-historical enterprises.

But why should we pay such attention to a set of theories that make art history more complicated? The growth of theory to its current predominance has coincided with wholesale re-evaluations not just of art but of what it is to be human in the twenty-first century. Whether theoretically denominational or polysemic, 'theory' frames the mindset of the present time. Just as it has become unfashionable for academics to produce speculative historical overviews or to identify overarching patterns in history, the history of art is now a set of histories – each conjunctional, local and discursive. The 'postmodern condition' or the 'crisis of confidence' of recent years has entailed some fundamental reappraisals of the kinds of 'facts' each discipline used to take for granted. As we have seen, the idea of the history of art as a history of great individuals had been steadily undermined, but thought-provoking writings, such as Roland Barthes's essay 'The Death of the Author' (1968), have dealt a blow to some of the unreflective adulation accorded to artistic genius. As Barthes put it, 'everything must be *disentangled*, nothing *deciphered*' (Barthes 1977: 147).

At the same time, the French philosopher Jacques Derrida described a 'decentred' intellectual universe. The old art history (and Derrida is writing principally about metaphysically loaded systems of language) used to place (white, bourgeois, heterosexual) 'man' at the centre of things. Anything that deviated from this centre was 'other' or marginal. But Derrida's universe contains no fixed centre and offers no assurances for art history of an artist at the centre of an art work whose intentions, emotions and desires are recoverable by us, the trained viewer. Derrida was ushering in a host of interpretations which would never stand as facts in a decentred universe. Parallel with the demotion of guaranteed facts, there have been a number of apocalyptic texts announcing the demise of history: Hans Belting's *The End of the History of Art?* (1984), Fukuyama's *The End of History and the Last Man* (1992) and Arthur C. Danto's *After the*

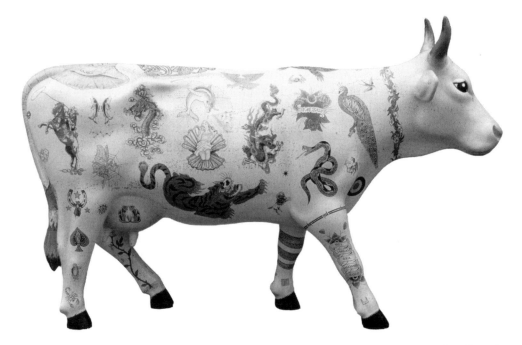

Figure E *Tattoo*, **painted by the inmates of HMP Wormwood Scrubs for CowParade London 2002.** Courtesy of CowParade Europe Ltd.

End of Art: contemporary art and the pale of history (1997). Danto identifies the pop artist Andy Warhol as the artist who, in the 1960s, single-handedly overturned the modern movement. According to Danto this heralded the end of art. The kind of rampant pluralism we experience today, in which contemporary art can be video art, installation, super-realism, abstract painting, is what he terms 'post-historical', and others might call simply postmodern. In some senses, then, postmodernism has firmed the resolve of those in an entrenched position whilst acting as a fillip to a confederation of irreconcilable positions.

We began this Introduction with the work of two artists, one working with the motif of the cow and the other with an actual cow. In a recent art project, *CowParade*, the cow has become the vehicle for a postmodern art practice (Figure E). The project involves artists from all over the world, who decorate a life-sized statue of a cow with their own designs or homages to other artists. These cows are combined into a herd and displayed in towns and cities worldwide – among them Chicago, Prague, London, Sydney and Oregon. The series is also viewable on a web site which allows viewers also to vote for their favourite cows and to participate in an on-line auction to purchase the cows or miniature replicas of the most popular. The almost flippant enterprise of decorating cows undermines the seriousness of so much art practice, but the distribution of knowledge about the project and the possibilities for future expansion make CowParade emblematic of the shifts and turns within modern art that this book explores.

Chapter by chapter

Chapter 1 introduces the key debates that underpin the period covered by this book. As the title 'What, when and where was modernism?' suggests, any certainties around modernism have been rendered unstable, especially since the 1970s and the arrival of a new term 'postmodernism'. The seemingly monolithic 'universals' of modernism – genius, essentialism, truth – have been called into question and subsequently revised. This chapter seeks to locate modernism in a set of practices and debates, and to open up the terrain to contemporary thinking. Many of the key terms and debates that take place throughout the book are introduced.

Chapter 2 offers an alternative view of mainstream modernism – as fundamentally pragmatic, optimistic and urban. Examining a number of artists who 'retreated from the urban' in the modern period, we see how modernism has had a difficult relationship with the spiritual and the mystical agendas of some of its key protagonists. Here we consider how and why some artists removed themselves from the city as the site of their modernity and chose instead to create from 'the interior'. We consider and question the claims of artists who used 'primitive' subjectivity and 'rural simplicity' as the basis of their quest for greater self-expression, and investigate the overlapping of the notions of 'subjectivity' and 'creativity'.

In Chapter 3 we concentrate on the changing nature of the public monument. Drawing on a wide range of older and contemporary examples, we explore the changing nature of public spaces and the function of monuments as visible manifestations of the changing relations of power and display.

and the lifelikeness of their work: apocryphal it may be, but the notion of good practice can be summed up in the tale of the Greek painter who painted on a wall grapes that looked so 'real' that birds actually pecked at them. The modern period is marked by a redefinition of art's function in depicting as 'real' a representation of the world of appearances. As we can see from the photograph of Duchamp's *Fountain* (see Figure 1.1), it was more than lifelike: indeed, it was actually 'real' – a ready-made urinal, but a urinal *masquerading* as art. Paradoxically, denying the status of a piece as art was one way of guaranteeing that status, as happened, for instance, with Marcel Broodthaers' 7 *This Is Not Art*. Like much of Broodthaers' work, the ensemble piece explored the status and construction of objects designated art by questioning the authority of display. Similarly René Magritte questioned the viewers understanding of the image in *This Is Not a Pipe*, which is a painting of a pipe with '*Ceci n'est pas un pipe*' written underneath. This work can be seen as part of modernism's ambivalent attitude to representation and to forms of mimetic realism. Put simply, the painting is a painting not a pipe.

By the late 1960s, a nascent postmodernism compounded the questioning of earlier modernist artists about what form and function art should take through the conceptual art movement, Ian Burn's *No Object Implies the Existence of Any Other* (1967) making explicit the loss of confidence in the ability of art to represent the *real* by painting the appearance of the world. Burn's work consists of text placed across a framed mirror, which reflected back the viewer, inviting the viewer to reflect on his or her own subjectivity. This work was part of a powerful impulse by 1966 to make art as ideas rather than mimetic representations of things in the world.

At times it is difficult to see just what it is that characterises 'art' in the modern period, especially as the examples cited thus far all seem to question or dispense with the boundaries of the discipline or actively undermine previously highly regarded concepts or beliefs. The skills traditionally associated with sculpting are clearly absent from the work of Duchamp and Broodthaers, yet the repeated reproduction of the works in art books testifies to their importance in art history. Modernism in art seemed to be implicated in a kind of crisis about what the work of a work of art should be, which is also to ask why so many artists fetishised objects perceived to fall outside the traditional categories of art. However, the questioning of what art should be was not the only impulse for the modern artist. In tandem with this questioning arose another, not always compatible, demand for artists to be self-reflexive about the medium that they worked in. Although not embraced by all artists, there was a requirement to self-consciously interrogate art's own internal, usually formal, functions, as we saw with the rise of formalism in music and dance.

A return to the reworking of sculpture and to ready-made art especially spotlights these issues. As we saw, as early as 1916 Marcel Duchamp had installed 'ready-made' objects, such as bottle racks, hatstands and bicycle wheels, in the art gallery. By 1917 the most famous of these ready-mades – *Fountain*, the urinal – had entered art history as an iconic object. Duchamp asked whether art was merely dependent on the sanction of the artist and its display, when he attempted to exhibit the inverted urinal anonymously, signed 'R. Mutt', at a New York Independents' exhibition. Perversely, it became art precisely because it was rejected, particularly since Duchamp complied with the rules laid down for the open submission of art works. An anti-institutional stance, a climate of spirited opposition and a conscious breaking of boundaries seem to have been prerequisites of modernist art. This tradition was established in the nineteenth century with the Salon des Refusés (Salon of the Rejected) (1863) in Paris when Edouard Manet (1832–83), in a defining moment, defiantly displayed art works rejected by the official Academy. To have one's work summarily dismissed by an orthodox institution subsequently became the sign of a serious enterprise and a mark of modernism. It is noteworthy that co-option into what was increasingly the modernist *revolution* was often retrospective and puzzled many artists whose radicalism went only as far as the paintbrush. Duchamp's inverted urinal, *Fountain*, unseen by the public, was, however, validated by an authoritative photograph taken by the American modernist artist, photographer and gallery-owner Alfred Stieglitz. To enter the pantheon of modernist icons therefore, art works in the modern period did not need to be actually made, exhibited or even really to exist, often achieving celebrity through notoriety, and fame through infamy.

Painting was equally marked by forms of iconoclasm. To the uninitiated, Kasimir Malevich's paintings *Black Squares*, exhibited at '0.10 Exhibition' in Petrograd in 1915, can seem like a puzzling rejection of any imagery (Figure 1.2). All content but for the paint seems to have been evacuated from the canvases, and yet the paintings have been the object of sustained historical and curatorial interest. Although the look of paintings and sculpture had certainly changed compared with, say, a Vermeer or a Donatello, just when and why remains contested. To pick up a point which we raised earlier, the net results of what appear to have been artistic abandonments were cultural forms that

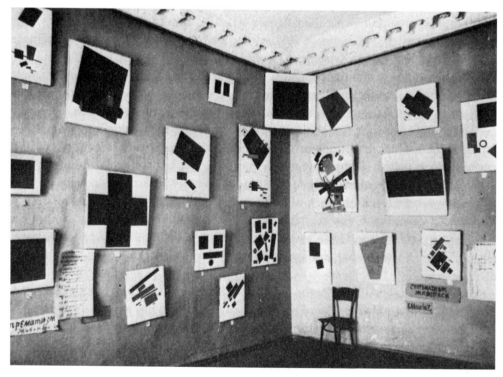

Figure 1.2 Kasimir Malevich, *0.10 Exhibition* in Petrograd, December 1915, with *Black Square*. Courtesy of the State Russian Museum, St Petersburg. Originally labelled 'trans-rational', the single-colour canvas was domestic in scale and was displayed in the same way as a religious icon across a corner of a room.

were principally experimental and innovative. As abiding principles, although simplistic and crude when we examine the course of twentieth-century art, they are a fair indication at least of what the practitioners of modernism thought it to be and of how it differed from what had gone before.

The examples Duchamp and Malevich provide are also an indication of a central paradox within modernism. If innovation, originality, an autonomous art (art that refers only to itself) and 'critical distance' (art that is a critique of orthodoxies) were programmatically central to modernism, then all that could be accomplished seems to have been achieved before the end of the First World War. If the iconoclasm of these two works could stand as a marker for modernism as early as 1915–17, what more could be achieved? If, in addition, postmodernism is taken to mean a rejection of notions of authenticity and originality, why had another fifty years to go by before modernism supposedly burned itself out? The two works stand in mutual tension. Duchamp's 'ready-made' was a rejection of his former painting practice, and certainly the early Russian avant-garde, of which Malevich was a member, had by the 1920s all but abandoned easel painting. As Raymond Williams (1989a: 69) points out, if real 'renunciation', abandonment of tradition, was supposed to have taken place, then there appears to have been no decision by most painters (Duchamp and the Russian avant-garde being significant exceptions) to give up oil paint as a medium. Nonetheless, as our first illustrations indicate, modern art seems to have had a negative or at least questioning attitude to making images of the 'real' world. At the apex of modernist cultural production, then, are iconosceptic, even iconophobic, images.

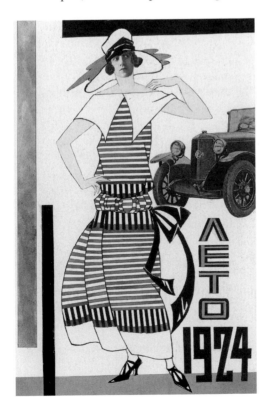

Figure 1.3 Liubov Popova, *Leto 1924* (*Summer 1924*). Cover design for a fashion magazine. Courtesy Galerie Gmurzynska, Cologne. In many of Popova's simple geometric designs she applied the abstract forms of her earlier architectonic paintings.

For the most part, traditional histories of art structured around movements and '-isms' such as impressionism and post-impressionism or abstraction and post-painterly abstraction, privilege painting and sculpture. Even where artists, like the Russian constructivists and futurists, designed clothes, made music, designed furniture and made films (Figure 1.3), it is with their paintings and sculpture that we are made primarily familiar.

The reproducible arts of photography, printmaking, craft and design still remain, by and large, categorised as lesser arts. This hierarchical approach to art's histories has helped sustain the exclusivity of the '-isms' approach. It has excluded, in part because of the often transitory and ephemeral nature of the works, much of Dada and missed out Fluxus and Situationism: groups that revelled in anti-art 'production' or mass-produced multiples working across media. Surrealism is often limited to a hagiography of repetitively familiar European names. The 'domestic' arts of quilt-making, lace-making and embroidery are entirely absent from the resolutely unpractical canonical modernism unless incorporated into a painting or sculpture for their formal beauty (see Plate V). The examples we have chosen are indicative of what Williams identifies as 'the machinery of selective tradition' (1989a: 69), which by and large saw art as an autonomous practice and therefore outside craft, design and most forms of photography which could have a practical function.

The version of modernism that dominates art history is concerned largely with painting, while sculpture is seen as a second-order art form. By the middle of the twentieth century, when writers and historians began to 'write up' a modernist art history, the emphasis tended to be on the works themselves separated from broader cultural networks. The nascent discipline acquiesced to the hidden power of historicism: the compelling human story. Biographical details of the artists' lives of alienation from social norms and their struggle to create new and ever more abstract works were the staple of many accounts. By the 1960s there was a hardening of the accounts of canonical art, mirrored in other disciplines, that insisted art be about art. Put simply, the dominant modernist tradition maintains that the demands of 'specialisation' and 'purity' required painting to be rooted into its 'own area of competence', defined by the American critic Clement Greenberg as 'paint' and an orientation towards the flatness of the canvas: as only these two properties were exclusive to painting. Barnett Newman's monumental *Cathedra* (1950–1), almost 17 feet across, complied with high modernism's (or Greenbergian modernism's) edict: to explore the medium of paint and attain flatness by forgoing illusionistic devices such as perspectival depth. Newman's vast canvases cannot be reproduced effectively in a book. The claims for the works, however, are equally vast. Distancing Newman from Piet Mondrian's (1872–1944) geometric abstraction, Greenberg maintained that, although his paintings consisted only of 'rectilinear and parallel bands of color against a flat field . . . [with an] emphasis . . . just as much on color as on pattern', Newman had 'simply aimed at and attained the maximum of his truth within the tacit and evolving limits of our Western tradition of painting' (Greenberg 1990a: 330). We should raise two issues here that have occupied historians and artists in about equal measure. Could it be that, far from the radicalism that we believed modernism to be, in its painterly manifestation at least, it was a form of conservatism after all? Or does radicalism lie in the ability of artists critically to assess the medium through the medium itself to lead to some kind of 'truth'?

When was modernism?

The answer to the question 'when was modernism?' is not a simple matter of establishing dates. It depends in part on what modernism is believed to have been. If it is merely a continuous series of stylistic changes, then, measured as technical radicalism, in some sense the issue is either very simple or very vexed. Beginning with Édouard Manet's 'unfinished' canvases of modern life around the 1860s, continuing to such works as *A Bar at the Folies-Bergères* (1882) (see Plate II) and finishing somewhere around American abstract expressionism in the 1950s with works such as those of Barnett Newman. That we should attempt to answer the question posed here at all would have seemed peculiar 200 years ago. In the eighteenth century, history and fiction were kindred forms and history was regarded as a literary art. Both possess a narrative structure; that is, both tell a story. The emphasis on narrative gave rise to a way of writing about the past as a story in a chronological sequence of events. One of the great scholarly enterprises of the age was the systematic periodisation of the past to order, sequence, classify and impose dates upon history.[4] Currently an understanding of our own relationship to the past is tempered by a 'crisis of confidence' in understanding the past through empirical data. Although we may now feel that history is something we 'make up as we go along', the result of such systematic scholarly activity was the structuring of a discipline of art history that developed through its own principles of periodisation: there was medieval, Renaissance, baroque and rococo, or their local equivalents.

Such an enterprise left contemporary art history with a legacy of fixed chronological boundaries, a structure to which it initially subscribed, adding supplementary movements and '-isms'. The history of art is replete with survey books featuring separate chapters dealing with the various '-isms'.[5] This in itself has created a quandary. What should be the object of study in the modern period, particularly given modern art's own fractious relationship with its objects of study? Is a chronological survey of '-isms', although the most popular way of working through the period, the only way of understanding modern art? Should art works be central to the 'curriculum' or should the curriculum be structured around artists, 'the sensitive antennae of society' (Barr 1975: 5), collectors, political events or the changing Zeitgeist? If around art works, then which do we select to study?

General surveys tend to treat modernism as having an exclusively French nucleus and defined geographic borders. Even when Spanish and Dutch artists are mentioned, they seem to have been co-opted into French culture and a modernity that is sited in Paris. In acknowledging this emphasis we might look beyond the narrower margins and begin a history of art with a broader look at art's position within a cultural framework and not as a separate sphere of activity divorced from the social. Where the social dimension impinges on traditional histories of art it is usually at the level of biography, as is evident in the monograph book form. Artists' biographical details may shed light on artistic activity but also on art's social context. Art history as a history of '-isms' combined with edited highlights of the lives of artists does, however, tend to focus attention on the salacious and the tragic, often substituting romantic ideas of individual struggle for any real engagement with the social and political framework that informed the making and reception of the art works.

A systematic approach

By the 1920s, the empirical model of scholarly activity required by modern art as it became increasingly 'difficult' was felt to need some kind of genealogy. Alfred H. Barr Jnr, scholar and founding director of the first modern art gallery, the Museum of Modern Art (MoMA), which opened in New York in 1929, created a now-notorious schema for modernism. Barr's attempt to define an historical trajectory for modern art adorned the cover of the catalogue for MoMA's 1936 exhibition *Cubism and Abstract Art* (Figure 1.4). It is emblematic of the difficulties facing those who attempt definitions in the current age of resistance to overarching defining characteristics. Barr's schema was provisional, and although he did later rework the chart he made no major revisions. The schema's narrow boundaries and its assumptions about which movements and artists are significant and on what grounds have led to charges of 'historicism' – constructing a history that is consistent with contemporary values – and 'teleological thinking' – constructing a system as if art inevitably progressed towards a 'natural' goal, in this case abstract art. Barr's diagram gives a graphic representation of a trajectory that flows from post-impressionism, through cubism and expressionism, the machine aesthetic and surrealism, to two forms of abstraction: on the left, non-geometrical biomorphic abstract art, typified by Wassily Kandinsky, and, on the right, geometrical abstract art, represented by Piet Mondrian. While compelling in its apparent logic and clarity, having the authority of a scientific diagram, Barr's schema has always been problematic. First, it contributes to the schism between 'conservative' practices and a perceived radicalism by aligning itself with technically 'progressive' practices. Second, it evacuates the social and political agendas that often informed the movements identified in favour of a deracinated art. In many ways the grid was emblematic of the dominant view of modernism – flat, repetitive, non-figurative, ordered and bordered. It may be emblematic of one definition of modernism, certainly familiar if we follow the line of art's need to purify and orient itself towards flatness (a point to which we will return), but it is important to grasp that modernism, though used to label/define certain art works, is also a set of ideas and beliefs about art works and as such, we will see, is unstable and often deeply subjective. Moreover, the dynamic, ever-changing practice of cultural activity in the twentieth century, the sheer diversity of cultural responses to modernisation, should militate against any homogeneous and totalising outcome, which Barr's schematic approach seems to endorse.

The legacy of Enlightenment thought

Leaving aside the twentieth century for a moment, we want to turn to the rationale for locating modernism in an earlier period. Writers often locate the onset of modernity in the eighteenth century in what has been termed the Enlightenment. Thierry de Duve identifies in the writings of Roger de Piles and Abbé Dubois a significant shift of emphasis in the notion of individual subjectivity characteristic of this period. De Duve maintains that *taste* is an important factor in the ideology that supports modernism, and he identifies a movement from a kind of collective idea of taste to a notion of taste as determined by the individual. It was during this period that the emphasis on *feeling* as the basis for judgements of taste emerged. This is not to say that a highly formed sense

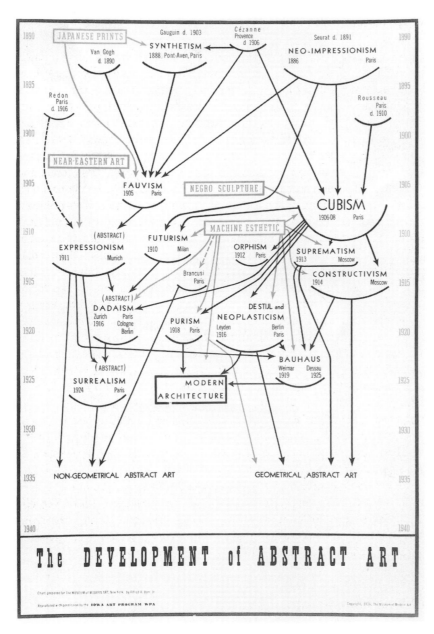

Figure 1.4 Alfred Hamilton Barr Jnr, *The Development of Abstract Art*, 1936. Cover of the exhibition catalogue *Cubism and Abstract Art*, MoMA, 1936. Offset, printed in color, 7¾ inches × 10¼ inches (19.7 cm × 26 cm). The Museum of Modern Art Library, New York. Digital image © 2003 The Museum of Modern Art, NY/Scala, Florence. Barr's schema is concerned with the development of abstract art and in its exclusive focus it concentrates on moments of 'breakthrough' and influence. This grid became a significant historical framework in modernist art history, charting the move towards non-geometric and geometrical abstraction located at the bottom of the grid. The chart identifies the key masters of modernism at the top of the grid as Van Gogh, Gauguin, Cézanne and Seurat, with the influence of Japanese prints, although subsequently accorded less prominence, as a crucial defining element.

of self had not existed prior to the eighteenth century; however, put crudely, the agency of the individual began to encroach upon the position previously occupied by God. To raise the question 'were we ever modern?' is, therefore, to enquire not only about dates but about reconfiguring notions of the individual. The later Enlightenment period was marked by a subjective enthusiasm or sensibility, manifest in a widespread concentration on the esoteric functioning of the internalised self rather than on the functioning of the state. This subjective sensibility was often accompanied by maudlin preoccupations and overwrought feelings. The quest for Truth was no longer a scientific issue but an issue of first-person self-consciousness: for example, the term 'autobiography' appeared at this time. The cult of individualism and rebelliousness, a sense of personal taste being central to defining the self, as constructed during this period is best summed up in Jean-Jacques Rousseau's credo 'If I am not better, at least I am different'.

The eighteenth-century Enlightenment is often called the Age of Reason, although Roy Porter cautions against this 'misleading' portmanteau term as many of its leading proponents, men of science such as Newton, saw 'experience and experiment, not a-priori reason, [as] the keys to knowledge' (Porter 1990: 3). However, during the period, there was considerable opposition to the authority of the aristocracy, the traditional repository of morality and taste. The French writer Denis Diderot (1713–84), responsible in part for *L'Encyclopédie*, the first published encyclopaedia, was opposed to the classical rules of beauty and believed, more democratically, that beauty resides in ordinary and everyday entities. He rejected the belief that *breeding* is the basis for taste and instead emphasised *experience*. More important for our purposes is the collapse of confidence in seventeenth-century doctrines such as the Divine Right of Kings and the challenges to aristocratic values. As we will see, 'lived experience' was to be pivotal for the prime movers of modernism, critics and writers who, like the nineteenth-century French poet Charles Baudelaire and the Edwardians Roger Fry and Clive Bell, and latterly Clement Greenberg and Michael Fried, valued engagement with the 'here and now' over any acquiescence to the extant classical order.

The German theorist Jürgen Habermas also located the origins of the modern period in the Enlightenment, in his influential paper 'Modernity: an incomplete project' (1990). He saw modernity as a continuation of the belief in an 'illuminating' age in which enlightenment was an attitude to problem-solving, sustained by trust in the power of logic to solve problems rather than by belief in a *deus ex machina*.

The Enlightenment project was profoundly influential, offering theoretical justification for dissent against traditional authority for both the American and French Revolutions. While its philosophical ideas reached every sphere of social life, it is its relationship with the arts that interests us here. Enlightenment philosophers believed that through a combination of science, technology and an autonomous art (art as a self-governing sphere of activity) all things, including nature, could be conquered and all social problems solved. Art was therefore seen as an implement with which to improve, both morally and socially, the condition of humanity. This was in stark contrast to the earlier function of art that, according to de Duve, was:

> to honour the dead, serve the Church, ornate bourgeois interiors, placate taste . . . but its function was never programmatically . . . to exert critical vigilance over the ethical realm. Once it appears in art works, this very function of critical vigilance –

precisely because it is new – radically severs them from their pasts; it forbids anyone to valorise art forms that failed to make the same break on their own.

(de Duve 1996: 432)

In part, then, the art works that became identified with the term 'modernism' contained some kind of moral imperative – an idea we will return to throughout this book. This is not, however, a transparent issue. The moralising tendencies of Victorian art, based largely on notions of self-improvement, were not directly equatable with the moral high ground that modernists occupied. What de Duve identifies has been described as a 'critical distance' (art that is a critique of orthodoxies). As we will see, moral action was often evacuated from the aesthetic programme of modernism, but, paradoxically, in order to engage in an act of pure aesthetics modernism was somehow to lay claim to another moral high ground.

An important Enlightenment legacy for modernism has been the construction of the notion of the artist-as-genius. It is possible to discern the legacy of the eighteenth- and nineteenth-century Romantic movement in the heroic (if short-lived) stage of the early avant-garde. Alienation and rejection were essential elements in the formation of artistic sensibility within Romanticism. The movement required a new form of subjectivity, one that we will examine more specifically in coming chapters, that at least in part opposed classicism's emphasis on order and restraint. The Romantic artist became identified, at least in myth, with the Byronic phrase 'mad, bad and dangerous to know'. Restraint was not the order of the day: landscape art in particular exalted in 'sublime' tragedies, and disasters abounded, with incipient industrialisation eroding the edges of nature. Facets of Romanticism were 'adopted' by the avant-garde: in particular, rejection of conventions, resistance to institutionalised forms of regulation, and the emphasis on the individual subjectivity and imagination.

This moment of rebellion is notable because in earlier epochs certainly no one expected a Vermeer or a Rembrandt to be technically innovative, to contribute to a manifesto or to declare the grounds of their 'critical distance' from the established order or status quo to create *their* art. We may have come with hindsight to value Rembrandt's ambiguous relationship with the worthy burghers of seventeenth-century Amsterdam, but that is not to view his art as advanced or in opposition to the dominant order. Early modernism, however, was marked by an avant-garde that looked for radical political transformations through artistic innovation and experimentation, and the declaration of that radicalism in print. In the case of the early twentieth-century Italian futurists, a manifesto could conceivably precede any art work. Filippo Marinetti published the first manifesto on futurist painting before any significant body of work had been produced. The declamatory nature of the manifesto is important in establishing an intervention in mass 'consciousness'. It is a statement of intent – the reverse of the private diary and letter form used by earlier artists.

Formalism: the creation, analysis and evaluation of the work of art outside social circumstances

There is often an assumption that an 'artistic death knell' ushered in the modern movement.[6] However, for some, such as the American critic Clement Greenberg, it was important to establish that modernism, within the parameters of his own definitions, was in a continuum with the past. Greenberg saw the development of modernism as a historical phenomena referencing the unsettling effect of photography on artistic practice in mid-century France (the first daguerreotype, a combination of printmaking and photography, was made in 1839) as part of the crisis that precipitated such dramatic changes in the way art looked and the crisis in what function art could have. This is not, contrary to modernist opinion, the first time that painting had been in crisis. In fact, history painting had come under threat in the eighteenth century when the introduction of mirrors into aristocratic homes resulted in the mass removal of 'old-fashioned' painted panels in favour of increased reflected light.

Greenberg is definite about dates and, perhaps more importantly, the way in which modernism manifested itself: the form that the works took. His writing does tend to suggest that modernism, after all a concept or tendency, was in some way self-defining, with a will of its own. Nonetheless, for Greenberg:

> Modernism showed itself more clearly at first in terms of technique, technique in the most immediate, concrete sense. That is how Manet broke with the recent past more momentously than did any other contemporary in his or any other arts. Not that he broke with all tradition. Harking back to a more distant past in Spanish painting, he found himself inspired to leap into the future.
>
> (Greenberg 1986a: 30)

If we return historically to the academic works of the nineteenth century we can see just how startling modern painting looks. The distortion of colour, the rejection of naturalistic conventions and the blatant rejection of the classical conceptions of the heroic in favour of the mundane still have the ability to disarm the viewer. Hung side by side with an academic work, such as the French winner of the Prix de Rome Adolphe Bouguereau's work the *Birth of Venus* (1879) (see Plate III), an impressionist painting by the technically, relatively 'conservative' painter Renoir *Monet Working in His Garden in Argenteuil* (1873) (see Plate IV) demonstrates both the continuities and divergences of art practices in that period.

By the beginning of the twentieth century, works showed scant regard for even the conventions of early modernism. Natalia Goncharova's (1881–1962) *Linen* of 1913 (see Plate V), with its distortion of scale, unheroic subject matter and anti-naturalistic composition, has so little resemblance to its academic and early modernist counterpart that it is easy to assume that technical change and innovation, an emphasis on *formalism*, was all that was important in the works designated 'modern'.

The definition of terms and the changing status accorded to them has often obscured understanding of modern art. Nowhere is this more evident than in the term 'formalism', which we have used several times. The conflation of terms generated, wittingly or not, around Clement Greenberg often make the period difficult to categorise. 'Formalism' and 'art for art's sake' are two terms often used interchangeably in writing about modern art. Rarely are sustainable definitions attempted (and not without reason). Attempts to cite modernism with a capital 'M' as an indicator of the type of modernism associated with Greenberg can be misleading. Greenbergian modernism is perhaps closer to a relatively useful definition of a dominant and defining history of modernism that both ordered the past and influenced the working methods of artists anxious for critical acclaim. Greenberg's work was based on formalist critical tendencies rooted in the theories of, among others, Clive Bell and Roger Fry, but the whole of modernism or indeed Greenberg's theories should not be co-opted under such a blanket term. Formalism, rather than a proclivity like modernism, better suggests the way in which works are read or subjected to aesthetic evaluation by the artist or viewer. Formalism is principally an approach that emphasises line, colour, tone and mass at the expense of the significance of subject matter. Alone it gives few clues as to the social context of art works. At first sight this is an apparently 'easy' theory of art, although it underwent several transformations, between 1912 and 1950, in response to the perceived direction of the modern movement in painting and sculpture. Developed between 1912 and 1914 by the English painters and art critics Clive Bell and Roger Fry, formalism privileges the aesthetic response as mediated through sight alone. Visual sensibility accordingly is a prerequisite of art appreciation, and a genuine aesthetic experience is both self-sufficient and disinterested. The strength of this approach is that it can embrace all art forms since a formalist response to any item or artefact from any culture or period makes no distinctions in relation to cultural context. However, there is also a philosophical dimension to formalism, harking back to the Enlightenment philosopher Immanuel Kant and, through him, to Plato. In brief, this is a system of aesthetic judgements and values which have their own internal intricacies, whereby beauty is not scientifically measurable but is appreciated through 'feelings' and 'aesthetic pleasure'. The crucial and defining feature of Kantian aesthetics is that aesthetic pleasure is disinterested; that is, the aesthetic response transcends the corporeal and the contingent. This aesthetic can obscure formal art appreciation as it often resorts to exclusivist ideas about painting and sculpture which are highly philosophical.

Given the apparently open agenda of formalism, it is curious that so little art finds its way into the pantheon of great works as defined through the process described by Clive Bell as an engagement with 'significant form' (Bell 1982: 67–74). By this he meant that art works of quality can be identified through their formal properties, which alone act as the marker of their significance. We saw in Alfred Barr's schema (Figure 1.4) how exclusive the canon of 'great works'/movements could be. Certainly it seems that the emphasis in modernism on the 'aesthetic response' has been exclusive rather than inclusive. If we return to the work of Duchamp and apply a formalist agenda, it becomes easier to see why works such as *Fountain* (Figure 1.1) were difficult to accommodate unless they stood in opposition to aesthetic taste. Kantian aesthetic responses can only accommodate partial readings of modernism, and *Fountain* was 'distasteful'.[7]

This approach in the modern period is not exclusive to critics such as Bell, Fry and Greenberg. The symbolist painter Maurice Denis maintained in 1890 that 'a picture . . . before being a battle horse, a nude woman, or some anecdote – is essentially a plane surface covered with colours assembled in a certain order' (Denis 1968a: 94). Perhaps the difficulty here is in maintaining a formalist 'eye'. Just how long can mere looking be sustained without recourse to other questions about what an art work is about, without reordering those works into some kind of subject matter with social, not aesthetic, considerations? Be that as it may, one of the compulsions of early modernism seems to have been to abandon subject matter and give primary consideration to the form a work should take.

Modern art and its objects

Modernism has become synonymous with specific modern paintings produced by the 'old masters of modern art', Cézanne, Monet, Picasso, Pollock. Although actual examples may be referred to as quintessentially modern, modernism is also a set of ideas and beliefs about those works, and so needs to be distinguished from the works themselves. To reiterate, these *works*, in what constitutes a canon of modern art, were themselves identified through a process of selection and validation that was considerably different from the academic procedures of the established academies of art in the nineteenth century. One sense of modernism, as we have seen, tends towards rejection of the values of the academy, perceived by a new generation of artists as conservative and repressive, and implicated in bourgeois notions of moral correctness as somehow corresponding to exactitude and 'finish' in a painting. For instance, Ruskin's attacks on the 'cockney . . . coxcomb' Whistler's hurried *Nocturnes* (Figure 1.5) were not merely attacks on incompetent painting: he saw their lack of verisimilitude as a moral affront. Manet's 'unfinished' and rather dishevelled canvases were not just poor painting (that could easily be accommodated) but were also a fall from moral grace.

In *The Birth of Modern Painting*, Gaëtan Picon writes of an earlier break with the past, in 1863, and of Édouard Manet (see Plate II) as the founding father of modern art:

> When the Salon des Refusés – the Salon of the Rejected – opened in Paris on May 15, 1863, it was as if History were staging an event which, in the order of painting, would show all the signs of a break with the past and a new beginning. . . . It was a drama with several leading characters but with one outstanding hero: Manet; and for which *Le Déjeuner sur l'herbe* – whether applauded or booed – might have supplied a title.
>
> (Picon 1978: 7)

The passage is important, as it raises several spectres. For many social historians in the 1970s and 1980s, the language of heroism and the presumption of a heroic rupture with the past contributed to the mythologising of art history's past. It is an indication of the radical debates (particularly under the aegis of the so-called new art histories) that have opened up the terrain of traditional art history, and which were written largely from a Marxist viewpoint. In fact, although rarely credited, John Berger was also writing critical, not celebratory, connoisseurial art history as early as the 1960s. Marxism permeated the new writing's seminal works: T.J. Clark's *Image of the People: Gustave Courbet and the 1848 revolution* (1973b) and *The Absolute Bourgeois: artists and politics in France 1848–1851* (1973a) altered the terms under which art history would be written. Clark stated his method in his introduction to *Image of the People*, entitled 'On the Social History of Art':

> When one writes the Social History of Art, it is easier to define what methods to avoid than propose a set of methods for systematic use. . . . So I begin by naming some taboos. I am not interested in the notion of works of art 'reflecting' ideologies, social relations, or history. Equally, I do not want to talk about history as 'background' to the work of art. . . . I want also to reject the idea that the artist's point of reference as a social being is, a priori, the artistic community. . . . Lastly, I do not want the social history of art to depend on intuitive analogies between

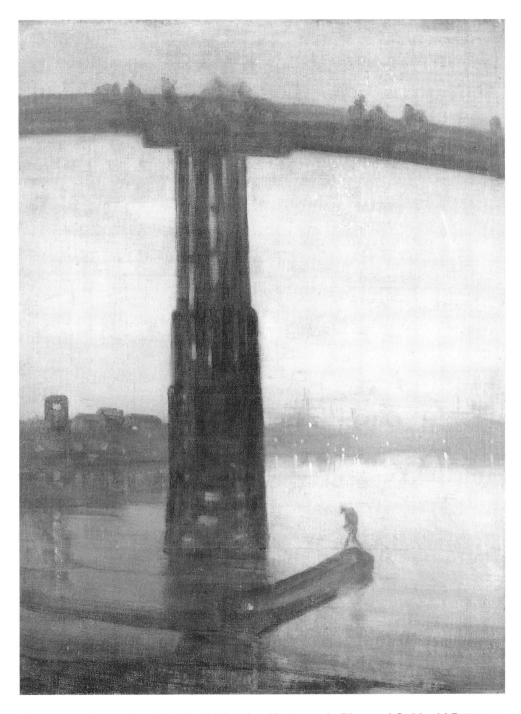

Figure 1.5 James Abbott McNeill Whistler, *Nocturne in Blue and Gold: old Battersea Bridge*, c.1872–5. Photograph © Tate, London, 2003. In a similar vein to Kandinsky, Whistler associated his work with musical equivalents: nocturnes and harmony.

form and content . . . that the lack of firm compositional focus in Courbet's *Burial at Ornans* is an expression of the painter's egalitarianism, or that Manet's fragmented composition in the extra-ordinary *View of Paris World's Fair* (1867) is a visual equivalent of human alienation in industrial society.

(Clark 1973b: 10–11)

The newer art histories do seem to be permeated with a set of puritanical negatives, but their aim has been to prise art from its esoteric rest home and push it back towards some form of social relevance.

The strength of the Marxist approach was its acknowledgement of the subjective nature of historical reconstruction. The assumption of a 'disinterested history' and, crucially, the assumption of a 'disinterested aesthetic' above and beyond the contingencies of historical reconstruction were laid bare by Marxist, socialist and feminist art historians. The central tenet of Marxist art history (and it is only fair to point out that there are many shades of Marxism – Leninist, Engelsian, Althusserian – named after their various exponents) is that art is influenced by the social and political circumstances in which it is produced. But the degree to which the social and political conditions in which a work of art is produced *actually* influence that work is controversial. Some (these are often called 'vulgar Marxists') argue that a work of art is the passive product of any given socio-economic situation, while others credit art as having more relative autonomy in the face of what they see as more remote socio-economic events: an artistic agency militating against any simplistic notion of cause and effect. (See, in particular, Hadjinicolaou 1982).

Marxism has usefully uncovered the arbitrary nature of the common-sense values of dominant discourses, which includes the centrality of the 'artist as hero' – in the crowd but not of it – in modernist discourse. The modernist artist is the anti-academic anti-traditionalist who breaks the boundaries and revels in the refusals. There is, however, plenty of evidence to suggest that Manet and many other modern artists craved official approval. The relationship between artist and authority and, crucially, display opportunities, patronage and galleries is a constant irritant in twentieth-century avant-garde culture. The gradual assimilation of oppositional art into institutional orthodoxy represents one of the failed utopias of the modern period. The collapse of the Eastern bloc combined with the poststructuralist rejection of totalising beliefs has contributed to a collapse of confidence in Marxism as a tool for analysis. However, it would be premature to dismiss the strength and rigour of the Marxist contribution to art history even as the light fades on the utopia that it seemed to represent.

To return to Gaëtan Picon's 'one outstanding hero', Manet, Picon centres the modernist tropes – innovation and rejection – around the artist. It is unlikely that a book on the Renaissance or the Baroque period would start with the artist. For other periods, innovation, originality and authenticity were not isolated in the gifted individual, whose subjectivity, through some notion of self-expression central to modernism, would reveal the truth about the age. This construction of the artist as hero is a primary marker of the modern period. The art works that would be *modern* art are defined and subjected to validations of a specific kind. If T.J. Clark and the feminist social historian of art Griselda Pollock wanted new ways of reading seminal modernist canonical works like Manet's *L'Olympia* (1863), other dissidents preferred Raymond Williams's approach to modernity and its objects – an approach characterised by analysis of the relationship between popular culture and fine art.

In traditional histories of modernism, an academic genre painting such as William Frith's *Paddington Station* (1862) (a Dickensian anecdotal narrative painting full of incident perpetrated by stock characters) is not included within the category of the modern. In sharp contrast, Claude Monet's 1870s narrative-free atmospheric paintings of railway stations are. This form of legitimacy does not take place naturally, nor is it a procedure that can be attributed to some abstract notion of the modern as somehow self-selecting. The procedures of selection are within given discourses supported by institutional validations, even when apparently oppositional. Merely rereading the original canon from a Marxist or a feminist perspective, a process questioned as 'new lamps for old', does little to diminish the authority of the canon itself. (See, in particular, Gretton 1986.)

'Modernism', as we have witnessed, has a hierarchical basis which privileges high cultural forms and practices, and subordinates graphic design, commercial and industrial photography and film. At the same time, it also created a hierarchy *within* painting practices which saw the Victorian narrative pictures such as the 'slice of life' paintings of Frith or Luke Fildes as wanting. To ask meaningful questions about modernism, then, is to ask questions about cultural value.

Avant-gardes

> The only modern art of significance and quality is avant-garde art, and any art that is satisfied with exerting functions that predate modernity (placating taste for instance) loses its value as well as its critical function simply by being retarded, retrograde. When push comes to shove, Rodchenko is an artist and Bonnard is not.
>
> (de Duve 1996: 432)

The term avant-garde has already been mentioned in various contexts without a real definition. It holds a crucial if ambiguous, even contradictory, position in relation to cultural practices in the late nineteenth and twentieth centuries. Although current confidence in it has been shaken, the avant-garde remains an important (if fictional) feature of modernism, especially in terms of its inclusions and exclusions. 'Familiar' problems of the avant-garde have been identified by Hal Foster as 'the ideology of progress, the presumption of originality, the elitist hermeticism, the historical exclusivity, the appropriation by the culture industry, and so on' (1990: 5). Foster's set of negatives is a concise deconstruction of areas once considered inviolable. A shift in 'feeling' for avant-garde culture seems to be manifest in the now not-unfamiliar tone of Foster's statement. In general, the public may not have liked the work of avant-garde artists, but there was a broad general agreement that it was progressive and original, even authentic. Its position was assured, and, even if remote, its very hermeticism, its 'otherworldliness', did not necessarily mark it off as 'elitist'.

The history of the avant-garde is not transparent. The avant-garde itself (and it was often self-defining) is notorious for mythically obscuring its own history. This is in part a consequence of the artist's often woebegone if sometimes heroic attempt both to court official recognition and yet to stay beyond the confines of orthodox sanctification. The strategies devised by artists, writers and musicians to establish themselves in opposition to the dominant order make up some of the most interesting artistic skirmishes of nineteenth- and twentieth-century art.

The 'avant-garde' is a military term and, as such, is instructive in setting the conditions of artistic endeavour since the late nineteenth century. A relatively new term, it singles out an important difference in modern art practice from what went before. The term suggests an element of danger, certainly of risk, a military metaphor applied to Western cultural practices. The advanced guard went into battle first. The rest, crucially in modern art terms, followed or, rather pejoratively, 'brought up the rear'. By these terms, Monet led with his impressionistic railway station, whereas Frith's detailed rendering of a railway station saw him pensioned out of the army altogether. It has, however, become all too apparent in the late twentieth century that the legions did not always follow the avant-garde. But this is to jump ahead. At least in artistic terms, to be 'in advance' was to return to our modernist trinity, was to be authentic, innovative and original. But what did it mean to be authentic, original and innovative in the mid-nineteenth century? The Industrial Revolution brought with it major social upheavals across the Western world, and particularly in England as it was industrialised earlier than its European counterparts.

One response to such apocalyptic changes can be found in the works of the young English artists who made up the Pre-Raphaelite Brotherhood. Formed in 1848, a date at which some commentators suggest the avant-garde got into its stride, the work of this grouping could constitute a radical practice. The Brotherhood was, after all, sufficiently 'anti-establishment' to constitute a critical relationship to society; its relationship with modernity was complex, and its imagery was technically, visually and symbolically innovative. It also had the right critical connections. In 1928 Roger Fry, subsequently associated with the formulation of the aesthetic response in relation to post-impressionism, wrote an introductory essay to the art collection at the Lady Lever Art Gallery, Port Sunlight, Merseyside, which is, however, unfortunately not available as a purchasable publication, being part of the Gallery's 'reserve'. In this essay Fry stated that 'it was against the trite sentimentality, the trivial facetiousness, or merely theatrical effectiveness of the motives which were current among the painters of the mid-century that the Pre-Raphaelites *raised the standard of revolt*' (Fry 1928: 18, emphasis added). All the characteristics which seemed to ensure entry into avant-gardism were in place: revolt, genius and what Fry defined as 'seriousness and conviction' – a kind of pictorial moral high ground. Fry identified crucial elements in the Pre-Raphaelite rebellion, particularly in the quality of Dante Gabriel Rossetti's 'poetical inventions, [and] the freshness and intensity of his themes' (Fry 1928: 19). Ultimately however, Fry 'conceded' that even Pre-Raphaelitism, in Britain 'the one distinctive and original movement of the period, fits readily enough into the Royal Academic conception of painting' (Fry 1928: 30). Fry acknowledges the Brotherhood's opposition to the Royal Academy but finally, with regret, condemns the works as 'illustrative'. The term became synonymous with 'inauthentic', that is, somehow mediated. So rebellion alone, even against the academies, is not enough, at least not for critics such as Fry. He required a sense of the pictorial, not of the illustrative, saying of Rossetti: 'he never showed himself a painter in the proper sense, his expression was laborious and heavy handed' (Fry 1928: 30). So although Fry's admiration for the Pre-Raphaelites is clear, the grounds of his disapproval comply with that estimation of the avant-garde that requires *in expression* technical innovation of a certain sort. Whatever a proper painter is, Rossetti, for Fry, was not one.

There must be a rejection of 'illustration', and, as Fry was to say of the American symbolist James McNeill Whistler, there must be instead 'a *direct* expression of imaginative states of mind' (Fry 1928: 30, emphasis added). The dominant account of Pre-Raphaelite works sees them as a retreat, not an advance, into the mythic past – an indulgence in the face of the reality of 'dark satanic mills' and Dickensian squalor. Whistler's work, on the other hand, seemed more connected to the 'here and now'. Pre-Raphaelitism can too easily seem like a mawkish antidote, even a panacea, to the modern world for those knowledgeable enough to draw on the poetry and symbolism of Dante, Malory and Keats (Figure 1.6). As we will see in Chapter 3, one of the defining aspects of modernism was its relationship to the *imagination* – the ability to realise an alternative to the present, to the morass of industrialisation. An engagement with modernity need not have resulted in the seemingly monolithic French model. However, the Pre-Raphaelite technique was deliberately archaic, not 'unreflective' illustration, and offered a glimpse of an alternative to the present. The movement was also programmatically self-conscious, one of the modernist tropes. At the risk of sounding jingoistic, the influence of British art on European art in the nineteenth century was considerable. John Constable is often cited because of the enthusiastic reception of his works by the French impressionists. The Pre-Raphaelites were, however, associated with symbolism, which did not come to dominate art-historical writing, at least that of the American and British persuasions.

The Brotherhood fails to enter the avant-garde, as it is defined in the Baudelairean sense of an engagement with modernity that requires paintings of modern life to be symbiotically linked to a new means of representing those living through an industrial age. Arthurian legends or the morality tales of life under capitalism were not enough. It was necessary somehow to be of that age and to show it through technical innovation as well as through a celebration of the heroes of everyday life. This apparent lack of technical innovation in painting is echoed in the debates over the radical nature of the writer Charles Dickens. On what grounds, Raymond Williams (1989a) asks, is the radical 'realism' of Dickens marginalised against the achievements of James Joyce, Franz Kafka, Virginia Woolf and T.S. Eliot? What were the grounds for privileging those who 'denaturalised' language over others who reflected it like a mirror? Avant-garde artists equally rejected what they perceived to be art that mirrored the world. However, it would be wrong to assume that the 'appearance of things' is a simple mirroring of the world, as even mundane things can assume symbolic or allegorical connotations in works of art. It is simply that Barr's belief that artists rejected images of things in the world because they were 'bored with painting facts' belies the complexity of representation.

In *The Politics of Vision* (1991) Linda Nochlin maintains that the term 'avant-garde' was first used in relation to art by the French utopian socialist Henri de Saint-Simon in the 1830s. Crucially for the early avant-gardists, social revolution was inextricably linked to the arts. The arts were not confined to the realms of the aesthetic alone. Nochlin quotes D. Laverdant's 'De la mission de l'art et du role des artistes' (1845):

Art, the expression of society, manifests, in its highest soaring, the most advanced social tendencies: it is the forerunner and the revealer. Therefore to know whether

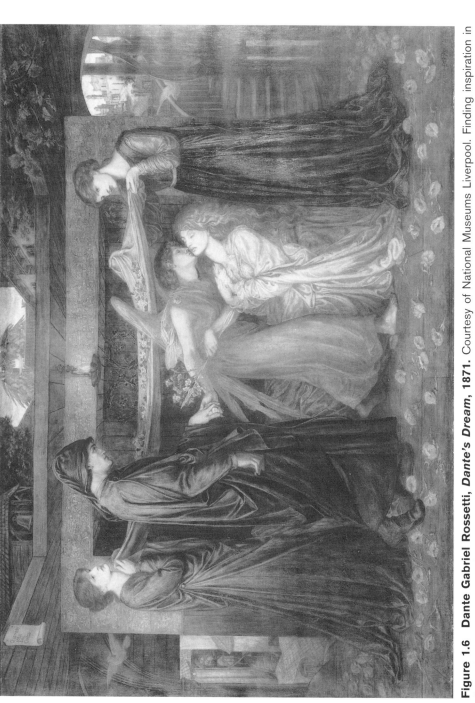

Figure 1.6 Dante Gabriel Rossetti, *Dante's Dream*, 1871. Courtesy of National Museums Liverpool. Finding inspiration in fifteenth-century Italian art and the poetry of Dante Alighieri; unrequited love and untimely death were central themes for Pre-Raphaelite painting here against a Florentine backdrop. Virgil's Dante and Beatrice are depicted here at the moment of her death.

art worthily fulfils its proper mission as initiator, whether the artist is truly of the avant-garde, one must know where Humanity is going, know what the destiny of the human race is.

(Laverdant, quoted in Nochlin 1991: 2)

This is a far cry from the requirements of academic technical competence in the subtle modelling of human flesh, the careful gradations of tone and the privileging of line over colour – to recall a classical past. Artists must now have a serious mission and a futuristic social insight beyond that of most mortals. This version of avant-gardism finds its apotheosis, according to Nochlin, in Courbet's major work *The Painter's Studio* (1855). Courbet's form of realism was championed by the French writer Charles Baudelaire. Courbet's allegorical work *The Painter's Studio* features a complicated array of characters and poses, with Courbet holding centre-stage. However, the essential element in avant-garde culture – that of alienation from bourgeois norms – does not make a more substantial appearance until Édouard Manet and the writers Flaubert and Baudelaire. It has been argued that Manet's *A Bar at the Folies-Bergères* (1882) (Plate II) combines the commitment to social and technical radicalism of Courbet with the isolation and alienation necessary for the advancement of what we have come to know as avant-gardism.

In Manet's work, irony and the irreverent reworking of art-historical sacred cows – for instance in his paintings *Le Déjeuner sur l'herbe* (*Luncheon on the Grass*) (1863) and *L'Olympia* (*Olympia*) (1863) (see Giorgione's pastoral idyll *Concert Champêtre* and Titian's *Venus D'Urbino*) – coalesce to create wilfully ambiguous paintings. According to the dominant version of avant-garde culture, these set the standard for avant-garde practices (a very different agenda from the postmodern reworking of old masters). Even at this juncture, however, the level of social or political commitment in Manet's work has been contested. Manet may have been isolated from his bourgeois roots but he never attempted, at least not through his art, to overthrow the established order, although there is plenty of evidence to show how disaffected he was from Napoleon III's Second Empire and its imperialist initiatives.

In a series of five works begun in 1868 (see Plate VI), Manet depicts the execution of the Emperor Maximilian, Napoleon's puppet ruler, abandoned in Mexico, one of Napoleon's less successful colonial interventions. Manet drew heavily on contemporary accounts of the execution, changing details in the works as more information was relayed through the newly laid transatlantic cable. Manet appears to have worked obsessively on the series until the following year. The series is overtly but inconclusively critical of Napoleon's failure to save Maximilian from execution by Benito Juárez's Mexican Liberal troops. It has been suggested that the soldier loading his rifle to complete the *coup de grâce* is a portrayal of Napoleon III; in addition, the troops resemble French rather than Mexican soldiers. Unlike other paintings of the execution, Manet's series was the subject of severe censorship. The lithographic stones, which would have created wider public access, were confiscated and the series of works was never shown in France in its entirety. In spite of Manet's clear political agenda and his attempt at a major modern history painting, one of the losses of avant-garde practices, the American critic Clement Greenberg felt able to state that 'the lasting shock [of the series] had to do with his handling of the medium and that alone. . . . Similarly, the Impressionists, coming in Manet's wake, caused shock or scandal by nothing other than the way they used paint' (Greenberg 1986a: 31).

The debate may seem a little remote from a position that now sanctions more inclusive agendas but it was an important issue in relation to avant-garde culture. The nature and extent of Manet's social and political commitment are crucial in establishing an avant-garde agenda. The modernist claim is that Manet's subject matter was a 'pretext for painting' and that his commitment to politics was, at best, secondary to the 'act of painting', a claim made even more extreme in Greenberg's writing, where the content of the work is disregarded in favour of paint handling alone. There is enough evidence, however, to suggest that Manet's paintings were no mere formal exercise – that he also had an explicit political agenda and that this was evident in his choice of subject *and* way of painting. For instance, the ambiguities evident in the Maximilian paintings can be accounted for, at least in part, by the need to evade the censors – not because he was concerned over charges of incompetent painting or indulging his pleasure in paint, but because the content of his work was politically inflammatory. Manet may have been alienated from the bourgeoisie, but in this particular instance he was supporting a liberal-bourgeois opposition (united in its condemnation of Napoleon III's ill-conceived ambitions).[8]

In his essay 'Modernist Painting', originally published in 1960 in Forum Lectures (*Voice of America*), and more widely in 1965 in *Art and Literature*, Greenberg continued to maintain the position that to paraphrase all content should be avoided like the plague, delineating the limitations of traditional art: 'Realistic, illusionist art had dissembled the medium, using art to conceal art' (Greenberg 2003a: 775). In addition, he wrote of a new emphasis on flatness and what he termed 'opticality'. Greenberg declared: 'Manet's paintings became the first modernist ones by virtue of the frankness with which they declared the surfaces on which they were painted' (Greenberg 2003a: 775). There is here a significant shift in emphasis, from what appear to be the concerns of Manet in the 1860s to the preoccupation of a critic writing a century later. It does highlight the difficulties faced in recovering artists' intentions, but also the difficulties of separating present concerns from those of the past.

The tensions in Greenberg's writings are indicative of the polarities that have characterised many of the histories of art produced over the past fifty years. How do artists reconcile the twin commitments of what appear to be separate spheres of activity – the aesthetic and the political?

Another example might be useful. Until recently Pierre Bonnard, the French painter of interiors and nudes in the bath, had an assured position within the avant-garde. However, the grounds on which the debate has been staged have shifted again. At just the point when avant-garde culture has gained institutional and public acclaim, the historians of art have pulled the rug from under the avant-garde. Bonnard is not to be considered avant-garde because the designation was, according to de Duve and others, bogus in the first place. It has indeed proved difficult in the nineteenth and twentieth centuries and beyond successfully to combine the political and the aesthetic, especially when there seemed also to be a requirement for innovation and originality. A caveat here, however: David Craven's work on the artists of Central America would suggest that the gap between art and politics can be successfully breached (see, in particular, Craven 1989). However, in the main geographical regions of modernism, de Duve's identification of the work of the Russian constructivist artist-designer-photographer Aleksandr Rodchenko as that of an artist through such works as *The Female Pyramid*, where he used acute camera angles to document the lives of Soviet peoples under Stalinism, and that of the French painter Pierre Bonnard, known through works such as *Nude in a Bath* as not the work of an artist, is axiomatic of a particular tendency, an illustration of the difficulties of classification within avant-garde culture. Traditional art history would include Bonnard for his technical innovations and close following of the precepts of *intimisme* (an art of closely patterned interior decorative work that concentrates on texture and surface ornament for effect and where the subject matter plays a part subordinate to the iridescent colouring) and largely marginalise Rodchenko for his politics and photography. De Duve ironically highlights the issues surrounding classification, insisting rhetorically:

> You are not a historian of art; you are a historian of the avant-garde. Such is the name of the practices that alone interest you. The name of art and the consensus that it begs are nothing but the retrospective sanction of these practices. It makes them autonomous, and in so doing alienates them; it endorses them, and in so doing drains them of power; it affirms them, and in so doing negates their negating impetus.
>
> (de Duve 1996: 20)

Aesthetic autonomy

The linking of the terms 'autonomy' and 'art' is a modern phenomenon, a result in part of the supposed loss of innovations in painting with the invention of photography, but also a response to the increasing commercialism of modern life under capitalism, an issue looked at in more detail in Chapter 8. In brief, this autonomy can be seen as the detachment of art from the realm of the social. Peter Bürger points to the central paradox in trying to explain art as an autonomous activity that exists outside of the social world because to refer to art's independence requires 'you . . . to refer to autonomous art's position within society' (Bürger 1984: 35). In this sense, Bürger continues, 'to suggest autonomy is a historically conditioned phenomenon turns into a denial, what remains is mere illusion'. Autonomous art, then, not only contains this central paradox but, as a construction of bourgeois society, the historical development of the avant-garde ironically precludes any possibility of an autonomous art. Hal Foster identifies this elitism as a problem within avant-garde culture that attempts to create a hermetic world, simultaneously 'revealed and obscured', sealed off from the social. This is to arrive at the position we identified earlier: although we can see that art works are positioned and even constructed within bourgeois norms, can they be reduced to them? Is there no possibility for art to transcend the conditions under which it was validated and consumed? It is important to grasp that, while art works are undoubt- edly formed in relation to social and aesthetic discourses, the variety of artistic responses to modernism would suggest that artists are not merely passive reflectors of dominant social and aesthetic discourses. In particular, the work of the international groups of surrealists, with their productive use of Freudian and later Jungian notions of the uncon- scious, stands as a riposte to the reductive theories that made art merely a reflection of bourgeois values. Through a strategy of 'making strange' the everyday, the surrealists hoped to force a re-evaluation of bourgeois norms.

For some theorists the question of autonomy remains a thorny one. Terry Eagleton cautions us:

> From Romanticism to modernism, art strives to turn to advantage the autonomy which its commodity status has forced upon it, making a virtue out of grim necessity. Autonomy in the worrying sense – social functionlessness – is wrenched into autonomy in a more productive sense: art as a deliberate turning in upon itself, as a mute gesture of resistance to a social order which, in Adorno's phrase, 'holds a gun to its head'. Aesthetic autonomy becomes a kind of negative politics.
>
> (Eagleton 1990: 370)

For Eagleton the only way out is to reject the aesthetic to make art against itself, an avant-garde strategy that will become a familiar one over the course of what follows.

Avant-garde and the relationship to bourgeois culture

As was put simply by Raymond Williams in *The Politics of Modernism*, 'hostile or indifferent or merely vulgar, the bourgeois was the mass which the creative artist must either ignore and circumvent, or now increasingly shock, deride and attack' (Williams 1989a: 53). All avant-garde movements were anti-bourgeois and yet all were assimilated by the structures of bourgeois society. As T.J. Clark put it: 'Bourgeois society is efficient at making all art its own' (Clark 1973b: 6–7). The relationship of modern art to the bourgeoisie is further complicated by the historical divisions within the bourgeoisie between 'petite' and 'haute', not unlike the English distinctions between lower- and upper-middle class.

These historical distinctions arose in France following the demise of the aristocracy as a force to be reckoned with after the Revolution of 1789. The triumphant bourgeois revolutionaries, perhaps displaying a characteristic insecurity in the face of aristocratic 'taste', either quickly assimilated or formed (depending on the extremity of your position) the potential for an 'acquisition of taste' in modern art. The haute bourgeoisie saw themselves as the arbiters of taste and the artistic heirs of the system of patronage. Having 'taste' at this point required a flirtatious but not dangerous liaison with bohemianism – a kind of frisson without the discomfort. The successive '-isms' of nineteenth- and twentieth-century art, predicated not on levels of skill that could be acquired but on art forms that required a new form of sensibility in order to be 'understood', were the perfect vehicle for protection against the philistinism of the lower orders. It is noteworthy that, by and large, even in terms of the north–south divide in Britain, the newly rich mill- and shipowners preferred the 'skilled' paintings of the Pre-Raphaelites and late-Victorian aesthetic movement to those of the 'incompetent' French school of daubers favoured by the sophisticated upper-middle class in London. This division is also evident in Australia in the art collections of Melbourne and Sydney, where the convict settlement of Sydney tends towards traditional Victorian painting, with the more 'sophisticated' Melbourne declaring its taste by collecting French painting. For instance, the 'competent' painter Sir William Orchardson was described by

Bloomsbury's Roger Fry as 'a man of refined but trivial sensibility' (Fry 1928: 31), thus moving what was later described by Bourdieu as 'cultural capital' out of the reaches of the nouveau riche. With the burgeoning upwardly mobile success stories of industrialisation, wealth was no longer adequate as a distinguishing feature of social class. The new rich had the money to differentiate themselves from the working class, but this was insufficient to impress. This is, of course, a fairly crude level of reasoning, though, as we saw in the Introduction, the sensibilities required of the new art, extolled in the theories of Clive Bell and at a more sophisticated level in Roger Fry's work, instead of giving universal access to all became the privilege of a certain class.[9]

The rapid move through the '-isms' of canonical art history, then, becomes a prerequisite of taste, and avant-garde culture is a necessary absorption of styles by the dominant fashion. The remove from so-called objective standards of competence required a level of critical substantiation and, crucially, spokesmen to identify the real 'challenges' in art. Members of the educated upper-middle class, confirming their status and power, were willing to act as a discriminating high priesthood in these matters. Pierre Bourdieu's *Distinction: a social critique of the judgement of taste* (1984), a sociological survey undertaken in the 1980s, adds weight to this proposition, in which the avant-garde continually redefined advanced art in opposition to the popular taste of the 'lower orders'. His work suggests that avant-garde culture and the elevation of certain art works, whether in literature, music or the visual arts, represent the class struggle fought out in the cultural arena. Bourdieu identifies a bourgeois strategy that accumulates what he calls 'cultural capital', a force which continually moves taste beyond the reach of working-class audiences. The challenging visual language of high-art icons, such as Picasso's *Les Demoiselles d'Avignon* (1907) demonstrates the point precisely. Within mainstream modernist histories this painting is accorded pre-eminence, Alfred H. Barr declaring, somewhat hagiographically, in 1943, that it was 'the first important cubist painting . . . in which Picasso's formidable and defiant genius reveals itself' (Barr 1988: 28). Originally an image of sailors in a brothel, the reworked final image depicts a bowl of fruit in the foreground and five angular female nudes with mask-like faces paying homage to Picasso's fascination with African masks. As far as avant-garde culture is concerned, there is a built-in time-lag between critical reception and popular acceptance. The acquisition of cultural capital is dependent upon an avant-garde; currently, where there is arguably no single avant-garde, this strategy becomes increasingly *passé*, since the 'shock of the new' rarely achieves its aim.

The time-lag principle is not only related to working-class taste; colonial and other cultures are also caught up in a deficit dependency model where their own art production is usually measured against the time that it takes avant-garde culture to influence their own 'indigenous' art, which is then deemed parochial or exotic. The benchmark of avant-gardism does not allow local and regional art production to be measured on its own terms.

Two avant-gardes

There was a period, however, when an avant-garde had greater cultural cachet. Raymond Williams identifies the complexity and vulnerability of avant-garde culture:

We have then to recall that the politics of the avant-garde, from the beginning, could go either way. The new art could find its place either in a new social order or in a culturally transformed but otherwise persistent and recuperated old order; all that was quite certain, from the first stirrings of modernism through to the most extreme forms of the avant-garde, was that nothing could stay quite as it was: that the internal pressures and the intolerable contradictions would force radical changes of some kind.

(Williams 1989a: 14)

Two avant-gardes are discernible (although the polarities do not always hold): on the one hand there is the avant-garde designated by its 'pure opticality' – its exponents being Roger Fry, Clive Bell, Clement Greenberg and Michael Fried; and on the other hand there is the avant-garde of Dada, surrealism, futurism and constructivism. Both are basically utopian art projects, but although their aims were the same their objectives were very different.

We have briefly alluded to Dada, a group of writers, musicians and artists that collaborated across art forms in Zurich in 1915. Dada's roots had been in the revolutionary art of the early Russian avant-garde, and it went on to inspire 'branches' in New York, Berlin, Barcelona and Paris. Implicit in the sheer variety and scale of their art (simultaneous poems, cabaret, noise, music, posters and paintings, illustrated in Marcel Janco's painting of an evening at *The Cabaret Voltaire*), Dada artists demonstrated a commitment to personal and political revolution. The term 'revolution' has lost much of its currency in the twenty-first century, applied as it is to processes as diverse as the manufacture of hair conditioner or triple beefburgers. In Zurich's Spiegelgasse, however, Dada's 'revolting' Cabaret Voltaire was in good company. The exiled Lenin, Russian leader of the Bolshevik Revolution, plotting revolution on a grand scale, lived across the street. Politics and art were inextricably enmeshed in Dada literary and polemical manifestos and anti-manifestos.

Hugo Ball was a leading Dada protagonist at the Cabaret Voltaire, and his *Gesamtkunstwerk* (complete art works achievable through cabaret) was a vehicle for Dada's engagement of the bourgeois in a war of attrition. Hans Arp wrote:

The bourgeois saw the Dadaist as a loose-living scoundrel, a villainous revolutionary, an uncivilised Asiatic, with designs upon their bells, safe-deposits and honours. The Dadaists thought up tricks to rob the bourgeois of his sleep. . . . The Dadaist gave the bourgeois a whiff of chaos, a sensation like that of a powerful but distant earth tremor, so that his bells began to buzz, his safe-deposits wrinkled their brows and his honour developed spots of mould.

(Arp, quoted in Richter 1965: 37–8)

The fate of much avant-garde culture is glimpsed by Hans Arp in 'Dadaland':

Revolted by the butchery of the 1914 World War, we in Zurich devoted ourselves to the arts. While the guns rumbled in the distance, we sang, painted, made collages and wrote songs with all our might. We were seeking an art based on fundamentals, to cure the madness of the age, and a new order of things that would restore the balance between heaven and hell. We had a dim premonition that power-mad gangsters would one day use art itself as a way of deadening men's minds.

(Arp, quoted in Richter 1965: 25)

There were other modernist responses to the clamour of war that illustrate the division of avant-garde culture, whose two branches shared a commitment to creative practices during a period of violent upheaval. Claude Monet, at Giverny in northern France, was coping with the distant noise of the guns while painting water lilies in his garden – a late series of garden paintings, colossal in scale, depict the lilies that dissolve into virtual abstraction. It is a moot point which of these avant-garde strategies has been the more effective or at least more historically significant to the history of art. In terms of traditional art history's 'selective machinery of tradition' (to recall Williams), Monet's formalism (and evacuation of politics) was valorised, while Dada's tactics are often presented as the antics of naughty schoolboys or ignored.

An additional contradiction of avant-garde culture is its distant relationship to the masses. André Breton, leader of the surrealist movement (sharing many Dada tendencies), wrote in 1929 in 'The Second Surrealist Manifesto': 'I do not believe in the present possibility of an art or literature which expresses the aspirations of the working class' (Breton 2003: 465). In surrealism the revolution of the psychic self, the inner world, was symbiotically linked with revolutionary Marxism. The surrealist's difficulty with political commitment was connected to the ease with which revolutionary techniques, formal experiments that would reveal the inner world, were appropriated as mere experiments or else rejected as distant from their politics. Surrealist automatist practices like frottage, grattage, decalcomania and montage were innovative but easily neutralised of any radical potential. In essence the surrealist quandary mirrors the avant-garde's precarious existence.

Radical art in terms of innovation was not seen as the only option to social revolution in the modern period, and it is a misreading of avant-garde culture always to see it as a break with the past, in spite of claims made by avant-gardists themselves. Lenin and Leon Trotsky recognised the achievements of bourgeois art forms, although they acknowledged their essentially conservative nature. A complete rejection of previous art forms was not therefore necessary. In *Literature and Art*, published in 1923, Trotsky states: 'Artistic creation is always a complicated turning inside out of old forms, under the influence of new stimuli which originate outside of art' (Trotsky, quoted in Timms and Collier 1988: 179). Lenin rejected new art forms advocated by both the Proletkult, a confederation of workers and factory art clubs producing art by and for the people, and the constructivists, employed in the same project, but using an abstract visual language in favour of building on existing bourgeois orthodoxies.

Antonio Gramsci, working in Turin in the early 1920s before Benito Mussolini's rise to power in 1922, and prior to a decade in prison, organised the Institute of Proletarian Culture, which bore affinities to the Proletkult in Russia. Gramsci also acknowledged the dynamism of bourgeois individualism, but advocated a redirection of that energy to mass culture. The rejection of the idea of continuities in favour of the modernist tropes of disruption, rejection and alienation was part of a strategy of social renewal. The continuities are, however, there, even if largely unacknowledged.

Art as commodity

> There are some people for whom the mere mention of art and money
> in the same book . . . is high treason, a hanging offence. To them it is
> as if money were a form of fiscal defoliant; set it among the fragile flow-
> ers of the art world and in next to no time you will have a wasteland.
>
> (Watson 1992: xxiii)

The co-dependence of art as art and art as commodity is a pronounced feature of
modernism. There are two aspects to this co-dependence: first, that modern art has
tended to depict the commodification of culture (for instance in the objects for sale in
A Bar at the Folies-Bergères), and second, that art aspires to the condition of commodity.
Peter Watson's observation, overblown perhaps, nonetheless highlights a prominent
feature of nineteenth- and twentieth-century art, a feature that has at times either
bedevilled art practice or been embraced by its practitioners and public alike. As we
have seen, avant-garde culture contains several paradoxes: one is the instrumental effect
of art markets on an art that aims to be autonomous and 'free' but at the same time
remains in thrall to the novelty factor of an art world hotfoot in pursuit of the new
and unfamiliar with which to *épater les bourgeois*.

One of modernism's more 'heroic' constants has been to evade commodity status and
to risk, or celebrate, a retreat from the world. From the Russian Proletkult movement,
through Dada, surrealism and the situationist international to abstract expressionism,
there have been attempts to evade the controlling mechanisms of market forces. Abstract
expressionism (dealt with in more detail in Chapter 6), it has been argued, attempted to
remove itself from the political arena and market forces, at the level of routine analysis,
by retreating into the aesthetic. The critic Greenberg acknowledged the ambiguous
position the avant-garde would need to maintain with its patrons. After all, even painters
need to eat. However, he declared that artists would need to remove themselves from
the commercial world, and frequently from the social world also, in order to survive, and
that this in itself was an act of heroism. The visual outcome on the canvas of this retreat
was a rejection of direct reference to the real world. Greenberg stated:

> Retiring from the public altogether, the avant-garde poet or artist sought to main-
> tain the high level of his art by both narrowing and raising it to the expression of
> an absolute in which all relatives and contradictions would disappear, and subject
> matter or content becomes something to be avoided like the plague.
>
> (Greenberg 1985: 35)

This utopian idealism that seeks to protect art from commodification becomes in its
turn another heroic failure.

With the possible exception of 'gift culture' – which is usually relegated to the realm
of 'primitive' economic forms, and therefore the academic preserve of the anthropologist, or else is marginalised to the periphery of 'sophisticated' capitalist Western
economics – the nineteenth and twentieth centuries have been marked by the total
assimilation of cultural activity within the orbit of commodification. As early as 1900,
the German philosopher Georg Simmel, writing in *Philosophy of Money*, acknowledged

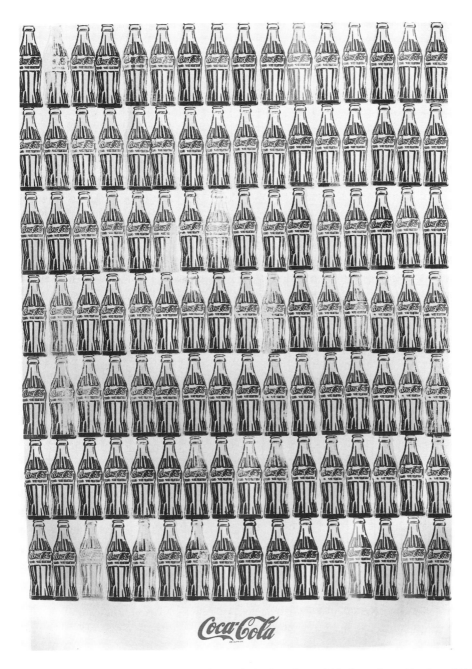

Figure 1.7   Andy Warhol, _Green Coca-Cola Bottles_, 1962, from the collection of Whitney Museum of American Art, New York. © The Andy Warhol Foundation for the Visual Arts, Inc./ARS, NY, and DACS, London, 2004. Photograph © 2001: Whitney Museum of American Art, New York. The seemingly endless repetition of the ultimate consumer success story, the Coca-Cola bottle, is part of Warhol's repertoire of advertising icons from Brillo pads to Campbell's soup cans. Silk-screened in grid-like formations, the work replicates the assembly-line presentation of bottles in a factory, or on the supermarket shelves, as well as alluding to the procedures of mass production in the printing process.

the inability of culture within a capitalist society to evade commodity status. Modern capitalism, he believed, would reduce all human creativity to the vicissitudes of the market place (see Simmel 1978).

Ever since the impressionists in the 1860s rejected the official Salon as the only legitimate financial marketplace and created an alternative art market with a dealer system, artists have both rejected (Duchamp) and embraced (Warhol) the process in about equal measure. As both the desired object of exchange value and increasingly since Manet's *A Bar at the Folies-Bergères*, with its conspicuous display of new mass-produced consumer goods, part of the imagery of modernism, commodification has permeated art practice and display. Andy Warhol's repetitive images of consumer culture and his imitation of the factory procedures of industry marked a break with the fetishising of the unique signature style of the artist and countenanced the 'trash' culture of the masses as the unlikely subject for great art (see Figure 1.7).

Currently, postmodernism's easy 'embrace' of commodity culture seems, at times, for instance in Barbara Kruger's *'Untitled' I Shop Therefore I Am*, an embrace that undermines the earlier modernist claim that a 'critical distance' was essential to its operations. This work is part of a series produced during the late 1980s that traded the palaces of art for the more overt advertising spaces of the billboard, the sides of buses and, here, the shopping bag. Kruger's pithy slogans, such as 'When I hear the word culture I take out my checkbook', questioned the supposed purity of art by exposing its commercial underbelly. Even the politically sanitised spaces of the white cube (as we will see in Chapter 7) have now embraced commodity as a framework for display. Recently several major exhibitions have committed space to commodity culture, shopping and consumerism. For instance, *The Chapman Family Collection* (2002) by Jake and Dinos Chapman reworked the unsullied purity of the tribal artefact by creating its own convincing versions of tribal figures, whose credibility is undermined by anachronisms such as bags of French fries and the trademark 'golden arches' of McDonald's.

The early commodification of art is evidenced by the purchase from the Royal Academy by Lord Leverhulme of Louise Jopling's *Home Bright, Hearth Light* (1896) (Figure 1.8) for use as an advertising image to promote Sunlight Soap, which he manufactured. More recently, in the 1990s the multinational clothing company Benetton ran various advertising campaigns which generated controversy for their aestheticisation of violence, death and human suffering. Benetton's imagery blurs lines that used to exist between art and advertising. Such imagery, unlike *Home Bright, Hearth Light*, generates controversy because it has nothing whatever to do with the product advertised. Under the guise of a social crusade, Benetton select causes such as AIDS, environmental disaster, war and famine, and violent death through organised crime to advertise the company. Although the image is not related to clothes, the tiny telltale bright green logo in the adverts is enough to indicate the fashion agenda. Such is the force of commodity culture that a discreet logo and unconnected image can sell clothes around the world.

Figure 1.8 (right) Louise Jopling, *Home Bright, Hearth Light*, 1896. Courtesy of National Museums Liverpool. The purchase of art works in order to advertise the products of industrialisation began during the Victorian period with the soap manufacturer Lord Leverhulme. This late-Victorian work extols the virtue of the clean home in an accessible aesthetic form, easily appropriated by mass advertising.

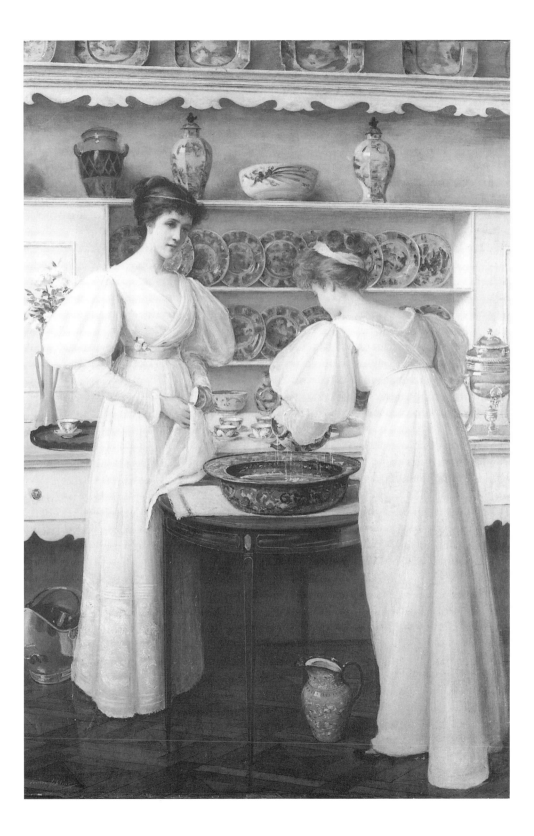

In spite of Simmel's early conviction, this phenomenon has been challenged by artists working at the edges of acceptability in making connections between advertising and the Holocaust. Tom Sachs' *Giftgas Giftset* (1998), shown in an exhibition in the Jewish Museum New York in 2002, takes the glamorous logo of luxury goods and places them on the Zyclon b canisters of the Nazi death camps. In *Giftgas Giftset* and the companion piece *Prada Deathcamp* (made of cardboard paper, ink, thermal adhesive and foam) Sachs draws attention to the Holocaust industries' relationship to consumption as well as to the repressive, controlling structures of the advertising industry. He uses the style labels of the fashionably wealthy to investigate the erosion of personal identities through totalising mechanisms such as merchandising and advertising.

Where is the avant-garde now?

We have suggested that there have been continuities and ruptures between modernism and postmodernism. The current position of avant-garde culture is relevant here. Critics such as Burger have commented on the failure of the historic avant-garde:

> For Burger the historical avant-garde also failed . . . the dadaists to destroy traditional art categories, the surrealists to reconcile subjective transgression and social revolution, the constructivists to make the cultural means of production collective – but it failed heroically, tragically. Merely to fail *again*, as the neo-avant-garde does according to Burger, is at best pathetic and farcical, at worst cynical and opportunistic.
>
> (Foster 1996: 13)

Robert Hughes, writing in the *Sunday Times Magazine* in 1979, felt confident enough to announce the death of the avant-garde.

> This sudden metamorphosis of one of the popular clichés of art-writing into an unword took a great many by surprise. For those who still believed that art had some practical revolutionary functions, it was as baffling as the evaporation of the American radical Left after 1970.
>
> (Hughes 1980: 18)

Other writers have sought to bury modernism. They point to things like the so-called technological revolution, the reappropriation of avant-garde strategies by the world of advertising and the supposed collapse of art into pure commodity as evidence of the demise of modernism – and as themselves markers of postmodernism.

However, announcements such as that of Hughes concerning the 'death of the avant-garde' are premature according to others. If modernism has ultimately failed, then what happens to all its relics, *Fountain* for instance? Contemporary art practice has found various uses for avant-garde culture. The first easily visible manifestation of the avant-garde's loss of purity came in postmodern architecture with the wholesale importation into one building of previously autonomous, apparently irreconcilable, styles. Returning to Sherrie Levine's photograph of Stieglitz's photograph of Duchamp's *Fountain*, her acknowledged plagiarism is representative of the next stage in the reassimilation of modernist strategies into the postmodern. It may be seen, on one level, as postmodernism's partial acknowledgement of the failure of the totalising tendencies of modernism, and of a lack of confidence in universal beliefs in general. The whole notion of a universal modernism has been found wanting. However, as Suzi Gablik argues in relation to Levine's 'duplicitous' strategy, postmodern art 'becomes the cheerful orchestration of collapse, the cracked mirror of culture where products must continually replicate other products, where artists become the authors of somebody else's work' (Gablik 1991a: 36–7).

The triumph of postmodernism, at least in the West, has been a Pyrrhic victory. Postmodernism's crisis is the crisis of confidence in the function of art and culture at the end of the twentieth century and beyond. One of the gains of postmodernism, however, has been its recuperative aspect. It allows for artists and historians to explore in the wider margins works and strategies neglected or dismissed by modernism. It allows also for local and specific art works that take account of cultural diversity and celebrate difference. Its other gain, a mistrust of hierarchies, has come at the expense of a sense of overall purpose. A loss of confidence in the unitary self and a unitary expression (explored in greater detail in Chapter 2) has opened up a space that takes account of poly-vocalities. In terms of the work generated under the rubric of postmodernism Faith Ringgold's series *The French Collection* (1991) can be seen as paradigmatic: a celebration of black people's intervention into Western art history. *The French Collection* takes masterpieces of modern art and domesticates them through the collectively embroidered patchwork quilt and fabric painting. In a series of images, Ringgold gently but firmly declares bogus the myths of masculine and white creativity. In *Sunflowers Quilting Bee at Arles* (1991), Van Gogh, clutching a vase of sunflowers in a field full of sunflowers, is placed in the background of the work, while Ringgold foregrounds a quilting bee[10] of black women working on a sunflower motif. The work, which contains a text-based border, operates at many levels, not least as a critique of the hierarchy of genres, in which textile work is found wanting, as we remarked at the beginning of this chapter. But it is a celebration also of the cultural diversity of art practice itself. An amalgam of formal fine-art practice (painting) and domestic handicraft (patchwork fabric), Ringgold's work is eclectic at the level of both subject and medium.

Ringgold's work is emblematic of postmodern plurality and witness to the partial erosion of the division between provincialism and internationalism. It is also an acknowledgement that there is no longer a unified field of art or a single practice that we call fine art. New subject alliances are being formed, and boundary-spanning rather than attention to the purity of the medium is the new art order.

Many artists now work across a field broadly defined as interdisciplinary; that is, a fusion of art with other subject disciplines such as philosophy, anthropology, science or architecture. Rather than work in what was termed multiculturalism, there are new forms of hybridity taking place that acknowledge what Okwui Enwezor (2003) sees as cultural toing and froing, not just across disciplines but also across physical distances and cultures.

The artist Simryn Gill, normally resident in Sydney, returning to her home town of Port Dickson in Malaysia, produced a series of photographs of local people, their identities suggested on two levels. They are surrounded by their possessions or work tools that situate them in their town and in the modern world. However, their faces are obscured by tropical fruit masks that confound the viewer and confront the ambiguities that make up modern cultural identities (see Plate VII). The images contain a mixture of the timeless exotica demanded by the tourist gaze as well as evidence of the industrialised world of a global economy, a far cry from the images of 'other' cultures that contributed to modernism's singular world-view, which we shall look at in detail in Chapter 2.

The strength of the modernist project was its sense of purpose, which increased in the face of opposition – part of its dissenting tradition of antagonism and alienation. The difficulty now, at least in Western culture, when art seems to have fused with global commodity, is that rebellion lacks cachet. As a consequence, art has arguably been deprived of its energy, and certainly its utopianism. Moreover, postmodernism has introduced a form of relativism and scepticism, with irony playing at centre-stage: a boon perhaps to previously excluded groups but somewhat repetitive in practice, with a repertoire of enquiry into the reified artworks of history. So far we have concentrated on modernism and postmodernism as urban phenomena engaged with the larger utopian projects of modernity. In Chapter 2 we look at modernism and postmodernism again, this time in terms of a search for rural and spiritual utopias and alternative art practices.

2 Retreats from the urban

> We have substituted for the idea of 'nature seen through a temperament', the theory of equivalence or of the symbol: we asserted that the emotions or spiritual states caused by any spectacle bring to the imagination of the artist symbols or plastic equivalents. These are capable of reproducing emotions or states of the spirit without it being necessary to provide the *copy* of the initial spectacle; thus for each state of our sensibility there must be a corresponding objective harmony capable of expressing it.
>
> (Denis 1968b: 105)

Although, as we saw in Chapter 1, many appeals have been made to the reasoning of Maurice Denis to support the purely aesthetic ends of artists' formal concerns, his idea of 'plastic equivalents' for 'emotional or spiritual states' will be our focus in this chapter. The notion that artists' authority rests in their first-hand experience of the thing that they are making into a work of art has always been open to question; for instance, no one expected the artist to have first-hand knowledge of ancient battles, of Diana bathing or of the creation of Adam. It was the artist's ability to approximate the spectacle that was valued. However, for modern artists the capacity to invent spectacles that they have not experienced is less significant than the artists having *actually* experienced the things (and in particular the emotions) that they make the object of their art. Denis's call was for art works which correspond to 'states of our sensibility' – not by representing the 'spectacle' or the cause of the sensation but via 'plastic equivalents' in colour and form (see Figure 2.1). This has then to be seen in the context of particular shifts which combine to privilege the artist as someone whose authority resides principally in his or her capacity to express interior moods and beliefs.

In this chapter we look at how artistic authority in the modern period is grounded in a notion of the artist's unique experience and particularly in his or her 'inner world' of feelings, impressions and sensibilities. We look at how the personal journeys of the artist's imagination (both physical and mental) became so important to modern – especially non-figurative – art in relation to the search for spiritual meaning. The image

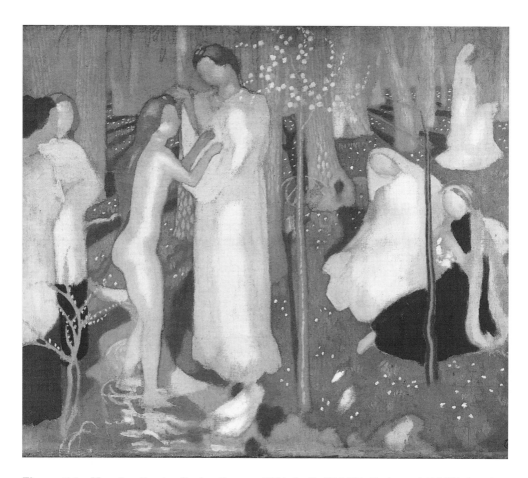

Figure 2.1   Maurice Denis, *Springtime, c.***1894–9.** © ADAGP, Paris, and DACS, London, 2004. Courtesy of the Metropolitan Museum of Art, Gift of David Devrishian, 1999. Like much European symbolist art, Denis's painting is a blend of personal and conventional iconography. Denis's neo-Catholicism led him to seek the divine in everyday subjects, which are rendered as remote and mysterious. This painting depicts three pairs of young women, each representing aspects of the sacred and the profane. The profane is being purified in the forest of Saint-Germain, symbolically at Easter time.

of the artist venturing out (or inwards), risking his or her senses (and sometimes sanity) in order to experience the limits of the imagination is very much part of the rhetoric of modern art. It is often attended by the notion that a physical retreat (usually from the urban environment) permits a psychic 'rebirth' of the artist. But it is attended also by the notion of a retreat that is mystical rather than physical. As we will see, the communion of peoples and their religious beliefs may be loosely characterised as mystical, although precisely what that entails depends upon whether one's system of belief is Buddhist, Christian, Hindu or something else. However, as we will see, a number of artists from the late nineteenth century onwards renounced conventional religious systems or sought out alternative spiritual experiences.

Imagination and 'the fiction of the self'

> Because no two people have the same intellect and senses, we cannot find the truth in representing things as we see them; they will always be distorted.
>
> (František Kupka, quoted in Henderson 1983: 105)

As defined by Raymond Williams, the imagination is 'mental conception, including a quite early sense of seeing what does not exist as well as what is not plainly visible' (Williams 1988: 158). The *imagination* was classified as a category of knowledge in Denis Diderot's (1713–84) *L'Encyclopédie* and it became the prime site of knowledge in eighteenth-century Romantic notions of the poet (such as Blake and Coleridge), even though it remained of secondary importance for scientists.

The imagination, however, played a less significant part in the pathology of the artist until the modern period. What is significant for our purposes is that when artists do start to privilege the imagination it is in a spirit of opposition. For Charles Baudelaire (1821–67) the imagination, 'the queen of the faculties', was diametrically opposed to the doctrine of 'truth to nature' and signalled the right of the artist to pursue 'his' fancies (Baudelaire 1965: 155). Baudelaire divided artists into two camps: the realists and the imaginatives. The realist seeks to copy nature, the imaginative to 'paint its own soul' (Baudelaire 1965: 162). Baudelaire's separation of 'nature' (the external world) from the 'soul' (the internal landscape) was very much part of the philosophical dualism we examine on pp. 58–60. But for the present the salient feature of the imagination is the way in which under modernism inferiority assumes superiority. The imposition by artists of form on their imaginings and the evolution of a personal iconography – either a unique signature style or a recurring set of motifs – is crucial to the modernist concept of art.

The perceived differences between art movements such as impressionism and symbolism (although Baudelaire's distinction pre-dates both) mark the differences between 'external' and 'internal' for the modern artist. Paul Gauguin, whose career spans both impressionism and symbolism, criticised the Parisian impressionists for being 'shackled' (his term) by their attempts to render impressions of nature – haystacks in different atmospheric conditions, Sunday outings along the banks of the River Seine, flowers in a vase. The impressionist pursuit of nature is summed up by Cézanne, who is supposed to have said, in awe, of Monet that 'he was only an eye, but my God what an eye'. Gauguin, however, had no truck with the impressionists' privileging of 'the eye' of the artist. On this matter he was fundamentally at odds with the impressionists because he believed that his 'internal eye' was more important than his physical or external eye. Gauguin used the phrase 'working from memory' to describe his method: nature may well have been the starting point for his art, but his imagination had the last word. In order to tap his imagination, Gauguin consorted with different experiences of nature – at Pont-Aven in Brittany (Figure 2.2), in Arles and finally in Tahiti. Gauguin's belief in the power of imagination over observation signalled (if you believe in modernist sea-changes)[1] a shift in thinking about the making of art whereby in order to nurture the imagination the body had to be exposed to new experiences.

Similar sayings in which the imagination is privileged can be found among the writings of Gauguin's contemporaries: Edvard Munch's well-known dictum 'nature is transformed

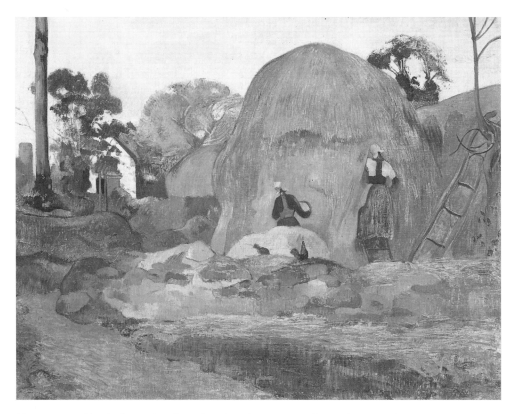

Figure 2.2 Paul Gauguin, *Les Meules jaunes ou la moisson blonde*, 1889. Musée d'Orsay. © Photo RMN–H. Lewandowski. Monet famously painted haystacks, recording the changes to the motif in differing atmospheric conditions. Gauguin's motives appear less scientific and he directed an art practice in terms of dreaming rather than seeing: 'draw art as you dream in nature's presence, and think more about the act of creation than about the final result'.

according to one's subjective disposition' and Gustave Moreau's 'I believe only in what I do not see and solely in what I feel' are typical of the rhetoric of the *fin de siècle*. The other-worldly and introspective themes that characterised the symbolist movement were part of the *fin-de-siècle* mind-set. Many ponderous 'cycle of life' schemes saw artists asking profound questions: Gauguin's *Where Do We Come From? What Are We? Where Are We Going?*, Picasso's *La Vie*, Munch's *Frieze of Life* and Klimt's *Beethoven Frieze*. Although it began in literature and poetry, symbolism became both a style and a source of subject matter for the visual arts around the 1890s. In Alfred Barr's 1936 schema (Figure 1.4) symbolism plays a pivotal role, but in terms of modernist art history it is generally viewed as something of a cul-de-sac. The dynamism of the 'modernist project' – within the narrow parameters of formalism – is apparently undermined by symbolism's eclectic blend of literary content and narrative. At a time when, we are led to believe, the overwhelming impulse of artists was towards a purposeful 'purification of the medium', the symbolists seem quirky and old-fashioned. Moreover, their interest in quasi-mystical thought was somewhat arcane and remote from the hubbub of modernity.

To go any further with the notion of retreat into the interior landscape we need to examine how the notion of 'the self' and, in particular, consensual notions of 'the artistic self' have been reconfigured in the modern period. In general terms, notions of *selfhood* came under review. The idea of the self – as unique, unitary, separate and distinct from every other self – is a privilege of modern society, one that not all cultures share; in fact many cultures have no equivalent word. The notion of 'self' is thus historically, socially and geographically specific. The right to individual liberty, for instance, is enshrined in the Constitution of the USA, though what constitutes 'individual liberty' is historically contingent. Historically, notions of selfhood are bound up with humanism, Romanticism and utilitarianism, but the modern sense of the self is also the outcome of other far-reaching shifts of thought. Theories such as nineteenth-century social Darwinism underscored the shift from aristocratic to bourgeois power as the survival of the fittest groups of individuals. For our purposes the salient features of this historical impulse towards Western individuality is the proposition that each and every self is 'unitary' – different from the next – existing both outside and beside other such selves.

The death of the author

The notion of the artist as self and the viewer as another self is a hallmark of the bourgeois construction of art, based upon the idea of the work of art as an autonomous and discrete object. Indeed, as we will see in Chapter 7, the very design of the modern museum facilitates the private meditation upon, or spiritual contemplation of, the work of art. It is a condition of the special relationship between the viewer and the work of art viewed that the artist should be a meaningful communicator of thoughts and feelings. Borrowing from film theory, the concept of the *auteur* – the assumption that the author, director or artist is the pivotal presence in the making of a book, a film or a work of art – helps explain the link between art work, artist and viewer. To regard a work of art as the 'personal vision' of its maker has led art historians to conclude that there must be a significant link between the biographical details of an artist's life and his or her work. We have substituted a focus on what the artist *does* for who the artist *is*. This is a feature of artist biopics, films about the lives of famous artists. For example, Henning Carlsen's film about Paul Gauguin, *Wolf at the Door* (1986), derives its title from the uncorroborated scene where Gauguin likens himself to a wolf that would rather starve than submit to wearing a collar. The film is set in the two-year period between Gauguin's first and his final stay in Tahiti, only a very brief sojourn in Gauguin's otherwise racy biography. Nonetheless, the film dwells on his *feelings* of dissatisfaction with France and his longing to be back in the 'primitive' society of the South Seas. Donald Sutherland's portrayal of Gauguin in the film draws heavily upon descriptions of Gauguin's behaviour, and the actor plays with the badges of his *auteur* status – his studied disaffection, bohemian dress and predilection for alcohol.

However, in recent years the idea of the history of art as a history of great individuals has been steadily undermined. Thought-provoking essays such as Roland Barthes's 'The Death of the Author' (see Barthes 1977) have dealt a blow to some of the critically unreflective adulation accorded to artistic genius. With specific reference to literary theory, Barthes highlights the conceits of authorship:

The Author, when believed in, is always conceived of as the past of his own book: book and author stand automatically on a single line divided into a *before* and an *after*. The Author is thought to *nourish* the book, which is to say that he exists before it, thinks, suffers, lives for it, is in the same relation of antecedence to his work as a father to his child.

(Barthes 1977: 145)

Barthes posits an alternative view that the 'modern scriptor is born simultaneously with the text and is no way equipped with a being preceding or exceeding the writing' (Barthes 1977: 145). Many subsequent postmodern thinkers have built upon Barthes's ideas, referring to 'the fiction of the self' – a fantasy, supported by language, arguing that unitary selves are something we have invented to reassure ourselves. As Robert Smithson has explained, 'the existence of "self" is what keeps everybody from confronting their fears about the ground they happen to be standing on' (quoted in Lippard 1997: 89). Counter-*auteuriste* theorists would say that the making of art is not the sole responsibility of the individual but the product of a set of external factors which have conspired to make that individual think that he or she *really* is responsible. While rumours of the death of the author have been greatly exaggerated, there appears to have been a significant shift towards an interpretation of art works that depends upon the position of the viewer as subject. Meaning is not something simply deposited in a work of art by the omniscient artist, but is actively constituted by the viewer based upon his or her subject position, as defined by class, race, gender or sexuality. Thus the intention of the artist in creating a work is apparently undermined by poststructuralist theories. For if the work of art is ultimately meaningful only from the position of the viewer as subject, then we can dismiss entirely what follows in this chapter. It is one of the paradoxes of postmodernism that notions of the viewer as subject undermine notions of the artist's subjectivity. It is fair to point out, however, that, while artists' intentions are no longer ostensibly the principal concern of art history, it would be premature to relegate artists' intentions to a cameo role, particularly when the 'intention' of so many artists was to 'find themselves' through their art.

Art and spirituality

One of the tasks of the spiritual in art is to prove again and again that vision is possible: that this world, thick and convincing, is neither the only world nor the highest, and that our ordinary awareness is neither the only awareness nor the highest of which we are capable. Traditionally, this task falls under a stringent rule: the vision cannot be random and entirely subjective, but must be capable of touching a common chord in many men and women.

(Lipsey 1997: 92)

We will see in Chapter 5 that there has been a tendency to view progressive modernism as rational and orderly. For instance, the view that Piet Mondrian's neo-plasticism was a hard-edged retort to the kind of expressionism that was dominating the modern movement in the period 1910–20 is characteristic of teleological modernism. 'Neo-plasticism' is a term which Mondrian borrowed from the philosopher M.J.H. Schoenmakers, and although it largely describes Mondrian's formal efforts to rid his paintings of everything bar red, blue and yellow on a black-and-white grid, it is also a term with metaphysical roots. It describes Mondrian's theosophical endeavour to make 'spiritual' art which was capable of communicating a universal truth. Theosophy was a set of metaphysical beliefs with roots in ancient mysticism which became popular in the late nineteenth and early twentieth centuries. The Theosophical Society's objective of a 'universal brotherhood of humanity' finds its visual counterpart in the claims made for much abstract art. Piet Mondrian's reading of 'universal truth' came via theosophy and stemmed, in part, from the neo-Platonic idea, which found favour with many exponents of abstraction, including Roger Fry in his essay 'Art and Socialism' (1961), that there were enduring qualities which lay behind the accidental or surface appearance of things. And it combined with Mondrian's interest in theosophy, in which artists find enlightenment from within by invoking the services of transcendental forces.

Although recent writers such as Suzi Gablik have proposed that we need to be sensitive to 'vaster realities' (Gablik 1991b: 57), it has been generally unfashionable (among Greenbergian modernists at least) to discuss the spiritual in art (although, as Chapter 6 will show, spiritual values do play a large part in the formation of post-war aesthetic theories). The importance of spirituality in the modern period, however, is both remarkable and quite often overlooked. The association of spiritualism (in the guise of a brand of esoteric mysticism) with Nazism in the 1930s and 1940s has discredited it with some of the Jewish intelligentsia and leftist writers who have been responsible for so much of the writing on the history of art. Similarly the rise of existentialism in the 1950s made an interest in matters spiritual seem like so much unfashionable hokum. Since then, many art historians have found it difficult to square the undeniable fact that artists were influenced by (and put on record their debt to) what might loosely be termed spiritual tendencies with the history of modernism and all that modernism's rhetoric entails. For instance, Wassily Kandinksy's *Concerning the Spiritual in Art* (1977; first published in 1911) has either been demonised as untheorised mysticism or misread altogether as an apology for a type of woolly formalism. Uninstitutionalised spirituality, then, is difficult terrain in the present theoretical climate of 'deconstruction', with its underlying objective of 'demystifying' the object of study. The rigorous and pseudo-scientific methods of 'deconstruction' may have dealt a crushing blow to the personal and the subjective, the mystical and the transcendental, but the postmodern climate paradoxically permits the spiritual after all. One of the ironies of postmodernism is that its central lack of faith in 'certainties' – especially the idea that 'modern man', as a rational being, has all the answers to all the world's problems – has permitted a place for the spiritual and the transcendental.

Although spirituality is not readily brought to mind in the Greenbergian formal appreciation that modernism engendered – in fact Greenberg evacuated it altogether – it was certainly part of the *fin-de-siècle* Zeitgeist. Many modern artists were affiliated to spiritual movements in the early twentieth century, such as the Theosophical Society, anthroposophy, Rosicrucianism and the cult of Mazdaism, all of which had a common interest in the spiritual questions that came to the surface during the 'age of anxiety' during the *fin de siècle*. In brief, the tone of these spiritual tracts speculated about the connections between the material and transcendent realms. Notions of the spiritual and the mystical gained credibility with the idealist philosopher Henri Bergson (1859–1941) in works like *Creative Evolution* (1907), which posited a notion of perception involving memory and the subjective construction of reality. Emanuel Swedenborg (1688–1772), the Swedish scientist and Christian mystic, had outlined notions of 'correspondences' or connections between the visible and invisible worlds. Rosicrucianism, a mystic brotherhood dating from the Middle Ages and committed to advancing occult knowledge, counted many French symbolists among its number. George Ivanovitch Gurdjieff (*c.* 1872–1949), a self-proclaimed mystic and founder of the Institute for the Harmonious Development of Man, retreated to Fontainebleau to develop his teachings, which were informed by Eastern mysticism. Gurdjieffian teachings encouraged a kind of individuality that transcended what Gurdjieff saw as the sleep-like state of the mundane existence and encouraged paths to self-knowledge which gripped the imagination of a significant number of artists and poets in the 1920s and 1930s.

In terms of modern art practice, the most influential of the spiritual movements was the Theosophical Society, which was particularly important to a number of artists, including Kandinsky, Mondrian, František Kupka and, post-Second World War, Joseph Beuys. The Society was founded at the end of the nineteenth century and became an organised religion under Madame Helena Petrovna Blavatsky (1831–91). Broadly speaking, theosophists believed in the visibility of spiritual states, in white magic and in a sixth sense, which they referred to as 'superconsciousness'. For the modern artist the idea of a state of consciousness additional to the mundane was seductive. Superconsciousness, in theosophical theories, is a state of intense perceptivity (brought on by clairvoyancy or hypnotism) in which the subject, in a state of trance, has his or her perception heightened and is able to 'see' things not readily visible. The resulting ethereal vision, typically 'seeing' the world from a great distance or things so close up that they look like worlds within worlds, was to be harnessed by a number of twentieth-century artists.

What is significant about spiritual movements such as theosophy (and the sway that they held over many modern artists) is that they were usually at odds with broader scientific trends in modern thinking. For example, mystics tended to renounce the subject–object division that distinguished between the thinker and the thought. They saw the philosophical fiction of the mind–body dualism as a damaging one which prevents the mind from recognising its essential 'oneness' with the world. Theosophists rejuvenated an age-old belief in the visibility of spiritual states. Theosophy is a doctrine of togetherness rather than of unitary selfhood; the 'higher self', or *atman*, is collective rather than personal, and this sits uncomfortably with the ideas of individuality we outlined above (although ironically not with the 'fiction of the self'). Moreover, in these spiritual and occultist beliefs a retreat into the 'higher self', through the superconsciousness or whatever, was positively encouraged. The 'external world' was often compared unfavourably to the 'inner world', where feelings, impressions and spiritual knowledge were sovereign.

František Kupka has some claim, along with Kandinsky and Francis Picabia, to having 'invented' abstract painting. Kupka was a theosophist and spiritualist (in the sense of being a medium for seances). In line with broad theosophical thinking, he rejected the idea that three-dimensional 'reality' was the only visual experience, and based his abstract paintings on 'inner visions' – sometimes brought on by clairvoyant trances. On the surface his early work such as *Disks of Newton* (1912) (see Plate VIII) blends several concerns (balls in movement, orbits of the planets) with his interest in the laws of Newtonian physics. However, Kupka's interest in spiritualism meant that he believed himself capable of splitting his consciousness during seances and observing the world from 'outside'. Years before the first photographs of the earth from space, Kupka was painting what he believed to be 'visions' of the cosmos. Although Kupka never claimed that his 'inner visions' were any more than fragments which 'float in our heads', he believed that his clairvoyant vision lent him a transcendence which enabled him to survey the cosmos.

Kupka shared Kandinsky's interest in 'thought-forms', or material shapes and colours which can be given to abstract moods and states of being. Both believed in correspondences between painting and music. In the years before the First World War, Kupka painted a series of 'Fugues' and Kandinsky numerous 'Improvisations'. Kandinsky's *Heavy Circles* (1927) depicts disks overlapping like a diagrammatic rendering of planetary motion. For Kandinsky, the circle was the most complex of the three primary shapes (triangle and square being the other two) because it was a mass of contradictions, being both 'quiet' and 'noisy', 'stable' and 'unstable', 'precise' yet 'inexhaustibly variable', and came as close as it was possible to get to the fourth dimension.

In a number of ways Kandinsky was deeply indebted to European symbolism. He believed, for instance, that the 'inner world' of the artist should be expressed in the artist's work, but, more importantly, he inherited the symbolist notion that a work of art has, as well as a material existence, an interiority – even, according to Georges Albert Aurier, a 'soul' (see Chipp 1968: 87). Kandinsky's writings are full of unresolved tensions between physical existence and spiritual transcendence. He believed that the arts alone could 'give free scope to the non-material strivings of the soul' (Kandinsky 1977: 14). What motivated Kandinsky to search for the spiritual is complex but the idea that the spiritual realm provided a retreat from the worst of 'external' modern life, what he calls its 'dark picture', undoubtedly occurred to him. Kandinsky saw the flight to the inner world of the spirit as a retreat from the uncertainties of the external world – as expressed by science, religion and morality. The 'spiritual revolution' he discerns in literature, music and art constitutes 'a little point of light' in the otherwise 'soulless life of the present' (Kandinsky 1977: 14).

At this point we anticipate an idea which we will see more of in Chapter 3, an idea that has become somewhat discredited under postmodernism, the notion of 'essentialism'. As we have seen, one of the principal tenets of theosophy was its valorisation of the internal over the external, but Kandinsky's search for universal essences was apparently contrary to scientific modernism. For instance, cubism is concerned with presenting the visual world in novel terms (although, of course, it is no less immune to the spiritual than other art movements – for instance the Paris-based art group, Section D'Or). Kandinsky was, however, influenced by European symbolism (or *Jugendstil*, as it was known in northern European countries) and was steeped in the symbolists' search for essences. Kandinsky may have produced art materially – oil on canvas or watercolour on paper – but he believed that art was at the same time non-material. He saw art as something striving to be 'pure art' or to overcome its corporeality and become pure essence.[2] Kupka also compared art and music: 'I believe I can find something between sight and hearing and I can produce a fugue in colours as Bach has done in music' (Guggenheim 1975: 184). Nor was he alone in seeing the objective of art in this way. Kasimir Malevich's idea of non-objective art as 'milk without the bottle' was formulated along similar lines. Hilla Rebay, the theosophical baroness who exhibited the work of abstract artists in New York in the 1930s, also compared non-objective painting to music (see Frascina 1982: 145). Moreover, Rebay thought that a 'higher intellect' was required both to produce and to consume non-objective art.

Dualism

> My work is impure; it is clogged with matter. I'm for a weighty, ponderous art. There is no escape from matter. There is no escape from the physical nor is there any escape from the mind. The two are in a constant collision course. You might say that my work is like . . . a quiet catastrophe of mind and matter.
>
> (Robert Smithson, quoted in Lippard 1997: 89)

In 1969 the earthworks artist Robert Smithson, claimed his work was about 'the interaction between mind and matter. It is a dualistic idea which is very primitive' (quoted in Lippard 1997: 89). The modern idea of an art practice which linked mind and matter was, by 1969, hardly topical and recalled early modern artists' search for 'pure art'. Smithson acknowledged that his sense of dualism was 'primitive', and what is significant for our purposes is that Smithson should even have been trying to resolve this perennial quest. Smithson's *Spiral Jetty* at Rozel Point, Great Salt Lake, Utah (1970) (Figure 2.3), approaches the scale on which ancient monuments were constructed, and is often interpreted as an attempt at connecting to a primordial past (see Lippard 1983). Ostensibly it is an example of earthworks art, which emerged in the 1960s in the spirit of the 'dematerialisation' of art to be examined in Chapter 8 (*Spiral Jetty* periodically 'dematerialises' – that is, it disappears under rising water levels and resurfaces only intermittently). However, to see earthworks art as only a form of self-expression that at the same time happened to reject the art market is to miss what was to many the deep spirituality of the earthworks art enterprise. As we will see in Chapter 3, the modernist rejection of traditional sculptural forms precipitated a sculptural practice based on 'essence' and a concentration on the autonomy of art. In a debt to the minimalism of the 1960s, Smithson rejects the museum as the site for display and seeks out ancient earthworks as a more meaningful, more authentic, art practice. However, it is Smithson's idea of a connection between ancient and modern, mind and matter, that is significant here.

Although poststructuralist theories tend to point to the maxim that all human experience is locally conditioned (by socio-economic and other factors), the idea of universal patterns which permeate all human unconscious expression has been compelling. Jung's concept of a 'collective unconscious' gave expression to it and Claude Lévi-Strauss, in *The Savage Mind* (1972), saw age-old mythic patterns recurring in cultures, while Madame Blavatsky similarly stressed the links between 'civilised' and 'savage' cultures. The continuity of fundamental human experience – across time and space – was, according to some, what lay behind the retreat to the primordial.

The dualism of mental–physical life that emerged in the Romantic period is one which is revisited (often with the trappings of scientific certainty) in the early years of the modern period. Philosophical dualism is as old as philosophy itself. Plato's idea

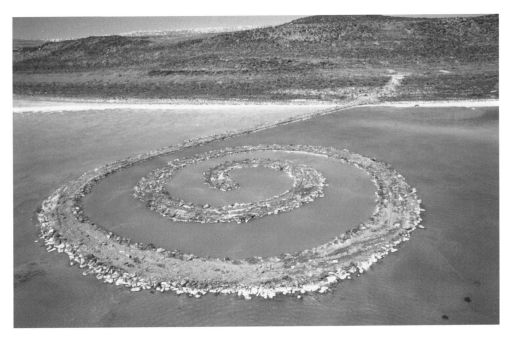

Figure 2.3 Robert Smithson, *Spiral Jetty,* April 1970. Great Salt Lake, Utah. Black rock, salt crystals, earth, red water (algae), 3½ feet × 15 feet × 1500 feet. © Estate of Robert Smithson/VAGA, New York/DACS, London, 2004. Courtesy of James Cohan Gallery, New York. Collection: DIA Center for the Arts, New York. Photo by Gianfranco Gorgoni. Smithson's monumental earthwork is constructed from black basalt and earth coiled in a 1,500 feet long spiral. The jetty is 15 feet wide but it is only intermittently visible since water levels in the Great Salt Lake fluctuate according to weather conditions. The idea for the spiral design was suggested by the Pre-Columbian Great Serpent Mound in Ohio and is itself a motif that is virtually trans-historic and transcultural.

that the intelligible world may be experienced separately from the sensory world is almost identical to the Christian belief that the soul continues to exist after the death of the body. Indeed the demarcation of the spirit and the body is common to many religions. The metaphysical idea of an 'outer' and an 'inner' self is paralleled by the dialectic between external and internal, material and non-material, conscious and subconscious, body and soul that informs many cultures. The Judaeo-Christian distinction between spirit and flesh and Descartes' mind–body dualism – summarised in the famous formula 'I think, therefore I am' – combined as potent philosophical forces.

Modern philosophy, as we will see in Chapter 4, tends towards subject–object dualism, distinguishing between the thinker and the thought – although, it has to be said, 'thinking' was narrowly defined in the modern period and the invitation to contribute was rarely extended to women. However, the realm of thought was sovereign in philosophical prophecies – Hegel, for example, had thought that man's spirit would eventually overcome matter. In *fin-de-siècle* Europe 'evolutionary transcendence' was highly fashionable, offering the possibility that evolution itself was inherently spiritual. Joseph Le Conte, the American Darwinian, published *Evolution: its nature, its evidences, and its relation to religious thought* in 1888–91. In a nutshell, his hypothesis was that 'man' was on the verge of evolving from a 'lower' outer life to a 'higher' inner life, throwing off the body and releasing the spirit.[3]

The Spanish artist Remedios Varo believed in 'spiritual breakthroughs' for women. Her paintings often contrast the mystical activities of women with the rational activities of male scientists. Scientists, she believed, consistently failed to recognise the higher reality of nature, while women intuitively understood its power. Varo saw herself and artists in general as explorers, in search of inner truth and spiritual meaning. Varo collected pre-Columbian art, studied Eastern religions and was fascinated by the occult and by alchemy, in particular. In the twentieth century, alchemy is no longer seen as an outdated search for a formula to turn base metal into gold; it has enjoyed a revival as a highly popular 'science'. Artists including Marcel Duchamp,[4] Salvador Dali and the surrealists certainly wrote about it, and Jung published *Psychology and Alchemy* in 1933. Varo's *Creation of the Birds* (1957) (Plate IX) shows the artist as a seated owl; with the divine help of a beam of light from a star and an alchemical still mixing colours for her palette, she creates a bird, which springs to life from the paper to follow other birds out of the window. The alchemical motif repeats itself in Varo's work – chiefly as a metaphor for female creativity. While the surrealists linked women to the supernatural and believed them to be the (unwitting) possessors of ancient magical knowledge, Varo turned this association to her advantage. She appropriated much occultism, particularly hermeticism (a heady brew of alchemy, Jewish mysticism and Hellenistic white magic). Varo adopted as a feminine prerogative the hermetic doctrine of 'as above, so below' – that is to say, living bodily life in imitation of the spiritual life; women, she believed, instinctively possessed ancient knowledge, while men were insensitive to anything outside the conventional intellect. Varo's sense of her own creativity was mirrored by the 'alchemical' transmutation of pigment in the act of painting, often rendered in her paintings by means of fantastic alchemical contraptions. Similarly, her often fey iconography suggests her interest in the supernatural. She personifies the artist (herself) as an owl, itself the symbol of wisdom, creating birds which are at once personal symbols and Jungian symbols of transcendence (see Kaplan 1988: 163).

Transcendence

> I collect shadow and light
> in my painting
> which nothing can hold
> art
> is transcendental
> realization of nature
> it is
> the vocabulary
> of imagination
> and spirit
> imagination
> is
> the will of art
>> ('Transcendence', Richard Pousette-Dart)

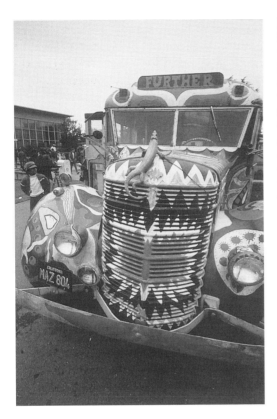

Figure 2.5 *On the Bus*. **Photograph by and courtesy of Gene Anthony, 1966.** <http://www.sixties.photos.com>. Ken Kesey and the Merry Pranksters decorated this 1939 Harvester bus in fashionable psychedelic colours and slogans, including the motto 'Further' at the front and 'Caution – Weird Load' at the rear. The 'magic bus' contained a changing number of passengers who travelled coast to coast, literally tripping, to express their alienation and separation from mainstream culture.

sentative of the dualism of body and mind. Paula Modersohn-Becker thought of the city and the country as diametrically opposed territories. In a letter of 1905 she described how at Worpswede her life was 'built mostly on inner experiences' and contrasted it with her 'outer life' in Paris (quoted in Perry 1979: 33–4). This sort of distinction was common among creative people who removed themselves to the countryside or to another country in order to foster an 'inner life'. The retreat from the urban often represented a renunciation of the excesses and complications of city life. For instance, the American transcendental poet and writer Henry David Thoreau rejected the material comforts of the city for an ascetic retreat to Walden Pond to consort with and find pleasure in the natural world. But, unlike Gauguin, Thoreau's retreat was indeed solitary. Living in self-imposed exile was more than a matter of finding a conducive atmosphere to concentrate on a great work of art, literature or music – a place where the imagination could roam free. The rural retreat was, as we shall see, indicative of yet other complex factors in the relationship of the modern artist to his or her work of art.

Ascent to nature and artists' colonies

The ideal or visionary is impossible without form: even angels come down to earth. By walking upon earth and looking up at the heavens, and in no other way, can there be an equilibrium. The greatest dream or vision is that which is regiven plastically through observation of things in nature.

(Max Weber 1910: 25)

Des Esseintes, the hero of Huysmans' *A Rebours* (1884) (sometimes translated as 'against nature' or, more properly, as 'against the grain' Huysmans 1997) argues that 'nature has had her day' and advocates an artificiality in refinements of taste which characterised the Aesthetes. The contrived anti-nature stance of the Aesthetes is, perhaps surprisingly, often echoed by modernist sophisticates. The well-known anecdote of how Mondrian once went to tea at Kandinsky's studio and took exception to the trees outside, insisting he be seated with his back to the window, is indicative of the kind of modernist myth-making that surrounds the symbolic renunciation of nature (and naturalism). According to the lineage of modernism mapped out by, among others, Alfred Barr, Mondrian's fabled (if feigned) hatred of greenery finds its correspondence in his hard-edged geometric painting. If we examine Mondrian's *oeuvre* under this rubric, then we see that he begins as a painter of embrowned windmills in a landscape; he moves on to analytical paintings of blossom on a tree under the influence of cubism, and finally arrives at neo-plasticism. We follow the artist from a painter of nature to the abstract painter of geometry, like so many others, and see this 'progression' as a badge of modernity, although we witness many regressions and false starts in this progression. And when artists seem to go backwards, from abstraction to figurative or classical styles (as Pollock, Severini, Malevich, the Delaunays and Dali all did), this is seen as retrogressive to modernism's teleological imperatives.

Mainstream modernism has often measured its modernity in terms of how far it dispenses with nature/naturalism. Many modern artists, such as the impressionist painters of Paris, never renounced nature: they painted in sleepy seaside resorts, took weekends on the River Seine, and many retired to consort with nature on a permanent basis. It is, however, especially difficult in the history of modernism to reconnect abstract artists with nature. One of the underlying difficulties is the mismatch between the received history of modernism and individual artists' relationship with nature. The received history of Western modernism tells us how, in the industrialised period following the end of the Franco-Prussian War in 1870, the French people were drawn towards the city and French artists to its *demi-monde* – seedy nightclubs and brothels. This is contextualised by writers such as Théophile Gautier and Baudelaire, who began to see nature – first in the sense of the countryside and later in the sense of 'naturalism' – as ugly. However, Wilhelm Worringer's argument in *Abstraction and Empathy* (1963), first published in 1908, equates naturalism with a faith in the organic world. Naturalism, he argued, provided the viewer with the necessary incentive to empathise with the work, whilst abstraction was a retreat into the 'world of the inert'.[5]

Nature was ingrained in the Romantic imagination, and it was a condition of Romanticism that writers and poets had a meaningful commerce with nature – for example Théodore Rousseau's retreat to Fontainebleau and the Romantic poets' relationship to the English Lake District and other lakes in Europe. In *Twilight of the Idols* Nietzsche had rejected the idea of a return to nature in favour of an 'ascent to nature', and many artists, writers and musicians sought personal ascendancy through a commerce with nature. Perhaps nowhere is this more apparent than in the number of artists' colonies that sprang up in Europe at the turn of the century – at Pont-Aven and Grez-sur-Loing in France, at Skagen in Denmark, at St Ives in Britain and at Worpswede in Germany, where Paula Modersohn-Becker and Fritz Mackensen worked.[6] The idea of the artists' colony as a retreat from the sophistication of the city as well as a place to escape the dictates of academies lured many artists. For example, Fritz Mackensen, the first of the artists to settle at Worpswede, had been actively involved in a student protest group in Düsseldorf and was a card-carrying secessionist.[7] Often these artists were aligned, in Germany anyway, with volkish movements. The volkish movement had been evident ever since German unification in 1871 and expressed itself in a dissatisfaction with urbanisation and materialism. The seemingly uncomplicated life of the peasant in the countryside, removed from the apparent crassness of urban existence, appealed to the young, idealistic artists who first began taking their summer holidays in Worpswede in the 1880s.

As Michael Jacobs has shown, many artist colonies were far from remote and they were usually close to railway networks (Jacobs 1985: 12). However, they did tend to lie outside the tourist circuit and were not generally considered picturesque or attractive by the travelling public. Just as the original Arcadia was a remote and wild place, so artist colonies were organised retreats for poets and painters in secluded areas of Europe and North America. The idea of Arcadia was constructed as a place of rural simplicity where men and women led an uncomplicated life and shepherds sang to one another in eclogues. Paintings such as *Trumpeting Girl in a Birch Wood* of 1903 (Figure 2.6) implicate the indigenous population of Worpswede in a closeness to nature of much the same kind as Gauguin had with the natives of Pont-Aven and Tahiti. The retreat to artist colonies was as much a social affair as it was a professional choice. In

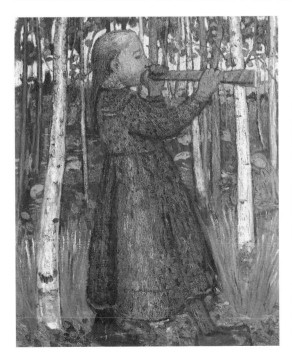

Figure 2.6 Paula Modersohn-Becker, *Trumpeting Girl in a Birch Wood*, 1903. Courtesy of Kunstsammlungen Böttcherstrasse, Paula Modersohn-Becker Museum, Bremen. The depiction of forest interiors (*sous-bois*) was not uncommon in artists' colonies and there are several paintings of the birch woods by Worpswede artists. Nina Lübbren sees this preference for forest interiors over more conventional landscape compositions as 'emblematic of the nature experience artists were seeking in rural artists' colonies. At the heart of the rural nature experience lay the sensation of immersion' (Lübbren 2001: 81–3).

fact, many paintings produced at the most established artists' colonies are representations of artists' lunches and social gatherings and not solely of landscapes and indigenous
peasant folk. As Nina Lübbren has argued, it was marshy, boggy or overgrown landscapes that were selected for *plein-air* study by artists within the various colonies in
Europe, rather than more conventional compositions:

> Rural artists' colonies managed to sustain, in a unique way, the ideal that the villages
> where *they* were located harboured special and distinct motifs and subjects that were
> completely other to the hackneyed sights turned out by those inferior 'spirits'. Place-
> myths constructed by colonists were able to cast 'their' locations as havens of
> anti-tourism despite their numerically substantial popularity, and despite the fact
> that most of the motifs in any given artists' colony were painted by dozens of painters.
>
> (Lübbren 2001: 156–7)

The poet in residence at Worpswede, Rainer Maria Rilke, was an early enthusiast of
the minimal landscape – that is, of the flat landscape as opposed to the jagged landscape of the picturesque or the rolling landscape of the Romantic. Another recurring
subject of paintings made in artists' colonies is the *sous-bois*, or undergrowth of the
forest interior (see Figure 2.6), and they dispense with the normally panoramic views
of academic landscape in order to focus on the restricted space of the thicket and the
rough vegetation lurking beneath the forest canopy.

What is significant about the artistic perception of a closeness to nature, in the light
of the ideas we have examined thus far, is two underlying suggestions. On the one
hand, 'closeness to nature' was seen as an 'ascent', and the quality of 'inner life' among
Worpswede or Breton peasants and Tahitian people was more important than their
material circumstances. But, on the other hand, the equation of 'peasant' and 'soil',
while keying in to Romantic mysticism, was consistent with nineteenth-century
doctrines of 'knowing your place'. Modersohn-Becker's interest in local folk culture
and 'back to nature' basics made her a formal precursor to German expressionism, but
these themes were also later to be identified with the 'blood and soil' ideology of right-
wing politics in Nazi Germany. Like science (as we will see in Chapter 5), the polemical
discourse on nature could be harnessed for different purposes. Much of both Hitler's
and Stalin's spin on socialist realism was imparted against a pastoral backdrop. For
instance, Stalin cast tractor drivers and farmers, just as often as coal miners or canal
diggers, as the heroes of the new Russia. Similarly, Hitler's Aryan race was conceived
in terms of semi-rural idylls of German workers ploughing German soil, producing
indigenous German crops for indigenous German people (regardless of the fact that
many workers on the land were the forced labour of 'inferior' races). Many artists
painted idyllic scenes of harvest or ploughshares as part of this 'back to nature' enthusiasm. For example, Erich Erler's *Blood and Soil* of 1942 is distinctly unmodern. Its
representation of the indigenous German country-dweller's closeness to nature is
supported insidiously by its appeal to the past and the 'naturalness' of nature. Official
Nazi art pictorialised *Lebensraum* (living space), in which the Aryan race takes control
of the land for the mutual improvement of blood and soil. Erler's bucolic representation of the family's fundamental closeness to nature makes the ideology of blood and
soil literal. Blood-and-soil depictions of nature typically omit any sign of mechanisation

in agricultural activity to reinforce the timeless bonds between the German people and the land they farm, in these paintings by hand or with a primitive plough.

The appeal to nature to support an insidious agenda was not new. We will see in Chapter 4 that it was patriarchy which turned the identification of women with nature into a complex negation of a biological fact in favour of an economic necessity. The 'division of labour' that came about in the Industrial Revolution subverted any notion of women's 'biological difference' into a passivity and an objectification predicated on a notion of woman's *essence*. The proliferation of images of nude women in the land-scape in Western painting represents, among other things, the quasi-superstitious belief that the reproductive system of a woman's body linked her preternaturally to the repro-ductive systems of 'mother nature'. But many women artists in the twentieth century have been active in making the identification between woman and nature a positive rather than a negative one. Women surrealist artists, for instance, actively engendered the connections between themselves and nature (and the preternatural). Male surrealist artists had already identified women with organic nature – referencing their sexual organs in flowers and depicting them in meaningful communion with animals. But those women artists, such as Remedios Varo, who came to be associated with the surre-alist movement appropriated these identifications and made their own iconography from the animal and plant kingdoms.

The artist and writer Leonora Carrington, like her friend Varo, painted magical birds and shared the same esoteric preoccupations. Carrington's *Self-Portrait* of 1938–9 shows the artist seated in a room with a lactating hyena and a rocking horse. A galloping horse is visible outside the window. In Carrington's personal bestiary the horse was the principal icon and is represented twice in this self-portrait. By looking at Carrington's short stories we can ascertain that the horse served several different icono-graphic purposes in her paintings. For instance, in the short story 'The House of Fear' (1937) it is the horse that acts as the physic guide for the heroine (Carrington herself?) (see Chadwick 1991: 78–9). Drawing upon a lifelong interest in Celtic symbolism, the horse is a magical means of travel, flying through the air in paintings and in her stories.

Retreats into the unconscious

Ever since Leonardo da Vinci exhorted artists to look at stains on dirty walls in order to find fantastic compositions of landscapes and figures, using external resources to alter creative centres has been a feature of underground avant-garde art practice. The possibility of accessing the creative centres of the primal and elemental self where 'pure' artistic intuition resides, stripped of all the external forces that shape and compromise artists, has been a compelling fiction for modernism. Methods used to displace the centre of creativity from the conscious – colloquially known as 'getting off your head' – included hallucinogenic drugs, alcohol, starvation, staring at cracks in walls, shamanism, automatic writing, dreams ('oneirology', as described in Freud's *The Interpretation of Dreams* 1976) and invoking chance. The common denominator in all those searches for ever more original and authentic sites of creativity was the uncon-scious. The unconscious was the site of the 'marvellous' for artists disenchanted with the world of conscious encounter. Moreover, it became a place of retreat for artists averse to the civilising processes and conventional gestures of mainstream modernism. A retreat into the unconscious, however, was more than just a riposte to mainstream modernism: it seemed to be a retreat from the rational world. In fact, the retreat into the unconscious was rarely an act of self-indulgent escapism: it was often political. Fuelled by Freudian notions of the unconscious as the site of 'real' motivations and desires, many surrealists believed the 'irrational' could reveal political and social truths stripped of any claims to reason. For example, André Breton had worked with shell-shock victims during the First World War and his experience of clinical 'hysteria' led him to conclude that, for Surrealists at least, a mental disorder could be a condition for creativity, what he called 'a supreme means of expression' (Breton 1972: 17).

In order to explain the regard that artists had for the unconscious mind, we must call upon psychoanalytic theory. The role that the unconscious mind plays in art was investigated by Freud at the turn of the century. Freud thought that unresolved child-hood experiences can trigger unconscious symbolism in the artist's work. Famously, he attributed Leonardo da Vinci's painting *The Virgin and Child with St Anne* to the artist's experience of having had two mothers – a natural peasant mother and his father's wife – an experience which he tries to resolve (unconsciously) by uniting the two women in one picture. Jung countered Freud's notion of a personal unconscious with a collective unconscious that governed, a priori, symbolic motifs in art. However, the artistic preoccupation with consciously representing the unconscious, whether personal or collective, rests upon a belief in its accessibility. For example, as we will see in Chapter 6, Jackson Pollock's belief that he was 'painting out of the unconscious' demonstrates not only its topicality but an underlying faith in an accessible unconscious. Pollock also was influenced by the spiritual teachings of Jiddu Krishnamurti (1895–1986), a protégé of the Theosophical Society, whose writings were popular in the United States and Europe from the 1920s. Also of importance to Pollock were the shamanistic sand paint-ings of indigenous Native Americans, for whom working in sand is an act which suspends the conscious mind for an intuitive response to the medium. Confidence in Pollock's belief in an accessible unconscious has been questioned by, among others, Jacques Lacan. Lacan suggests that the very notion of an unconscious has to be under-stood as a constructed category (constituted in and by language) which is contingent upon social and historical conditions. A case in point is the work produced by the American abstract expressionist Willem de Kooning after he was diagnosed as having Alzheimer's disease in the 1980s. De Kooning's paintings from this period were bought and sold in the same manner as his earlier work, thereby raising the question of their status as art. On the one hand, we privilege the unconscious in a work of art, but in de Kooning's case some would argue that his lack of consciousness negates the status of his paintings as art.

A much-vaunted way of tapping the unconscious was through improvised and spon-taneous gestures, which reportedly bypassed the rational controlling mind. 'Chance' was particularly valued since, theoretically at least, chance is the opposite of intention (Breton 1972: 26). André Breton's *Manifestos of Surrealism* (1924) advocated elements of chance (shuffling words cut from a magazine and dropping coloured squares on to paper) in the same way that Freud conceived of psychic automatism (Freudian slips, free association and word games). For Breton, these strategies constituted 'the absence of any control exercised by reason' (Breton 1972: 26). The jury is still out on just how random and beyond conscious control the laws of chance actually are (and how independent of intention chance can ever be). All the same, chance has played an important part in some artists' perceptions of twentieth-century modernism. It was, after all, the 'accidental' encounter between Kandinsky and one of his paintings, laid on its side in his studio, that reportedly led to his development of abstract painting. Whether or not this often-told tale is true is less important here than the artist's perception of a chance encounter.

The invocation of chance that preoccupied the surrealists took on many guises. Ithell Colquhoun, the English surrealist artist and writer, systematically investigated automatism in the 1930s and 1940s and published the results in an article entitled 'The Mantic Stain' (1949). Colquhoun was actively involved in various forms of occultism (so much so that she was expelled from the English surrealist group by its Marxist element). Her painting *Sea Star I* (1944) is the product of what the surrealists called decalcomania – where a painted surface is pressed against another and then pulled apart again to reveal a textured surface. The chance evocation of form by the process of decalcomania in *Sea Star* creates a symmetrical pattern suggestive of a variety of different forms. Colquhoun's friend André Breton described the process of decalcomania as one that created 'submarine flora, unfathomable fauna . . . delirious broughs of grottoes, black lakes, will-of-the-wisps' (Breton 1997: 87). Clearly, in terms of its debt to pure 'chance' decalcomania has fairly predictable outcomes. So chance does not entail a total abandonment to chaotic fortune, but it can describe a state of removal in which conscious control is put on standby.

More extreme retreats to the unconscious are the stuff of art-historical legend. Jean Dubuffet's interest in the delirious mind and in mental functioning in its most pre-rational stages could be seen in the context of a long line of artists, including Richard Dadd, Vincent van Gogh, Camille Claudel, Egon Schiele and Leonora Carrington, all of whom had at some time or another been declared 'insane'. Dubuffet collected what he called *art brut* (literally translating as 'raw art') from 1945. *Art brut* was work produced by psychiatric patients, criminals and clairvoyants. Like a number of others (most notably André Breton and Hans Prinzhorn), Dubuffet valued 'instinct, passion, mood, violence, madness'. His *Paysages aux ivrognes* (*Landscape with Drunkards*, 1949) (Figure 2.7) is characteristically painted in the spirit of *art brut*; naive, simplified figures are seemingly hastily drawn out in thick impasto. In a lecture entitled 'Anticultural Position' (given at the Art Club of Chicago in December 1951), Dubuffet described how the West could learn from the 'caprices of savages' (by which he seems to have meant the producers of *art brut*). He resisted what he called 'acculturation' and was irritated by claims that 'modern man' was more civilised, more sensitive to beauty and more intelligent than either his ancestors or his counterparts outside the West.

Attempts to transgress the kinds of artistic practices that had come to be orthodox by exploring the unconscious, seeking what Paul Klee called 'the primal beginnings of art', gathered a certain momentum in the 1960s with the recreational use of LSD. Sadie Plant's collection of *Writings on Drugs* (1999) surveys the literature on drug taking and argues that drugs are akin to technology in the sense that they are a way of changing the 'wiring' of the brain. The 'rewiring' that LSD permitted was most closely associated with the psychedelic art movement of the 1960s and the activities of artists and writers such as Timothy Leary. When artists, writers and musicians first started to talk about a psychedelic movement, LSD was not yet a banned substance (although a prohibition in

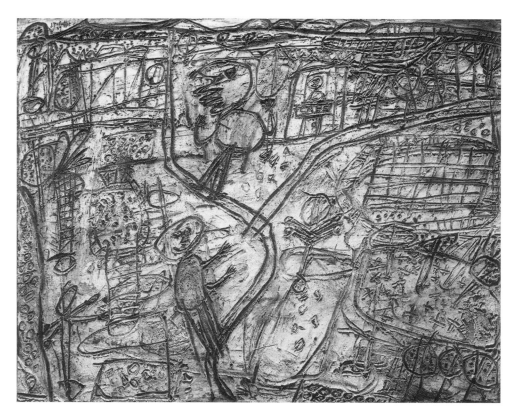

Figure 2.7 Jean Dubuffet, *Paysages aux ivrognes*, 1949. © ADAGP, Paris, and DACS, London, 2004. Courtesy of the Menil Collection, Houston. Part of a series of so-called 'Grotesque Landscapes' produced in 1949. Dubuffet applied his paint with a palette knife in a thick impasto and worked at the surface, scratching and scraping away and adding more paint, to create what he termed 'a world of fantasmagoric irreality'.

1966 led to a worldwide ban). The effects of taking the drug included hallucinations and distorted sensory awareness, reportedly opening 'the doors of perception'. In return, psychedelic art mimicked the hallucinatory effects of the drug through the creation of immersive environments – collages of sound, burning incense and pulsating, kaleido-scopic lights. An article on the new phenomenon of 'Psychedelic Art' published in *Life* magazine commented on how psychedelic artists 'go after every available nerve ending from the eyes to the soles of the feet' (Joel 1966: 64). The article offered the advice that 'The voyager who wants to blast off into inner space has the choice of many routes' (Joel 1966: 64). In point of fact the routes to inner space were fairly circumscribed and a num-ber of artist-led venues for experiencing the psychedelic appeared in the 1960s, but oper-ating on similar lines. Jackie Cassen and Rudi Stern collaborated on multimedia performances in New York, and in London Mark Boyle created psychedelic light shows with his partner, Joan Hills, under the title of the Sensual Laboratory. From his New York loft Richard Aldcroft offered 'ecstatically beautiful – or terrifying' – experiences (often termed Be-Ins in the 1960s) by means of a kaleidoscopic light show, which he called the 'Infinity Projector' (see Figure 2.8). What they all had in common was that the luminous effects created by pulsating or kaleidoscopic projections of light and colour were intended to induce in the viewer a state of contemplation at the very least, ecstasy at best. There were sufficient examples of the new art practice to warrant the first Exhibition of Psychedelic Art, organised by the pioneering multimedia commune USCO at the Riverside Museum in New York in 1966.

Whether or not we believe that there is a place called the unconscious where modern artists can find inspiration for the 'authentic' art work, we are faced with an overwhelming number of artists who have held this view. As we often link modernity to the forces of technocracy, industrialisation and urbanisation, the idea that modernity could be played out in opposition to these forces may seem to negate modernity. However, the retreat from the urban, like the Pre-Raphaelite 'retreat' to the Middle Ages, is just as much a response to the experience of modernity as the embrace of the machine by the futurists or the Bauhaus. They are all linked by the common factors of formal experimentation, idealism, anti-bourgeois politics and a critical engagement with modernity. However, the retreats of artists from the urban, from the conscious to the unconscious, from flesh to spirit, from materiality to non-materiality and from outer to inner have been both a productive impetus for many modern artists and a compelling 'fiction' for the avant-garde.

In 2003 urbanites flocked to see a light installation at Tate Gallery London representing the sun. Olafur Eliasson's *Weather Project* was commissioned for the Turbine Hall of Tate Modern at Bankside. Using the same mono-frequency lamps that are generally used in street lighting, Eliasson created a large sun-shaped disc of sodium yellow light in the cavernous entrance hall. Literally employing smoke and mirrors,

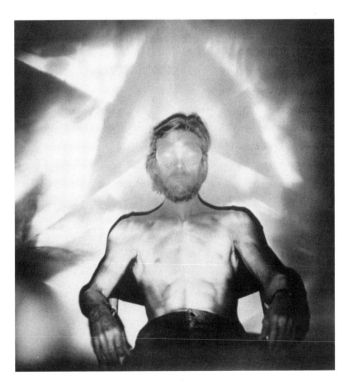

Figure 2.8 Richard Aldcroft being assaulted by images from a Kaleidoscopic machine, 1966. Courtesy of Getty Images/Time Life. The Infinity Machine, also known as a proleidoscope, was a metal box with a lens which projected celluloid particles moving in a gel on to the walls and ceilings of so-called Be-Ins. To be in these immersive environments of light and sound (and smells) allegedly heightened sensory awareness to promote spiritual and aesthetic insight.

Eliasson convinced visitors that they were indeed experiencing a virtual weather effect. A series of machines generated a fine mist that blurred the mechanical supports of the sun and created a sickly acid glow in the hall. Because the artist placed mirrors across the ceiling of the Turbine Hall, effectively doubling the impression of height in the space, *Weather Project* generated some unforeseen responses in visitors. To be sure visitors interviewed by the press described their feelings of awe, talked about their hair standing on end and even about feeling spiritually moved, but many of them were also lying on the floor and staring up at their own dimly lit reflections above. The unintentional prospect of participating in *Weather Project*, whether that amounts to basking in the glow of the artificial sun or to acts of communal self-surveillance, contributed to the popularity of the work. However, the title of the piece, *Weather Project*, belied the more prosaic research that preceded its plastic realisation in the Tate. In the lead-up to the project Eliasson interviewed staff at the gallery, compiled and analysed data and concluded that society's interest in the weather was indeed capable of comment. An oblique marketing campaign on buses and posters whetted the public appetite for the forthcoming installation as if to underscore the fact that the weather is such a frequent topic of conversation among residents and visitors to a large city. What started out, at the outset of modernism, as the individual exploration of nature has at the beginning of the twenty-first century become capable of being participatory. As concerns with environmental issues grow we are not content to nominate one artist as spokesperson for nature, but, rather, recognise that artists such as Eliasson are exploring environmental issues on behalf of and with an audience.

Monuments, modernism and the public space

For the sake of a single verse one must see many cities, men and things.
... One must be able to think back to roads in unknown regions, to
partings one had long seen coming.
(Rainer Maria Rilke, *The Notebooks of Malte Laurids Brigge*)

The power of the metropolitan development is not to be denied. The
excitements and challenges of its intricate process of liberation and
alienation, contact and strangeness, stimulation and standardisation, are
still powerfully available. But it should no longer be possible to present
these specific and traceable processes as if they were universals, not
only in history but as it were above and beyond it.
(Williams 1987: 46)

It is just possible that in the twenty-first century the West's attachment to cities will seem
at best eccentric and at worst an aberration. Mike Davis (2002), in *Dead Cities: a natural
history*, was not alone in predicting an end to our love affair with the environmentally
unforgiving urban existence. Since nineteenth-century industrialisation, cities have been
the focus of accelerating communication, social transformation, revolution and reaction.
Increasingly, however it seems, the technological revolution makes where we live
irrelevant to our working lives: the global village is accessible at the touch of a keyboard.
Modernism, however, was played out against a predominantly urban backdrop, driven by
migration to the cities during industrialisation, where rapidly changing social relations
transformed artistic production, consumption and display. Artists' responses to modernity
and all the technical and economic changes wrought in its wake, as we have seen, have not
been uniform. Although the city was central to modernism it had as its 'other' the countryside and, for many artists, it prompted extended explorations in 'exotic' and 'primitive'
locations. It is one of the ironies of modernism that, although an urban phenomenon, it
had a symbiotic relationship with nature. Its 'offer' of authenticity (as we saw in Chapter
2), while deeply romantic in concept, could propose an alternative to the modern urban
world. In this chapter we return to cities' public spaces – spaces currently challenged as
the boundaries between public, corporate and private are increasingly blurred.

The city

Received modernist art history has for the most part placed Paris at the centre of modernism,[1] although latterly Singapore and Tokyo have been identified as its postmodern successors. Beyond the actual physical spaces of global cities lies another metropolis – the virtual city and the disembodied encounter with Cyberia. This chapter will explore artists' and historians' responses to the changing realities that cities have presented. It begins by looking at the often-neglected memorial monument of the civic square and the public place. If the equestrian statue of the Renaissance square, with its harmonious relations of scale and proportion, seems unproblematic to the tourist in search of history, the European monument in the nineteenth and particularly the twentieth centuries strikes a somewhat discordant note.

Many of the works we will look at have been designated *realist*. It is worth noting at the outset, however, that what we understand as *realistic* in a work of art is always culturally determined. Whether we know it or not, we are bound by a tacit understanding which determines for us whether works look correct or real. This is not a question merely of familiarity, although familiarity unquestionably plays a part. Our perception of nature itself is culturally determined and informed by pictures and sculptures. The monument's *realism* in the nineteenth century contributed to our understanding of reality itself. The rapid transformation of our understanding of 'the real' in the late twentieth century is echoed in the transitory and often ephemeral nature of the monument in the modern period. The monument, or memorial monument, acts as a lexicon of shifts in cultural practice. It is therefore an important site of a culture's rites and rituals, which contribute to a collective or at least 'collected memory' (Young 1993: xi). However, the privileging of the individual subject within modernist art practices enabled a shift from public to private in which the monument's primary function was subject to revision. For instance, when the monument is displaced or removed the formation of historical memory is fractured; and when modernist art practice moves from the public domain to the private sphere of individual contemplation the notion of a public monument loses some of its cultural privileges.

On monuments and memory

In September 1996 Michael Jackson's monumental *Moonwalker Statue* (Figure 3.1) temporarily towered above the River Vltava in Prague, emblematic of Jackson's 'History of the World' tour. The statue stood in front of the faltering timepiece, the metronome, erected to mark the passing of the Cold War and the re-entry of what was then Czechoslovakia into Europe. The site's former incumbent had been the statue of the Russian leader Joseph Stalin. The socialist realist monument (Figure 3.2) popularly referred to as 'Stalin and the Bread Queue', had been removed in 1963, following Nikita Kruschev's de-Stalinisation programme of the 1950s. These changes are significant in charting, in the modern period, the fugitive state of the monument – usually a signifier of solidity and stability. The ideologies represented by monuments and, crucially, their modes of representation, are what concern us here. The simulated-bronze statue of Jackson may, on one level, seem to signify a return to the unreconstructed kitsch that

Stalin's statue, in Western terms, used to represent. The designation 'kitsch' was a modernist indictment of much socialist realist work – a term of approbation used by Clement Greenberg in his 1939 article 'Avant-Garde and Kitsch' (Frascina 1985: 21–32). Accordingly, the term 'realism' itself, the accurate or naturalistic recording of visual appearance in the world, became an impediment to truth-telling in the modern period. Socialist realism, the official doctrine for all the arts in Russia from 1934 onwards, cannot be *real* by modernist criteria. It is marked twice in its 'regressive' anti-modern tendencies: once by its dependence on previous, often naturalistic, bourgeois art forms and again by not merely recording the visible world but actively constructing a partisan realism – an optimistic art of, and for, the masses.

However, kitsch is now a form of parody widely used in postmodern practice, especially by artists critiquing established notions of taste. As we saw in Chapter 1, taste was the principal criterion for establishing quality within modernism, and to subvert modernist notions of taste is a typically postmodern device. For instance, Jeff Koons's

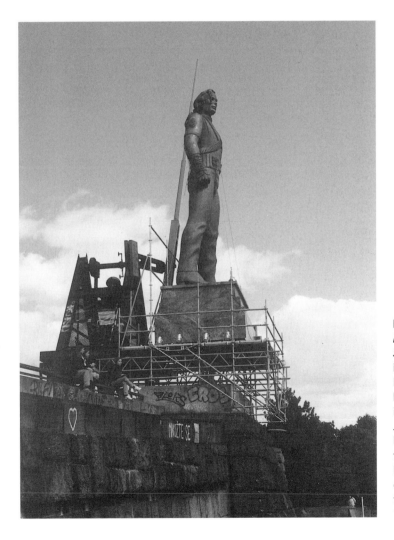

Figure 3.1
***Moonwalker Statue*, temporarily in Prague, 1996.**
Photograph Pam Meecham. The inflatable statue of Jackson as military hero with attendant tanks was part of the kitsch armoury used during the *His*tory of the World tour in 1996.

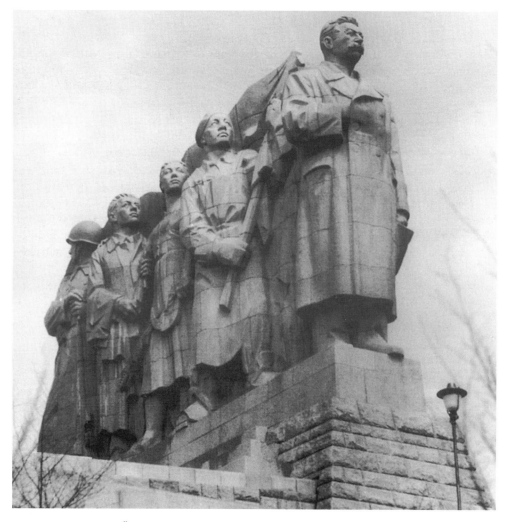

Figure 3.2 Otakar Švec, *Monument to Stalin*, 1955. The officially sanctioned monument conformed to the political strictures announced by Andrei Zhdanov in 1934. Although there was initially little aesthetic guidance, all works were expected to be populist in form and accessible to the masses. By the 1950s, however, an aesthetic had been imposed of which this statute is exemplary.

huge puppy made of flowers, which temporarily embellished the entrance to Spain's Guggenheim Gallery in Bilbao, used 'bad taste' in an ironically knowing way. Of course, Michael Jackson's statue might operate at the level of parody – as an ironic spin on capitalist reworkings of socialist realism – or it might be simply an unwitting pastiche.

The statue of Jackson in heroic posture and pseudo-military regalia mocks notions of authenticity (its creators could make no claim to formal innovation), and in its iconoclasm it reconfigures the function of the monument in Western culture. The statue's form bears more than a passing resemblance to socialist realism, but could be said to stand in triumphant antagonism to it. The statues of Stalin and Jackson seem to stand as binary opposites – for the demise of the totalitarian Soviet bloc and the economics of Communism, and for the triumph of liberal free-market economics. Compared, the two statues raise the question of the changing nature of public art. As we will see, in direct contrast to earlier public art that represented a perceived consensus, under late capitalism sculptures in public spaces seem to occupy a position of ambivalence – either in conflict with dominant values or complicit in the blurring of boundaries between public, private and corporate.

Postmodernism has been seen positively by critics such as Francis Fukuyama as the 'masterstroke' of capitalism, ushering in a utopian age of the consumer.[2] *Moonwalker Statue* can be seen as emblematic of post-Marxism and as a harbinger of a global advanced capitalist society in which the ideological battles symbolised by the Berlin Wall would have no place. Culture, in the new millennium of neo-liberal politics, becomes the ultimate commodity. This commodification, however, is now explicit; that is to say, by and large, under modernism art works often disguised the economic activities of capitalist society. As we saw in Chapter 1, latterly artists often make the culture–commodity relationship overt, particularly in works such as Barbara Kruger's '*Untitled*' I Shop Therefore I Am, which was emblazoned on carrier bags. Of course, the statue of Michael Jackson, too, is a monumental advertising campaign. The relationship of advertising to art was part of the pop art phenomenon in the 1960s and has been most recently recycled on U2's 1997 'Pop Mart' tour and in several art shows, such as *Shopping* at Tate Liverpool (2002). As we saw in Chapter 1, during the 1960s Andy Warhol used packaged consumer goods made into multiples to critique art's original status: an anti-purist aesthetic. Currently the utopian promise of happiness through consumerism is bolstered by many formerly radical art techniques. 'Appropriation' and 'quotation' are recurring themes within postmodernism, evidenced in contemporary advertising campaigns where the combination of once-radical techniques such as montage, collage and documentary-style photography make surrealist-like images that fuse art and commodity with technical brilliance.

Even such an obvious juxtaposition as two statues representing Jackson and Stalin bears witness not only to the cult of the personality, instigated under Stalinism in the 1930s and revamped as the cult of the pop star, but also to postmodernism's fragility. The triumph of capitalism, the crumbling of Communism and the creation of a new consumerist Eden have been lauded as historical inevitabilities. To suggest a historical programme that is both purposeful and intentional is to impute to 'history' – in the sense of the passage of time – a motivation of universal scale. It also is an indication of a confidence in the present such as may reflect only a partial view of the new world order. While the former Soviet Union and its satellites rarely used corporate advertising, like other cities of the world they now have a new set of monuments – the signs of the mega-corporations like Benetton and Coca-Cola which advertise under the banners of 'The United Colours of' and 'We Are the World'. The new monuments around the bloc are now the ubiquitous yellow arches of McDonald's and the Starbucks.

The arrival in the early 1990s on Wenceslas Square (the site of the 1968 Russian invasion of what was then Czechoslovakia and of the Velvet Revolution of 1989) of McDonald's registered a new utopia, the globalism of the multinational and the *homogenising* of cultures. The march of McDonald's throughout the globe (now showing signs of abating) has been an astonishing phenomena, nowhere more so than at the site of revolutionary nationalism in Prague, Wenceslas Square, and in particular at the McDonald's outlet opposite an equestrian statue of the king and saint Vaclav (Wenceslas) by Myslbek (1912). John O'Neil identifies this process not through the 'yellow arches' alone but through the loss of the specific to the generalised:

> Defamilized meals – the ultimate goal of McTopia – constitute a further step in the democratization of American taste that begins with the infant addiction to sugary foods. . . . The result of such gastronomic levelling is that America is the only country in the world where the rich eat as badly as the poor – a demonstration-effect that serves to underwrite the globalization of McTopia.
>
> (O'Neil 1993: 137)

Under this rubric, the familiar yellow arches of McDonald's become synonymous with a 'democratic' levelling which is of course profit led and assumes, as its accessory, an unthinking, passive consumer. However, in spite of the seemingly negative aspects of the global village, it can be argued that consumers, including those within so-called subcultures, are not just passive recipients but have the capacity to create a 'critical distance' – in the modernist sense of the term, taking what is appropriate or useful from Western commodification while maintaining local identities.

The rapid social transformations that have taken place in the East and the West since 1989 signify radical changes that blur the boundaries of many previous sedimented beliefs. Jackson's *Moonwalker Statue*, along with the 'cultural imperialism' of Coca-Cola and McDonald's, call into question many certainties, not least the status of kitsch and high art's relationship to advertising and new technologies. It has been argued (mostly by Marxist critics) that art's search for the 'holy grail' of originality will result in its own annihilation – and the fusing of art and advertising is just one manifestation of this. Modernist attempts to avoid commodification, evident in early modernist rejection of commercial art, may seem futile, but the nihilistic view that total commodification has been inevitable may well be premature. Even to pose this question is an indication of the difficult terrain which the arts have traversed since the nineteenth century.

We want to return to a period in history dominated by the public or state rather than the corporate monument. In 'Moscow', written in 1927, Walter Benjamin commented on the visible absence of monuments in the streets of Moscow, saying that Moscow was village-like, 'augmented by landscapes', compared with other European cities where 'there is hardly a square . . . whose secret structure was not profaned and impaired over the course of the nineteenth century by the introduction of a monument' (1979: 203). These nineteenth-century monuments' artistic role was usually overlooked in favour of a public role, and the two are rarely conflated. Located in prominent positions, and as official monuments lacking avant-garde credibility, they have little artistic currency. Official monuments, such as those of monarchs and heads of state and war memorials, are significant visual expressions of state values subordinating artistic ones. However, they do more than simply mirror official state values: they contribute to their very formation. That is to say, monuments help construct memory – not only recording what and who is remembered but also dictating the form that those memories take. The form of the monument in the twentieth century becomes crucial in this respect.

Agitational monuments

Ironically, these important signifiers of state values displayed in urban public spaces have become so familiar as to be all but invisible to passers-by, though their power has not been lost on those in authority. A memo written in 1918 by Lenin suggested that those without work could usefully be employed clearing discredited Czarist monuments from the cities (Lodder 1993: 19). The Russian filmmaker Sergei Eisenstein, acknowledging the propaganda potential of the ruined monument, shows the destruction of a statue of Alexander III by revolutionaries in the opening sequence of his epic film *October* (1927–8).[3] Even though iconoclasm has a long history, the pulling down of the monument is as important as is its erection, as the much televised removal of monuments following the war in Iraq (in 2003) demonstrated. The act of 'dismembering' the Alexander III monument, after all no more than an act of vandalism, was enough to register in the audience the changed political order brought about by the fall of the Romanov Dynasty. It registered also Eisenstein's belief that all art is ideological, and none more so than public sculpture. The primacy of monuments and monolithic sculpture in the new Communist epoch was acknowledged and debated. Monumental forms to immortalise the new regime, part propaganda, part utopian, were needed to replace the fallen symbols of the autocratic regime.

Broadly speaking, the new revolutionary monuments were pluralistic in form and content, experimenting with both avant-garde forms and more traditional academic art practices. Lenin had originally requested non-permanent monuments to the revolution. In his 1918 'Plan of Monumental Propaganda', Lenin had advocated transitory and accessible works not made of granite or bronze. The works were not intended for contemplation and relaxation but were to be temporary street art, an agitational art, part of the vibrant celebration of a proletariat revolution. The pluralism associated with the early honeymoon years of the revolution did not survive for long (although the polarisation of avant-garde versus totalitarian socialist realism has been overstated). Generally, however, by the mid-1930s socialist realism, the official state art that celebrated the 'reality' of the revolution, had solidified the monument to the proportions of Vera Mukhina's towering (24-metre) *Industrial Worker and Collective Farm Girl* – two idealised figures, holding hammer and sickle aloft (Figure 3.3). It is a commonplace observation that totalitarian regimes monumentalise their ideologies, but monuments throughout the West also represent dominant forms of power and celebrate the values of government.

The place of the monument, as we have seen, is no longer assured – those of the most recent past being the most quickly removed. It is one of the disquieting characteristics of the modern period, seen most concretely (but not exclusively) in the removal of the monument, that our relationship with the past has been eroded. Eric Hobsbawm identifies this as living 'in a sort of permanent present lacking any organic relation to the public past' (Hobsbawm 1994: 3). The remaining monuments celebrating Communism were hastily removed from the former Eastern bloc after 1989, although amnesty was granted in the Czech Republic to those of Soviet war heroes who had fought against Fascism. Some statues were recycled but most, unless destroyed or melted down, were consigned to warehouses or aircraft hangers – like *Lenin at Louny* in the Czech Republic (Figure 3.4) – to await possible rehabilitation in a social realist theme park.

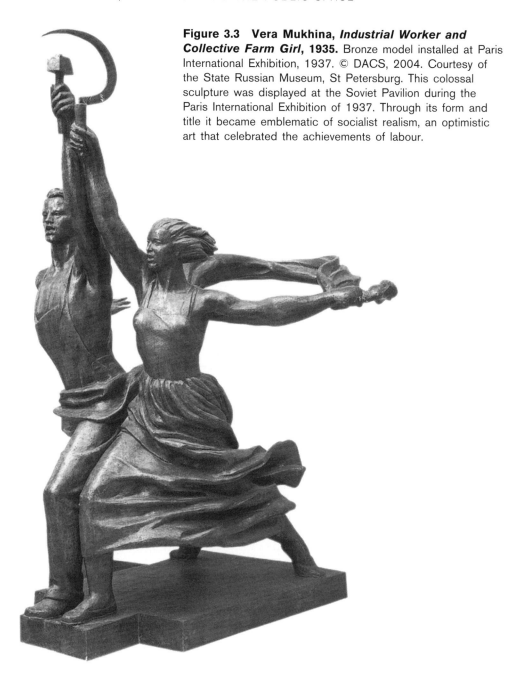

Figure 3.3 Vera Mukhina, *Industrial Worker and Collective Farm Girl*, 1935. Bronze model installed at Paris International Exhibition, 1937. © DACS, 2004. Courtesy of the State Russian Museum, St Petersburg. This colossal sculpture was displayed at the Soviet Pavilion during the Paris International Exhibition of 1937. Through its form and title it became emblematic of socialist realism, an optimistic art that celebrated the achievements of labour.

Tatlin and the unrealised monument

Ironically, it is the monuments that were not completed – those which act as counter-monuments and 'unrealised projects' – that Western art history valorises. Vladimir Tatlin's constructivist tower *Monument to the Third International*, described by Mayakovsky as 'the first monument without a beard' (Lodder 1993: 90), was never built

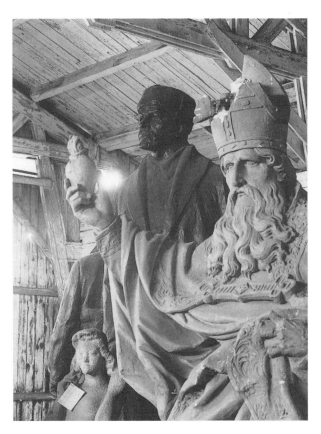

Figure 3.4 *Lenin at Louny*, Czech Republic, 1997.
Photograph Pam Meecham. Removed from public spaces, for safe keeping within eighteen months of the Velvet Revolution the disgraced monuments, Lenin, party workers, a trade unionist executed by the Germans, and militia men, were placed in an aircraft hanger at Louny where they keep company with Czech poets, saints and garden statues awaiting repair or rehabilitation.

(see Figure 3.5). It survives, however, in various guises. Tatlin's dynamic constructivist *Monument to the Third International* (named after the organisation formed to oversee the International Socialist revolution), which should have rivalled the Eiffel Tower in Paris, was aborted at an early stage – emblematic in many ways of the revolutionary socialism that Stalinism interred. The proposed 300-metre high monument constituted an attempt to synthesise formalist innovation with revolutionary politics – an entirely different type of structure 'uniting in itself a purely creative form with a utilitarian form' (Punin, quoted in Lodder 1993). The monument of three revolving glass and steel structures in spiral form would have housed suspended solids: a cube, pyramid and cylinder. The structure would then have functioned as a communications network for the revolution, at once an assembly hall, an administration centre and a radio station, with the capability of projecting revolutionary watchwords on to the clouds. The massive construction would have straddled the River Neva in what was then Petrograd.[4]

The critic and avant-garde apologist Nikolai Punin, writing in defence of Tatlin's monument, argued against the use of classical and Roman sculptural forms to celebrate the new order: because of their connotations of heroic individualistic posturing and their static quality, 'thinkers on granite plinths' could not represent the proletariat. Geometric shapes, Punin maintained, were more appropriate for the people. The spiral form in particular (even prior to the Revolution) had become a useful symbol for socialist monuments (see Lodder 1993: 25). Although such abstract forms were held to be universally

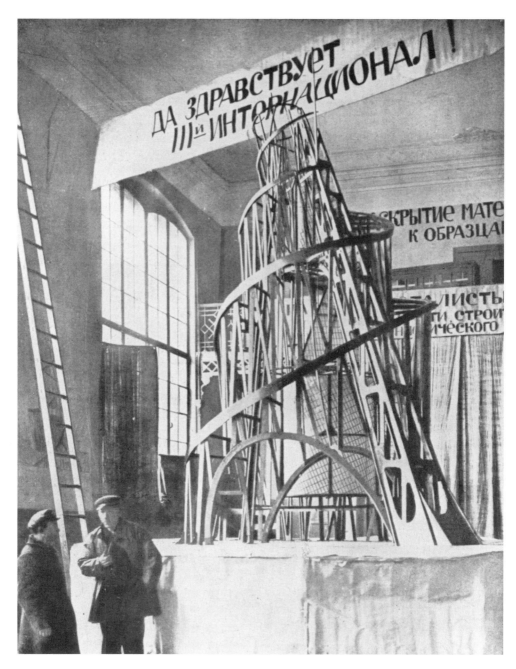

Figure 3.5 Vladimir Evgrafovich Tatlin, *Model for a Monument to the Third International*, 1920. © DACS, 2004. Courtesy of Moderna Museet, Sweden. Popularly known as *Tatlin's Tower*, the wooden model shown here would have been impossible to construct but has had an immensely important afterlife as a symbol of the failure of avant-garde culture and utopian communism in the Soviet state. It is also a reminder of the Russian avant-garde's enthusiasm for the emancipatory possibilities of mass-media technology.

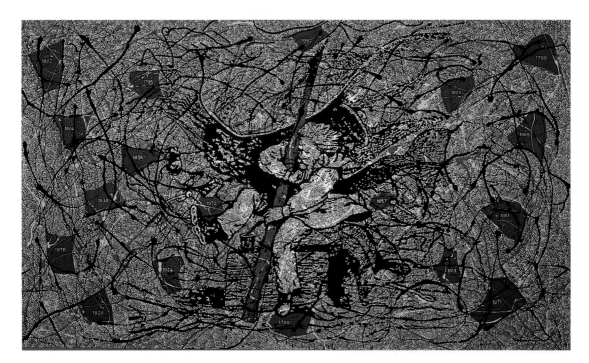

Plate I Gordon Bennett, *Myth of the Western Man (White Man's Burden)* 1992 Worked in synthetic polymer paint on canvas measuring 175 × 304 cm and thus smaller than Pollock's *Blue Poles: Number 2, 1952* that measured nearly 210 × 480 cm, Bennett's central figure is borrowed from a school primer illustrating the journeys of the Victorian explorers Burke and Wills. The dates placed onto the surface of the canvas reference significant events in the histories of Aboriginal and Torres Strait Islander peoples. Courtesy of Art Gallery of NSW © Gordon Bennett.

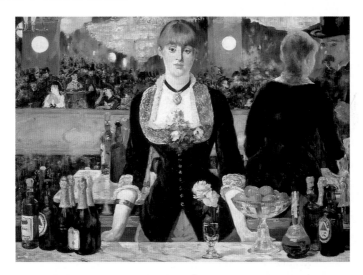

Plate II Édouard Manet *A Bar at the Folies-Bergère* 1882 This much-discussed painting of a famous Paris nightclub for the *demi-monde* has been written of in terms of its modernity: of the images of Bass bottled beer and the electric lighting. Historians have also concentrated on Manet's innovative painterly techniques – the way that the paint was applied to create the effects. However historians have also seen the work as emblematic of changing power relations under industrialisation. The ambiguities and disjunctions of scale (found in the barmaid's mismatched reflection in the mirror and the looming overly large male figure in the top right-hand corner) have been discussed in terms of complex political and social references rather than as formal innovations, a frequent modernist claim. Courtesy of Courtauld Institute of Art Gallery, London. Oil on canvas, 96 × 130 cm.

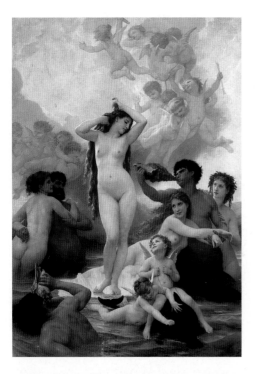

Plate III   William Adolph Bouguereau *Birth of Venus* 1879 The standard of finish, that is, the degree of polish and exacting attention to detail expected of academic paintings is evident in this work as is the other central condition for an academic work in this period: an idealised figure often, as in the case here, taken from Greek mythology. Courtesy of Musée d'Orsay © Photo RMN / H. Lewandowski.

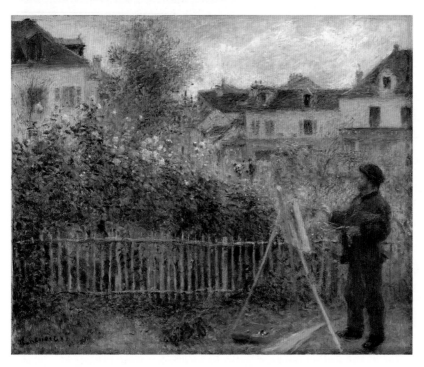

Plate IV   Pierre-Auguste Renoir *Monet Painting in his Garden at Argenteuil* 1873 The painting of Monet working outside on a small canvas pursuing his subject of flowers, shows the different working practices of the new art. Although Renoir's painting is relatively large (50 × 105 cm) its scale is not heroic compared with academic works. Even in reproduction it is possible to see the lack of finish in this work, its almost hasty application of paint. Courtesy of Wadworth Atheneum, Hartford. Bequest of Anne Parrish Titzell.

accessible, Lenin famously thought Tatlin's tower resembled a huge coffee grinder. John Berger does point to the paradox of abstraction and the social conditions of the time, asking 'what can Tatlin's *Monument to the Third International* mean to a peasant with a wooden plough?' (Berger 1969: 46). The continuing presence of Tatlin's tower in art-history books (usually as an elegy to 'a world gone wrong') is the real reason for its survival in memory. That the structure could ever have been built is a matter of conjecture, but its presence is a testament to its very lack of monumentality – it serves as witness to a failed modernist and political utopia, a salutary if nostalgic lesson for the West.

In the West

Tatlin's work was part of a general rejection by modernist artists of both the form and content of the nineteenth-century monument. The anthropomorphic (human-form) monument, in particular, lost its place in the city. Within early modernism (mid- to late nineteenth century) there was a scaling down of sculpture and painting as part of the move towards the private consumption of art in smaller bourgeois homes. Sculpture became the equivalent of the easel painting – portable, intimate and collectable but 'hardly heroic' (de Duve 1996: 25).

Those modernist artists in the twentieth century who were in opposition to official culture held an ambivalent position on the monument's 'life' in the public domain and on its status as 'official' art. Placed above eye-level, usually on a plinth, the monument was positioned, both physically and symbolically, in relation to the space (often a city square) which it was to occupy. It is worth noting that, with a few exceptions, the plinth or pedestal of traditional sculptures no longer held the avant-garde artist's interest. Whether in the city or, latterly, in the minimal earthworks of Robert Smithson and the Christo and Jeanne-Claude's 'wrap round' landscapes and islands (such as the 1968–9 *Wrapped Coast – One Million Square Feet, Little Bay*, Sydney, Australia), vast tracks of desert or canyon, the sites used often ruptured the previously symbiotic relationship between sculpture and location.

The change from public to private artistic contemplation by the 1890s had made it difficult for artists to register the conditions of modernity from the monuments of *grands boulevards*. The stuff of impressionist painting had been the fleeting glimpse of *la vie moderne* rather than the solid statue. For instance, Camille Pissarro, in such works as *Boulevard Montmartre: afternoon sunshine* (1897), one of a series of over 300 paintings completed in the last decade of his life, took the city as his subject matter. As was the case with most of his city paintings, the bustling Boulevard Montmartre was painted from an upstairs window or balcony and shows the effects of weather and time of day on the city street. Paris had been transformed under Napoleon III in the late 1850s by the building programmes of Baron Haussmann. The spectacle of the city could be viewed from the new vistas opened up by the huge boulevards, which created open spaces in which to view monuments.

Significantly, the monumental for the impressionists, with notable exceptions such as Pissarro's paintings of the statue of Henry IV, was not to be found in the Place de la Concorde or the Arc de Triomphe, but in the icons of modernity – the railway stations (the cathedrals of the age) and the Eiffel Tower. The new monuments were such edifices as London's Crystal Palace, the riveted wrought-iron structures of indus-trialisation, together with Baudelaire's new 'heroes of modern life' – the marginalised and transgressive populace of modernity: ragpickers, prostitutes and entertainers. The wide boulevards offered increased shopping and leisure facilities, public parks and modernised bars, but they also displaced large sections of the Parisian population. These people themselves supplanted the old heroic statues as the new corporeal monuments of modernity, inevitably 'ephemeral . . . fugitive . . . contingent' (Baudelaire 1964: 13). The new edifices of international exhibitions and shopping arcades were the subject of endless paintings, and they registered just how far modernity was marked by the new consumerism and 'conspicuous display'. The downside of modernity, however, was registered by the entirely unmonumental – the detritus of shopping arcades, brothels and bars inhabited by the urban underclass. Fragmentation and alienation quickly entered the visual vocabulary of artists and writers associated with early modernism.

In Europe in 1850 the rural population still outnumbered the urban population. However, cities began to absorb the population from the countryside and to attract people from other nations. Cities therefore became the focus of modernism partly because the émigré had been absorbed into the city. For the modernist poet Rainer Maria Rilke, creating a single verse was resolutely connected to the subjective nature of modern experience found in the restless life of the émigré. The solitude of poets such as Henry David Thoreau and Emily Dickinson could be countered by the modernist imperative to experience the vibrancy of the new cities. The internation-alist, rejecting the domestic sphere, found the alienating experience of cities, roads and regions central to the modernist diaspora. The modernist artist, poet, writer was the antithesis of domesticity and, with few exceptions, modernism was a largely masculine affair. Modernism had as its lead player the 'rootless cosmopolitan', who was often literally stateless or committed to internationalism and a rejection of national bound-aries. The fixed monument bearing a relation to the architecture and squares of the city and its national culture no longer seemed the appropriate form for the transnational artist. In its 'fossilised' traditional form, the monument failed to tell the truth about the conditions of modernity which seemed to be such an imperative for modernists. 'Truth' became a modernist trope, most famously with Cézanne, who wrote to Émile Bernard in 1905: 'I owe you the truth in painting and will tell it to you'. Rilke, confronting what he saw as the 'colossal reality' of Cézanne's paintings, said: 'the good simple truthfulness, it educates you; and if you stand beneath them as acceptingly as possible, it's as if they were doing something for you' (Rilke 1991: 50).

Arriving at a truth is never guaranteed, and is compromised even further when subjectivity is factored in. In many respects the homelessness of the monument mirrors the modernists' sense of rootlessness. The quest for truth could not be located in the permanent. Modernist artists increasingly transgressed boundaries and borders in what appears to have been an intellectual, physical and spiritual restlessness.

Sculpture and the public

What we have outlined so far demonstrates how the near-invisible street monument can act as a barometer of changing social and artistic relations, and as such is an important social site. Modern sculpture, outside of the monumental, was held in lower esteem than painting. The American artist Ad Reinhardt's quip that sculpture was 'something you bump into when you back up to look at a painting' is not without some waspish substance. Whilst Michelangelo had considered sculpture to be the only real art and painting as something for women, modernism tipped the balance towards painting. Modern sculpture's relationship with painting prior to the minimalist challenges of the 1960s was of only secondary order. Modernism is usually explained in relation to painting. Even Clement Greenberg's essay 'Newness in Sculpture' largely discusses sculpture for what it was not, that is, painting (Greenberg 1986b: 60).[5] Abstract painting did have an equivalent in sculpture but it was largely unsuccessful. Apart from the 'ready-made', which bears some comparison with chance or 'automatism' in surrealist painting, it proved difficult to translate the concerns of modernist painters into sculptural equivalents.

For Leo Steinberg, 'flatness was the analogue in art of the experience of modernity' (Batchelor 1997b: 16), leaving sculpture in Reinhardt's no-man's land – acting as a controlling mechanism for the circulation of the public around the gallery space.[6] Modernism has also found sculpture difficult to accommodate within the tropes of individual expression. Subjectivity seemed easier to render in paint. And modernist painting lent itself effortlessly to private contemplation, while sculpture remained an important carrier of public rites, and anthropomorphic statues its most acceptable manifestation. It is one of the paradoxes of modernism, then, that its quest for universals resulted in an art that was so unpopular with the general public that, as Albert Elsen has observed, 'in terms of international public acceptance, no modern sculpture has ever matched Bartholdi's Statue of Liberty' (Elsen 1974: 155).

The new sculptures of, say, Constantin Brancusi and Barbara Hepworth became increasingly remote from public places by seeking autonomy – becoming objects of aesthetic contemplation independent of state ideological 'interference'. Sculpture, until the move back to the public sphere in the earthworks of the 1960s, found its peripatetic home in the new galleries and modern museums – especially in their sculpture gardens and touring shows. Much of Brancusi's work, for instance, was bequeathed to the French nation and remains in his studio, where it is displayed for our contemplation. Of course, there were modern artists who worked in public places, but the extent to which the parameters of their project had changed is remarkable. If the modernist monument was more like a private symbol intervening in a public space, then of what could the monument be a public reminder?

The heroic public monument had received a much-needed fillip in the nineteenth century through the work of Auguste Rodin. Fundamental to his work was a sense of the overtly 'public'. However, the artists who aspired to modernity rejected Rodin's 'theatricality' and his 'restless surface' (Hamilton 1984: 463) in favour of a constant tenet of modernism – 'direct' simplicity. The Romanian artist Constantin Brancusi worked from primitive, folk and children's art. Simplicity, he believed, defined a sculptural syntax that was unencumbered by past conventions. Like many of the early modernists, Brancusi utilised the work of peasants, children and primitives as if they had no past or present and could therefore be representative of an originality outside their own local histories.

Brancusi's monumental totemic sculptures were 'direct carvings' – intuitively formed in the spirit in which, he believed, African tribal masks and Romanian folk art were made. Brancusi sought an authenticity that neo-classical sculpture seemed to lack. His obelisk-like structures were often more primeval than primitive. In sculpture, the use of the 'primitive' (always problematic in a postcolonial age) did not enter the vocabulary of sculpture as it had that of painting. 'Expressive' painting that exaggerated and distorted to gain effect in sculpture was interpreted as simplicity. Drawing on the formal vocabulary of African carving, in 1918 Brancusi produced *Endless Column*, the first in a series of works usually roughly carved from wood. In the 1930s variations were built in Tirgu Jiu, Romania. The almost 100-feet tall *Endless Column* of 1937 (see Figure 3.6) was thought of as a mystical ladder, being part of what Brancusi described as a search for the 'essential core of visible matter'. He explained: 'what is real is not the external form, but the essence of things ... it is impossible for anyone to express anything essentially real by imitating its exterior surface' (Brancusi, quoted in Hamilton 1984: 462). Brancusi, like many other artists, was expressing the age-old metaphysical question of what lay at the heart of the cultural form – its essence. To this end he simplified forms – in the case of the column, into repeated, rhomboid, six-surface, modular structures. The fifteen complete modules and two half-modules were moulded from a carved wooden shape and then cast in iron and 'threaded' on to a square internal

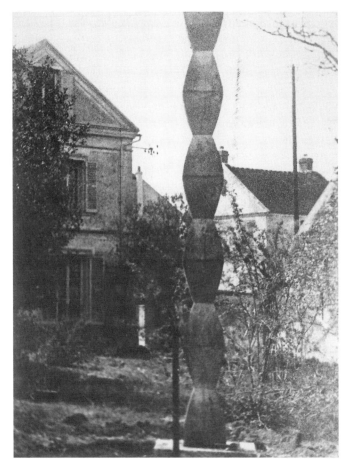

Figure 3.6 Constantin Brancusi, *Endless Column*, 1937–8. 9 inches × 6¾ inches gelatin silver print. © ADAGP, Paris, and DACS, London, 2004. Courtesy of Philadelphia Museum of Art: The Louise and Walter Arensberg Collection. Photo by Lynn Rosenthal, 1992. The modular endless column seen here in its 1937 manifestation was central to Brancusi's art practice from 1920.

steel column. The original finish of highly polished golden brass soon deteriorated, but initially, at least, shone a bright yellow. Brancusi's search for essentials through elemental forms such as eggs – a motif for 'self-contained perfection' and creation – became a private contemplation on the form of the sculpture itself, a far cry from the public declarations of nationalism embodied in heroic statues such as Bartholdi's *Liberty*.

To generalise, modernist sculptures eliminated visual hierarchies in a move akin to high modernism's 'all-over painting', typified by Jackson Pollock (see Chapter 6). Brancusi's sculpture rarely had a centre and a periphery; in spite of the height of the columns, the individual blocks do not appear to diminish. The sculpture is viewed as a whole and, since contemplation was the primary objective, any tactile element was of secondary importance, or irrelevant.

The essence

'Essence' designates the set of properties considered to be definitive of something – animal, vegetable, mineral or a work of art – qualities that constitute 'the specific what-ness of something' (Eagleton 1996: 97). These essences, however, are not always readily observable properties; as Herbert Marcuse put it in 'The Concept of Essence', essence is 'an isolation of the one true Being from the constantly changing multiplicity of appearance' (1968: 43). This metaphysical concept 'essence' has come under attack from a number of quarters: from Marxists, who think that essentialism is a romantic fiction; from new art historians, who think that essences are unstable; and from poststructuralists, who conclude that 'things' are not of an (ir)reducible nature. The Austrian philosopher Ludwig Wittgenstein was an important voice in undermining confidence in the universal values of, say, Kantian notions of beauty. He argued against essentialism and what has come to be termed a 'family resemblance' view, maintaining that, rather than a work of art having a single essence, the connections between works of art cannot be reduced to beauty or truth but involve a network of differences and similarities. His work has been influential on a later generation of deconstructionists such as Jacques Derrida. Wittgenstein's theories were important in uncovering the importance of context – that is, the practices and conventions of a given period – in reading an art work. However, to write off essentialism altogether would be premature. The American philosopher Arthur Danto argues against the open concept of art that we have received from Wittgenstein and in doing so embraces a view that accommodates even non-art objects such as urinals or found objects. For Danto, what he calls the *indiscernibles* are crucial in identifying an artwork, not the *perceptible* properties; hence his tendency to emphasise interpretation, which he largely situates within the historical conditions under which an art work was produced and a symbolic embodied expressionism related to metaphor. Terry Eagleton has spoken of postmodernism's antipathy to essentialism, largely within social relations:

> There are indeed reductive, falsely eternalizing, brutally homogenizing uses of the concept of essence, and they have wreaked especial havoc in the fields of gender and ethnicity. Essentialism there means something like 'reifying to an immutable nature or type', and has been a potent weapon in an arsenal of the patriarchs, racists

and imperialists, even if it has also been brandished by some feminists and ethnic activists themselves. But if every concept which can be deployed for radical ends was discarded because it was used against them, the discourse of radicalism would be threadbare indeed.

(Eagleton 1996: 103)

'A criterion for whether a city is modern: the absence of memorials'[7]

There is another issue we might consider – the changing status of decoration under modernism. The German arts and crafts school Bauhaus was enormously influential in the 1920s and early 1930s. Founded in 1919, it developed a radical programme of integrated arts. The increasing specialisation of architecture in particular, however, resulted in the separation of the disciplines into 'purist' camps. The austerity and uniformity of much modern architecture made sculpture, as decoration, superfluous. The geometric ordering of the city under architects and planners like Le Corbusier[8] might admit a sculpture but it would take an abstract, mystical, often Eastern, form. In general, then, decoration became outlawed as buildings without ornament were seen as works of art in their own right. The Austrian architect Adolf Loos went so far as to associate decoration with decadence and crime in 'Ornament and Crime', an article written in 1908. By association, therefore, sculptural adornment, so popular under art nouveau, was rendered obsolete. New York's modernity, for instance, can be registered in the dearth of its monuments; the city's buildings stand as substitutes. By the middle of the twentieth century the individual identity of cities had been replaced by an international style more suited to corporate capitalism than civic authority.

This is to emphasise only one aspect of modernism, but, nonetheless, artists who have worked on fixed sites for public commissions have run the gauntlet of artistic populism. Often viewed merely as an adjunct to an urban space, public sculpture is required to conform with public or corporate taste – what Robert Morris despairingly called 'urban decoration for urban sites'. In some cases, for instance Richard Serra's *Tilted Arc*, the subject of an ignominious court case and removal, or Rachel Whiteread's *House*, also the subject of controversy and removal, the public work's primary function seems to be the debate it generates.

Into the community

The conceptual artist Joseph Beuys (1921–86), also a founder member of the German Green Party, worked on monumental projects that draw together some of the issues about art in public places looked at so far. Conceptual art was another attempt by artists to avoid the straitjacket of commercialisation and the conformity of gallery art. Often 'dematerialised', the final art product was sometimes irrelevant, the process given primacy over output. New public art outside the gallery is something of an oxymoron since, ironically, most art collections are public. However, the term is used to designate art that, although increasingly difficult to define, is in a public space. Conceptual art often took the form of interventions into public spaces using non-traditional material: text, video, billboards, hoardings.

This was the case with Beuys's *7,000 Oaks* project, developed for the international quinquennial art exhibition 'Documenta 7', held in Kassel, Germany in 1982, in which he created a living sculpture. Atypically, the mutability of this monument is inbuilt. *7,000 Oaks* exists in different locations in different cities, and transfiguration is a crucial element in its conception. Although referred to as oaks, many of the trees are other species, but, seen with their companion, a large piece of basalt rock, they are an unmistakable feature on many streets across the globe. Talking of *7,000 Oaks*, Beuys stated:

> [M]y point is that . . . these 7,000 trees . . . each would be a monument, consisting of a living part, a live tree, changing all the time, and a crystalline mass (basalt columns) maintaining its shape, size and weight. This stone can be transformed only by taking from it, when a piece splinters off, say, never by growing. By placing these two objects side by side, the proportionality of the monument's two parts will never be the same. We now have six and seven year old oaks, and the stone dominates them. In a few years' time, stone and tree will be in balance and in 20 to 30 years' time we may see that gradually the stone has become an adjunct at the foot of the oak or whatever tree it may be.
>
> (Beuys, quoted in Demarco 1982: 46)

The work *7,000 Oaks* is, therefore, an organic monument, implicating the public in Beuys' ecological agenda. Beuys' work was part of a wider attempt to return art to the community and make of art something accountable.

Permanent commissions for public spaces have encountered difficulties beyond the requirements of pleasing public taste and meeting civic budgets. Just what we celebrate of the past, or of the future, is no simple issue. The need to commemorate the past is strong, and the memorial monument is still part of most countries' culture. The difficulty in a pluralistic age is how we represent 'others'. The term 'the other' was used by Simone de Beauvoir, writing in 1949, to clarify the position of the female in relation to the centrality of the male – 'he is the subject, he is the Absolute – she is the other' (de Beauvoir 1949: 16). This term has subsequently been used to designate the marginal group in relation to the dominant order. This awareness of power relations has contributed to a loss of confidence in shared universal values which previously assumed a totalising, universal human nature. Sculptors of monuments which are commissioned to speak for others, then, are placed in an unenviable position.

The counter-monument

Horst Hoheisel's *Monument to the Aschrott-Brunnen* (1987) (Plate XI) is an apposite example of the counter-monument, an acknowledgement of the inability to speak for the other. In 1908 a civic monument for the city of Kassel was funded by a Jewish industrialist. The Aschrott-Brunnen monument in City Hall Square was originally a 12-metre high, neo-Gothic pyramid fountain surrounded by a pool. It was destroyed by members of the National Socialist Party in 1939. The reasons for rebuilding this monument after the war are complex. Memorial monuments usually celebrate triumphs rather than the state's decimation of cultures and peoples. Hoheisel's solution was a design that made explicit the relationship between the present and the past. The monument was not designed merely to replace the previous structure. In making the form a 'negative monument' Hoheisel hoped to relate the present to the past as the only way of understanding both. The negative monument acknowledges the destruction of the first. Like many other memorials to the Jews, it reinforces through its negation of the monument the remembrance of absence. The spectator stands on the flat site of the monument and listens to the periodic fountain that flows down around the inverted pyramid. Hoheisel stated:

> I have designed the new fountain as a mirror image of the old one, sunk beneath the old place in order to rescue the history of this place as a wound and as an open question, to penetrate the consciousness of the Kassel citizens so that such things never happen again. That's why I rebuilt the fountain sculpture as a hollow concrete form after the old plans and for a few weeks displayed it as a resurrected shape at City Hall Square before sinking it, mirror-like, twelve meters deep into the ground water. . . . The pyramid will be turned into a funnel into whose darkness water runs down.
>
> (Hoheisel, quoted in Young 1993: 43)

For Hoheisel, the need to tell the truth could not be represented by a simple reconstruction or replacement of that which was destroyed. His counter-monument was designed as an allusion to the original and as an illusion, forcing the spectator to confront the former's absence.

Other memorial monuments to the Jewish people have raised the spectre of remembered loss. It seems that public mourning and the commemoration of the recent past are as problematic as the debate around what form the monument should take. To portray the Holocaust abstractly – the preferred option of Richard Serra's and the architect Peter Eisenman's design of a colossal 'garden' of stone pillars (in Berlin) – raises issues around the need to mourn or commemorate within a perceived realism. Although many of the memorials to the First World War contain figures, few artists attempting to work with the Holocaust have chosen anthropomorphic monuments, despite hostility to the idea of 'abstracted' mourning.

Christian Boltanski's *Missing House* registers that which was 'lost' as an imagined space. The delays in the completion of Rachel Whiteread's memorial to the Jews, *The Nameless Library*, built on the Judenplatz in Vienna, has proved equally labyrinthine in concept and execution. Now constructed, Whiteread's work comprises 266 square metres of concrete – a white rectangle. The sides of the structure contain impressions of thousands of books, and embedded in the structure are the names of the concentration camps where Jews were interred in the Second World War. Whiteread's monument *The Nameless Library* is built close to Or Sarua Synagogue as a memorial to over 65,000 Austrian Jews who died as a result of Nazi persecution. Its position on the Judenplatz is not unproblematic, as the architectural integrity of the original square is broken by the sheer scale of the building. However, it can be argued that, like Hoheisel's negative form monument, its power lies in its refusal to offer comfort.

The commemoration of specific cultural groups, often sub-cultures or groups outside the dominant class, is a preoccupation of many contemporary artists. Whiteread's (*Untitled*) *House* was a memorial to another community, in this case the relocated working-class population of Bow in the East End of London. The internal spaces of the empty house were filled with light-grey concrete and the exterior walls of the terraced house were removed, leaving a ghostly reminder of the private space of a family home. Never conceived as permanent, *House* was demolished after a single casting vote by Bow Neighbourhood Councillors, who then ordered its demolition. (*Untitled*) *House* itself was consigned to memory (or at least to photographic and video records) when the concrete cast was removed in 1995.[9] (*Untitled*) *House* and *The Nameless Library* can be seen as part of what has been characterised as a melancholic postmodern 'sense of loss'. In her casts and imprints Whiteread fashions the presence of an absence. The monument to the European Jews 'lost' in the Holocaust also bears witness to their loss. Although problematic and a cliché of learning, the debates that fuel the controversy over what constitutes a suitable monument to lost communities are likely to be the lasting legacy.

These examples illustrate a major debate in twentieth-century cultural practice: what kinds of monuments can be built and, more crucially, what forms can they take? James Young maintains that

> the fundamental dilemma facing contemporary monument makers is [thus] two-sided and recalls that facing prospective witnesses in any medium. First, how does one refer to events in a medium doomed only to refer to itself? And second, if the aim is to remember, that is refer to a specific person, defeat, or victory, how can it be done abstractly?
>
> (Young 1993: 11)

The issue for the modernist memorial monument is its very self-referentiality. Does the modernist insistence on the autonomy of the art work necessarily lead to its political irrelevance? And, conversely, does mimetic illusionism – the anthropomorphic statue – always fail as art? But there is an ambiguity here: Whiteread's *House* looked like an 'abstract' sculpture, with geometric shapes bearing scant resemblance to the physical world. Yet it was also the cast of an actual house and therefore *real* in a very concrete sense (both literally and metaphorically, as it happens). Although by no means unproblematic, the term 'realism' in its post-war manifestation came to be associated with the 'thing itself'. Broadly speaking, to refer to a work of art as 'realist' meant that it added to the world of things; it was not just illusory or a reflection of things already in existence. These works required an engagement with an invented (imagined) realm, although this was nevertheless predicated on an engagement with the ordinary and the mundane.

It can, of course, be argued that the failure of the permanent monument in the twentieth century is simply a manifestation of the collapse of shared values; cultural diversity and pluralism will not admit of a universal vision shared by all. That, however, would be to simplify the significance of the monument to the process of *the formation* of unified values, even if 'the common memory' is illusory.

The complexity of this issue can be read in Australian attempts to forge one nation out of a history of the violent oppression during frontier conflicts. Although traditional

Aboriginal art has typically been displayed as ethnographic artefacts in museums such as the Pitt Rivers in Oxford. The *Aboriginal Memorial* (1987–8) (Plate XII), however, is shown in an art gallery. It was created for the Australian bicentenary year, 1988, marking the beginning of colonisation. The memorial in the National Gallery of Australia is dedicated by its makers to the indigenous Australians who defended their land and perished in the 200 years of white settlement. In this work speaking for others is avoided as the memorial was made by indigenous peoples. The work's position inside a classic Western art gallery signals attempts at reconciliation on two levels: the political and the artistic. Cheek by jowl with icons of Western art such as Pollock's *Blue Poles: number 11* (1952), the traditional form of Aboriginal art no longer registers as ethnographic anonymous craft but as part of a continuum of art production. However, in its specific political context, it rejects the aspiration to universalism of much modernist art. Through its traditional form and function it resists assimilation.

Artists at war

> Art isn't supposed to be practical, but when it is it's great.
>
> (Lippard 1990: 118)

It is a common observation that most public monuments celebrate violence or incorporate an aggressive element. The depiction of the conqueror and the vanquished is an important element of Western public monuments; even the caryatids that adorn civic buildings were to the Ancient Greeks representations of a defeated nation. Unlike their European counterparts, eighteenth- and nineteenth-century American monuments often celebrate the virtues of the 'common man' rather than those of the state. However, in trying to create monuments to the American Civil War (1861–5) artists had become familiar with the divisive potential of the memorial, which cannot merely represent a victor. That is, in attempting to reunify a divided country, granite and stone reminders of one side's success are at best tactless. The American war in Vietnam raised this spectre again, but at a time when artists were increasingly preoccupied with the 'self' and an art constructed around notions of private contemplation.

The 1950s were marked by an increasing tendency among artists to engage in an art of 'monumental vision' and making 'cathedrals of ourselves' (Barnett Newman 1968): an art of individualism. If art had become increasingly centred on its own practices, the Vietnam War was a watershed for many artists previously disengaged from political activities. The legacy of McCarthyism and the anti-Communist witchhunts, as we will see in Chapter 6, had contributed to an unprecedented retreat to the studio. The Vietnam War reopened the debates started in the 1930s around the social responsibilities of the artist. The monuments that were created around this war, however, were largely the inverse of traditional monuments.

Lucy Lippard has argued that Robert Smithson's earthwork at Kent State University in 1968 became an 'unintentional monument' when the National Guard opened fire on anti-Vietnam War demonstrators. Smithson's work, although political only in the sense that works cannot be in the world and not be political, became the focus of anti-Vietnam protests and a photograph of the work was exhibited as an anti-war poster.

The work consisted of an abandoned woodshed on the university campus that Smithson partially covered with earth, creating an 'ambiguous grave-ruin' (Lippard 1990: 20). The symbolic resonance of the work altered as the killings at Kent State became the focus for anti-war activism. It mobilised many artists who were politically active but engaged in 'abstract' art practices that seemed inadequate to express the anger and grief felt at the US government's involvement in the war in Vietnam. It was the Peace Movement that not only, often under the aegis of the Art Workers' Coalition (AWC), was active in the making of art works that brought the war to public attention in a critical non-celebratory way, but also exposed the institutional collaborations that simultaneously funded the museums and art galleries and the military-industrial complex.

As well as Smithson's 'unintentional' monument, there were several monuments that commemorate conflict. The Los Angeles 60-feet high *Peace Tower* was a temporary collaborative piece initiated in 1966 by the Artists' Protest Committee. The tower, built by Mark di Suvero and Mel Edwards, consisted of 400 panels by artists from all over the world. The artists were some of the best known then working, including Judy Chicago, Philip Evergood, Robert Motherwell and Ad Reinhardt. What is interesting about the collaboration was its synthesis of diverse art practices from figurative to non-objective art. It is also worth noting that the tower is rarely written about, despite its enormous significance to the period. It was intended to stay as a visual analogue for the war, to be removed only when the war finished.

As we have seen, monuments are not always realised. Many of Claus Oldenburg's plans for monuments referencing everyday consumer goods[10] fall into this category. Oldenburg's work is part of a much broader rejection of abstract expressionism that we look at in greater detail in Chapter 6. Suffice it to say that pop art involved an explicit, if sometimes ironic, engagement with consumerism, illustrated by Oldenburg irreverently producing a plan to replace the Statue of Liberty with an electric fan, and for huge trowels and clothes pegs to be placed in unlikely places. Pop art directly challenged what was increasingly seen as abstract art's esoteric retreat from the world.

Oldenburg's first constructed project was *Lipstick Ascending on Caterpillar Tracks*, for Yale University, placed in position on Ascension Day 1969. It had been commissioned by students (the Colossal Keepsake Corporation) and was situated near the official war memorial on Hewitt Plaza. Yale, until then a bastion of male privilege, had just become co-educational, and the introduction of the lipstick on campus was knowingly anarchic. For Oldenburg, it was reminiscent of Tatlin's tower and should have incorporated a telescopic element. Most of Oldenburg's monuments have not been permanent and have incorporated change – movement and sometimes metamorphosis. In this case, however, graffiti and erosion through weathering wrought unwanted changes, and *Lipstick* was removed in 1970. Crucially, monuments were for Oldenburg a celebration of the present; he argued: 'Why should monuments commemorate something that happened 100 years ago? It should reflect what is going on today' (Oldenburg, quoted in Lippard 1990: 35).

The traditional monument has tended to confound gender politics. That is, the female is often used to represent what she does not possess – justice, liberty, equality. The female form as monument, typically either classically robed, therefore historically unsited, or unrobed and so socially unspecified, has been the allegorical repository of state values that often excluded the female. The monument, as we have seen, also contributes to the formation of state values. Allegory, as Marina Warner points out, has a double intention, conveying one meaning but also saying something else. Of Parisian monuments she comments:

> [O]nto the female body have been projected the fantasies and longings and terrors of generations of men and through them of women, in order to conjure them into reality and exorcise them into oblivion. The iconography appears chiefly in public commissions and in the edifices where authority resides because the language of female allegory suits the voices of those in command.
>
> (Warner 1985: 37)

The very visibility of the female form in public statues is paradoxical given that it was used to reinforce patriarchal values.

In terms of the Vietnam War, Oldenburg's monument made use of a common motif, that vanitas of appearance, the lipstick, to subversively analyse the transience of human existence and the erroneous confidence placed in technological order and the machinery of war. The use of the female form or of associated female 'ephemera' in anti-war works reintroduces the figure into art at a time when it had seemed conspicuous by its absence. Oldenburg's *Lipstick*, in its first incarnation, had been a huge plastic inflatable. Max Kozloff points to the inherent radicalism of Oldenburg's work: 'one thing sculpture is quite simply not allowed to be, if it has any pretensions to the mainstream, or any claim to historical necessity, is soft' (Kozloff 1967: 26). Subsequently reworked in a metal case, the retractile lipstick conformed to phallic symbolism. The missile was conflated with male sexual aggression, but, ambiguously, the lipstick too became a weapon. In this sense, the lipstick both conforms to the use of the female form as a clichéd repository of patriarchal values and subverts it. Significantly, in this period the Women's Movement, in part arising out of the activism of the Peace Movement, established itself as a major force in Western art practice.[11] In tandem with the feminisation of modernism Oldenburg's monument also breaks the rigid anti-chromatic format of most Western public sculptures and monuments. The absence of colour, the concentration on black, grey and at best bronze, is remarkably uniform throughout the Western world. Public taste seems to require a denial of colour, a chromaphobia.

This is in part gender-related. The nineteenth-century writer Charles Blanc identified colour with femininity, considering it of a secondary order to the more 'masculine' design or drawing. There is a long history of colour being subordinated to 'purer' disciplines like drawing and, more pertinent to the subject under consideration, sculpture. Colour is often related to sensuousness, eroticism even, and therefore in a culture burdened by a legacy of censoriousness and hierarchies is regarded as a sign of frivolity. Colour has also acted as a marker of the primitive or, in pop art's case, a populism associated with bad taste. David Batchelor states: 'to this day "seriousness" in art is usually available only in shades of grey' (1997a: 2). Oldenburg's *Lipstick* is therefore transgressive precisely because it blends serious intent and playful imagery. It transgresses the etiquette expected of traditional war memorials – the social site of violence made visible. Traditional war memorials often use the female form to embody abstract notions such as peace, justice and liberty, though Oldenburg's use of the lipstick to stand for the female is also the application of a piece of pop irony.

There are further works to consider in relationship to the memorial monuments to the Vietnam War. Maya Lin's *Vietnam Veterans' Memorial* in Washington, DC (Figure 3.7), was dedicated in 1982 and is now situated amongst a growing collection of memorials in Washington Mall's Constitution Gardens close to the White House. The memorial was a belated tribute to the soldiers in combat (hostilities ceased in 1973), who found themselves in an uneasy, even hostile, relationship to the country for which they had fought. The monument is a V-shaped low wall of polished black granite that reflects back the image of the viewer. It is an earthwork which appears to descend into the ground and is partially buried in the soil. Carved into the granite are the names of the 58,135 US casualties, listed according to date of death. Coincidentally, Maya Lin won the open competition to design the monument with an anonymous entry when she was a young graduate at Yale University. The significance of this monument registers some of the changes that the history of monuments outlined so far has made. We have seen that modernist works have been largely unsuccessful in combining the public and private spheres, but Lin's work is an exception. It has not remained isolated and unexplained or remote from the community. Its apparent self-referentiality – it has no illusionistic devices or decorative features – has been overcome and it stands as a successful 'interactive' abstract work: the monument is touched, has rubbings taken of the names and is a repository for gifts. The monument is not a celebration of war. It does not glorify but literally inscribes the cost of war. In this crucial sense, then, the memorial monument has 'critical distance' – creating an ambivalent relationship with the dominant order. The new art of the public space may offer the possibility of a new critical relationship for groups marginalised by the central contradictions of a public art. The issue of Maya Lin's sculpture, however, highlighted the official ambivalence to abstraction's ability to be read in different ways. The fact that Maya Lin's monument can be registered as an anti-war monument resulted in official censure. Placed near Lin's work is Frederick Hart's bronze figurative work of three GIs (Figure 3.8). Hart's more traditional rendering of the heroic figurative monument was erected as if to act as a counterbalance to compensate for the lack of specificity of Lin's monument. As an index of postmodernism, a newer bronze group, also overlooking Maya Lin's monument, features women in auxiliary wartime service supporting wounded soldiers.

The growing collection of memorial monuments to war multiplying in Washington, DC, is not just an act of remembrance, it is part of the attempt to recover retrospectively the histories of people written out of memory. The Korean War of the 1950s has been largely absent from significant memorial sites. So the late arrival of a *Korean War Veterans' Memorial* in the 1990s, positioned within sight of Maya Lin's Vietnam memorial, raises several issues. The *Korean War Veterans' Memorial* looks at first like a compromise between variant forms of the Vietnam memorial discussed above. Its large black wall, like Maya Lin's work, reflects back the image of the viewer, but closer inspection reveals the etched images of military personnel. In addition it features traditional anthropomorphic statues, built to scale, in front of the wall, positioned as if crossing a field of combat. Bearing a resemblance to the museum dioramas of a bygone age, the tableau attempts to render the realism of war in its details of a moment of action and even in the imitation of the rough terrain over which the soldiers fought. Each soldier is realistically rendered in lead, but the effect of the material is to give the figures a ghostly pallor: their ethereal presence is reinforced by their images

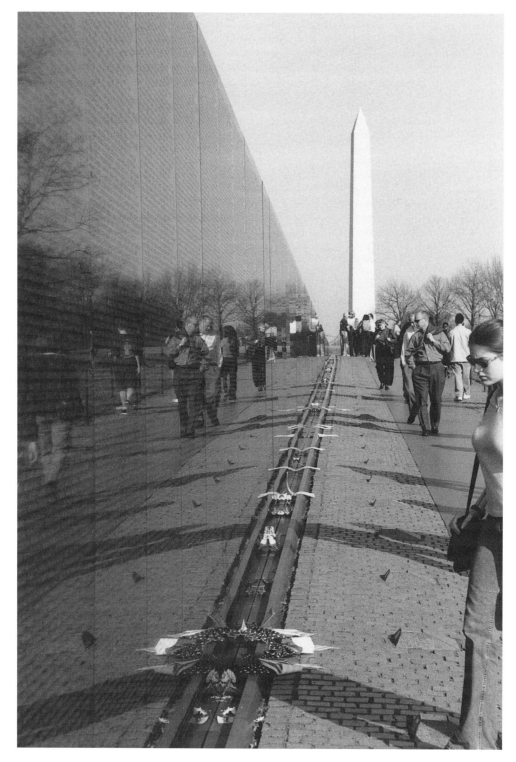

Figure 3.7 Maya Lin, *Vietnam Veterans' Memorial*, 1980–2, Washington, DC. Photograph Pam Meecham. The memorial monument is 450 feet in length and is made of granite. It bears some comparison to the traditional wailing wall of more ancient cultures.

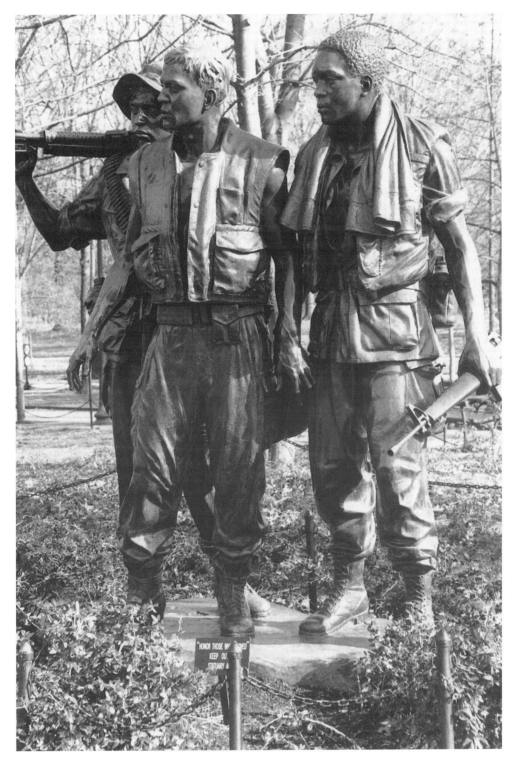

Figure 3.8 Frederic Hart, *GIs' Monument*, 1984, Washington, DC. Photograph Pam Meecham. The figurative bronze work was placed within sight of Lin's abstract memorial and throws into sharp contrast Lin's commitment to seeing the memorial as a place to overcome grief not as a place of propaganda.

reflected on the black wall. The monument's representation of a narrative, with a platoon leader appearing to shout instructions to the radio operator at the rear, confounds any reading of the work as a traditional symbolic monument. Instead, the *Korean War Veterans' Memorial* is a life-sized tableau of a moment of war, seen through the prism of Hollywood war films.

We have seen that many public monuments have the – overt or covert – theme of violence. The graphic representation of violence in the twentieth and twenty-first century has presented a set of complex issues. Armand Fernandez's monument to the conflict in the Lebanon (erected outside the Ministry of Defence building in Beirut) unusually incorporates actual instruments of war. Layers of tanks are contained inside a ten-storey concrete structure, the gaping holes in the concrete revealing glimpses of weapons, while the tanks' guns protrude from inside the monument. The 5,000-tonne assemblage uses real Soviet tanks, contained in what resembles a shelled building but is actually a composite of sandbags and concrete, in effect combining the destructive weapon with the destroyed. Like Maya Lin's abstract work, the *Lebanese Monument to Peace* appears to reference modernism's tropes, such as monumentality, ready-mades and industrial processes. However, it is one further example of the kind of solution to the ongoing problem of 'representing the unrepresentable' that inverts several conventions of the traditional war memorial. Like a violent parody of the ready-made, the monument incorporates the 'real' in the form of actual tanks. In tandem with the edicts of modernism it forgoes the use of precious materials, instead using concrete, which underscores the brutalist character of the project, aesthetic and political. Fernandez saw the work as a *memento mori* and a continual reminder of the catastrophic consequences of war.

The formation of unified values in a postmodern age, however, is perhaps neither desirable or possible, and so the potentially democratic idealism of the public monument has proved elusive. The cultural move from an autonomous and independent sculpture back to the public sphere inevitably raises the spectre of popular culture. The *Moonwalker Statue* of Michael Jackson, while in part mythic, bears at least some relation to an actual person, even if Jackson's self-aggrandisement has literally as well as metaphorically reconstructed that person.

The fate surrounding the statue of Rocky Balboa, the fictional boxer played by Sylvester Stallone in the Rocky film series (1976–85), is pertinent here. The film prop is a larger-than-life bronze of the 'working-class boy made good' – the apotheosis of the American dream. In the film the statue is displayed on the steps of the Philadelphia Museum of Art, which contains the major collection of Duchamp's 'ready-mades'. Marcel Duchamp, as we have seen, questioned what constituted art and art's relationship to the space in which it was displayed. The ensuing battle, therefore, over whether a functional piece of work, like the film prop made by Thomas Schomberg, could be an art work had illustrious parallels in high art. The museum authorities wanted the work removed after the filming was completed despite the statue's enormous popularity. It was eventually relocated to a sports stadium.

Regardless of its status as 'art', the statue of *Rocky* functioned not as iconoclastic avant-gardism, as in Duchamp's *Fountain*, but as popular culture. Its appeal as an icon of the 'common man' triumphant made it the second-largest tourist attraction in Philadelphia after the Liberty Bell (Senie and Webster 1992: 231). The partisanship the statue evoked undoubtedly polarised the debate to one of elitism versus popular culture. But the issue of how a fictional character can function as a contemporary monument is unresolved. Unframed by art's validating institutions, the status of *Rocky* as art is not assured. The elision of the divisions between high art and popular culture is one of the much-vaunted ambitions of postmodernism. However, overcoming the distinctions between art and non-art may prove more difficult in fact than in theory.

Virtually real monuments

> With the television image – the television being the ultimate and perfect object for this new era – our own body and the whole surrounding universe become a control screen.
>
> (Jean Baudrillard, quoted in Foster 1990: 127)

We began this chapter by looking at the city as the locus of modernity. As we enter the twenty-first century our experience of the city has become increasingly complex. While not everyone travels, no one who watches television stays entirely at home. We experience other places through the medium of the screen, and arguably the modern monument is now the movie. Although Laurie Anderson's *Blood Fountain*, a proposed 50-feet tall monument for murder victims, was on a grand scale, it was to be experienced via a small video projection which superimposed the blood-pumping work on to Columbus Circus in New York. In the main, modern artists have been as interested in critiquing the function of monuments as exemplars of platitudinous officialdom as in looking for alternative projects to celebrate. For instance, with his *Memorial Projection: a proposal for the city of New York* of 1986, Krzysztof Wodiczko laid out his resolution

> not to 'bring life to' or 'enliven' the memorial nor to support the happy, uncritical, bureaucratic 'socialisation' of its site, but to reveal and expose to the public the contemporary deadly life of the memorial. The strategy of the memorial projection is to attack the memorial by surprise, using slide warfare, or to take part in and infiltrate the official cultural programs taking place on the site.
>
> (Wodiczko 1996: 424–5)

Artists' current preoccupation with new technologies is part of a tendency towards a virtual, rather than a direct, experience of creating art works. It might be useful to recall that for Brancusi and his peers the direct experience of carving was crucial to the authenticity of what was produced. Since new technologies are eminently reproducible and do not possess the same inherent claims to originality, the authentic experience has now shifted to the beholder. One of the earliest examples of interactive artwork is Jeffrey Shaw's *The Legible City* (see Figure 3.9), which is an interactive video installation. Here the dematerialised experience of the city is ciphered through a notion of virtual reality. The viewer is the participant, who maps the terrain of the city by cycling through New York courtesy of a real-time animated computer-graphic projection which functions by means of electronic sensors. The screen contains text storylines by different people in Manhattan or Amsterdam, from taxi drivers to Donald

Trump. In the Amsterdam experience Dirk Groeneveld included actual events in the city's fifteenth- to nineteenth-century history reconstructed from archive documents. The vocabulary used was based on the old Dutch language and the text made to approximate the literal scale and colouring of the replaced buildings. By cycling across storylines new texts can be made, and each cyclist creates a new reality. The virtual bike ride around the two cities (a screen that corresponds to a map on the bike indicates the cyclist's actual location), by being interactive, combines several notions of the *real* and of *virtual reality*. Shaw states that, 'between reality and representation, between the city and its simulation, there is the psychogeography of the vicarious experience' (Shaw 1996: 487).

The use of the low-tech cyclo, the traditional Vietnamese pedal-powered taxi, became emblematic of Vietnamese technological inferiority during the Vietnam War as images of Hanoi were televised around the world. It also, however, played a central part in the war as the conveyer of secret messages and is part of a cultural identity threatened by Western culture. The cyclo is the central motif in the work of Japanese-born Jun Nguyen-Hatsushiba. As a metaphor of the past and a powerful image of the complexity of our relationship with that past, the cyclo is used by Nguyen-Hatsushiba to explore ritual and the way that the cyclo, an antediluvian pre-technologised relic, can work

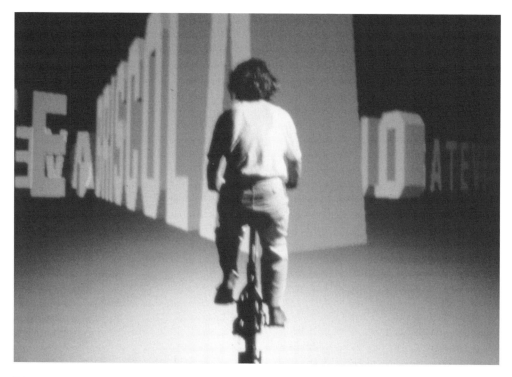

Figure 3.9 Jeffrey Shaw, with Dirk Groeneveld and Gideon May, *The Legible City*, 1989–91. Courtesy of Jeffrey Shaw. In the video installation the architecture of the city is replaced by text, although the text conforms to the original physical plans of the city. The cyclist is at liberty to choose the direction the bicycle will travel. The computer-generated images are played out in 'real time' in order to simulate the experience of cycling.

beyond nostalgia to draw the past into the present. The fate of the cyclo is uncertain, as it clashes with the desire to modernise a culture through the automobile or becomes merely a tourist 'must do'. In his 2001 *Memorial Project Nha Trang, Vietnam – Towards the Complex – For the Courageous, the Curious and the Cowards* (see Plate XIII), Nguyen-Hatsushiba abandons his reinventions of the cyclo to create a narrative on a single-screen video. The underwater film sequence shows a small cavalcade of cylos being pushed across the surface of the seabed towards a 'memorial site' of mosquito nets.

It has been a constant of both modernism and postmodernism that the art work's subject has often been an absentee. We saw in Chapter 1 that modernism had a fractious relationship with the art object. The depiction of the human figure has also undergone rapid transformations, so that it is missing from many works – as we have seen, monuments as much as paintings or sculpture. The use of video and DVD has added a further layer of pathos to memorial projects. Traditionally the camera recorded a presence; however, many artists use the camera to record an absence. Some artists have refused to depict the subject precisely because the camera records what is there rather than what is not. Zarina Bhimji's work is part of a continuum of negative monuments like that of Hoheisel, Whiteread and Smithson. Although her film is about the diaspora caused when General Idi Amin expelled thousands of people for whom Uganda had been home, and about the subsequent murder and torture of many thousands more, the victims are only referred to through the soundtrack and empty buildings. Bhimji's soundtrack often registers as distant murmurs and suggestive but indecipherable sounds. The indistinct and unsaid take the place of the pretensions to clarity and truth of documentary filmmaking. Bhimji's elegiac 24-minute film *Out of the Blue* (2002) registers the landscape of Uganda together with its empty buildings. The images of the deserted buildings are preceded on the video by images of landscapes more suited to a nature programme. However, the images of the lush, tropical landscape are transformed by fire as part of a strategy that moves the viewer from contemplation of the beauty of the landscape to the political realities of the dictatorship.

The extent of the impact of mass media on our perception of reality has been difficult to assess. However, the theorist Jean Baudrillard holds up the example of simulacra to show how our sense of self has altered in the modern world. Put simply, a simulacrum is an identical copy without an original. We cannot, so the theory goes, separate our reality from the means of *representing* that reality. The impact of digital imaging and the organisation of information (its transmission and retrieval), and the way that we learn, is therefore in and through simulacra. Of course, these theories have implications extending beyond the visual arts. Baudrillard cites a historical shift which suggests that we in the West no longer produce things – machines or materials – we just manufacture information.

In art terms the influence of Baudrillard has been complex. Although theory is not always mirrored by practice, Baudrillard's attacks on modernist 'sacred cows' such as 'authenticity' and 'originality' have seen some artists taking cover under a knowing, ironic art practice that refers to other art practices. These are works that have a currency only within discourses of art, and therefore art becomes only about art and requires a knowing audience. (Vik Muniz, in Chapter 6, makes more sense when one is familiar with Hans Namuth's famous film footage of Jackson Pollock at work.) Baudrillard's theories have become an endorsement for a form of self-reference which can be viewed as socially irresponsible – although he is ambivalent about the shift that he himself has registered. At its most nihilistic, postmodern culture recycles fragments of the past, a process characterised as just 'playing with the pieces' (Storey 1997: 165). As John Storey maintains, if Walter Benjamin claims that mechanical reproduction has destroyed the 'aura' of the art work, then Baudrillard argues that the 'very distinction between original and copy has now been destroyed' (quoted in Storey 1997: 126). This process is easy to see in film, of course, where to make reference to an original print makes little sense. There are only copies, no original.[12]

There have been calls to 'boycott Baudrillard' and to resist those claims that reduce 'all our experience to the thinness of the television screen', since we are not 'passive victims of a mediated information flow' (Wheale 1995: 62). However, the Baudrillardian collapse of certainties has precipitated a crisis in our understanding of representation and realism. For Baudrillard, in the universe of simulation 'reality becomes ambiguous, paradoxical, certainly undecidable – so it no longer has a use-value, one can no longer say, "this is real, this is rational, this is true"' (Williamson 1996: 308). Baudrillard (1988, 1993) explores the relationship between fantasy and reality most accessibly in his references to America's notion of itself and to Disneyland. Disneyland, with its sanitised environment and its lack of urban detritus (vagrants and litter), simulates an American utopia. Baudrillard claims that Disneyland is presented as imaginary so that we can believe in the 'real' America. And this, he argues, is not real either. It is not a question of false representation of reality, but of an 'act of concealment'. The real is no longer real, we are constantly told; in fact, it is simulated, and so we need an act of fiction (Disney) to convince us of our reality.

To make sense of reality, then, we refer to fiction as if it were reality (Rocky's statue conforming, in part, to this). But the issue is more complex than the mere escape from reality into fantasy. The fantasy exists – and Disney is only one of myriad fantasies – in order to convince us of the 'realness' of our own lived experience. Storey maintains that it is 'not a retreat from the "real" but the collapse of the real into hyperrealism' (Storey 1997: 165). Hyperrealism, then, is a characteristic of postmodernism, although it is not consistent in its manifestations. What is real in the Baudrillardian sense is a dissolution of the fantasy, Disneyworld, into everyday reality. We may well be engaged in a 'false realism' (Jameson), since postmodernism is rarely consistent in its manifestations. In the cities of the Pacific Rim, in Singapore and Tokyo, the parody and pastiche of Western culture produce another set of realities.

Bypass monuments

If unofficial monuments and counter-monuments have figured highly in the urge to celebrate or commemorate, artists have also been concerned with looking over the unseen or overlooked, to draw attention to unheroic histories. Cornelia Parker takes as her subject the soil that has been removed from an unstable monument, in this case the leaning tower of Pisa. Using her trademark exploding fragments, Parker's (2002) *Subconscious of a Monument* was installed at the Frith Street Gallery, where the clay clods hung, as if airborne, from floor to window height across a room in apparent contradiction of the laws of gravity. The work also included three glass wall pieces on which fragments of soil had been randomly dropped. The effect physically destabilised the viewer in a ghostly echo of the predicament of the unstable tower at Pisa. Parker's declared interest in the 'unmade' rather than the ready-made chimes with modern art's obsession with the non-regulatory, the unofficial and fragmentary. She states:

> Sculpture was always about making these permanent, solid things. For a long time my work has been about trying to erode monuments, to wear them away and to digest them, and then create a moment, a fleeting thing. I had monuments falling. Instead of being huge edifices that go upwards towards the sky, they were falling down. . . . It was about suspending. . . . Nothing was solid, nothing was fixed, everything has a potential to change, so it was the opposite of the monument; it was the moment.
>
> (Tickner 2003: 370)

This registering of a history through moments and fragments can be found in earlier works by the situationists. In 1957 Guy Debord and Asger Jorn collaborated in a memorial project consisting of snapshot collages of their pre-situationist existence to commemorate the founding of Situationist International. The book *Mémoires* (1958) was made up of scraps of texts and images from high and low culture laid out in no obvious coherent order in a 'collaged re-collection'. Frances Stracey has argued that 'the dispersed structure of these morsels of memory serve [*sic*] to commemorate the past in a form that challenges conventional models of the memorial, understood as an entombment or freezing of the past' (Stracey 2003: 59). By pillaging and reappropriating the detrius of consumer culture Debord and Jorn are heirs to the Baudelairean appeal to celebrate modern life on the streets of the city but also to Walter Benjamin's search for modernity in the arcades of the new consumer culture. The book then operates as a memorial not just to Debord and Jorn but to those who fall outside official memorial culture, those who trespass at the margins of official history and have no 'legitimate' memorial. Some of the images consisted of collages of a disparate collection of images and text pieced together with splattered ink. Moreover, the abrasive outside cover of *Mémoires* was of sandpaper; it aimed to act as an irritant in the archiving process.

Almost in the manner of a Byzantine icon, the collages of Kurt Schwitters also act as portable memorials for a fugitive past, although his Merzbau of pasted, cut and torn fragments gleaned from the streets of Hanover evolved to take over large sections of his houses in Hanover, Norway and the Lake District in England after he fled Nazi Germany.

There is one further monument that we want to discuss in relation to 'non-sites' for monuments that modern artists have preferred over the conventional or official monument. Memorialising the ordinary, everyday and overlooked, Robert Smithson worked amongst the 'non-sites', ruins of the industrial landscape. In *The Monuments of Passaic* (1967) Smithson immortalised the pontoon bridges, drainage pipes and concrete of a highway under construction. *The Monuments of Passaic*, a section of the twenty-four gelatin silver prints (7.6 × 7.6), documents the terrible beauty of industrial wasteland, which to Smithson was post-industrial ruins; that is, ruins before they have even been constructed, rather than a structure reduced to ruins at a later stage. With *Land Art* in general and Robert Smithson in particular, 'sculpture' finally achieved the heroic status that it had arguably failed to attain under modernism. Smithson explored the margins between monuments and sculpture, parks and industrial sites, insisting that the exhibition in the gallery was a place of 'cultural confinement' conditioned by 'fraudulent categories' where works of art became 'politically lobotomized' (Smithson 2003: 970–1).

Spontaneous monuments

Bypassing official dictates and rituals on the required decorum for public expressions of grief, spontaneous monuments representing private grief and outrage have reached endemic proportions, with votive candles, poems, toys and temporary shrines replacing the rituals and reliquaries of officialdom. In so doing, the spontaneous monument blurs the boundaries between public and private that Louis Althusser (1918–90) maintains are a separation constructed to sustain class divisions. He suggests:

> The distinction between the public and the private is a distinction internal to bourgeois law, and valid in the (subordinate) domains in which bourgeois law exercises its 'authority'. The domain of the State escapes it because the latter is 'above the law': the State, which is the State *of* the ruling class, is neither public nor private; on the contrary, it is the precondition for any distinction between public and private.
> (Althusser 2003: 929–36)

It can be argued that the communal expressions of grief that take place at the site of loss are a response to the lack of confidence in established forms of authority such as church and state. The unregulated placing of messages, photographs and requests for information at the site of an act of violence, from a car crash to an act of terrorism or a football stadium tragedy, has become a prominent feature of public grief, most graphically seen in the Missing Posters at the 69th Regiment Armory, New York, following the destruction of the World Trade Center in New York in 2001 and in the placing of flowers and messages at the gates of Kensington Palace following the death of Diana, Princess of Wales, in 1997. They are also a return in Britain to a previous generation's unofficial street shrines marking the death of local men killed in the trenches of the First World War. Unlike most monuments, which are placed symbolically some distance from the actual incident or site of loss, the spontaneous monuments are site-specific, the visiting of the site being an important element in a new form of ritual. The ritual is fuelled by the mass media's promotion of images that create confidence in a relationship with the (often unknown) victim. The spontaneous monument is also immediate and bypasses the distancing devices of monuments devised by committee. Moreover, in staying outside officially sanctioned etiquette the memorials often incorporate protest as well as remembrance not endorsed by officialdom. There is a sense of continuity, however, with the traditional anthropometric monument, in that, like the majority of public monuments, the spontaneous memorials commemorate violent and untimely death.

We want to return, in the context of local and community grief versus the official monument, to Maya Lin's *Vietnam Veterans' Memorial*. The memorial was conceived as a site of healing; it is referred to as 'the wall that heals'. Part of the cathartic possibility of the memorial lies in the wall functioning as the reliquary of an earlier age through the touching of names and the placing of mementos, letters to the dead and photographs at the site of the wall. There is a travelling replica of the memorial, made of aluminium, which loses its position as an earthwork, the structure of the Washington original, to take up a reduced size (half-scale) and take its place temporally in local communities. The monument is adapted to local and specific needs and as such constitutes a metaphor for the fugitive status of the postmodern monument that is temporary, mobile and often subject to local needs rather than the demands of the nation-state.

At the start of the twenty-first century the etiquette for monuments has undergone significant changes that are marked by a less rigid code of practice than formerly. The once-static signifier of permanent state values in *solid* form has been replaced by a mass of ambiguities in both form and function. Often at once local and global, decisive and yet uneasy, grand and yet unassuming, the monument has taken on a mantle of impermanence and negotiation.

The nude in modernity and postmodernity

In 1969, during one of their early outings into 'bagism', Yoko Ono and John Lennon were interviewed by journalists. Bagism was the couple's own art movement, playfully parodying '-isms' and an attempt to depersonalise the cult of fame and to confound the kind of judgement that is made on the basis of appearance alone. By (dis)appearing in public in a large bag for two, Ono and Lennon not only preserved their visual anonymity, but challenged the assumptions that viewers make on the basis of gender, ethnicity, age and dress. And yet, ironically, what interested the journalists interviewing Ono and Lennon was not the purpose of the performance but whether they were naked inside the bag. That this mattered at all to anyone outside the bag, on the one hand demonstrates that the press had completely missed the point of bagism, but on the other also shows how the connections between nudity and art had become a cliché in the popular consciousness (see Figure 4.1).

Images of the nude are commonplace in Western art and have been a staple of painting and sculpture since the Renaissance; so much so, in fact, that the nude is now enshrined in art practice and has come to be regarded principally as an art form. However, the male and the female nude carried rather different historical meanings, and in art-historical studies in recent years both have come to be regarded as more than just art forms. For instance, notions of the female nude as the 'privileged object of connoisseurial voyeurism' have been eloquently deconstructed in Marxist and feminist art history. And, in turn, writings about the male nude have been revised in the wake of 'queer politics'.

That it was the female and not the male nude that came to dominate the visual language of early modernism is indicative of an overwhelming shift away from the values embodied in the idealised, heroic, timeless classical male nude of the eighteenth century. While the classical male nude is clearly dependent upon an accurate, if idealising, representation of the human form, in modernism there appears to be less need of a model. For instance, Matisse's and Picasso's nudes often bear little resemblance to the sitter. Ironically, modernism's tendency to distort the female form has simultaneously resulted in an artist–model relationship that ascends to mythical proportions. The modernist myth of bohemia, as Frances Borzello (1982: 86–98) points out, brought out into the open the artist–model relationship. Implicit in the bourgeois construction of the bohemian artist is the idea that 'his' creativity is closely linked to the female

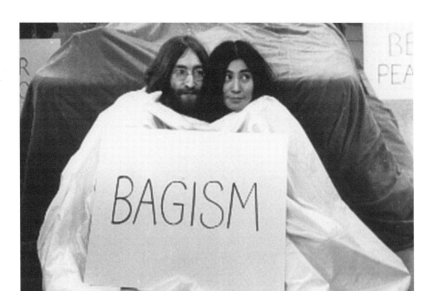

Figure 4.1 **John Lennon and Yoko Ono, *Bagism*, 1 April 1969.** Courtesy of Getty Images/ Time Life. The photograph was taken just days after their wedding when the couple were being interviewed in London for a television programme. The concept behind bagism was that people could interact without prejudice since the anonymity of the bag prevented them from making judgements on the basis of looks, age, gender and race.

model. The female sitter fulfils a triple role as model, mistress and muse, but, in addition, she becomes an important sign of the male artist's modernity. In this chapter we examine how the female nude became a crucial element in the formation of art designated *modern*; that is, the female nude – especially the prostitute but also the female body of the barmaid and the working-class woman – became emblematic of modernity. We saw in Chapter 1 how the move from academy to studio, the appeal to middle-class patronage, the evolution of a personally expressive iconography and the position of women in modern society under the division of labour brought about by industrial capitalism combined as conditions of modernity. Furthermore, these socio-economic factors combined to make the female nude a complicated carrier of meaning. The nude became, on one level, deeply implicated in the politics of representation and, on another level, a metaphor for the modern artist's own sense of alienation.

It may surprise us today that the fixation with the nude female body in art practice is thus conterminous with modernism – particularly when eighteenth-century academic training had been dominated by the male figure. Before the authority of the academies was challenged by artists working in a less orthodox idiom in the second half of the nineteenth century, their institutional apparatus had upheld classical models of painting and sculpture. Classical art was an exemplary art practice that taught students to improve upon nature, idealising the subject of the human figure according to a set of prescribed ideas about composition – proportion, harmony and colour. Interestingly, however, it was the male rather than the female figure upon which these principles were visited in the academies. Classical male nudes were heroic exercises in paint or marble.

Michelangelo's *Adam* on the ceiling of the Sistine Chapel or Jacques-Louis David's *Intervention of the Sabine Women* (1799), in which the men fight with only cloaks and shields affording cover for their bodies, are, in this sense, works of the highest order, and the male nude therefore is made to carry important ideological meanings. This grand rendition of a story from Ancient Roman history is enacted by warriors improbably fighting in the nude. David's male nudes were inspired by Ancient Greek statues of gods and athletes and their nudity is symbolic of the higher moral purpose and heroism of the battle. The women's carelessly exposed breasts, however, are symbolic of their helplessness in an unguarded moment of utter despair as they try to separate the warring factions. Some feminist writers, Lynda Nead for example, have differentiated between the treatment of male and female nudes, where the male figure stands for elevated and timeless values while the female is left to stand for the 'merely' beautiful (Nead 1992: 29). Nead identifies the male nude with notions of the 'sublime'; that is, the highest category of aesthetic appreciation in eighteenth-century Romanticism. It is therefore not without significance that it was the female nude – by its very passivity open to any number of patriarchal constructions – rather than the ordained male nude, that became an icon of the fragmentary nature of *la vie moderne*.

The male nude

From the eighteenth to the twentieth century the 'life class' has occupied a central place in the academic training of artists. Entry to the life class would be preceded (and supplemented) by a study of anatomy and by drawing from the antique. All academies and, later, art schools retained plaster models of well-known antique statues and friezes for students to copy. The root cause of this kind of organisation within the academies was the dominance of history painting as a genre. History painting describes art that has a biblical, literary or classical content, such as David's *Intervention of the Sabine Women* (1796–9), which is ostensibly an ancient story about the peace effected by the Sabine women between the Romans and their enemies the Sabines, but which had a significance for the new French Republican order after years of revolution. History painting was at the apex of the hierarchy of genres – above landscape, still-life or portraiture – into which art was subdivided. History paintings were often weighty and serious in tone, with a moral or exemplary message, like David's painting, which was considered to earn them their place in the hierarchy. It was impossible to have history painting without the human figure, and the idealised heroic male nude body was its bedrock. This is not to say that all history paintings depict nudes. They do not. But the preparatory sketches and sometimes detailed studies that preceded them were nearly always nude figure studies of the historical characters. It was only in the final stages of an art work's creation that figures were swathed in drapery or clothed in antique costume.

The nude was therefore a prerequisite of history painting – in the sense that drawing from the nude was a necessary condition of the painting. The precious place of the nude was bolstered by the economics of the art market in the eighteenth and nineteenth centuries. Ultimately, it was the nude that offered the best hope of patronage among art buyers and it was the vehicle through which ambitious artists hoped to gain official recognition. Nineteenth-century notions of artistic excellence were synonymous with how well an artist could convey history and, by implication, how well he could paint or sculpt the nude. Given that 'academic studies' (decorative drawings of nudes in mock-classical poses) dominated the public art exhibitions of the 1870s in Europe, it is perhaps not surprising that artists should have continued to subscribe to the codes and conventions of academic nude painting. Equally, and as numerous feminist art historians from Germaine Greer to Griselda Pollock have pointed out, the exclusion of women from life classes (and from academies and art schools for most of the nineteenth century) militated against their success, particularly in the genre of history painting. And when women were eventually permitted to draw from the nude (around the turn of the twentieth century in most European countries), male models would be provided with 'posing pouches' or loin cloths.[1]

Margaret Walters explained that the male nude carried many more meanings than the female nude, citing political, religious and moral meanings as personified by the male nude body: 'The male nude is typically public: he strides through city squares, guards public buildings, is worshipped in the church. He personifies communal pride or aspiration' (Walters 1978: 8). However, Abigail Solomon-Godeau points to evidence of a crisis in representing the male at the end of the eighteenth and beginning of the nineteenth century. She has shown how the confident, virile and heroic males of neo-classicism gave way to languishing youths offered up for erotic display. The standards set by the male nude only later came 'to symbolize the obsolescence of academic precepts and values' (Solomon-Godeau 1999: 43) and the male nude was therefore rejected by more radical artists, who used the female nude as a mode of dissent. On the rare occasions that the male nude does resurface within modernism the types of criticism and analysis that ensue are wholly compromised by the lack of critical discourse to describe the reception and perception of male nudity. A case in point is Thomas Eakins painting *Swimming* (1884–5) (Plate XIV), which pictured the artists' friends and pupils bathing at a local beauty spot. The picture has been the subject of some speculation in recent years regarding its content. Some see the presentation of naked male bodies in the painting as evidence of homoeroticism or, more specifically, Eakins' own homosexual desire. It is worthy of note that, even though the painting is currently being revised through the lens of queer theory, this ultimately perpetuates the formation of the gaze as a male one and closes down the possibility of sexualised male nudes for the female gaze.

Another notable exception to the modernist prohibition of the male nude is to be found among Seurat's studies for the large and ambitious painting *Bathers at Asnières*. These included a Conté-crayon drawing of a naked young boy seated on the banks of the river (Figure 4.2), as well as drawings of the same figure topless. What is remarkable about Seurat's nude is its absence of heroism and lack of gratuitous sensuality. Because Seurat's work is modern (the boy is not an athlete or warrior or a god, he is one of Baudelaire's 'heroes of modern life') the semi-naked male continues to carry specific messages. In this instance the boy's profile would have betrayed his class origins to anyone interested in physiognomy in the nineteenth century. Moreover, his rounded, sloping shoulders marked his body as belonging to the labouring classes rather than to the pampered leisured classes discussed by Solomon-Godeau and painted earlier in the same century. If anything of substance can be drawn from these limited incursions into the otherwise dominant territory occupied by the female nude, then it is that the male

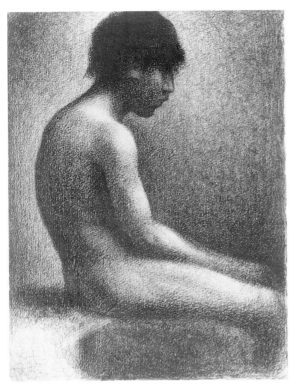

Figure 4.2 Georges Seurat, *Seated Boy with a Straw Hat* (study for *Bathers at Asnières*), 1883. Courtesy of the National Gallery of Scotland. There are numerous figure studies for *Bathers at Asnières*, including versions of the seated boy that appears in the foreground of the finished painting. This nude study was most likely completed in Seurat's studio and in other versions the boy is wearing trousers. In the completed painting the topless boy sits on a white smock, which implies that he is employed in one of the local trades, perhaps as a boat-builder or carpenter, and the tricolour in the background suggests that it is Bastille Day and therefore the boy is on holiday.

nude is not articulated for the female gaze. The virtual disappearance of the male nude from the art produced under modernism is in and of itself remarkable, as is the fact that when the nude male body does reappear in the 1960s, it is with the advent of performance art and at a time when male (and female) artists are readily disrobing to make their point (see Chapter 8). As the Guerrilla Girls pointed out in their poster campaigns of the 1980s, proportionately the overwhelming number of art works from the modernist period depict female nudes (they cite the statistic that 85 per cent of nudes in the Metropolitan Museum in New York are female, asking the question 'Do women have to be naked to get into the Met?'). So why is it that the male nude was not a site of modernity, not an object of modernist experimentation and not a metaphor for the disorienting effects of life under industrialisation?

The genealogy of the female nude

When Thomas Eakins painted the American sculptor William Rush decorously assisting his naked model to step down from the posing dais (1907–8), he (unwittingly) exposed several ambiguities in the conventional portrayal of the female nude. Eakins's painting may be read as a conventional, rather sentimental, image of male chivalry – possibly reflecting what he *knew* of Rush's character. However, it is also an image which disturbs Kenneth Clark's well-known distinction between 'the naked and the nude'. This distinc-tion was made on the basis that the naked was *knowing* and the nude *distinterested* – as one of being 'huddled and defenceless' versus 'balanced and confident' (K. Clark 1980: 1). The idea of the nude as being somehow 'clothed in art' and therefore desexualised is an important one, which, in part, derives its authority from the Kantian notion of a 'disinterested aesthetic'. That Eakins's unnamed model is shown with pubic hair marks her, in Clark's terms at least, as 'naked' rather than 'nude' – even though, we presume, the sculptor Rush intends to transform the naked woman into a conventional nude. While Clark clearly ranks the nude above the naked, the Marxist art historian John Berger reverses the ranking since, he claims, 'to be naked is to be oneself' (1972: 54). For art historians such as Lynda Nead, Berger's theoretical counterpoint merely inverts the opposition of 'naked' and 'nude'. Nead challenges the peculiarly Western set of binary oppositions that characterise philosophical discussions of art and shows that they do not, in fact, stand up to much close scrutiny. Nead shows how John Berger, in reversing Clark's differentiation of naked and nude, merely elevated the naked (into which Eakins's representation of Rush's studio might fall) as a private act of love, but failed to place it within an understanding of the broader cultural constructions of 'love' and 'the naked'. For Nead this is a perverse answer to Clark and is in an equally false position since it supposes that the naked somehow lies beyond the realm of 'cultural intervention' (Nead 1992: 14–16). Naked or nude, semi-clothed or fully clothed, the female body can never be an innocent category, beyond cultural definitions and, as we will see, it is a perpetual carrier of overwhelmingly male signs.

As Eakins's painting demonstrates, one (academic) artistic convention that distinguished nakedness from nudity was the absence of pubic hair. Classical female nudes were always without pubic hair (except, interestingly enough, in the preparatory sketches). Early modern artists, generally speaking, did little to overturn this convention in painting or sculpture. The issue of pubic hair is neatly concealed by a convenient hand in Manet's otherwise 'naturalistic' *Olympia*. Even photographs of nudes discreetly side-stepped the issue, hiding pubic hair with drapes and clamped thighs. In 1917 the police closed a Paris exhibition of Amedeo Modigliani's paintings, which included *Reclining Nude*, on the grounds that 'they have hair'.[2] Pubic hair, however, does feature in works designated 'pornographic' photography and it does feature in artists' drawings, for example in Degas's images of brothels (see Figure 4.3). In this respect, pubic hair is one of the signifiers of sex, and its explicit depiction is usually reserved for pornography. Gustav Courbet's *L'Origine du monde* (1866) (Figure 4.4) was a private commission which undoubtedly served an overtly pornographic use for its owner (and for more than 100 years it remained in private collections). It depicts the isolated torso and parted thighs of a 'naked' woman lying down with the covers raised to her armpits. There is little ambiguity here; this is the erotic orifice, surrounded by 'realistic' pubic hair. However, its high-art pretensions are hinted at by the epic tone of its title.

From the brothel drawings of Degas to Picasso (who admired and bought Degas's brothel scenes) the implicit and explicit associations of the modern nude are of prostitution. Baudelaire's call for *la vie moderne* was embraced in French literature, where books such as Emile Zola's *Nana* and Gustave Flaubert's *Madame Bovary* enlisted the prostitute or 'fallen woman' as a symbol of modernity. This is in stark contrast to the Enlightenment, when Denis Diderot, writing in the *Salon Review* on François Boucher in 1765, remarked:

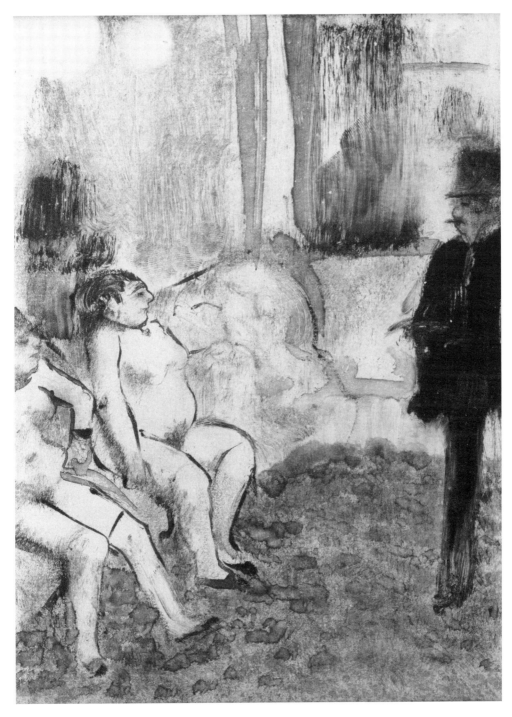

Figure 4.3 Edgar Degas, *Le Client***, 1879.** Musée Picasso. © Photo RMN. Like Picasso and Toulouse-Lautrec, Degas made multiple studies of the everyday life of the brothel between 1875 and 1885. Degas's brother destroyed around seventy of the 120 drawings of brothel scenes following the artist's death.

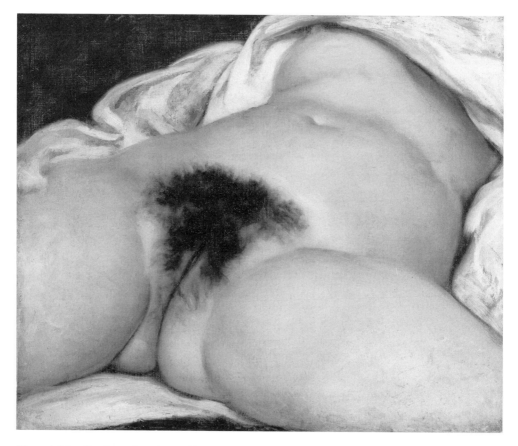

Figure 4.4   Gustave Courbet, *L'Origine du monde*, 1866. Musée d'Orsay. © Photo RMN–H. Lewandowski. Commissioned by the Turkish diplomat and celebrated collector of erotic art Khalil Bey, the *Origin of the World* is still troubled by its pornographic status. The Musée d'Orsay has only put the work on display since 1996 and many web sites devoted to Courbet's work demur from illustrating this one.

> [T]he degradation of his taste, his colours, his composition, his characters, his expression, his drawing has followed the depravity of his morals step by step. What do you expect an artist to put on his canvases? Whatever is in his imagination. And what can a man have in his imagination who spends his entire time with the lowest kind of prostitutes?
>
> (Diderot, quoted in Eliot and Stern 1979: 111)

However, ever since John Berger pointed out that the bikini-clad woman on a car bonnet (at, for example, a 1970s motorshow) signified 'For Sale', semiotic theories of the reclining nude have been under review. Semiotics shows how conveying meanings to members of the same culture relies upon a symbolic order of signification which exposes, in Berger's example of the scantily clad woman on the bonnet of the car, how one cultural code operated in the 1970s.

The complex system of signs we have invented for ourselves often blurs the real significance of things; the naturalising and the normalising of the depilated nude indicates how conventions can arise out of representation. The conventional nude is neither natural nor normal, but the result of centuries of consolidated art practice. It was only when modern artists ruptured these conventions that the conventions themselves were exposed. The critical reception of Courbet's *Les Baigneuses* (*The Bathers*, 1853) (Plate XV) was one of those instances where scandal revealed the hypocrisy inherent in the conventions of a 'disinterested aesthetic'. Executed on the grand scale (90 inches × 96 inches) normally reserved for heroic images of classical bathers, Courbet's painting is a knowing repudiation of academic codes. Slyly alluding to the iconography of *Noli me tangere* (representations of Mary Magdalen and the resurrected Christ) in the gestures of the figures, this painting was an affront to French Second Empire bourgeois norms. The conventional 'bather' would have been a milky-skinned, aristocratic, teenage beauty tastefully dabbing herself by a stream in an Arcadian landscape. Courbet's bather, however, was a ruddy-faced older woman, and she was washing rather than bathing. The conventional bather never actually looked in need of a bath; Courbet's bather, according to his critics, did.

Courbet's conspicuously working-class bather was castigated at the time of the painting's exhibition for being too old, too ugly and too dirty. Paintings of the lower classes certainly existed in the mid-nineteenth century, but they too followed established conventions – generally those of genre painting, which rendered the working-class subject as either pathetic or foolishly humorous, but never with gravitas. Courbet's *Les Baigneuses* not only rode roughshod over academic conventions but crossed with several conventions associated with pornography. In the painting Courbet depicts the servant with rolled stockings, as she might appear in a pornographic photograph or a print of the period. Moreover, the bather she attends has discarded her very contemporary clothing on the branch of a tree, rather than having been recently disrobed of a classical mantle or shift. This marks the bather as being in a state of undress – naked rather than conventionally nude. False dichotomies or not, these binary oppositions of naked and nude have been cleverly deployed by modern artists, overturning the old order. What is significant for our purposes is that replacing the nude female body with the naked female body should constitute an act of male artistic rebellion.

Representing the female nude

After thirty or so years of scholarship, feminism now has a relatively well-established position within art history. Its impact, in simple terms, has been to bring to light the art produced by women which was hitherto neglected by the canon-forming dominant discourses of art. Crucially, however, many feminist art historians have worked not solely to rehabilitate forgotten women artists, important though this is, but to look at the operations of the system that supports the privileged status of male artists. Feminist art historians have challenged the very ideological base of a mainstream art history which has hitherto been paraded as 'natural' and 'neutral'. This is part of a broader thrust against 'disinterested' scholarly activity, which clearly includes the perception that the nude is principally an art form, a subject for dispassionate scrutiny.

Feminist art history, like lesbian, gay and postcolonial art history, is one in which the ideological position of the critic or historian radically impinges upon her interpretation of art history in general and art works specifically. Of course, orthodox art history, when written in the interests of white, male heterosexuality[3] and with a Eurocentric agenda that relegated non-Western art forms to a lesser category, is similarly conditioned; but orthodox art history had become such a standardised approach to art that it was able to masquerade as 'natural' and 'neutral'. Feminist art historians fundamentally reject the claims to universalism that used to be made on behalf of literature, music, art and culture in general. They expose how art has often been silenced in terms of the politics of race, gender and sexuality. They foreground questions of difference – principally of gender but also of racial, cultural and sexual difference. But we should not think that the insights that feminist art historians have brought to bear, during a very self-analytical period of feminism, are applicable only to 'marginalised' art forms; on the contrary, any such tokenism would be detrimental to the possibility of their criticisms serving as a blueprint for the analysis of other power relations and so providing models for change management. The issues of representation, in particular, that feminism has called into question have a resonance for all aspects of representation, not just representations of women.

For example, Piero Manzoni's *Living Sculpture* (1961, Milan), in which the artist put his signature on the body of an attractive young naked woman so as to designate her as a 'living' sculpture, may be 'revised' in the light of a feminist theory of art history.[4] While the 'old art history' might well have appreciated the 'gesture' – the artist is ostensibly punning the notion of creativity by simply signing his model – a feminist art historian would doubtless pose questions. Catherine Elwes describes *Living Sculpture* as a work which 'represents woman as sexed commodity. She also embodies the traditional model/mistress/muse who supplies material and sexual and spiritual nourishment for the delicate palate of male genius' (Elwes, quoted in Kent and Moreau 1985: 164). Elwes's interpretation of what is at stake here is indicative of the kind of sea-change in thought that feminism has brought about. Crucially, as Parker and Pollock put it, 'art is not a mirror. It mediates and represents social relations' (1989: 119). *Living Sculpture* therefore is typically probed in terms of the power relations between the artist and the model, the representation of the woman and the context in which the work was made. All the 'givers' of the old art history, in particular the notion that the nude is principally an art form – that is, an object of the 'disinterested' connoisseurial gaze – are called into question by feminism. However, undermining the idea that the nude is visually autonomous, that it is nothing but an arrangement of aesthetically pleasing colours and shapes, has been an uphill task.

The relationship between an image and the reality it purports to represent is, according to many contemporary critics, inherently political. This stems in part from the work of poststructuralist theorists, who have identified a connection between 'texts' (or, for our purposes, 'images') and 'power'. Michel Foucault's reworking of the influential proposition 'knowledge is power' questioned the nature of knowledge itself and, in so doing, emphasised the ideological constructions that underpin the relationship between knowledge and power (Foucault 1994). For example, representations of women, racial minorities or disabled groups are inevitably constructed according to dominant ideologies; and it is not until traditionally marginalised groups represent themselves that their practice exposes the power relationships implicit in mainstream art. Indeed, many other art-historical givens have been rendered obsolete by pluralism and cultural diversity. The depiction of the nude in modern art is a given which has been revised by feminists precisely because the representation of a nude women *is* political. Artists do not *present* the nude, they *represent* her.

What we have established is the apparent ease with which the female body came both to represent abstract concepts and to also function symbolically as a metaphor for artistic alienation. A feature of artistic alienation in the modern period has been to look beyond the borders of Europe for inspiration. Clearly, the representation of the nude is doubly marked by artists' preoccupation with cultures outside their national boundaries. Edward Said, a Palestinian cultural theorist who lived and worked in the United States, was highly influential in exposing the specific representations of the East in the West. With specific reference to literature, Said writes:

> The things to look at are style, figures of speech, setting, narrative devices, historical and social circumstances, *not* the correctness of the representation nor its fidelity to some great original. The exteriority of the representation is always governed by some version of the truism that if the Orient could represent itself, it would; since it cannot, the representation does the job, for the West and *faute de mieux*, for the poor Orient.
>
> (Said 1995: 21)

Current theories of alterity, particularly those laid down by Said, foreground many of the functions of representation; which is to say, *knowing* the 'other' in terms of providing an accurate and impartial representation is impossible. Edward Said's exemplary investigation of Western literature explored relations between the Orient and the Occident (the East and the West), and exposed Orientalism as a peculiarly Western discourse based largely upon stereotypes of turban-wearing despots, boasting exotic harems of scantily clad odalisques attended by eunuchs. *Orientalism* (first published in 1978) and *Culture and Imperialism* (1993) deal mainly with representations of the East in literature, but Orientalism was also a fashion in art – typified by Eugène Delacroix's exotic Algerian scenes. What needs to be established here is that in representing the 'other' Delacroix's perception was coloured by his position as a white male who belonged to a colonial nation.

Being female is no guarantee of having better *knowledge* of the 'other'. There are many examples of paintings of the female nude by women artists that subscribe to overarching masculine principles of erotic display. For example, Elisabeth Jerichau-Baumann's undated painting *Odalisque* subscribes to the stereotypes of the female nude propagated by her male counterparts. However, as Reina Lewis has demonstrated, women's images of Oriental nudes are fundamentally different at the point of reception. She shows how Oriental nudes by women artists were validated by Western ethnographic discourses (Lewis 1996: 119) and derived their authority from the rendition of nationality rather than eroticism per se. Both male and female artists, unwittingly or not, colluded with and even informed Oriental discourses, simultaneously confirming, rather pejoratively, the Orient as 'non-Western'. While Near and Far Eastern people were regarded as 'exotic', the 'savage' black Africans had long been part of the slave trade and existed in a debased relationship to white Europeans. The slave trade made it economically advantageous to construct the African as mentally inferior and (as we will see on pp. 125–9) called upon the services of medicine, anthropology and Darwinism to support this thesis. The West's economic relationship with the East, however, was not uniform. Depending upon exactly which part of the East the figure represented came from, the odalisque was correspondingly higher in the hierarchy of races than her black African equivalent.

Returning to Said's damning observations about the West's representation of the 'poor' East, we come to two positions: first, a dominant position, which presumes the right of representation and, second, the basic condition of 'otherness', which is 'to be spoken of' rather than 'to speak for oneself'. Neither position is arbitrary – both have arisen out of a set of complex historical circumstances in patriarchal, imperialist and capitalist trade dealings. The act of representing peoples under direct colonial rule or as disadvantaged economic partners of the West is therefore also political. The 'politics of representation' is evident in the value judgements implicit in the hierarchy of races, the appeal to the erotic-scientific curiosity of the West and the confirmation of imperial sovereignty. Even though the conventions of Western representation assume a power over the subject depicted, in fact Western art profits greatly by its commerce with the East. As Edward Said argues, 'European culture gained in strength and identity by setting itself off against the Orient as a sort of surrogate and even underground self' (Said 1995: 3). His point is important, since the influence of other cultures can be clearly seen in the art of the West. It is important to note that the avant-garde artists' claim to originality is, as we will see, predicated upon a much older engagement with a perceived exotic 'other'.

Subject and object

> One of the things that any painted object does is to resist significa-
> tion at some level because of its very objecthood. And the female nude
> – because of *its* objecthood – may be seen as almost emblematic of
> that level of resistance.
>
> (Armstrong 1986: 223)

The formation of the artist as 'subject' and the nude as 'object' has grown out of a tradition of philosophical inquiry which seeks to distinguish between thinkers and what they think about. It has become customary to assume that the subject is that which acts and the object is that which is acted upon. However, this distinction is seen to be inadequate in many cases of modern art. As we saw in Chapter 2, some artists searching for the spiritual renounced the subject–object dichotomy altogether; furthermore, the distinction fails to hold when the subject, as we will see in Chapter 8, can also be the object in terms of being a work of art – as in the case of performance art.

To compound the complexities of this subject–object discourse, epistemological shifts over the past twenty or thirty years have questioned the basis for knowledge about notions of subject and object. For instance, poststructuralists regard the subject as that which thinks and acts, but only in so far as the agency of the subject is qualified in some way. Thus in terms of dealing with representations of the nude, we start with the caveat that the subject has first to be recognised as a person or a set of people – whose language, ideology, even subconscious desires have been preconstituted in some way. In other words, the artist's representation is, in itself, an enactment of larger cultural forces, not an unmediated act of self-expression. With this in mind it becomes evident that however we qualify the precise nature of subject and object we come back to a set of conventions – whether visual or linguistic – which in the case of modern art designate the nude object as passive and the artist subject (or viewer) as active in terms of constituting meaning. In particular, the conventions of looking and being looked at (surveillance and display) present a set of problems for contemporary art history.

Film theorists first put forward the proposition that the construction of the spectator in mainstream cinema is gendered. What film theorists mean is that in practice women are 'objectified': they are displayed for the visual pleasure of male viewers (both within the film itself and in the audience that watches the film). Scopophilia, or the 'pursuit of visual pleasure', is a tendency which the film critic Laura Mulvey has argued is overtly masculine.[5] Blending psychoanalytical criticism with feminist film theory, Mulvey argued that mainstream Hollywood cinema fetishises the female form as embodied in the 'perfect' figures of Hollywood actresses. The audience, although comprised of men and women, shares an identification which is overwhelmingly masculine, both in terms of identifying with the male protagonist and adopting male desire in looking at the female on screen. Alongside both goes the cultural alignment of male as active and female as passive. For a female viewer to experience the same (active) 'visual pleasure' she has to adopt the position of the male viewer or assume the 'male gaze'. Visual or scopophilic pleasure, then, has come to be seen as an entirely masculine enjoyment.

Theories of female spectatorship often begin by problematising the mechanisms of the male gaze. In *Speculum of the Other Woman* (1985a) the French psychoanalyst Luce Irigaray rejects altogether the suggestion that women merely adopt the 'male gaze' rather as if looking in a flat mirror, and offers the exclusively female alternative analogy with the speculum (which has a convex surface that renders any object reflected in its surface as curved) to feminise women's reflections of themselves. The analogy gets to the biological centre of difference, although many women find it problematic that the mirror which enables them to understand themselves should be a speculum – the gynaecological instrument used for internal examinations.

Feminist, lesbian, gay and postcolonial critics have pointed out that claims for any sort of universal gaze are suspect because *man*, in the humanist sense of the word, is invariably constructed as white, Western, middle class and male. Nor is *he* really free to determine *his* own existence, but is in fact constrained by conditions of class, race, gender and sexual orientation. Numerous books in recent years have amply demonstrated that film has always been watched 'subversively' by groups whose identification is unconventionally drawn to minor characters and villains; or else who reroute the overt message of the film to serve an alternative agenda. Mulvey herself has revised her theory in order to accommodate other subject positions of visual pleasure.

For the art historian, another aspect of scopophilia, in large part also imported from film theory, is the theory of voyeurism. Film theorists have pointed out that the audience's vicarious enjoyment of watching a film in a darkened room is voyeuristic because pleasure is derived from the viewers' awareness of seeing without being seen. This has a particular resonance in Western art when so much that may be categorised as 'the nude' relies upon the premise that in the scopophilic display of the female nude she *herself* is unwittingly presented; that is, she has no power over her representation.

A classic case study of the nude (and one which has been amply deconstructed) is Degas's presentation of female nudes 'innocently' performing their ablutions for the spectator. Following Baudelaire's imperative that the artist should work from modern life, Degas depicted nudes which were highly specific to Paris in the 1870s and 1880s. Degas's matter-of-fact rendition of the private act of bathing (as opposed to the alfresco bathers of academic art) has been seized upon by art historians considering the mechanisms of the gaze. In each case an unsuspecting woman is surveyed by a (presumably) male viewer. As such, they have been viewed principally in terms of their status as modern 'snapshots' (based on Degas's well-documented use of photography) of fragmentary and fleeting moments in everyday life and have been applauded as such by modernists. Degas's unusual perspectival stances, his peeping-Tom views 'through a keyhole' and his use of flattened perspectival space have equally been upheld as markers of his boundary-breaking modernism.

Until relatively recently, questions about the nature of Degas's 'male gaze' have hinged on the issue of his modernist 'snapshots' and the privileges of his 'keyhole' vantage points, even though some of Degas's contemporaries found the inherent misogyny of his gaze the most remarkable aspect of his nudes. In more recent years, the question of Degas's misogyny has attracted the attention of critical scholarship, much of it influenced by feminism. Charles Bernheimer, deconstructing Degas's nudes, has returned to the critical reception which his work received at the end of the nineteenth century. In 1889 the French novelist J.K. Huysmans interpreted Degas's pastel drawing *Woman in a Tub* as proof of the artist's 'attentive cruelty' and 'disdain for flesh' (Bernheimer 1989: 161). He characterised Degas's view of his subject thus:

> [T]he penetrating, sure execration of a few women for the devious joys of their sex, an execration that causes them to be overwhelmed with dreadful proofs and to defile themselves, openly confessing the humid horror of a body that no lotion can purify.
>
> (Bernheimer 1989: 162)

This is quite a shocking response to works of art which subsequent formal appreciations in the twentieth century have come to regard as masterful exercises in the linear modelling of the female form, especially in their innovative use of pastels.

It can be argued that formalism is fundamentally irreconcilable with other readings – especially, in this instance, psychoanalytical readings. Psychoanalytical readings allow the 'return of the repressed', whereby both the subject and the object's underlying motivations are revealed. In Huysmans' terms, Degas's women bathing are read as psychologically revealing, and Huysmans claims that the penetratingly voyeuristic gaze of the artist is actually 'punishing' woman for her abject sexuality. Subsequent scholarship on Degas's gaze has tended to focus on his alleged misogyny. On the one hand, some art historians have argued that Degas's gaze puts him in erotic possession of the subject. On the other hand, there are those who have argued that Degas's work actually confounds the mechanisms of objecthood and subjecthood so implicit in the

Western construction of the male gaze. For this to be, we have to read these images from the point of view of the subject and to believe that the subject is not as frail as we have previously held. The awkwardness of her pose, the vulnerability of her naked-ness and her lack of classical credentials are not disempowering but are, in fact, overwhelming proof of her resistance. On the basis of a subjective reading of the woman bather's complete absorption in the act of washing herself (that is, she is not looking back at the artist with complicit coyness), she retains her physical integrity. The validity and sustainability of either argument aside, what each tends to do is to weaken any simple binary division between active bestowing object and passive recipient subject.

The formal nude

The art critic of the *Mercure de France* G. Albert Aurier (1865–92) wrote in 1891 of Renoir's *Nude in the Sunlight*:

> Why show her as intelligent, or even stupid, why show as false or as disagreeable? She is pretty! . . . Why should she have a heart, a brain, a soul? She is pretty! And that suffices for Renoir, and that should suffice for us. Does she even have a sex? Yes, but one suspects it to be sterile and only useful to our most puerile amusements.
>
> (Aurier, quoted in Dijkstra 1986: 182)

The subject matter of a woman bathing in a stream in an unspecified sylvan glade is familiar in art history. However, at the time it was first exhibited Renoir's technique for rendering the sunlight dappled through trees was criticised in the pages of *Le Figaro* for showing flesh as though it were decomposing. In this context, Aurier's statement is a defence of woman as motif. The fact that women have been repeatedly represented in modernist art by no means implies that their bodies signify 'women'. On the contrary, a nude woman is rarely anything but a motif. The art-historical etiquette for describing the nude is to use the pronoun 'it' rather than 'she' or 'her'. This distancing from the personal (including the fact that the models are often anonymous and interchangeable) is characteristic of centuries of art practice. The nude, then, is not appreciated osten-sibly as a picture of a woman but as an abstraction upon the theme of nude woman (K. Clark 1980: 79ff.). In terms of the modern period, the formal characteristics of the nude have often been represented as a pretext for modernist experimentation with form. This modernist mission to extend the notion of artistic beauty into cubist, expressionist and surrealist stylisations of the nude and in depictions of anti-bourgeois subjects is meaningful mainly because these modes of representation would previously have been regarded as overwhelmingly ugly and profane. The starting point for any aesthetic eval-uation of the art object was based on a consensual notion of beauty. As a criterion for judging art, the aesthetic implies that 'beauty' (in itself a loaded concept) resides in the art object and that 'taste' is the viewer's capacity for appreciating the beautiful. As a facility for appreciating nudes, the aesthetic lays claim to that kind of universalism which, we reiterate, is always suspect. Nonetheless, the championing of beauty in works of art that were consistently regarded as ugly and profane is profoundly important to our citing of the female nude in this endeavour.

That the female body should be the starting point for so many formal experiments is remarkable given the apparently enduring standards set by the male nude in the eighteenth century. Many seminal works in the modernist canon are based on the female nude: Manet's *Olympia*, Cézanne's *Grand Bathers*, Picasso's *Les Demoiselles d'Avignon*, Henri Matisse's *Pink Nude*, Henry Moore's *Reclining Nude*, Willem de Kooning's *Woman* series – these take more and more radical liberties with the female form. In Moore's work, the female nude evaporates altogether into rotund forms recalling the fleshy contours of a conventional reclining nude. The crux of the issue here is why formalism and the female nude overlapped at this crucial time in the development of modernism.

Formalism, as we have seen, is the critical practice of focusing on the artistic technique of the art work at the expense of its content or subject matter. As stated elsewhere, formalism evolved in line with developments in modern painting and sculpture. As we have seen, it is not the remit of the modern artist to make facsimiles of nature. In the early phase of modernism artists were concerned with equivalence – that is, with approximating the sensations evoked by, say, landscape. For this reason, modernism gave artists creative licence to explore abstract patterns and gestures which had more to do with private self-expression than with shared visual perception.

Formalism has aligned itself with the claims that the work of art is an autonomous object and, as such, one that can be 'understood' from a relatively objective standpoint. For the formalist 'understanding' and 'perception' are one and the same thing. Formalism was conceived at a time when visual perception was a branch of optics which assumed that we all see everything in roughly the same way, irrespective of conditioning factors; that is, we all see objectively. Theories of visual perception have altered significantly in the twentieth century. Rudolf Arnheim's *Art and Visual Perception* (1974) (first published in 1954) established perception itself as a subject for analysis within art-historical discourse, laying down criteria for how and why we perceive the visual field as we do.

To return to the construction of the gendered gaze and visual pleasure, others have since argued that visual perception is, in fact, always ultimately subjective, since the one doing the perceiving is in the grip of ideological forces. In 1891 when Albert Aurier wrote about Renoir's *Nude in Sunshine* as principally an aesthetically pleasing picture of a pretty woman, he was in thrall to the perceptive structures of his class, race and gender. This is not to claim the moral high ground but simply to acknowledge how the conditions in which judgements are made change; Aurier's comments now jar mainly because formalism, according to more recent scholarship, no longer holds sway.

Interestingly, those artists who worked in the formalist idiom, linked to abstract expressionism but resistant to the call to abandon content, vented their urge to abstract by distorting the female figure. Willem de Kooning's well-known *Women* series of paintings is abstract expressionist in style in the sense of contributing to the development of an idiosyncratic handling of paint but the central motif, one or two women, usually nude, is all too apparent amid the broad gestural brushstrokes of action painting. In the 1950s in the United States, artists who wanted to continue to work with the female nude in the face of calls to abandon content felt that they had to justify this philosophically. De Kooning's work ran counter to the goals of the other abstract expressionists and he defended his attachment to the figurative and to the female nude on several occasions. In one interview de Kooning explained how his interest in the series of *Women* paintings began: 'I began with women, because it's like a tradition, like the Venus, like Olympia, like Manet made Olympia. . . . There seems to be no time element, no period, in painting for me' (quoted in Prather 1994: 127). De Kooning's *Two Women in the Country* (1954) (Plate XVI) appears late in the overall series, which began as early as 1938, and the two women who were its subject were taken up again in 1947. The reception and interpretation of de Kooning's *Women* paintings was, and continues to be, mixed. When they were first exhibited at the Sidney Janis Gallery, New York, in 1953, they caused controversy. De Kooning's expressive brushwork was seen as an aggressive act against women in general and his comic presentation of the nude suggested to some that the artist's perception of women was misogynistic.

The anxious nude: death, disease and dangerous women

> If 'unconscious' and 'irrational' are the main attributes of primitivism, these very attributes are fundamental in the construction of woman as 'other'. In the context of art these classifications of art operate in two ways in that they constitute particular objects to be represented, 'the native' and 'woman', which as a 'represented' are paradoxically invested with the 'essence' of difference.
>
> (Philippi and Howell 1991: 239)

In 1853 Théophile Gautier referred to the nude woman in Courbet's painting *Les Baigneuses* as 'a Hottentot Venus'. This was a topical term during the nineteenth-century so-called 'scramble for Africa', in which European nations raced to colonise valuable (and sometimes worthless) African territories. Sara Baartman was the original 'Hottentot Venus'.[6] She was a black South African who was exhibited in Paris and London as a medical curiosity at the start of the nineteenth century (after her death even her preserved genitals were displayed for medical practitioners in Paris). During her lifetime her buttocks were regularly caricatured in the popular press and protruding buttocks came to be a stereotypical attribute of black women. More significant for our purposes is how the myth of the 'Hottentot' came to be twisted and entwined with myths of European women – especially the prostitute.

The underlying marker of black women's bodies as representative of primitive sexual insatiability stems from the myth that black men and women were sexually 'uninhibited'. Sander Gilman (1985) has shown how the 'Hottentot' and the prostitute were regularly twinned as examples of the excesses of female sexuality. While images of the 'Hottentot Venus' now seem like gross and offensive racial caricatures, for much of the nineteenth century they carried the aura of 'scientific fact'. Havelock Ellis's *Studies in the Psychology of Sex* (published in seven volumes between 1897 and 1928) and Freud's *Three Essays on the Theory of Sexuality* (published in 1905; see Freud et al. 1949), identified, respectively, the black woman's buttocks as a sign of racial inferiority and all women's genitalia as primitive. Gautier's reference to Courbet's *Les Baigneuses*, then, is actually not just a weak reference to the swarthy complexion of the woman in the water, but a highly loaded reference to the association of lower-class women (and by association prostitutes) with the 'lascivious' black African.

In the West, as Foucault has demonstrated in *Madness and Civilisation* (1990), so-called empirical knowledge is used to prop up the pseudo-scientific construction of women. In this case anthropology – a 'disinterested' study of other peoples – contributes, with one or two minor adjustments, to the alterity of European women. Importantly, the study of women through sexology, anthropology and medicine removed the object of study from the exotic and erotic representations of women and into a discourse of biological inferiority. Paradoxically, the presumed 'desexualised gaze' of anthropological voyeurism was current at a time when the depiction of women in mainstream art was becoming more overtly sexualised and blatantly erotic.

Fin-de-siècle anxieties about imminent social collapse, the end of the old order and the ushering in of new and potentially dangerous forces were played out with gusto in the art and literature of the period. Artists literally rehearsed the decline and fall of the old order in images of a world gone mad. Many thought that Europe would follow Babylon, Ancient Greece and Rome into collapse. The role that women played in these nightmare visions of the *fin de siècle* was as a sort of universal inverse of their role in the old order. There was, for instance, a genuine fear among governments and political commentators that emancipating women at home would precipitate the emancipation of colonial subjects abroad. Using women as markers of the inverse of civilisation is a recurring 'displacement activity' for the dominant order. Certain fears tend to be heightened at particular moments: 'displaced anxieties' are evident in 1950s sci-fi films about invaders from outer space or in 1990s films about vampires. On one level these 'texts' may be read literally in terms of their storyline, but their subtext is very pertinent to fears of the time – of Communist invasion in the 1950s and more recently of contaminated blood in the wake of the AIDS epidemic. Representations of women – in particular representations of female sexuality in the modern period – shift to carry metaphorically the fears of the time. As Elaine Showalter argues, legislation to regulate the sexual behaviour of women (especially prostitutes) in the *fin de siècle* was, although couched in the language of sexual purity, in actual fact motivated by the resurgent fear of syphilis (see Showalter 1991: 188ff.). The nineteenth-century belief that female prostitutes were the carriers of venereal disease, combined with evidence that prostitution was endemic – a result of the move from the countryside to large industrial conurbations – and the Victorian invention of family values, resulted in morally regulative imagery. Images of 'fallen women', brothels and dangerous women from history were offset by images of 'the angel in the house' and scenes of maternal duty.

It is no coincidence that female sexuality (especially 'deviant' female sexuality) was increasingly the subject of scientific analysis in the nineteenth century. Biological folk-lore had it that women's physical and mental well-being could be guaranteed only through marriage and motherhood. At a time when women were agitating for the vote, pressing for the right to inherit property and enter the professions, women in art (and literature) were sensationalised as femmes fatales. The negative stereotyping of women in art was often a less than subtle attempt to unsettle the commonplace view of women as harmless – under-educated and ill equipped for entry into the professions or government. Nudes, like their clothed counterparts, were cast as dangerous women – Eves, Judiths, Delilahs and Salomes, biblical heroines who used their sex to lull men into a false sense of security before dispatching them altogether. The painter Edvard Munch, for example, fashioned multiple images of femmes fatales, giving them titles such as 'Vampire', 'Harpy' and 'Maiden and the Heart'. The print called *Jealousy II* (1896) was directly based on events in 1892, when Munch was involved in a bizarre ménage of poets and artists in Berlin. *Jealousy* probably depicts the beautiful muse of this circle. The naked woman offers an apple to her latest lover whilst her presumably thwarted or erstwhile lover looks harrowingly out from the front of the image. The presentation of the male as a victim of predatory female sexuality is a recurring motif in *fin-de-siècle* art and poetry.

It is one of the paradoxes of modern art that, although the female nude was apparently nothing more than a pretext for painting, a pure form existing in a realm beyond base sexual desire, the conflation of the female form with 'the primitive' suggests a more complex order of engagement. This contradiction has been exposed by the occasional twinning of feminist and black or non-Western criticism and has thrown up some interesting areas of overlap. For example, the types of discriminatory discourse that confirmed the cultural superiority of the Western male were, in fact, often predicated on the rhetoric of primitivism and female otherness.

Once a pejorative term for anything that was 'foreign' or had preceded Western classicism, 'primitivism' became a way of describing non-European cultural artefacts – such as Oceanic, pre-Columbian, African or Aboriginal carvings and textiles. Used more properly, it describes the West's obsession with otherness rather than the tribal artefacts themselves (Rubin 1984: 5). But because 'primitive' objects were highly collectible in the early years of the twentieth century the term also came to describe the work of Western artists who copied the effects and incorporated the designs of non-European artefacts into their own art. The term is more problematic today since implicit in our understanding of the primitive is the 'cultural supremacy' of the West, which has made exchanges between Western artists and tribal 'artists' unequal and implicated the latter in a culture of appropriation. What is vital, however, for the production and consumption of images of female nudes within modernism is the slippage between constructions of the primitive and constructions of women, which, as far as we are aware, is without a male equivalent. We should ask why, at the inception of the modernist movement, styling the female nude according to the pictorial habits of an African 'sculptor' was seen as a worthwhile formal exercise for Western artists.

Why would modern European artists, representative of the most self-assured and powerful nations on earth, turn for inspiration to the cultures of peoples they thought were vastly inferior? The German expressionist artist Ernst Ludwig Kirchner was a collector of African artefacts who, after 1907, began styling his nudes in deference to the primitive (see Plate XVII). A founder member of the German expressionist group of artists Die Brücke, in Dresden, Kirchner exemplified the artist who thought that an engagement with the primitive would liberate the soul. At a time when many ethnic artefacts were entering German museums in Berlin, Munich and Dresden, many avant-garde artists were studying them in the same way their predecessors would have copied from the antique. The received history of primitivism, then, was that it was a licence for artists to throw off the shackles of European convention and to lose their Western inhibitions – not least their moral inhibitions. Collapsing contemporary ideas of the 'primitive' with notions of the 'natural', the primitive came to be seen as a corollary to bohemia. As Raymond Williams observes, primitivism was a modernist strategy for breaking with the past (or side-stepping it altogether) on the basis that the primitive was 'innately creative, the unformed and untamed realm of the prerational and the unconscious' (1989a: 58). Kirchner's work represents a widespread trend in twentieth-century art to romanticise the so-called 'primitive' – to see it as a place where things were simpler and spiritually more valuable. However, for many since, faith in the integrity and ethics of primitivism has been shaken.

Kirchner's rendition of the primitive nude would, stylistically speaking, mark him as an expressionist, rather than a cubist or a surrealist. It is on this question of style that so much twentieth-century art history has been founded – and has subsequently foundered. However, in terms of content – especially the artist's construction of the nude woman – it is the paintings that are particularly revealing of European values in the period. As Desa Philippi and Anna Howell have shown, the identification between a non-Western 'other' and a 'primitivised' notion of European women is part of the 'fantasy of cultural coherence' which confirms white male rule (1991: 238ff.). But it is also a link which has been positively fostered by 'ethnic' and 'feminist' artists since the 1970s. The ideological connection between women and nature (as we saw in Chapter 2) was common currency among modern European artists. Kirchner showed his female nudes to be natural to the sea, to the forest and to nature in general. The recurrent symbolism of women and nature shows just how issues of gender difference were crucial to early twentieth-century ideas of the primitive and the natural. Our problem is how to retrieve meaning from such notions when the grounds of modernism – in particular the grounds on which we used to value such notions – have shifted.

The primitive was often underscored by social Darwinism. Darwinism made the case that extinction was the result of physical weakness or unfitness for purpose. The eighteenth-century fable of intercourse between black Africans and apes was reborn in nineteenth-century colonialism through fear of miscegenation between blacks and Europeans, supported by social Darwinism. What came to be known as the 'science' of eugenics was called upon to 'explain' a number of social ills. By the turn of the century eugenics had become a means of countering the deplorable state of health among the 'cannon fodder' of Europe's armies. A survey of volunteers in the Boer War had shown that a large number of British men were physically inferior to required standards and the British government set up a commission in 1902 to investigate the causes of physical deterioration. Baden-Powell's Boy Scouts' Movement, founded in 1908, was an indirect response to this perceived inferiority, aiming to promote a healthy outdoor life to improve the physical condition of potential soldiers. Social Darwinism, however, perversely proved the fitness for purpose of non-Europeans. It is interesting, in this respect, that the Munich 'Degenerate Art' Exhibition of 1937, an exhibition of art confiscated by the National Socialists, 'demonstrated' the inferiority of modernist (especially expressionist) art by showing it alongside a conflation of 'negro art' and the art of the insane. The technical radicalism of European primitivism was effectively dismantled in Nazi Germany on the grounds that it was not Aryan. It was considered a hybridised art practice which had 'interbred' with tribal art and represented the work of 'prehistoric stone-age culture-vultures and art stammerers [who] may just as well retreat to the caves of their ancestors' (Adolf Hitler, in a speech inaugurating the Great Exhibition of German Art in 1937; quoted in Chipp 1968: 482).

It is another paradox of modernism that, as we saw in Chapter 3, the female figure can be made to represent that which she does not possess – liberty, justice, freedom. The female nude has proved a useful repository of anxieties about political emancipation, sexual deviancy and miscegenation in the modern age. The female nude, then, is more than just a formal site of modernity, a place where modernists experiment with technical radicalism: the female nude is the very site on which male fears, fantasies and projections are played out.

The nude as the site of postmodernity

Postmodernist claims to redress the excesses and sins of modernism – especially in its racial and gender biases – might lead one to expect that art classifiable as 'postmodern' would have its focus elsewhere than on the female nude or areas of the female anatomy. Postmodern artists continue to focus on the female nude as a crucial part of their art practice, but regularly and knowingly critique the subject of the nude. In a sense, then, such work can be differentiated from the formal experiments of modernism by the motivation of artists working on the female nude.

The deconstruction of the primitive in the 1980s by black women artists such as Lesley Sanderson, Sonia Boyce and Lubaina Himid has validated one kind of postmodern approach to the thorny issue of representation. Himid's *Freedom and Change* (1984) (Figure 4.5) is based on Picasso's *Two Women Running on the Beach* and reworks notions of white male power and the eroticisation of the black female in order to deconstruct myths of the primitive. If reappropriation of the primitive is no longer a preoccupation of women artists working in the past ten years, the female nude, as a site of postmodernity, is by no means exhausted.

The Palestinian artist Mona Hatoum's video art work *Measures of Distance* (see Figure 4.6) shows the artist's mother in the shower. The screen is overlaid with the Arabic script from letters written by Hatoum's mother to her daughter, and there is an accompanying soundtrack of English and Arabic dialogue between mother and daughter. The function of the nude mother in Hatoum's video work is neither erotic nor salacious. As we will see in more detail in Chapter 8, the piece raises interesting questions about the politics of women's writing about themselves, not least in terms of memory and identity. But in terms of the contemporary politics of representing the nude (even if that nude is a family member) postmodernism is clearly radically different from modernism. Hatoum's mother is shown nude, not just because she is being filmed in the shower, but because her unclothed body acts as a sign of her identity, particularly as constituted in and by her maternity and her ethnicity.

John Hilliard's *Close Up* (1994) is a postmodern attempt to unsettle a modernist voyeuristic view of a naked woman. *Close Up* refers implicitly to Courbet's *L'Origine du monde* (Figure 4.4) in that it borrows the pose and has a similar cropping of the frame to encircle a naked woman's torso, but it also makes an explicit reference in the sense that the object of the artist's gaze is really the close-up of the woman's vagina. Hilliard's cibachrome shows a woman sprawled with her head turned away from the

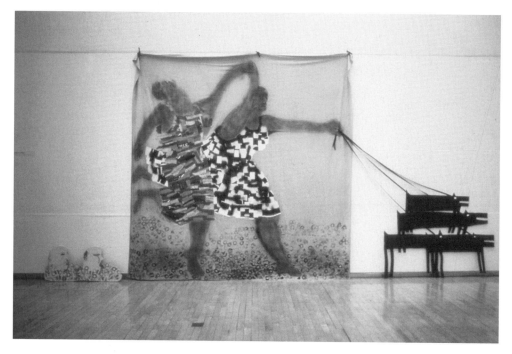

Figure 4.5 Lubaina Himid, *Freedom and Change*, 1984. Courtesy of the artist. A mixed-media work, painted wood and fabric, which takes the poses of the figures from Picasso's *Two Women Running on the Beach (The Race)*, painted in 1922, and replaces their classical shifts and exposed breasts with the colourful patterned dresses of Caribbean fashion. To the side of the women the heads of two white men with their tongues exposed salaciously watch the running women.

camera lens. This image is covered by another photograph, which is an enlarged view of the (same) woman's pubis and vagina. In certain respects *Close Up* is very close to the conventions of pornography and could even be labelled 'obscene'. What validates it as art is its reproduction in particular publications, together with the gravitas afforded it by the backing of art's institutions and the sacred spaces of the 'white cubes' in which it is exhibited. It is worth remembering, however, that such institutional backing is not an invariable guarantee of an item's status as art, as such a well-publicised case as the work of the American photographer Robert Mapplethorpe serves to show.[7]

Hilliard's *Close Up* could be seen to confound the voyeuristic gaze by magnifying and isolating the female sex organ and depriving the orifice of its 'erotic identity' (Durden 1997: 20). Hilliard's 'close-up' is, of course, also a pastiche of Courbet's *L'Origine du monde* and exists alongside myriad other double-coded and cross-referenced works of art that are, as a result, classed 'postmodern'. The difference is that the original *Origine* was a private piece of erotica produced for the dubious delectation of a Turkish emissary; and it was not intended as – nor was it for at least 100 years – an object for public viewing. Hilliard's work is fundamentally different both at the point of conception and at the point of reception. It is 'saved' from being obscene or pornographic (at least in terms of art-historical consensual notions of art), not solely because of its claim to 'art' status, but because it claims to be a critique of the issues, not part of the issue itself. If, however,

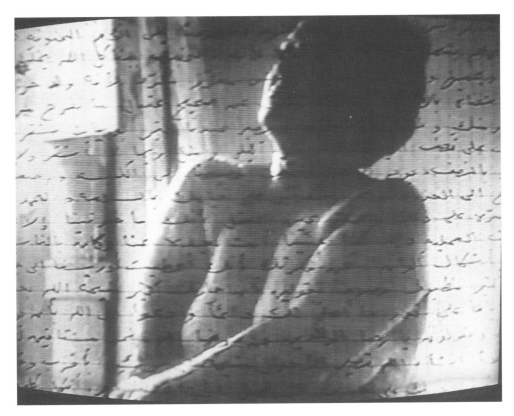

Figure 4.6 Mona Hatoum, *Measures of Distance*, video still, 1988. Courtesy of the artist. The fifteen-minute video is based on the reunion of the artist with her mother in 1981 following a period of separation. The film shows the artist's mother in the shower washing herself, while the scene is overlaid with text in Arabic script. The artist's voice-over reads from the text and makes the pain of compulsory separation of mother and daughter apparent.

Hilliard's work were to be sold as 'top-shelf' material, it seems that his 'intention' would in this respect become a matter of little relevance.

The nude, pornography and obscenity

Hilliard's work raises issues that have vexed feminists, art historians and every other related discipline for many years, namely, at what point does a work of art cross a line and become merely pornographic or, worse still, obscene? The whole issue of art and pornography is complex terrain. Various ideological stances on pornography are polarised between pro- and anti-censorship debates. The liberal position is that there is no evidence that pornography is harmful, while the position of the moral right-wing and many feminists is that it is.[8] According to Lord Longford's well-known definition of the 1960s, pornography is 'something that [gives] incentive to action'; latterly this has found subsequent resonance in the extremist statement 'Porn is the theory, rape the practice' (Morgan

1977 [1974]: 165–6). The vitriolic nature of many of the debates around pornography in the 1970s and 1980s was particularly evident in the attacks on, and the defences of, women artists who wilfully and sometimes literally matched their gynaecology with their creativity (see Chapter 8). At the same time, the feminist definition of pornography as sexual exploitation is countered by art that 'explores' rather than 'exploits' female sexuality.

Current obscenity laws are unclear about what actually constitutes obscenity, and these laws vary from country to country and, in the United States, from state to state. The first obscenity law in Britain was passed in 1857 in a climate of fear that easily reproducible photographic pornography might pass into the hands of the working classes. The next obscenity act, in 1959, sought to legislate against anything that had 'the power to deprave or corrupt'. This marker is open to interpretation and famously failed to nail Penguin Publishers in 1960 when they were taken to court for publishing D.H. Lawrence's 1928 novel *Lady Chatterley's Lover*. Indeed, subsequent inquiries into pornography and obscenity moved that text should be exempt from all such accusations of obscenity. The visual image remains subject to policing and continues to be conceived of as possessing the 'power to deprave or corrupt'. For artists and performers working outside of the pornography industry, the images or performances most commonly threatened with the obscenity laws are those that feature male and female genitals or contain real or simulated sexual acts. But more often than not, if the works are legitimised as genuine works of art, then the threats are seldom real. The controversial stage show the *Puppetry of the Penis* has been 'nearly closed' at several venues on the grounds of obscenity. Billed as 'the ancient art of genital origami', the show consists of two Australian performers making puppet shapes (the Eiffel Tower, a hamburger, the Loch Ness monster) with their penises. The former 'porn star' Annie Sprinkle ran shows in cities in America, featuring a bosom dance and inviting members of the audience to view her cervix (see Figure 4.7), which were regularly threatened by obscenity laws.

Traditionally, as we have seen, classical and neo-classical images of the nude had obscured the vagina. But vaginas had preoccupied the moderns. Picasso spent the last year or so of his life obsessively drawing female genitalia. However, public exhibitions of the resulting images have infrequently and only recently been exhibited. Only as recently as 2001 at the Jeu de Paume in Paris has there been an exhibition devoted to *Picasso Érotique*. Duchamp worked secretively for twenty years (1946–66) on *Étant donnés*, a tableau of the partially revealed torso and parted legs of a woman in a landscape (see Figure 4.8). Visitors to the Philadelphia Museum, where the work has been displayed since 1969, have to peer through one of two cracks in the door to see the tableau within. No matter how hard they strain to extend their field of vision they can never see the woman's face, only the torso and centrally positioned genitals. So when Judy Chicago 'reduced' her dinner guests in the 1970s to a set of vulvas she was representing a paradigmatic shift in thinking whereby female artists reclaimed the vagina from an exclusively male preoccupation. Her ambitious multimedia work took the artist and some 400 participants five years to complete. It consists of a triangular table, 48 feet long on each side and containing thirty-nine place settings, laid with dinner plates that are also genital portraits of thirty-nine women from history and mythology. Chicago's strategy for putting women back into history has received a mixed press. The negative press centred on two opposing readings of the piece: that it is an 'obscene' presentation of vulvas or that its presentation of the vulva can explain historical gender differences. Of course, *The*

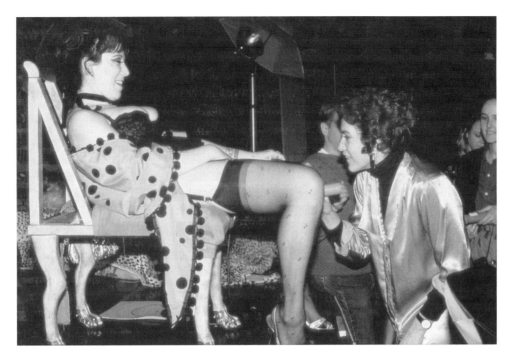

Figure 4.7 Annie Sprinkle, *Post-Porn Modernist*, 1992. Photo Les Barany. Courtesy of the artist. Annie Sprinkle took *Post-Porn Modernist* on the road between 1989 and 1996, giving a series of live performances. Annie Sprinkle's performances gave her verbal personal autobiography, a critique of the porn industry in combination with performances including the 'Bosom Ballet' and the 'Public Cervix Announcement'.

Dinner Party was very much of its time, and in more recent years such gynaecological ripostes have been roundly condemned as 'biological reductivism'. However, it is important to note that these acts of 'making visible', from a female perspective, uncovered a great deal of prejudice. But, as we will see in Chapter 8, using one's genitals to make a political point has had a great deal of artistic currency. Duchamp's tableau *Étant donnés* was a secret work of art to be peeped at through a crack in a door; so when Annie Sprinkle publically invites audiences to view her cervix by shining a light along a speculum inserted into her vagina, is she critiquing modernism or merely reliving it?

Barbara Kruger has exhibited a sculpture depicting Marilyn Monroe on the shoulders of Bobby and John Kennedy, wearing the billowing dress made famous in *The Seven-Year Itch*. The title, *Family*, hints at the artist's ironic presentation of the Kennedy brothers with Marilyn Monroe, but the work itself extends the comical irony of the spectacle of Marilyn sitting astride the shoulders of the two brothers, both rumoured to be her lovers. The prurient gaze of the viewer is further invited when, from closer inspection, it is revealed that Marilyn is not wearing the white knickers seen in the film; in fact she is not wearing any underwear. The work may be called postmodern in many ways: stylistically it refers to socialist realism in its kitsch construction of a life-sized superreal monumental figure; but it also makes a knowing reference to the much-publicised alleged sexual relationship between Marilyn and both Kennedy

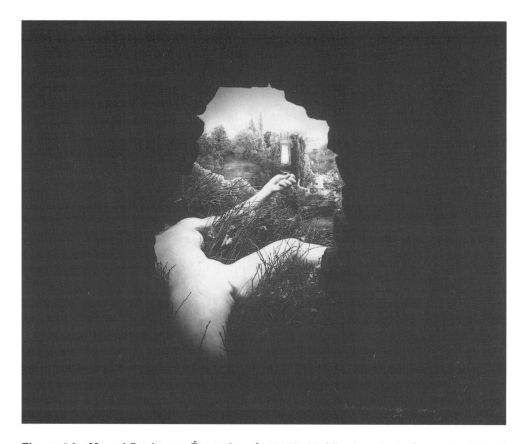

Figure 4.8   Marcel Duchamp, *Étant donnés*, 1946–66. Mixed media. © Succession Marcel Duchamp/ADAGP, Paris, and DACS, London, 2004. Courtesy of Philadelphia Museum of Art: Given by the Cassandra Foundation. This epic installation was 'secretly' worked on by Duchamp for twenty years in his New York studio although it was not publicly exhibited until 1969, after the artist's death. This state of semi-secrecy prevailed for some time since Duchamp stipulated that photographic reproductions of *Étant donnés* could not be published for fifteen years. The artist also left detailed instructions on how to assemble and disassemble the tableau.

brothers. The use of Marilyn as an icon by Andy Warhol, for instance, is well known. But Marilyn's ironic status has become multi-layered. Appignanesi and Garrett's *Postmodernism for Beginners* (1995) contains a cartoon figure of Marilyn with a speech bubble announcing: 'Only by metonymy do I exist as a possibility for men'. Metonymy, the substitution of a name for what is really meant – Marilyn really means sex – is postmodern irony. Of course, for many women self-awareness of their metonymic status can backfire – for example the singer Madonna's book *Sex* (Madonna and Meisel 1992) – and the emancipatory politics of gender still sits uncomfortably with the representation of the nude. As we will see in Chapter 8 there has been a semantic shift in recent years which means that the term 'nude' has been supplanted by the term 'body'. The unclothed body, particularly as a means of self-representation, is no longer the site of modernity (in the sense of dealing with universals, essences, ideals) but the site of personal history, identity and self-awareness.

5 From the machine aesthetic to technoculture

Since it is correct to say that culture in its widest sense means independence of Nature, then we must not wonder that the machine stands in the forefront of our cultural will-to-style. . . . Consequently, the spiritual and practical needs of our time are realised in constructive sensibility. The new possibilities of the machine have created an aesthetic expressive of our time, that I once called the Mechanical Aesthetic.

(van Doesburg 1975: 93)

In 1914 the Italian futurist Luigi Russolo toured Europe with his noise machines, or *intonarumori*. These consisted of a set of wooden boxes which hid noise-making contraptions designed to make diverse sounds when hand-cranked (see Figure 5.1). For Russolo, noise *was* art and this belief was central to the claim of his 1913 manifesto 'The Art of Noises' (1973). There are several key points that this 'art work' demonstrates in terms of the emergence of a 'machine aesthetic' in twentieth-century modernism: first, that a machine should have been the origin of the art work; second, that there is not a trace of traditional fine art practice here; and, third, that as an important postscript to the work Russolo went on to develop his noise machines into a keyboard – the forerunner of the electronic synthesiser.

In this chapter we will see how ideas about the machine and, later on, about technology have created not only a set of images for twentieth-century art, but a powerful set of metaphors which have reconfigured the way in which we think of artist and viewer, subject and object, and even mind and matter. Generally speaking, since the Enlightenment 'science' has been a generic term and 'technology' – what Moholy-Nagy in 1922 defined as 'the invention, construction and maintenance of the machine' (quoted in Benton and Benton 1975: 95) – the application of science, the expression of science in society. As a branch of knowledge, 'science' can sometimes seem to be in opposition to 'nature'. Eighteenth-century Romantic notions of the sublime, for example, were given visual form through images of volcanoes and storms; perversely, 'science' offered the potential to harness natural forces to power the sublime machines of the Industrial Revolution. However, the applications of science have a frightening potential to go horribly wrong (witness the metaphoric representation of the consequences of disturbing

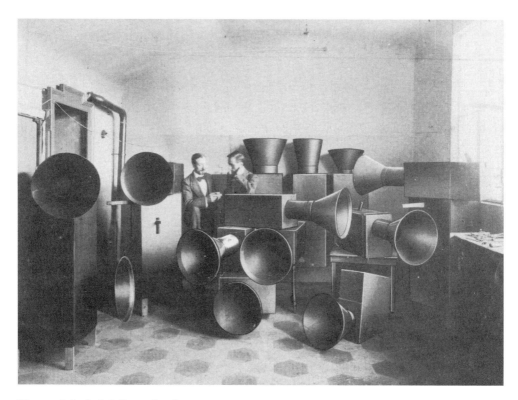

Figure 5.1 Luigi Russolo, *Intonarumori*, 1913. Courtesy of Archivio Storico, Fondazione Russolo-Pratella, Varese, Italy. Image courtesy of the Biblioteca Comunale Centrale, Milan. With his assistant Ugo Piatti, Russolo constructed ever more elaborate forms of noise-making instruments from 1913. The first public concert was given in 1914. The intoners were played by a lever and a crank which determined the pitch and tone of the noise. Unfortunately the originals have not survived, although there have been several reconstructions of the machines and re-enactments of the performances.

the natural order in novels such as Mary Shelley's *Frankenstein*, first published in 1818). At times when science fails to meet our spiritual and physical needs we often appeal to nature (for instance new-age mysticism or alternative medicine). Our attitudes to science, then, are never fixed but are ever-changing according to technology's many incarnations and, more importantly, what science proposes to add to our futures.

The belief in inexorable technological 'advancement' has spawned both utopian and dystopian premonitions, and the idea that the machine could be alternately a harbinger of disaster and a means of salvation is recurrent in twentieth-century and twenty-first-century popular culture. In this chapter we start with an examination of the positive and negative metaphors of the 'machine aesthetic'; we consider how its leitmotifs of speed, gigantism, repetition, standardisation, efficiency and noise provided both positive metaphors of harmony and strength and negative metaphors of human alienation in an increasingly mechanised and artificial world. We will also see how the shift from 'machine aesthetic' to 'technoculture' is marked by a continuing radical reordering–disordering of the world, both utopian and dystopian.

Futurism

As we saw in Chapter 1, within the received history of modernism the key feature of modern art practice was its rejection of everything perceived to be orthodox, even old-fashioned. According to conventional modernist wisdom, modern artists had been enthused by the rhetoric of 'the permanent revolution', which insisted that they do something novel – that they innovate rather than imitate. This may not seem a radical proposition nowadays, but then artists had for centuries been accustomed to copying established models; they were trained, for instance, to imitate antique sculpture and Old Masters' paintings. So when modern artists such as Manet or Cézanne appeared to lead rather than follow this was seen to be a paradigmatic shift. However, the progressive inclinations of the avant-garde were not necessarily futuristic, and the emergence of an art movement which was self-consciously futuristic in outlook was a shift within a shift. 'Futurism' describes the activities of those artists and designers who collected around the impresario Filippo Tommaso Marinetti in 1909; 'futurists' were self-labelled because of their enthusiasm for all things new, the machine especially.

At this point we encounter a fundamental dichotomy in the received history of the modernist mission. When the futurists hijacked modernism they took it to places its original exponents had never expected it to go. Modernism had never been synonymous with scientific and technological advances (except, perhaps, to stretch the point, in cases such as Seurat's pseudo-scientific theory of optical mixing). Manet's *la vie moderne* referred to the fleeting and ephemeral experience of modernity, not mechanisation per se. Even Baudelaire's advocacy of the city and rejection of Jean-Jacques Rousseau's nature did not automatically lead to mechanolatry. On the contrary, French modernists such as Cézanne remained in thrall to nature, obsessively painting and repainting landscapes. As far as the futurists were concerned, French modernism, in the early twentieth century at least, was in stasis. Even cubism, the new '-ism', seemed to the futurists to be obsessed with the inert – at first with viaducts in the South of France, and then with still life on table tops. The cubist concession to modernity was the fragmented representation of mass-produced industrial products rather than apples or mountains.

The futurists, however, were not interested in stationary objects. They were involved in all sorts of activities, including theatrical and live events, sound poems and costume designs (although the 'history of art' has curiously presented futurism as merely a 'history of paintings', with one or two sculptures by Umberto Boccioni).[1] The futurists' mischievous modernism was not only a brash enthusiasm for machinery, it embraced everything which augmented, or came with, the machine. In 1913 Antonio Sant'Elia, the Italian futurist architect, was designing plans for a city (*città nuova*). Sant'Elia's city was a utopian metropolis designed on a monumental scale. The *città nuova* (new city) should be regarded as a series of illustrations rather than precise architectural plans constructed according to scale and topography. The designs are of a visionary landscape of stepped, multi-storey buildings with external lifts and multiple traffic systems. Committed to a programme of technological innovation, Sant'Elia incorporated in the *città nuova* the latest technology (and some technology which was not yet available) – steel-and-concrete terraced skyscrapers, multi-storey walkways, detached lift shafts and slender linking bridges.

The call to order

> This is our century – technology, machine, socialism. Make your peace
> with it. Shoulder its task.
>
> (Moholy-Nagy 1975: 95)

The 'call to order' (*rappel à l'ordre*) was an expression, signifying a return to moral
fundamentalism, given to government policy designed to restore rationality to post-
First World War France (and later to Italy) after four years of turmoil. Although it
was implemented by means of socio-economic legislation, the 'call to order' was simultaneously interpreted by many artists as a suspension of experimental avant-garde
movements, such as cubism, and a resumption of the monumental classicism[2] that
seemed to have held civilisation together for over 2,000 years.

Underpinning this return to classical order was a drive towards 'purification' which
aimed to purge art of its excesses. This rationalisation of the visual arts tended in many
cases towards advocacy of a sober and impersonal aesthetic based upon geometrical
shapes and primary or muted colours as opposed to the flamboyant distortions of expressionism. Purism, a short-lived Paris-based art movement led by the architect Charles
Édouard Jeanneret (hereafter Le Corbusier) and the painter Amédée Ozenfant was one
such manifestation of the return to order. Le Corbusier and Ozenfant jointly published
their manifesto, 'Purism', in *L'Ésprit nouveau* in 1920, aligning the 'call to order' with
their own wish to 'purify' cubism, which appeared to them to be in an overblown,
near-baroque phase. They meant to impose the same spirit of rationalisation on painting
as was already present in architecture. The manifesto explained: 'The highest delectation of the human mind is the perception of order, and the greatest human satisfaction
is the feeling of collaboration or participation in this order' (Benton and Benton 1975:
90). Purism, they argued, can be achieved only by combining enduring primary
elements, or what were termed 'plastic constants' – enduringly simple forms which
rationalised whatever they 'depicted' – nudes or vases of flowers. In his *Accords* (1922)
(Figure 5.2) Ozenfant worked with a standard – prefabricated – set of sizes and compositions, uncomplicated shapes and colours. It is not difficult to understand this kind of
response to the uncertainties and devastation of war, and the appeal of making sense
of the world in terms of 'plastic constants'.

This reaction stands in stark contrast to the 'irrational' responses of surrealism. The
proto-surrealists, forming in Paris at the same time, totally disregarded the 'call to
order', since, they felt, it was precisely Western 'order' and 'rationality' that had led
to the mechanised slaughter of so many during the First World War. The surrealists,
who formally came together in 1924, believed that 'irrationality', rather than the 'call
to order', was worth pursuing.

The visual decorum of the purists, meanwhile, stripped away the apparent excesses
of pre-war art, especially of European symbolism, and rationalised the kind of abstraction that had emerged around expressionism. These underlying values of purity, balance,
serenity and order are just one set of motifs that the 'First Machine Age' (a term coined
by Reyner Banham in 1960) fostered. The rhetoric of purity had cropped up earlier,
in the work of the Viennese architect Adolf Loos, whose architectural design solutions
staked their future on flat-roofed building and geometric cantilevering. Loos's book

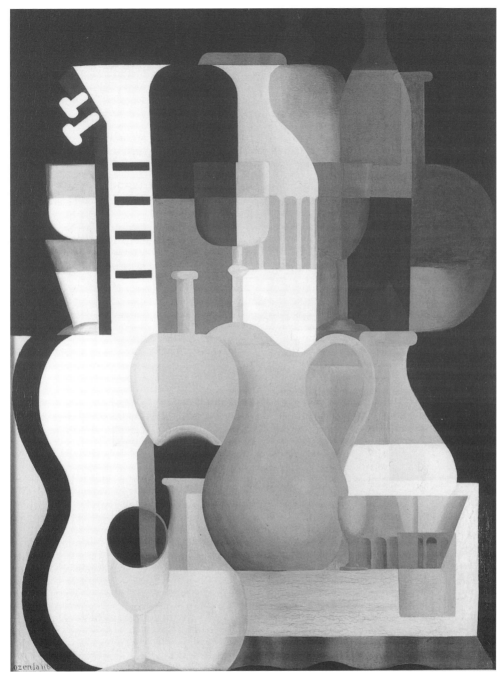

Figure 5.2 Amédée Ozenfant, *Accords*, 1922. © ADAGP, Paris, and DACS, London, 2004. Courtesy of Honolulu Academy of Arts, Gift of John W. Gregg Allerton commemorating the fortieth anniversary of the Academy of Arts, 1967 (3478.1). The still life is constructed in strict observance of purist rules. The economy of detail, simplicity of line and highly ordered composition are driven by the impersonal purist aesthetic, which called for the creation of reason and order out of the apparent chaos of nature.

Ornament and Crime was first published in 1908, although it was not published in France until 1920, when it was reprinted in the journal *L'Ésprit nouveau* (the literary organ of the purists), and in it Loos joined Le Corbusier and others in calling for a rational simplification of architecture. Adolf Loos equated decoration with sinister purpose. His memorable claim, in *Ornament and Crime*, that the two terms were synonymous rested on his observation that 'criminals' nearly always sported 'ornamental' tattoos. Loos's book was clearly part of an escalating rejection of art nouveau or what had been called 'the battle of the styles' in architecture and an attempt to resolve the differences into a single international style. The so-called 'international style' of architecture was wholly devoid of ornamentation, extraneous detail, frivolity and gratuitous detail. Not only did Loos equate architectural ornament with the excesses of European art nouveau but with the kind of ersatz ornament which poorly imitated the lavish craftsmanship of a bygone era.

Reyner Banham ascribes Loos's sense of simplicity to his belief that 'freedom from ornament is the symbol of an uncorrupted mind, a mind which he only attributes to peasants and engineers . . . laying further foundations to the idea of engineers as noble savages' (Banham 1996: 97). As we will see, the idea of the mechanic as ennobled somehow by being a machine operative was a feature of the 'First Machine Age'. The term 'technocracy', which describes a state of 'rule by technicians', had been coined by the Californian engineer William Henry Smyth in 1919 and was developed by Thorstein Veblen, whose book *The Engineers and the Price System* (1921) inspired a brief spell of technocratic idealism in the United States in the 1920s. In contrast to the technocratic idealism of the United States, the European surrealists made a map of the world in 1929 in which space was allocated on the basis of a country's spiritual and magical predilections. Thus, Mexico, Canada and Ireland, with, respectively, indigenous Indian, Inuit and Celtic communities, were relatively huge, while countries that privileged the measurable against the spiritual were reduced to the size of a pinhead or, like the United States, omitted altogether.

The 'machine aesthetic'

> The machine is as old as the wheel, the wings of Icarus or the Trojan horse. But it is only in our century that it has transcended its utilitarian functions and acquired a variety of meanings, esthetic and philosophical, which are only distantly related to its practical uses.
>
> (Baur 1963: 33)

The precise signification of 'machine aesthetic' requires a careful introduction since it does not describe a distinct group of individuals or even a 'movement' in art (in the conventional art-historical sense of 'movement'). Rather, it is a characteristic that marked certain groups, individuals and movements during the first half of the twentieth century. The machine aesthetic is properly a label for some aspects common to a range of affiliated movements in the First Machine Age of the second two decades of the twentieth century – very generally, purism in France, De Stijl in Holland, suprematism and productivism in Russia, constructivism at the Bauhaus and precisionism in

by the possibility of an egalitarian art practice in which (as we will examine in more detail shortly) standardisation was a positive feature.

The flipside of positive images of the mechanthropomorph was the mechanoid monster. For instance, *The Rock Drill* (1913–14), by the sculptor Jacob Epstein, now visible only through re-constructions, shows a visored figure straddling a pneumatic drill supported by a tripod. The title *The Rock Drill* innocuously describes the machine, but more disturbing is the mechanthropomorphic figure, complete with a hybrid foetus between its carburettor ribcage, that sits astride the 'phallic' drill. *The Rock Drill* tends now to be read (with the benefit of hindsight) as a prophetic piece – a dreadful portent of the First World War, a mindless monster fulfilling its programming regardless of conscience or consequence. The efficiency with which machines dispatch their orders becomes a nightmarish aspect of modern times, one which the sculptor regarded as 'the terrible Frankenstein's monster we have made ourselves into' (Cork 1976, vol. 2: 479). Epstein himself symbolically emasculated *The Rock Drill* after the First World War when he severed the drill and the driller, exhibiting only the torso of the driller with its limbs removed.

A further way in which the 'machine aesthetic' weaved itself into the consciousness of the period was via the self-consciously utilitarian language of the avant-garde. This is particularly evident in the differences between the languages of expressionism and of constructivism. As we will see, 'expressionism' and 'constructivism' were generic terms for several types of art practice in Europe and North America in the first half of the twentieth century. In his various utilitarian manifestos the constructivist Vladimir Tatlin conceived of the artist as a technician or 'inventor' (as opposed to a creator), a socially useful individual whose work in the studio mimics industrial processes. Tatlin's three-dimensional constructions were the antithesis of the painterly, expressionist art prevalent in Europe around the time of the First World War and engendered a 'culture of materials' that is sometimes mistakenly confused with 'truth to materials'. The vocabulary of the constructivists was demonstrably different from that of earlier modernists. They claimed to 'construct' or 'assemble' rather than paint, cast, carve or model art works. Tatlin's *Counter Corner-Reliefs*, for instance, typically constructed from sheet metal, expressed a fundamental opposition to the precocity and 'aura' of easel painting and in particular to the semi-mythical view of the solitary artist-genius expressing 'himself' in the medium of paint or stone.[3] Constructivism coincided with other confident announcements of the 'death of easel painting' – in the sense of brush-and-palette activity. For example, Nikolai Tarabukin's 'From the Easel to the Machine' (1923) reflected the belief that traditional methods of art-making had been exhausted by 400 years of convention and repetition. In contrast, artists affiliated to the machine aesthetic flirted with the syntax of the factory and, like Diego Rivera, cast themselves as 'a worker among workers'; or, like László Moholy-Nagy, dressed as engineers (see Figure 5.6). The semiotics of Moholy-Nagy's choice of clothing is significant: unlike the bohemian's greatcoat or the smock of the expressionist, the boiler suit worn over a collar and tie was more suited to the workshop than to the studio.

Finally, the machine aesthetic was part of the Zeitgeist, the spirit of the age, a palpable sea-change in the mood and temperament of some artists. When Meyer Schapiro, in his influential 1937 essay 'The Nature of Abstract Art', linked Diego Rivera's paintings of factories, Dada's 'burlesque with robots' and the futurists' regard

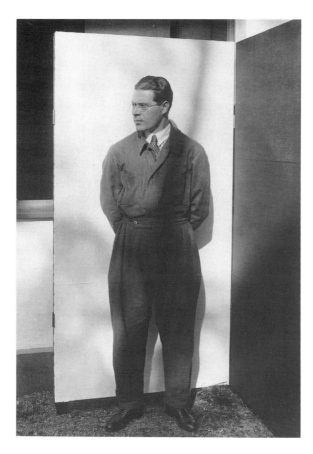

Figure 5.6 Lucia Moholy, Portrait of László Moholy-Nagy, Dessau, 1926. © DACS, 2004. Courtesy of the Bauhaus-Archiv Berlin. Moholy-Nagy's down-to-earth conception of the artist often put him at odds with the other teaching staff at the Bauhaus. Even his choice of day-wear (the engineer's boiler suit) announced his fundamental differences with the expressionist, smock-wearing contingent at the Bauhaus.

for energy and speed (Schapiro 1978: 206–7) he was summing up a shift in styles and attitudes. This was the 'Jazz Age' and the upbeat tempo and rhythm of jazz music and dance infiltrated the work of many artists, filmmakers and designers. Unlike Kandinsky, who listened to Schoenberg and compared his expressionist paintings to symphonies, Mondrian painted while listening to popular jazz pianists and was 'inspired' by the staccato drum beats and syncopated rhythms of the 'boogie-woogie'. Mondrian moved to the United States in 1940 and settled in New York for the final years of his life. *Broadway Boogie-Woogie* is a double homage to the city and to the artist's new-found enthusiasm for jazz. Many critics and historians have remarked on the arrangement of small mosaics of primary colour that seem reminiscent of the grid plan of New York City and the rhythmic qualities of boogie-woogie music.

A modernist schism

> Beauty is everywhere: more perhaps in the arrangement of your saucepans on the white walls of your kitchen than in your eighteenth century drawing room or in the official museums.
>
> (Léger 1975: 96–7)

In his pamphlet 'Where Artists and Technicians Meet' (1925–6), Walter Gropius made a distinction between 'the technological product made by a sober mathematical mind and the "work of art" created by passion' (Benton and Benton 1975: 147). Gropius's distinction is a sound one. In real terms, he was pointing to a fundamental difference between expressionism and constructivism. Each of these terms tended to act as an umbrella to describe all sorts of European and North American art movements which, as we have seen, adopted dissimilar styles and syntax and engaged in artistic sabre-rattling. This perception that mainstream modernism was subsumed by two overarching trends was confirmed in Alfred Barr's map of modernism entitled *The Development of Abstract Art* (see Figure 1.4). According to Barr, by 1936 the course of modern art had split in two. On one side there was 'non-geometrical abstract art' (growing out of expressionism) and on the other 'geometrical abstract art' (growing out of constructivism). Non-geometrical abstract art traced its line of descent from surrealism and expressionism, while geometrical abstract art stemmed from purism, constructivism and De Stijl, via the Bauhaus. Interestingly, Barr's schema puts the machine aesthetic in a box at the centre of this lineage. But, even more telling, by 1936 expressionism and constructivism were, with the exception of a historical link via the Bauhaus, apparently irreconcilable.

The art groups ranged on the side of the machine aesthetic were, again according to modernism's conventional wisdom, part of the backlash against the kind of romantic individualism that expressionism seemed to support. As an antidote to expressionism, geometrical abstract art revealed a broad disenchantment with the cult of the solipsistic and self-indulgent artist. Fernand Léger summed up this attitude in 1924: 'I have more faith in it [the machine] than in the longhaired gentleman with a floppy cravat intoxicated with his own personality and his own imagination' (in Benton and Benton 1975: 98). This is a far cry from the early modernist's heightened sense of self-expression, exemplified in Cézanne's maxim 'Let us strive to express ourselves according to our personal temperaments' (from 'A Letter to Emil Bernard' (1906), quoted in Chipp 1968: 21). Léger's faith rested on a vision of the pragmatic engineer who presided over the technocracy rather than on the hazy idealism of conventional painters. It is possibly not without significance that a number of those artists who subscribed to the machine aesthetic had come from non-fine-art traditions: El Lissitzky had a degree in engineering but took up illustration because he could not find work, Theo van Doesburg studied acting but gave it up because he could not make money at it, and Moholy-Nagy trained as a lawyer but turned to art as a therapy while convalescing from wounds sustained in the First World War. On one level these artists defied the Romantic notion that artists are born, not made, but then the fact of their improbable conversions rather lends credence to the idea that they were fated to be artists from the start. There is an irony in the West's urge towards individuality: that, although artists such as Moholy-Nagy appeared to have been opposed to the cult of Romantic individuality, it is extremely hard for us to do other than merely replace one set of Romantic images of the artist with another.

This dualism within modernism was played out in microcosm at the Bauhaus in Germany. Opened in 1919 as a regional arts and crafts school with an emphasis on bringing together the fine and the applied arts, the Bauhaus was at first indebted to expressionism. However, in 1923, in a lecture entitled 'Art and Technology: a new unity', Walter Gropius announced that technology was to be the pet project of the

Bauhaus. On one level this shift may be interpreted as a survival tactic in the face of budgetary strictures and the climate of accountability towards the arts in Weimar Germany five years after the First World War.[4] Indeed, the change in policy at the Bauhaus was aided and abetted by the relative stabilisation of the German economy, which, at the Bauhaus, permitted an injection of new staff. Yet the zeal with which the Bauhaus reinvented itself appears to be evidence of more than just a nascent business-like attitude, it seems to have been genuinely in keeping with the pragmatic and technocratic spirit of the age. Thus, when Walter Gropius enthusiastically reconfigured the Bauhaus, renamed the workshops 'laboratories', employed artists who imitated technicians and pursued the possibility of creating prototypes for mass production, he was not displaying the tendencies of the maverick.

At the Bauhaus of the 1920s Walter Gropius, Oskar Schlemmer and László Moholy-Nagy effectively outlawed the kind of unreconstructed expressionism that had come to be associated with the institution's early years.[5] Chiding his colleagues, 'you are all sick Romantics', Moholy-Nagy opposed the rhetoric of expressionism, rooted as it was in Romantic notions of the self, on every level. He modelled himself on the engineer working scientifically and in anonymity and, as we have seen, dressed rather pointedly in a boiler suit. Moholy-Nagy renounced the Romantic idea that as an artist he had to struggle towards a 'unique signature style'. To this end, his work brazenly undercut the humanist view of artistic practice as an original and wholly autonomous effort which is elevated above all other manual ones. For instance, *Light–Space Modulator* (1923–30) resides somewhere between machine and work of art (Figure 5.7). It is a revolving kinetic sculpture which reflects and projects light – 'a light fountain' made of metal and mirrors. Made in collaboration with the German engineering firm AEG, *Light–Space Modulator* is a summary of the activities that Moholy-Nagy encouraged at the Bauhaus: industrial collaboration, constructivism, photography (especially pictograms) and film.

This call for an art practice that was primarily productive was also in evidence in revolutionary Russia. 'Art into Production' was the slogan of Aleksandr Rodchenko and Vavara Stepanova, who published 'The Programme of the Productivist Group' in 1920 and called themselves, appropriately enough, 'the Productivists'. Their manifesto contained exclamations such as 'Down with art! . . . Long live the constructivist technician!' (Rodchenko and Stepanova 1975: 92) and its tone was not dissimilar to the fighting talk at the Bauhaus after 1923. Productivism, although a short-lived art movement (1920–2), also came at a significant time in the history of Russian avant-garde art. Productivism sought to fulfil practical and utilitarian ends. Rodchenko and Stepanova had also turned their studios into workshops which they used to explore the kinship between technology and art. Rodchenko was disillusioned with easel painting which he in fact 'gave up' in 1921 to concentrate upon the relatively mechanised processes of photography, photomontage and graphic design. For him 'art has no place in modern life', but photography, particularly experimental photography as opposed to 'connoisseurial photographs', was the ultimate anti-bourgeois, anti-art practice. Rodchenko's acute-angled photographs were intended to emphasise technical, as opposed to 'connoisseurial', aesthetics so that photography could be pressed into the service of the revolution.[6]

The tendency in Western art history to privilege easel painting has marginalised the experimental photography and film that were consistent with the principles of the

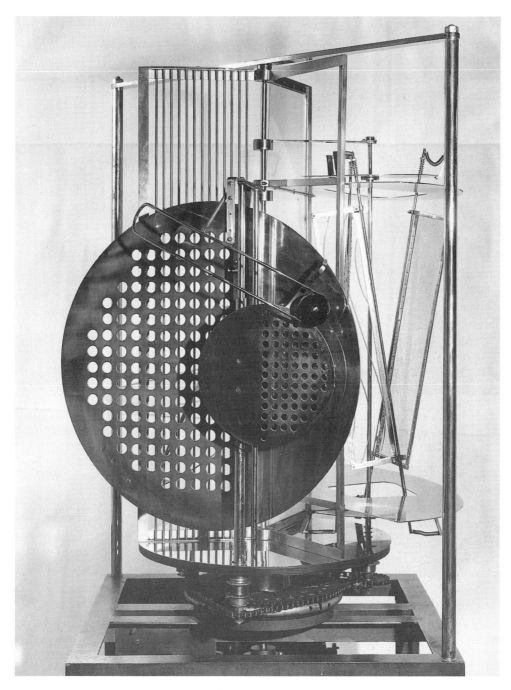

Figure 5.7 László Moholy-Nagy, *Light–Space Modulator*, 1923–30. © DACS, 2004.
Courtesy of the Busch-Reisinger Museum, Harvard University Art Museums, Gift of Sibyl Moholy-
Nagy. Although this piece has some claims to being the first kinetic sculpture, it does not move
for the sake of novelty. Rather, its moving parts are constructed to create light and shadow
effects. Moholy-Nagy's 1930 film *Lightplay, Black White Grey* depicts the device in movement
and demonstrates the interplay between light and shade.

machine aesthetic. This is puzzling: Alfred Barr argued in the 'Russian Diary' (1926; see Barr 1986b), in line with Lenin, that it was film and not easel painting that was the most significant art form, because it had the capacity to reach a mass audience. However, the fact that even an arch-modernist like Barr was unconvinced that easel painting could weather the massive upheavals of the revolutionary period ultimately failed to prevent the relegation of early revolutionary art forms to the subordinate status as propaganda in the received genealogy of twentieth-century art history.

As we have seen, the language used by art groups under the sway of the machine aesthetic is significantly different from that of their expressionist counterparts. However, another aspect of the importance of the separatist language of the machine aesthetic is that it came at a time when the very function of artists was called into question. This reappraisal of the role of the artist in society crops up periodically throughout the twentieth century but particularly, as we will see in the next chapter, in the 1930s in North America. However, in the 1920s the notion of a socially useful artist who not only served the interests of the state but connected with the lives of ordinary people seemed a real possibility. It is evident that the machine aesthetic played more than just a stylistic part in the revolution. Rodchenko served the Communist Party in designing advertisements whose uncomplicated design communicated direct messages to a largely illiterate proletariat.[7] With copy by the playwright Vladimir Mayakovsky, who called his slogans 'street poetry', Rodchenko's advertisements for Krasnyi Aviator cookies of 1923 provided straightforward imagery for the new urban masses and bore the hallmarks of the frank and highly legible image-making that represented a utopian implementation of the machine aesthetic. The advertisements utilise the clean and geometric outlines of constructivist design with Mayakovsky's state-bolstering slogan 'everywhere we advance the idea [of Soviet aviation supremacy], even in the case of sweets'.

Another significant aspect of the machine aesthetic, which we alluded to briefly in respect of Léger's standardised figures, was the idea of an egalitarian aesthetic achieved through standardisation. Stemming from the demise of aristocratic privilege, the idea of a universal beauty which may be found in the commonplace gained momentum from Enlightenment thinking and became a standard modernist claim. As early as 1751 the rationalist philosopher Diderot described 'the Stocking Machine' as 'one single and prolonged act of reason'. The Italian futurist Gino Severini explained in 1922 how 'the aesthetic pleasure created in us by a machine can be thought of as Universal, we may conclude that the effect created by a machine on the beholder is analogous to that produced by a work of art' (Severini 1975: 96).

By the 1920s universal beauty was, in keeping with the kind of rhetoric that artists on the left tended to adopt, a rallying cry for an art practice that was not embedded in the cult of personality. It is not insignificant that so many artists 'standardised' their means of production, usually by opting to work with a restricted visual vocabulary of geometric forms (Mondrian, Léger) or crude ready-mades (Tatlin, Moholy-Nagy). It is perhaps the ultimate irony of this project that, although many artists tried to depersonalise their art, removing all traces of the 'unique signature style', works by Léger, Moholy-Nagy, Mondrian or Tatlin are still recognisable as the products of individual artists. Moreover, these works have been displayed by art galleries and museums as the products of individual genius rather than as the outcome of collective enterprise.

In spite of this fundamental paradox, claims to a modern universalism persisted throughout the inter-war period. On one level it is possible to see universalism as yet another form of inoculation against individualism. However, this is only a partial explanation, for the claims to a modern universalism were utopian in spirit and often part of a socialist agenda. However, it is a commonplace observation that capitalism is not well disposed towards standardisation. Although its mode of production operates most efficiently through standardisation and repetition on the commodity conveyer belt, capitalism promotes the myth of specialism. Certainly, the erosion of some of the privileges of Western individuality was an important prerequisite of utopia, and artists such as Moholy-Nagy thought that the machine was a great social leveller which had the potential to equalise relations in society.

Artists' utopias had their corollary in popular culture. For instance, the film *Things to Come* (1936) was a lexicon of the international style, with sets inspired by the very latest in modernist design. Although *Things to Come* is a work of science fiction, the well-known definition of science fiction as 'reality ahead of schedule' points to a utopian future. The film (based on a story by H.G. Wells) traces the 100-year utopian redevelopment of 'Everytown' after it is destroyed by war. As a design for a model society, the notion of utopia had emerged periodically over a considerable period: the term derives from Thomas More's *Utopia* in the early sixteenth century (though the notion of an ideal state goes back to Plato's *Republic*) and figured prominently in William Morris's writings on utopian socialism in the nineteenth century. The important point about utopian ideas in the context of twentieth-century technocracy was that they functioned at the grass-roots social level and at the more abstract level of the democratic. Rather than paradise for the few, utopia is a perfect society for the many. The premise of *Things to Come* – that the old society has to be dismantled before utopia can be created – goes hand in hand with the notion that war clears away the debris of the old and that utopias are preceded by dystopias.

Dystopias

As we have seen, many early twentieth-century artists affiliated to the machine aesthetic were engaged in a utopian project to create order and harmony through the machine. But the flipside of utopia, dystopia, has also been a fertile undercurrent of modernity. The 'brave new world' prophesied by some was criticised by others on the ground that technocracy is dehumanising. The positive metaphors of harmony and strength afforded by the utopianism of the machine aesthetic were countered by negative metaphors of alienation. Antonio Gramsci, the Italian Marxist social theorist, borrowed his theories of alienation from Karl Marx, arguing that modern labour processes alienated the individual from labour itself. Gramsci believed that standardisation through mechanisation threatened the uniqueness of the individual, a belief echoed in popular fears that the machine would dislodge men and women from nature, surrounding them with artificiality – gadgets, standardised environments, gigantism, excessive noise and speed.

Moholy-Nagy thought that the machine had the potential to free ordinary men and women from the burden of repetitive labour, but there were many others who contested the relationship between machines and their human operatives. In the film *Modern*

Times (1936) Charlie Chaplin parodied the robotisation of human functions in the factories of North America. In one scene, prolonged exposure to assembly-line repetitions drives the protagonist, played by Chaplin, to become temporarily unhinged. Hypnotised by the numbing procession of bolts on the assembly-line which he has to tighten simultaneously with two spanners, Chaplin falls into the hidden mechanisms that power the factory and is transformed into an automaton carrying out the machine's instructions, with comic consequences.

Modern Times is also a critique of what came to be called 'Taylorism' or 'Fordism'. Frederick Winslow Taylor was the pioneer of 'time and motion' studies who advocated that labourers should work like machines in brisk, repetitive and time-saving motions to maximise efficiency in the factories of North America. Taylor and Henry Ford (in whose motor factories Taylor's methods were implemented) sought to improve workers' efficiency by regulating the 'time and motion' of each worker, rationalising every movement along an assembly-line. In *Modern Times*, Chaplin's parody of the excesses of Taylorism points to a very real fear that they blurred the boundaries between the working body and the machine – in particular that this method of production might result in an actual mechanthropomorphism.[8]

The belief that the mechanised world was 'disenchanted', depleted of all the qualities that had previously provided comfort – especially spiritual meaning – is an undercurrent of dystopia. However, for artists such as Theo van Doesburg, the very fact that machinery had removed 'man' from 'nature' actually facilitated the spiritualisation of human life (van Doesburg 1975: 93). Van Doesburg contrasted the materialism of 'handicraft', which he believed 'reduced men to the level of machines', with the 'new spiritual artistic sensibility' afforded by the machine (Banham 1996: 151). However, the scientific liberation of men and women from religious dogma and superstition went hand in hand with a new sense of human alienation in a mechanised world that offered no redeeming sense of belonging or purpose. This critique was echoed by Gramsci, who exposed morally reprehensible industrial practices that reduced the work of the labourer to soul-destroying, dehumanising, mechanical tasks. Gramsci castigated industrialists, especially Henry Ford, for being exploitative and uninterested in the 'humanity' or 'spirituality' of their workers (Gramsci 1971: 303).

At the same time, Marxist theories of 'technological determinism' asserted that, although many of the changes in society are brought about by changes in technological 'tools', it is in fact the 'social relations of production' that are the most salient features of any given period. To follow the Marxist line of reasoning, the combined interests of governments and capitalism shape technology into an insidious form of social control. There was nothing 'neutral' about technology. It was not a self-perpetuating mechanism but one which was controlled by the existing dominant order, and it replicated that order by serving its interests.[9]

The themes of exploitation and the alienation of labour are still persistent elements of dystopia. The critic and interdisciplinary artist Coco Fusco has curated art exhibitions on these very themes. Fusco argues that technology has created a new apartheid: women workers from Mesoamerica (geographically the middle of the Americas) and the former Eastern bloc make technological commodities which they cannot afford to buy. In video and performance pieces based on the disappearance of the *maquiladora*, Fusco's work shows how the commodification of black and Latino women's bodies (via

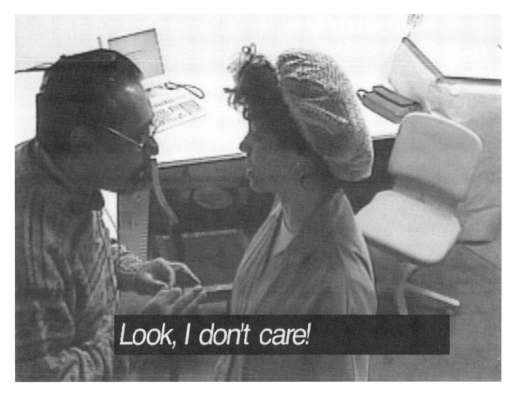

Figure 5.8 Coco Fusco, *Dolores from 10 to 10*, video installation, 1998. Video still courtesy of the artist. This video installation is based on the true story of one woman, a *maquiladora* worker in Tijuana accused of trying to start a union at her employer's plant. It recreates the management's attempts to get the woman to resign by locking her in a room without food or drink until she capitulated. *Dolores from 10 to 10* is Coco Fusco's interpretation of what the surveillance cameras would have seen during the woman's twelve-hour ordeal.

the international sex-tourism circuit) is symbiotically related to their status as 'forced labour' on assembly-lines in the electronics industries along the US–Mexico border (see Figure 5.8). Moreover, these women make the technology for surveillance equipment that will be used to control and monitor the activities of other workers. There is a counter-culture potential in technology, however; global action with other electronics workers in Korea, the former Eastern bloc and Ireland, for instance, is entirely enabled through the use of electronic communications. It is also important to register that Fusco's video work is frequently shown on public television, bypassing the museum altogether, in an attempt to gain access to a wider audience.

Video art

> [V]ideo posed a challenge to the sites of art production in society, to the forms and 'channels' of delivery, and to the passivity of reception built into them. Not only a systemic but also a utopian critique was implicit in

> video's early use, for the effort was not to enter the system but to trans-
> form every aspect of it and – legacy of the revolutionary avant-garde
> project – to redefine the system out of existence by merging art with
> social life and making 'audience' and 'producer' interchangeable.
>
> (Rosler 1996: 258–9)

The emergence in the 1960s of a branch of art practice that calls itself 'video art' is not far removed from the utopian spirit of the machine aesthetic seventy or so years previously. Mediated through the channels of mass media, video art holds out the possibility of a democratic practice in opposition to the perceived elitism of high modernism. 'Media' is a generic term to describe the systems by which information (and entertainment) are transmitted. The Canadian media guru Marshall McLuhan argued that the existence of mass media – in its most ubiquitous forms of television, radio and newspapers – is more significant than the content or message that they transmit: 'The medium is the massage' – a phrase which uses McLuhan's love of wordplay to pun the way in which the media massage us – not so much in terms of *what* is communicated as in terms of *how* it is communicated.

As we saw in Chapter 1, the 1960s were marked by social, political and economic upheavals that, broadly speaking, ushered in a period of competing interests. Although video technology undoubtedly developed in the 1960s, the genesis of video art itself gained a fillip from the emergence of counter-cultures in the 1960s, since video could be pressed into the service of representing 'others'. The use of mass culture and mass media by oppositional groups seemed to offer the chance for 'others' to control their own representation in art and re-present those images to an audience via familiar modes of transmission. The use of popular culture and familiar graphic modes of communication became the common currency of dissent from the 1960s onwards.

Although the media generally replicates the values of the dominant order, oppositional groups engaged with enthusiasm in the battle for custody of, control of and access to mass media. Ironically in the case of video art, its appropriation by marginalised groups required a critique of the medium, of technology which argues for a choice of alternative means–ends systems and therefore, for marginal groups, the subversion of the medium by the message. For instance, in the 1960s Nam June Paik's work keyed in to anxieties about the long-term effects of television viewing on the public, in particular that the medium would induce mindless apathy and passivity, or the 'narcotisation' of the viewer. Paik's video art took the view that television has a democratising potential but only if the medium itself is subjected to critical exploration. In this respect, Paik's association with the subversive strategies of Fluxus is evident in his works, which make visible the controlling mechanisms of network television. By making explicit the connection between art and politics, Paik's work exposed the fiction of technological neutrality. In this sense it is no coincidence that Paik uses the neo-Dada techniques of collage and décollage since they were recognised tools with which to deconstruct images and reveal concealed agendas. Paik's video collage *Good Morning Mr Orwell* (1984) was a global satellite project which pieced together and reconfigured prerecorded images from television footage with live avant-garde performances via international satellite from Peter Gabriel, Robert Rauschenberg, Laurie Anderson, Merce Cunningham, Alan Ginsberg and John Cage. On the first day of the new year of 1984 artists contributed to a live interactive satellite broadcast between New York, Paris and Germany. The live performers were collaged with prerecorded snippets of television footage and the tapes were subsequently edited into a two-channel video installation. Paik intended the piece to refute George Orwell's predictions for the year 1984 with an ironic free play of images and communications, quite the opposite of Big Brother's one-way surveillance.

When the majority of people receive their information through television pictures, painting can seem an outmoded site of cultural production, increasingly redundant in an age of electronic reproduction. However, this idea of the redundancy of painting is problematic. Television's innovative potential has never been realised. Television, according to Hall and Fifer,

> was not the communications medium it claimed to be but, rather, a one-way channel, broadcasting programs that sanctioned limited innovation and whose very means of production were invisible to the home consumer. Television through its management by corporate monopolies or state run systems had become a seamless hegemonic institution.
>
> (Hall and Fifer 1990: 71)

In sharp contrast, as Martha Rosler observes, early video art was 'not only a systemic but also a utopian critique' (Rosler 1996: 259) because, for the reasons outlined above, its medium was arguably more democratic, bypassing as it did the corporate structures that controlled public television. The cultural optimism of Marshall McLuhan's 'global village' suggested a contraction of the world and the utopian belief that 'global connectivity' would result in democratic communication.[10] Although in theory video art allows a democratisation of the arts, in stark contrast to high modernism's explicit embrace of a self-sufficient practice, in fact video art can be just as esoteric as any abstract painting.

The technological sublime

Mention was made at the start of this chapter of the Italian futurist architect Sant'Elia and of his designs for a utopian city. The scale on which this city was planned was such that, had it been built, its users would have been forced to assume vertiginous vantage points on top of skyscrapers and multi-storey walkways. Not unlike Russolo's *Intonarumori*, Sant'Elia's plans for *città nuova* tested the limits of sensory tolerance. His gigantic cityscapes would have dwarfed their inhabitants, who would have been whizzed up and down by high-speed elevators, surrounded by multi-storey walkways and cars would have raced around on specially constructed roads. In 1913 *città nuova* pre-empted the technological advances of the twentieth century that have enabled exhilarating physical experiences of the world not previously possible: flying over cities, standing on tall buildings and travelling at great speed. *Città nuova* had the potential simultaneously to thrill and terrify its inhabitants – it was technologically sublime, in the sense of the sublime as a mixture of 'pleasure and displeasure, terror and beauty'.

The sublime, a notion formulated in the eighteenth century by Immanuel Kant, was an experience that could be prompted by 'an outrage on the imagination, and yet it is judged all the more sublime on that account' (Kant 1952: 91). Kant was thinking typically of raging oceans, but we could also add precipitous cliffs, menacing weather systems and torrential waterfalls; that is to say, 'outrages on the imagination' in the sense that they offered the distant (and it is important that it is distant) prospect of danger. In the twentieth and twenty-first centuries, experiences of the sublime have been extended to include those which have been made possible by technology. The Enlightenment sublime, a mixture of terror and awe, could therefore attain a sort of modernist equivalence in the machine aesthetic's breathtaking leitmotifs of gigantism, speed and noise. However, at the end of the twentieth century the experiences of speed, vertigo and so on have become everyday features of Western capitalist existence, so that it is now perhaps difficult to reconstitute the mixture of pleasure and terror which characterised the machine aesthetic's sublime. In the early twenty-first century, just what might approximate the sublime is identifiable only through 'indirect communication' – the sublime through simulation rather than direct experience.

Terry Eagleton defines one aspect of the sublime in Enlightenment-like terms as its 'chastening, humiliating power, which decentres the subject into an awesome aware-ness of its finitude, its own petty position in the universe' (Eagleton 1990: 90).[11] In addition to being described in terms of the physical experiences of speed, noise and gigantism, the sublime has been located in matter that is barely perceptible, and then only with the aid of sophisticated equipment. For example, the physicist Stephen Hawking (1988) sees a kind of sublimity in the microcosmic particle system. Similarly, sublimity can be experienced in notional spaces that are 'unrepresentable'.

William Gibson coined the phrase 'cyberspace' in his novel *Neuromancer* (1984), which presents a dystopic vision of the future. Cyberspace is a computer-generated virtual environment that, unlike mere technological artefacts, holds out the promise of a capacity to reconstitute every aspect of human existence. A space and yet a non-space, cyberspace is a notional environment of pure digitalised information.[12] Cyberspace also offers the utopian prospect of the body of flesh transcending its corporeality and 'existing' as pure intelligence in a virtual world.

Although the body is clearly present in virtual interaction, since the body is the device through which we interface with the technology – for instance by means of touch, sight and sound – it offers the conceit of an out-of-body experience.[13] For example, Greyworld create sound installations using the sound system Koan to make generative art. Generative art involves programming a computer to 'generate' – in the sense of 'setting in motion' – its own drawing or sound. In the case of Greyworld's installations, the invisible application of technology, underneath floors or hidden in handrails, is predicated nevertheless on a physical presence in the sense that each bodily encounter generates a different sound.

Virtual reality

> VR [virtual reality] technology, far from including the body in a virtual environment, actively excludes the physical body, replacing it with a body image. One does not take one's body into VR. One leaves it at the door while the mind goes wandering, unhindered by a physical body, inhabiting an ethereal virtual body in pristine virtual space, itself a 'pure' Platonic space, free of farts, dirt, and untidy bodily fluids.
>
> (Penny 1995: 62)

Ways of thinking about technology have undergone changes in line with the shift from modernist to postmodernist thinking. For instance, in the 1950s, the first generation of computers was widely regarded with modernist enthusiasm as a rational and 'transparent' technology with the capacity to control and arrange complex data into a manageable system of mathematical algorithms. The invention of the 'postmodern computer', with its 'opaque' technology (graphic interface, mouse and double-click icons), in the 1980s separated the user from the mathematical operating systems. This shift from the 'transparent' modern to the 'opaque' postmodern is, according to Sherry Turkle (1995: 20), in keeping with the postmodern notion of the 'opaque' brain. As Lyotard maintains, new technologies tend to be conceptualised as substitutes for 'mental and/or linguistic operations' rather than as substitutes for mechanical operations. The effect of this is to collapse the Cartesian philosophical distinction between mind and matter. As Lyotard puts it, 'maybe the human mind is simply the most complex combination of matter in the universe' (Lyotard 1989: 19–20).

The corporeal world of physical experience has a parallel world in cyberspace which often mimics the Euclidean space of the three-dimensional world and the Western idea of the frame and adds to them the computer graphics, animated sequences and audio soundtrack derived from film. Western culture is, after all, oriented towards books, film and televisual display. Representing the world in digital form began with computer interfaces that were almost entirely text-based, but in recent years there has been a change to a more visual interface which resembles either the layered pages of a book or a television screen, with a sense of three-dimensional space.

The advent of virtual reality has added another dimension to our interface with the machine – that of virtual interaction. 'Interactivity', in which the user (rather than the viewer) is also author and editor of a multimedia encounter, is unlike television, video and film, in which it is only possible to 'delegate' one's looking. Successful interaction requires both induction into the technological sphere and sustained involvement in real time. Paul Virilio, in *The Art of the Motor* (1995), argues against the humanising of the language of technology. Pointing out that phrases such as 'interactive user-friendly' are far from being just that, Virilio contends that such language use constitutes a metaphor for the enslavement of humans to intelligent machines (Virilio 1995: 135). This is an extreme view but one that indicates nonetheless the way in which language is used to obscure the often insidious relations between people and new technologies (particularly, as Coco Fusco shows, in the workplace).

Virtual reality began as simulated environments for military training exercises.[14] Subsequently, a lucrative spin-off of this technology 'allowed' civilians to enter virtual worlds of combat, game-play and sexual conquest. Of course, we have always possessed the capacity to enter into an imaginative world of game-play, literature being a significant example; however, virtual reality holds out the emancipatory offer of participatory interaction and, with the aid of a teledildonic suit, *actual* physical sensation. The ability to put on suits to replicate the sensations of 'real' war or sex or even remote exploration of places as distant as the other side of the world or outer space marks the transition of this technology from the laboratory to the domestic space.

Traditionally there is something passive about viewing, but, as we have seen, in virtual interaction the viewer becomes the 'user' or even the author of his or her experience. The current state of actual reality falls short of the promise of virtual reality. Its currency resides in the speculative philosophical debates that surround the possibilities of the technology – such as altered perception and a paradigmatic shift in the status and use of what we call knowledge. The popular equation that knowledge equals power is undermined by the impact of new technologies which question what exactly constitutes knowledge, sweeping away centuries of certainties. This is precipitated in part by a crisis of confidence in institutional structures and in part because access to and acquisition of 'knowledge' are relatively fragmented experiences devoid of connectivity with traditional historical narratives. In brief, there has been a shift away from traditional forms of disseminating knowledge to electronically retrievable information, rendering obsolete the power structures inherent in formal educational infrastructures.

The digital world of cyberspace can recreate complex natural structures or fashion totally new illusionistic environments. The group TechnoSphere has developed a web site where users can design an artificial 'life-form' or 'creature' and send it to live in an online environment (see Plate XVIII). The 'creature' has to be assembled from a set of prescribed shapes and each user makes a hybrid creature which inhabits TechnoSphere, interacts with other creatures and keeps its 'creator' informed of its actions via email. Unlike the high-maintenance Tamagochi (cyberpets) of the mid-1990s, TechnoSphere 'creatures' have an independent existence in which they are at the mercy of other creatures in cyberspace. TechnoSphere is a space which is navigated in one of two ways: the user can 'see' through the 'eyes' of the creature; or the user can assume the vantage-point of a Steadicam, moving around or above the creature, flying over the landscape of TechnoSphere. Virtual reality raises some fundamental questions about the relationship of the human body to virtual space, and particularly about its boundaries. We will explore in more detail the implications of new technologies for our perception of the body in Chapter 8, where we will see how, for instance, the creation of digital alter egos – avatars – has created the possibility of a disembodied experience of self.

The Internet provides extensive and, more importantly, interactive ways of storing, displaying, retrieving and linking information and images. But is interactivity really a substantial alteration to the relationship between artist and viewer? The American artist Dan Graham's video installation and performance work *Present Continuous Past(s)* (1974) consists of two video monitors and two cameras which record the viewer in real time (time travel and the temporal relationship of the body to real time are common contemporary preoccupations). One surveillance monitor is in simultaneous playback mode, but the other monitor has a time-delay transmission which represents an image of the viewer recorded a few seconds previously. In some installations the sequence is simultaneously broadcast through mirrors. Dan Graham contrasts two models of time: 'the traditional Renaissance perspective static present-time . . . as the (self) image(s) in the mirror(s), and the time of the video feedback loop' (Longhauser 1993: 17). Thus the mirror reflects the present, the video camera records the continuous reflection in the mirror and the recording appears eight seconds later on a television monitor. Graham's work is principally a critique of capitalism, especially when he sets up these devices in shop-window displays within the gallery space. However, his preoccupations – time-delay, mirror reflections and the status of the viewing subject as both the producer and the product of works such as *Present Continuous Past(s)* – are also critiques of perception in the postmodern world, where technology has radically altered our sense of time and space.

As Marshall McLuhan observed, in contradiction to much contemporary science, human memory is 'set down through fixed chronology. We remember events by memorizing dates'[15] (McLuhan 1989: 170). Computers have supplanted some of the functions of human memory with what has been called the 'conceit of total recall'. However, computers generally employ non-temporal markers; for example, we tend to use spatial references for navigation and orientation ('point and click' graphic interfaces). The question of computer time in relation to real time is philosophically problematical. Hyperreality happens so quickly that it is estimated that one Internet year equals at least two and perhaps as many as seven calendar years. The experience of altered perception in relation to time and space that Dan Graham's work articulates is further problematised by the technological construction of a virtual reality. Even though real time is marked in three-second human pulses, the sense of time passing can be quicker or slower: from the dilation and contraction of time in film to the experience of forms of electronic communication, such as email and video-conferencing. As Virilio puts it, 'telecommunications tools, not content to limit extension . . . are also eradicating all duration, any extension of time in the transmission of messages, images' (Virilio 1997: 9). Suzanne Treister's web site and CD-ROM *No Other Symptoms: time travelling with Rosalind Brodsky* (1999) (see Plate XIX) work within the conceit of time travel. Rosalind Brodsky is Treister's fictional alter ego, a twenty-five-year-old woman working in a futuristic company that develops virtual-reality systems. Following a systems overload Brodsky comes to believe that she is a time-traveller with unique access to the past. Her 'drifting body', clothed in Treister's dress designs and carrying a series of attaché cases, passes through Moscow in 1917, 1958 and 2017; she visits Freud in Berlin and Lacan in Paris; she materialises on the film sets of *Dr Zhivago* in 1965 and *Schindler's List* in 1994. In Treister's biographical introduction she explains, 'Brodsky fetishizes history. She becomes a necrophiliac invader of the spaces containing the deaths of her ancestors, through the priviledged(sic) violence of technology' <http://ensemble.va.com. au/tableau/suzy/>. This Internet and CD-ROM simulation is immaculately plotted, following McLuhan's observations on memory and chronology. A diary records all the time-travelling events, costumes and attaché cases are archived and photographic 'records' of each occasion are posted.

Mechanthropomorph to cyborg

[T]he machine is us, our processes, an aspect of our embodiment. We can be responsible for machines; *they* do not dominate or threaten us. We are responsible for boundaries; we are they.

(Haraway 1991: 177)

Your species requires a visual reference point.

(Zen, *Blake's 7*)[16]

Until recently everything handmade has seemed to be under our own authority. However, the seemingly inexorable progress of the technological revolution suggests that technology may be able to evolve for itself. For instance, science fiction has many dystopic images of machines that become sentient, and nowhere is this more prevalent than in our cultural notion of the evolution of the cyborg. Unlike Léger and the artists of the First Machine Age, who depersonalised their subject by depicting people as mechanthropomorphs, many recent artists and filmmakers have to an extent humanised the computer by attributing to it personality traits and idiosyncracies. The computer is often given a human name, and our interaction with it is interpersonal. Portrayals of computers in popular culture are given the semblance of individuality. HAL in *2001: a space odyssey* (1968) is a melancholic 'character' who is even punished for disobedience; Commander Data in the TV series *Star Trek: the next generation* (1987–94) is an android with an almost tragic 'desire' to understand the life-forms 'he' encounters. Similarly, in *Blade Runner* (1982) two of the central characters do not know whether they are 'real' or androids that have been implanted with fake human memory. In *Robocop* (1987, 1990 and 1993) parts of the human body are synthesised with a robot, and a battle for control ensues between the human mind and the mechanical body. In the three *Matrix* films (1999 and 2003) the humans flit between a virtual reality that is chic and endows them with superhuman powers and the underground squalor of their dystopian reality in a battle with their robotic overlords.

The flipside of this is that some postmodernists tend to regard the human body not as a set of genetic sequences but as electronic circuitry. Merce Cunningham's 'digital choreography' of the 1990s creates dances on the computer screen that reverse the relationships between the performer and the machine enacted in the various mechanical ballets of the 1920s, by using dancers to physically enact a computer programme for choreographing dance. The computer normally notates a choreographed piece in order to record every dancer's part for performance at a later date. Cunningham's inversion of this is to create the ballet digitally first, with the dancers then matching the digital aesthetics of the programme. It is ironic that a cyborg invested with collective human intelligence should still be represented in a recognisably human form. This continual veneration of the body is, perversely, at the same time a denial of the body. As we will see in more detail in Chapter 7 when we examine notions of self and identity, Donna Haraway's 'Manifesto for Cyborgs' of 1985 (see Haraway 1991b) uses the cyborg as a metaphor for a decentred or postmodern sense of self. She argues that the cyborg is a model which has the potential to cast off Western notions of individuality and dominant notions of selfhood (in stark contrast to Paul Virilio's negative analysis).

Synthetic life-forms have been used as a potent metaphor for lost histories. If cyberspace is the final frontier, then, like video art thirty years ago, it has the potential to be a virtual democracy where cultural differences become invisible. However, the homogenising tendencies of electronic production have militated against such difference. Keith Piper's *Robot Bodies* (1998) (Plate XX) explores the metaphorical relationship between the image of the robot in science fiction and the history of black people in popular culture. Pointing out that the robot Sojourner Truth sent to Mars in 1997 was named after a black slave, Piper critiques notions of a culturally diverse future for artificial life-forms and simultaneously recovers the history of black peoples. Piper's use of digital technology is significant. As a multimedia artist and a black artist working in Britain, Piper makes explicit connections between notions of cultural displacement and new technologies that are non-linear, intertextual and multifaceted. Technology does, however, have the potential to be instrumental in forging national identity, as Kurdish nationals, for example, who have been historically dispersed can be 'reassembled' and united through digital technology, for instance via digital television networks (Byrne 1999).

Cyberculture

> I think lust motivates technology. The first personal robots, let's face it, are not going to be bought to bring people drinks.
>
> (Mike Saenz, quoted in Jones 1995: 48)

> The very terms we use to describe our experiences of cyberspace, such as fluidity, merging, dissolution, networks, morphing, also imply fantasies of escaping into or subsuming the other . . . movements into a new frontier of 'personal freedom' which are also the fantasies of colonialism. History should give us pause for thought, warning us to be wary of assigning too much progressive potential to easy dreams of inhabiting an other.
>
> (McPherson 2002: 188)

In 2001, the Tribes Gallery in New York mounted an exhibition entitled *Dystopia and Identity in the Age of Global Communications*. The exhibition, consisting of work by sixty contemporary artists, presented utopian and dystopian responses to the state of the world in a period of millennial tension. For example, Christoph Draeger's *Oil* (1998) projected giant views of oil slicks taken from news footage on to the gallery walls. Other contributors used the CD-ROM and the Internet to make their points. Marina Grzinic's *Axis of Life* combined the artist's graphic interface on the themes of birth, death, body, love, history and geography with a plethora of Internet links to related sites. Grzinic exhorts the user: 'Be my guest, take a lift to the reconstructed Eisenstein, or to the dead fields of the present – to Vukovar, the Croatian ghost city near the Serbian border. Or maybe you would like to jump in the life of the great Russian suprematist artist Malevich and take part in Malevich's funeral. . . . Yes, we are obsessed with History, Geography, Sex and Body'. The exhibition *Dystopia and Identity in the Age of Global Communications* seems, then, to present technology and cyberculture as a legitimate vehicle for artistic expression but also as a vehicle for critiquing issues such as the globalisation of capitalist culture, the dangers of uninhibited technological determinism and private greed and aggression.

The large numbers of women contributors to the *Dystopia and Identity in the Age of Global Communications* exhibition may be taken as evidence that new technologies are a vehicle for some kind of freedom of expression that has previously been denied to excluded groups. Modernism's engagement with the machine has been undeniably gendered. While women surrealists were granted custody of, and implicated in, a close relationship with nature, women did not possess the machine. As we have seen, the language of the machine was industrial and the metaphors for the machine aesthetic were often masculine. However, in recent years women have acquired more than a walk-on part in both the technological industries and the imagery of technology. On the one hand, this can be a reluctant co-option, as Coco Fusco reveals when she points out that women workers are the ideal workforce in the electronic industries since their smaller hands are more adept at manipulating microparts. Correspondingly, images of women figure increasingly in cyberculture. For instance, the animated character Lara Croft from the best-selling computer game *Tomb Raider* is an 'Indiana Jane' character who battles her way through increasingly challenging combative levels. On one level Lara Croft can be seen as an emancipated heroine and on another as a gross stereotype – a cyberspace pin-up with improbable vital statistics. On the other hand, cyberculture (including net-art, virtual communities and intercultural communications) is sometimes conceived of as another frontier – an uncharted territory with the illusion of infinity and the prospect of a free-for-all. The illusion of freedom in cyberspace, as a 'space' to be enjoyed by cyber-libertarians regardless of class, race, gender and health, is just that, an illusion, according to many. Coco Fusco rejects the idea that cyberspace is raceless:

> [I]t is difficult to avoid concluding that scientists, web designers and other digital artists are appropriating black cultural tropes to represent psychic freedom in cyber-space . . . in the same way that modernists turned to Africa to represent irrationality. These observations confirm that image makers, regardless of their tools, continue to borrow from the already known to imagine what they cannot see.
>
> (Fusco 2001)

As the boundaries between biology and technology are arguably dissolving, so the relationships between humans become unstable. The prospect of artificial intelligence and life online has contributed to a radical shift in interpersonal relations. For instance, email communication involves a different set of social interactions which abandon the conventions of formal and informal letter-writing. Cybersex – electronic intimacy with virtual pin-ups or other consenting (online) individuals – is another area in which technology allows a new dimension to human relationships. As we have seen, the interaction between humans and machines remains problematic, but some critics argue that this is a predominantly male problem and that women may well profit from the shift in power relations brought about by new technologies. Donna Haraway, for example, states that she 'would rather be a cyborg than a goddess' (1991a: 181), and Sadie Plant offers the thought that 'machines and women have at least one thing in common: they are not men' (Plant 1993: 13), maintaining that, in essence, 'woman' *is* a virtual reality because she plays 'other' to men in a patriarchal society. Both are optimistic, seeing the emancipatory potential of technocultures for women. Conducting our operations through a tactile world of touch-screen interfaces amid dispersed networks of information (an early feminist strategy) could, they argue, circumnavigate patriarchal modes of expression altogether.

The tide of opinion among contemporary cultural commentators would seem to refute any idea that an individual can enter cyberspace in order to play with identity and multiply selves as part of an emancipatory project. As many observe, the jury is still out on whether or not the rise of cyberculture is necessarily a benign prospect. Neil Postman's pessimistic view of new technologies are listed in his book *Technopoly* (1993), which describes a state of mind in contemporary Western culture possessed by an uncritical adulation of technological tools, a 'deification of technology'. Technopoly is what happens to society when the defenses against information glut have broken down . . . it is what happens when a culture, overcome by information generated by technology, tries to employ technology itself as a means of providing clear direction and humane purpose.

(Postman 1993: 72)

Geert Lovink has recently reviewed the history of the Internet and speculates on its uncertain future. Acknowledging the corporate and state agendas that control the Internet, Lovink (2002) calls for cyber-citizens to reclaim cyberspace. Lovink's 'cyber-libertarian' ideology is essentially optimistic; however, the ironic reclamation of cyberspace by an artist such as Keith Townsend Obadike demonstrates that digital technologies really reflect the hopes and ambitions of privatised, corporate culture, 'branding' all aspects of life. Obadike, an American-born artist, auctioned his blackness on the auction web site eBay. The 'heirloom' was put up for sale with the warning not to use his blackness when, for example, 'seeking employment, making or selling "serious" art, shopping or writing a personal check, making intellectual claims, or while voting in the United States or Florida'.

Apart from the fact that new technological developments have allowed artists to communicate their art in different media, we are left wondering whether there are real differences that distinguish contemporary art practice from what has gone before. There are certainly recurring themes in the work of artists using new technologies (but then there were recurring themes within modernism). The formatting of work conceived and executed with new technologies can be repetitive (but then styles were repetitive within modernism). And the strategies of appropriation, subversion, displacement and irony are surely the remnants of familiar avant-garde strategies from way back. Or perhaps it is simply too soon properly to review the relatively recent practices of artists operating via new technologies.

Modernism and realism in US art

The history of avant-garde painting is that of a progressive surrender to the resistance of its medium; which resistance consists chiefly in the flat picture plane's denial of efforts to 'hole through' it for realistic perspective space.

(Greenberg: 1986a: 10)

It is ironic but not contradictory that in a society politically stuck in a position to the right of centre, in which political repression weighed as heavily as it did in the United States, abstract expressionism was for many the expression of freedom: the freedom to create controversial works of art, the freedom symbolized by action painting, by the unbridled expressionism of artists completely without fetters.

(Guilbaut 1983: 201)

In 1953 the American artist Robert Rauschenberg, best known for his mixed media 'combines' (art works that combined diverse media and techniques), asked Willem de Kooning for a drawing that he could obliterate. Rauschenberg's *Erased de Kooning Drawing* (Figure 6.1), perhaps a homage by a young and relatively unknown artist to a major figure in American art, was an ambiguous gesture. The act of creation-through-destruction can be seen as both a tribute and a dismissal, at once metaphorical and literal. The erasure of an abstract expressionist work, existing now only in memory and the indentations on the blank paper, was perhaps a forerunner of the conceptual work (simplistically put, an art of ideas, not necessarily of outcomes) that came to dominate the American scene by the 1960s. The act of erasure was also a gesture that radically critiqued the modernist trope of self-expression – an ironic commentary on the residual Romanticism that dominated abstraction. The erasure of abstract expressionism and the questioning of authorship, creativity and originality that found their apotheosis in 'pure' abstraction have been major preoccupations of contemporary artists since the 1950s. The assaults on the nature of subjectivity and the myth of the artist are, however, often replaced by another layer of myth. It is not, perhaps, until the 'unmediated' 1980s and 1990s interventions of Sherrie Levine – who, as we saw in Chapter 1 re-presents photographs by 'modern masters' such as Edward Weston, either without changing them or by merely presenting a negative to emphasise the technological processes involved in creation – that authorship, particularly in its most masculine manifestation, and the myths of creativity are laid bare. In her 1981 *After Edward Weston*, she worked in flagrant disregard of Weston's copyright, and appropriated the image of Weston's son by re-photographing the work of the old master of Western photography, famed for his photographic originality and formalism. However, Rauschenberg's much earlier act is significant in establishing the necessity of acknowledging the importance of usurping the claims of abstract expressionism.

The image that Rauschenberg erased was a female figure and suggestive stylistically of de Koonings' *Women* series from the 1950s (see Plate XVI). The drawing de Kooning gave Rauschenberg was heavily worked and deeply indented, so traces of the rubbed-out image remain. Rauschenberg's work would, in turn, become the subject both of homage and enigmatic appropriation by the pop artist Andy Warhol. Pop art of the 1960s traded in the unique signature style of abstract expressionism for an unabashed impersonal and reproducible collaborative and commercial art. By using commercial techniques like silk-screen printing, drawing on imagery from advertising and paying scant attention to 'finish', the artistic 'purity' of abstract expressionism's serious endeavour was mocked. However, Warhol's anti-signature style, the evasion of individuality in artistic practices, becomes in turn its own 'unique' style label, instantly recognisable and therefore marketable (see Figure 6.2).

Referencing, indexing and artistic 'incest' are, of course, nothing new in art production. As we saw in Chapter 1, Manet had referenced Old Masters in his paintings, but arguably Manet's homage had not undermined the nature of the artistic process.[1] He, as the author of the work, is still very much in evidence. But Rauschenberg and, more latterly, Levine were making an entirely different point, and their works can be seen as examples of palimpsest. Palimpsest, the removal of the original to make way for another, is historically a reference to parchment on which text is written over previous text. Palimpsest is a metaphor commonly used by deconstructionists, particularly Jacques Derrida. Deconstruction is not just a reversal of strategies or a neutralisation of binary opposites: it is a process of displacement. Deconstruction is a strategy for reading texts and images which 'attempts to make the not-seen accessible to sight' (Derrida 1976: 163).

The erasure of the de Kooning, emblematic of American abstract expressionism, came at a complex moment in US art history. The reworking of another artist's work – by appropriation or erasure – has been identified as a postmodern preoccupation. It was not just a way of finding a new style, although in the search for novelty that underpins the art market this undoubtedly played a part; it was symptomatic of a 'crisis of confidence' both in the centrality of the artist and in the unique act of creativity.

Abstract expressionism is commonly identified as the pinnacle of high modernism. It stands at the apex of notions of individual self-expression and artistic freedom. However, a closer scrutiny of the movement within its historical context reveals a raft of major issues, not least of which was the transition of the avant-garde from adversarial culture to a petrified modernism. The erasure of a work by de Kooning, when seen within the broader political and social world of the post-war USA, is symptomatic of a crisis of confidence in the institutional success of a seemingly oppositional culture.

Figure 6.1 Robert Rauschenberg, *Erased de Kooning Drawing*, 1953. © Robert Rauschenberg/ VAGA, New York/DACS, London, 2004. Courtesy of Leo Castelli Gallery, New York. Ironically mounted in a gold-leaf frame, the ghostly work consists of faint traces of ink and crayon on paper.

Far from hanging on to its radical credentials, abstract expressionism was seen by many to have sedimented into mainstream orthodoxy. Just how the avant-garde came to renege on its radical promise is part of a broader story of exclusions and preoccupations in the USA in the 1950s that has its origins in the pre-war era of the 1930s.

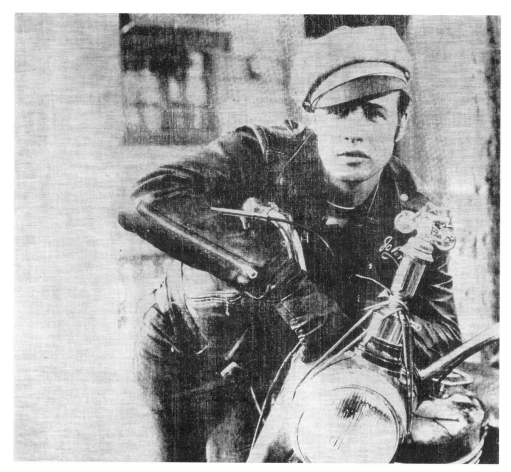

Figure 6.2 Andy Warhol, *Marlon Brando*, 1966. © The Andy Warhol Foundation for the Visual Arts, Inc./ARS, NY, and DACS, London, 2004. Courtesy of the Froehlich Collection, Stuttgart. In the 1960s, Warhol's embrace of commodity culture, whether ironic, critical or celebratory, consisted of an extended repertoire of the consumer products of capitalist culture, including celebrity culture, with images of *Liz, Elvis* and *Marilyn*. Here we have the legendary Marlon Brando in a still from László Benedek's cult 1953 movie *The Wild One*. The 'what have you got?' brand of rebellion played out by the film's leading characters echoed society's increasing unease at the repressive suburbanisation of the US during the 1950s. In a form of artistic rebellion against protocols for printmaking, including 'correct' registration, Warhol's slightly off-kilter repeat-patterned screen prints were produced within a pseudo-factory system.

Reconstructing the art of Depression America

Histories are constructed into totalities which operate through what Foucault called the 'principle of exclusion'. Nowhere is this more apparent than in the history of modernism in the US. A model of *culmination* drives the standard history of US art, obscuring other histories along the way, and, crucially for our purposes, the relationship between histories. Even chronological accounts of US art are complicit in a 'selective tradition' and are seldom merely descriptive of development, neutral descriptions or style labels. Each

Although hugely influential in bringing to public and political notice the plight of the tenant farmer, Bourke-White's most famous work, *You Have Seen Their Faces*, also faced the accusation of sentimentality. The photographs were collected together as a series in a documentary photo-essay book written with Erskine Caldwell. The photo-documentary essay was an important part of Depression culture in its impulse to search out and celebrate the 'real' American and the American Way. The choreographer Martha Graham's work in the 1930s is similarly apposite because it is customary to read Graham's dance in formal terms and to acknowledge her preference for mythic subject matter over political relevance. She is remembered largely for her pioneering 'dancing modernism', a corollary to abstract expressionism. However, Graham's choreography in the 1930s had an overt socio-political basis. *American Document* (1938) and *Frontier: an American perspective on the plains* (1935) were considered testaments to American democracy threatened by the collapse of the US economy. Unlike any of her later works, in the ballet *American Document* Graham used the spoken word to control meaning: the 'silence' of traditional ballet was broken in order to underscore a political reading.

The rejection, by the 1940s, of the content, form and function of New Deal art works went hand in hand with the rejection both of the period's social basis for art practices and of its reconfiguring of the artist as citizen. The archetypal New Deal art work and its location in a public building can be seen in Lucienne Bloch's 1936 *Cycle of a Woman's Life*, a mural painted for the recreation room of a women's house of detention in New York City (see Figure 6.6). In an interview entitled 'Murals for Use' Bloch commented: 'As for the matrons, outside of the fact that their concept of an artist was shattered when they saw me work without a smock and without inspired fits, they were delighted to witness a creation of a 'genuine hand-painted picture' (Bloch 1973: 77).

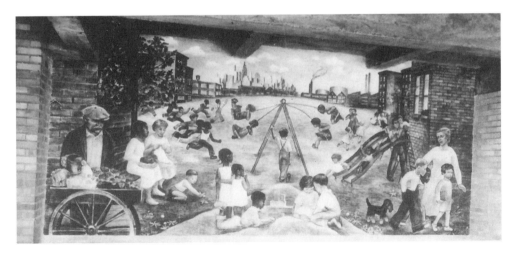

Figure 6.6 Lucienne Bloch, *Cycle of a Woman's Life*, 1936. Mural in Women's House of Detention, New York City. Courtesy of US National Archives photo # 16-AG-6272-A, reproduction by Photoresponse. Lucienne Bloch's mural *Cycle of a Woman's Life* was designed for a women's prison in Manhattan, New York. The life-cycle was a familiar motif in New Deal murals. In this instance the depiction of a multi-racial group of playing children formed part of a gently coercive rehabilitation strategy for women prisoners. The exemplary social scene operated as part of a recuperative practice.

The 1940s saw the premature closure of publicly funded arts projects, principally the Federal Arts Project (FAP) (1935–43) and WPA. The resurgent economics of war did allay the need for uplifting *American* art works, in favour of artists working shoulder to shoulder against Fascism, but the rejection of the projects was not entirely an economic issue. Post-1939 the politics of the New Deal was called to account. With the collapse of confidence in the utopianism of International Socialism in general and the Soviet Union in particular, which we will deal with in more depth later (pp. 181–2), confidence in left-wing values and, by extension, the form and the content of the art works that had promoted them diminished.

The post-war period saw a rise in what was termed the 'first-person aesthetic', which went in tandem with a rejection of advocacy for social causes and even for a socially relevant art. The former social crusader somewhat abruptly took on the mantle of outsider. The reasons for the shift away from the artist-citizen to the artist as alienated outsider in opposition to mainstream values (among whom Jackson Pollock was archetypal) can be traced to the increasing dominance of a formalist aesthetic and post-war monetary and political values. Any easy correlation between the economic and political and contemporary cultural production, however, would be dangerously reductive, as these issues alone do not account for the *forms* taken by art works after the war.

It is important to recognise that, although modern art practice moved into a new phase or style deemed more appropriate for a post-war world, the rigid divisions between the 1930s and the 1950s have been critically endorsed by modernist historians. For them this change required a rejection of previously held social and political commitments. There was, however, much continuity that we will refer to that has been largely repressed in favour of 1950s triumphalism. For example, in her influential book *American Art since 1900* Barbara Rose declared:

> [T]he WPA is a unique but crucial chapter in American art. This is so despite the fact that, outside of a few sketches or reconstructions, such as Gorky's Newark airport mural or de Kooning's sketch for the Williamsberg housing project, the WPA programs produced almost no art of any consequence that has survived.
>
> (Rose 1975: 126)

The statement 'no art of any consequence' is a denial of the diversity of practice supported by the Left in the 1930s. As we saw earlier, Stuart Davis was supporting a line taken by members of the AAC, an independent collective of artists and writers during the 1930s. The AAC supported the view, articulated by Davis, that there was no single aesthetic, no cohesion of styles: the common agenda was broadly political, not asethetic.[3] (See, particularly, Contreras 1983.) By the early 1940s the FAP increasingly came under attack. The project was defended, however, by MoMA, particularly by its curator A. Conger Goodyear and the director Alfred H. Barr Jnr, who said he was 'greatly encouraged by the quality of the WPA and believed that it would be a serious blow to American culture if it were to be discontinued'. There was still in the 1940s a positive idea of eclecticism rather than a monolithic programme of political correctness. However, the break-up of the AAC in the 1940s and the retreat of the Left effectively silenced some artists and writers committed to a plurality of aesthetics. In attempting to disclaim their artistic roots in the political radicalism of the 1930s, many artists and critics have diminished the artistic experimentation that took place before the war. For instance, the abstract expressionist Robert Motherwell's rejection of Depression culture was total; in a heated television debate he declared: 'Nothing good came out of it, really nothing' (H. Phillips 1963: 4).

The artists that Barbara Rose cites approvingly from this period are those who were to become major figures in abstract expressionism in spite of their 1930s output. Pre-war American painting, characteristically categorised as regionalist and right-wing or as involved in social protest and essentially left-wing, is usually relegated to a footnote in history, a cul-de-sac on the way to the real business of art – the 'pure' painting of the 1950s. Art from the 1930s receives little academic or critical acclaim beyond a 'roots' approach to abstract expressionism promoted by Rose and Irving Sandler (1970). The *esprit de corps* generated by Roosevelt's New Deal programmes for unemployed artists during the Depression years is usually credited in terms only of its contribution to the unifying of so stylistically disparate a group as the abstract expressionists. As the monopoly of formalist aesthetics is unravelled, reassessments of the period are taking place and artists that received little critical acclaim, such as Jacob Lawrence, William Gropper, Ben Shahn and Philip Evergood, are being renegotiated (see Plate XXI).

Mexico: national school verses internationalism

In tandem with a rejection of much of the 1930s work came a diminishment of the influence of Mexican art and politics, significant factors in the aesthetic and theoretical formation of a generation of US artists. This can be seen most graphically at an institutional level in the Torpedo diagram produced at the MoMA during the early 1930s and revised in the early 1940s. Consistent in design with the contemporary fashion for both streamlining and the machine aesthetic, the torpedo diagram shows the ideal modern art collection. In the second torpedo, formulated some nine years after the first, the nose contains in equal measure the United States and Mexico (see Figure 6.7).

By the late 1950s, and until relatively recently, Mexican art and American modernism were held in a false binary relationship as attempts to create a genealogy for a quintessentially American abstract expressionism obscured a Mexican presence. The rejection of the influence of the revolutionary Mexicans José Orozco, David Siqueiros and Diego Rivera on the evolution of abstract expressionism was marked. In part, the charge against New Deal art work as all 'murals of men in dungarees' parodied the images of peasants and workers familiar in many Mexican public commissions. Mural art is mentioned by modernist historians as a debt of the 1950s to the 1930s but it is reduced to a question of scale: to that of the abstract expressionists copying the monumental scale of Mexican mural painting – see, for instance, Rivera's *Detroit Industry* mural (1932–3) at the Detroit Institute of Arts. This is perceived as the *legitimate* legacy of the Mexicans. As for their ideological bequest – their Marxist politics or their insistence on a socially relevant art – debates at the AAC demonstrate just how indebted the latter were to the theoretical and political position of the Mexicans (see, in particular Siqueiros 1975).

It is part of the persistent legacy of histories written in the 1950s and 1960s that modernism evolved in Paris and then migrated to New York in the post-war period. This myth has persistently militated against the recognition of other centres of modernist cultural activity. For instance, there were artists' colonies in Mexico that

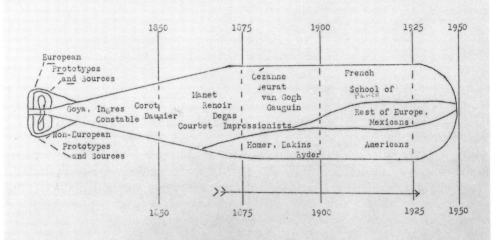

In the past nine years the torpedo has moved a little farther and the Committee would sketch it today in the following form:

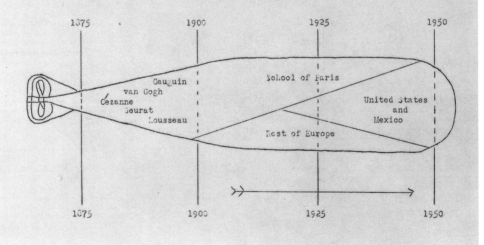

Figure 6.7 Alfred Hamilton Barr Jnr (1902–81), Torpedo diagrams of the ideal permanent collection of MoMA, 1933–41. Prepared by Alfred H. Barr, Jnr, for the 'Advisory Committee Report on Museum Collections', 1941. The Museum of Modern Art Archives, New York: Alfred H. Barr Jr. Papers, 9a.15. Photo © 2003 The Museum of Modern Art, NY/Scala, Florence. The diagram was prepared by Alfred Barr to illustrate his 'Report on the Permanent Collection in 1933' and for the *Advisory Committee Report on Museum Collections* in 1941.

attracted many US artists; Stuart Davis, who spent the summer of 1923 in the south-west, was only one of many to find inspiration in the politics and landscape of Mexico. However, it is not just recognition that was problematic; misrepresentation too became an issue for cultures outside a geopolitically defined modernity. The difficulties facing cultures outside mainstream modernism is perhaps best exemplified by the work of Frida Kahlo, who remarked: 'I didn't know I was a Surrealist until André Breton came to Mexico and told me so'. Kahlo is an important figure in Mexican art, since although her work was championed by surrealists such as Breton she saw herself as a Mexican realist and eschewed the internationalism of modernism. Moreover, her heavily auto-biographic imagery drew on Mexican spiritual sources, visualized in *retablos*, votive imagery painted on metal – quite unlike European surrealism, which drew strength from Freudian psychoanalysis. In *Self-Portrait Dedicated to Leon Trotsky* (1937) (Plate XXII), constructed within a stage setting, Kahlo wears traditional Mexican clothes, including a *rebzo* (Mexican shawl). This declaration of her cultural identity is consistent with Kahlo's political commitment to a country threatened by US imperialism. The scroll that she carries is inscribed with a dedication to Leon Trotsky, who lived with her and Rivera for a short time in 1937. In her use of her own Mexican and feminine identity she rejected modernism's conceit in speaking for others.

Many American and European artists had strong links with Mexican revolutionary cultures at the level of both the political and the aesthetic. Tina Modotti's photograph *Woman Carrying a Flag* (1928), *Mexico*, was part of a repertoire of farm labourers and working people, in this particular instance taking part in a political rally. They are, however, often read as formalist evocations of the beautiful rather than read for specific political content. Mexico and the expansion westwards to places 'unmarked' by European culture played a more important role in artistic production than art history's emphasis on East Coast avant-gardism would suggest. Davis, taking a cue from Mexican politics, wrote against the elitism of the art world in tracts such as *Federal Art Projects and the Social Education of the Artist*.

The Mexican Revolution of 1910, like the Russian Revolution of 1917, saw artists mobilised in the service of a revolutionary culture, resulting in an overtly politicised art. In an address to the AAC in the 1930s, David Siqueiros, drawing on the experience of the League of Revolutionary Artists and Writers in Mexico, argued that revolutionary art should be accessible to the greatest number of people. Similarly, writing in *Modern Art Quarterly* in 1932, Diego Rivera argued in an article entitled 'The Revolutionary Spirit in Modern Art' that all art was propaganda and that even apolitical art – that is, 'art for art's sake' or 'pure' art – had 'enormous political content'. He continued:

[A]ll painters have been propagandists or else they have not been painters. Giotto was a propagandist of the spirit of Christian charity, the weapon of the Franciscan monks of his time against feudal oppression. Bruegel was a propagandist of the struggle of the Dutch artisan petty bourgeois against feudal oppression. Every artist who has been worth anything in art has been such a propagandist.

(Rivera 2003: 424)

The revolutionary ferment in Mexico profited from the arrival of the Russian revo-lutionary Leon Trotsky, expelled from the USSR in 1929 by Joseph Stalin for criticising the doctrine of 'socialism in one country' and the Comintern's policies, particularly on

Fascism. In Mexico Trotsky continued to attack what he saw as a false claim by Marxism to provide a 'universal system'. Trotsky held to a belief in the non-rational side of politics. It was not surprising, therefore, that in 1938 he should publish in the American Marxist publication *Partisan Review* with the surrealist André Breton,[4] who shared Trotsky's commitment to the irrational. Their resulting collaboration, 'Manifesto: Towards a Free Revolutionary Art', written in anticipation of the Second World War, in essence repeats the call for a combination of politics and art while acknowledging art's own internal laws. They wrote:

> [I]n defending freedom of thought we have no intention of justifying political indifference, and . . . it is far from our wish to revive a so-called 'pure' art which generally serves the extremely impure ends of reaction. No, our conception of the role of art is too high to refuse it an influence on the fate of society. We believe that the supreme task of art in our epoch is to take part actively and consciously in the preparation of the revolution.
>
> (Breton et al. 1968: 485)

The manifesto maintained that the artist was not to imitate the model of socialist realism (see the discussion of socialist realist monuments in Chapter 3, pp. 81–2). For the revolutionaries Trotsky, Rivera and Breton, 'the artist cannot serve the struggle for freedom unless he *subjectively* assimilates its social content, unless he feels in his very nerves its meaning and drama and freely seeks to give his own inner world incarnation in his art' (Breton et al. 1968: 485; emphasis added). There is the by now familiar ring of 'art for art's sake' being part of a bourgeois conspiracy. Rivera would have found little solace in Roger Fry's creed: 'Art, then, is an expression and a stimulus of this imaginative life, which is separated from actual life by the absence of responsive action' (Fry 1993 [1961]: 26). Rivera would have found more consolation, perhaps, in Greenberg's Marxist-inspired writing of the 1930s. However, an engagement with the social, for the Mexicans, did not necessarily result in the kitsch, in the sense of bad taste, that Greenberg was anxious to avoid. In 'Avant-Garde and Kitsch', the issue for Greenberg was how easily art with 'content' could become a tool of propaganda. He advocated a complete withdrawal from the world to save art from the kitsch culture of capitalist economics, which he characterised as one of 'vicarious experience and faked sensation' (1985: 25). It is perhaps worth noting how far the parameters of the language of purism have changed: 'vicarious experience and faked sensation', as we will see, seem to be exactly the point in much of the late twentieth- and twenty-first century arts culture.

To recap, these debates were part of the intellectual climate for many artists who subsequently changed their art practice from one of social engagement to one of apparent social disengagement within, during and after the Second World War. The revolutionary potential seen in the unconscious and irrational realism of surrealism and the Mexican muralists was marginalised, leaving Jackson Pollock's work dependent on the surrealist practice of automatism and mural-painting scale. His early realist works, such as *Cody Wyoming* (1934–8), are not considered anything other than a rehearsal for his mature signature-style work. During the 1930s Pollock worked on several small-scale paintings, such as *Cody Wyoming* and *Going West* (1934–5), that celebrated a pioneer past and a mythic sense of frontier (see, in particular, Celeste-Adams 1986).

These kinds of paintings can also be seen as a major tendency in 1930s art, part of a strategy of renewal and affirmation in a period of national self-doubt. The broadly representational works in a form of baroque realism were produced under the influence of the regionalist painter Thomas Hart Benton (1889–1975). Pollock's work in the 1930s with David Siqueiros's workshop in New York is represented as an aberrant, politically naive moment during the Depression. However, the system of drip painting Pollock eventually used appeared in 1942 and was used consistently from late 1946, and stems from this earlier Mexican influence and is perhaps also influenced by Max Ernst, who worked in a spontaneous mode in the early 1940s. Siqueiros experimented with new industrial paints called nitrocellulose, with which he created free-form images, earning himself the nickname 'El Duco', after the paint brand name. Pollock was also influenced by his experiences of scenery backdrop painting techniques in theatre and by Native American sand painting, the point being that his work was not the product of an intuitive, precognitive act but was rooted firmly in wider cultural practices.

The revolutionary alliance of surrealism and Marxist politics is not without its basic contradictions, and it was no guarantee of an artistic high ground. There was a basic discrepancy between the revolutionary tenets of Marxism and surrealism. Breton was aware that the surrealist view of the unconscious as a means of tapping the artist's individual centre of creativity collided with the Marxist, particularly the Trotskyite, use of art as a political weapon. Reconciliation between the polarised positions of Marxism and modernism seems unlikely.

A further rejection: early modern American art

The term 'abstract expressionist' came into common usage in 1946, with additional terms like 'action painting' (1952) or 'American-type painting' or just the 'New York School'. Conventionally, American abstract expressionism has its roots in European modernism through its use of the language of the sublime, the transcendental and the revelatory. However, American art had its own artistic abstract precedence in the work of the nineteenth-century American symbolist Albert Pinkham Ryder. Ryder's works have deteriorated badly but we can get some sense of the process at play in the works of Frederic Fairchild Sherman, who says of Ryder's seascapes:

> [O]bviously unreal in themselves, they embody the very reality of the tragedy of the sea, and by appealing to the *imagination* rather than the *intellect* release subconscious presentiments of indescribable verisimilitude that are no more truthful mental images of remembered scenes than the paintings themselves are faithful transcripts of nature.
> (Sherman 1963: 82; emphasis added)

Ryder is an important reference point. He was considered important enough to be included in the *Armory Show* of 1913. Moreover, paintings such as Ryder's *Flying Dutchman* (see Figure 6.8) certainly influenced Pollock, who claimed in 1944 that Ryder was the only American 'master' who interested him. According to Naifeh and Whitesmith, Pollock's early tutor and mentor Thomas Hart Benton, the American scene and regional painter, introduced an 'incompetent' Pollock to the work of Ryder, maintaining that Ryder was an example of someone who 'couldn't draw the boat as finely as contemporaries like Winslow Homer, but could capture in his turbulent brush strokes its pitch and roll on a roiling sea' (Naifeh and Whitesmith 1989: 184). Ryder said of his own work: 'the artist should fear to become the slave to detail. He should strive to express his thoughts and not the surface of it. What avails a storm-cloud accurate in form and detail if the storm is not therein?' (Ryder, quoted in Baur 1976: 100). It is important to note that Ryder's ideas were highly conditioned by eighteenth- and nineteenth-century Romanticism; and, crucially, it was this aspect of Ryder's work that the young Pollock assimilated. Of course, Pollock's historicism can be misleading, particularly when it implies that art can be ahead of its time.

However, the influence of Ryder's thinking and work finds a resonance in Pollock's and other artists' work, suggesting an older and distinctly American pedigree for abstract expressionism. However, conventionally modern American art *appears* to have started

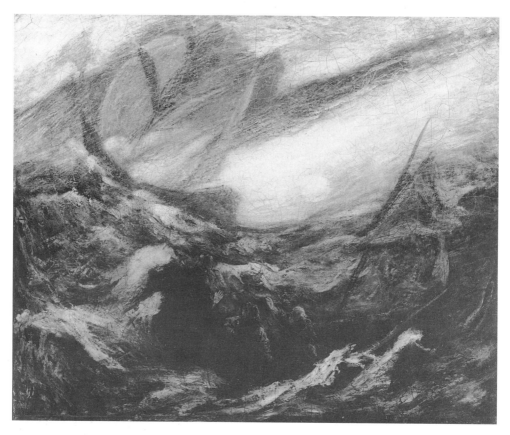

Figure 6.8 Albert Pinkham Ryder, *Flying Dutchman*, c.1887. Courtesy of the Smithsonian American Art Museum, Gift of John Gellatly. The similarities in working practices between abstract expressionism and Ryder can be read out of the painter's own words; 'I threw my brushes aside; they were too small for the work in hand. I squeezed out big chunks of pure moist color and taking my palette knife, I laid on blue, green, white and brown in great sweeping strokes' (Pinkham Ryder 2003: 63). It is noteworthy that the scale of Ryder's work is small compared with Pollock's major works.

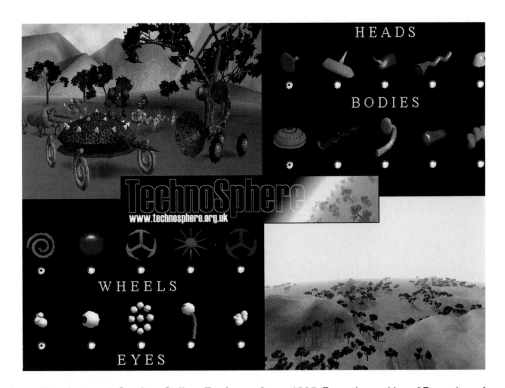

Plate XVIII   Jane Prophet and Gordon Selley *Technosphere* **1995** From the realtime 3D version of *TechnoSphere*. Created in 1995 by Jane Prophet and Gordon Selley, the planet TechnoSphere is a cyber terrain with its own digital ecology. Internet users are able to create creatures to inhabit Technosphere but they have no control over the fate of their creations. Over one million artificial creatures have 'lived' and 'died' in TechnoSphere since its launch. Courtesy of Jane Prophet.

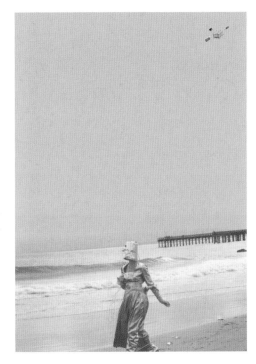

Plate XIX   Suzanne Treister *No Other Symptoms: Time Travelling with Rosalind Brodsky* **1995** Treister has worked on a series of on-line projects, perhaps the best known being *Time Travelling with Rosalind Brodsky*, which she has been developing since 1995. Rosalind Brodsky is in Treister's phrase 'a delusional time-traveller' who believes that she is working in the time-travel industry and has been erroneously sent back into the twentieth century. In the on-line reality constructed by Treister, Brodsky fantasises her vivid encounters in history. Courtesy of the artist.

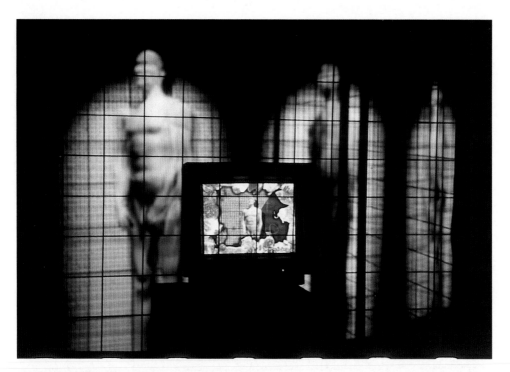

Plate XX   Keith Piper *Robot Bodies* 1998 Installation at Bluecoat Gallery, Liverpool. An interactive installation that draws a direct analogy between the robot and racial identity. The artist has explained that '[b]oth are visibly "others" and as such are assigned particular roles within the cultural and economic order ... they can be assigned grueling tasks in hostile and alien environments' (Piper, 2001). Courtesy of the Bluecoat Arts Centre and FACT. © Foundation for Art and Creative Technology.

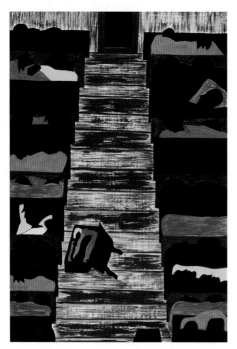

Plate XXI   Jacob Lawrence *The Trains were Crowded with Migrants* 1940–1 Part of the Migration Series (Panel 6), Lawrence's narrative pictures tell the story of African American people's post-slavery migration to the North. The work continues the themes of earlier series of works – Toussaint L'Ouverture (1937–8), Frederick Douglass (1938–9) and the Harriet Tubman series (1939–40) – that celebrate the heroes and heroines of abolition and the proto-Civil Rights Movement. © ARS, NY and DACS, London 2004. Digital image © 2003 The Museum of Modern Art, New York/Photo Scala, Florence. Gift of Mrs David M. Levy. 28.1942.3. Tempera on gesso on composition board, 45.7 cm × 30.5 cm.

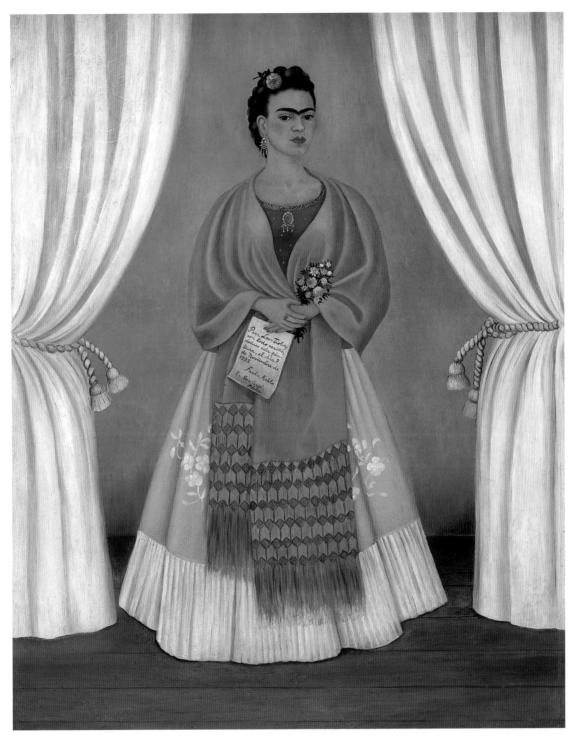

Plate XXII Frida Kahlo *Self-Portrait Dedicated to Leon Trotsky* 1937 In this work structured around a theatrical setting, Kahlo depicts herself wearing traditional Mexican clothes, around her shoulders the *rebzo*, a Mexican shawl. The scroll she holds is inscribed with a dedication to Leon Trotsky, the exiled Russian political leader. National Museum of Women in the Arts, Washington DC. Gift of the Honorable Clare Boothe Luce. © 2004 Banco de México Diego Rivera and Frida Kahlo Museums Trust. Oil on masonite, 76 × 61 cm.

Plate XXIII   Mark Rothko *Light Red Over Black* 1957 Rothko's paintings of layers of virtually translucent colour have been related to landscape and even entombment, however they bear no recognisable equivalence to things in the world beyond simplified shapes and are probably best read through the effects of layers of saturated colours of floating rectangles. © 1998 Kate Rothko Prizel & Christopher Rothko/DACS 2004. Photograph © Tate, London 2003.

Plate XXIV   Nancy Spero *Helicopters And Victims* 1967 Initially worked on drawing paper, the later works in the series were a collage of archival quality paper placed on top of Japanese rice paper which created a fragility at counterpoint to the brutality of the images. Courtesy of the artist. Gouache and ink on paper, 91.4 × 61 cm.

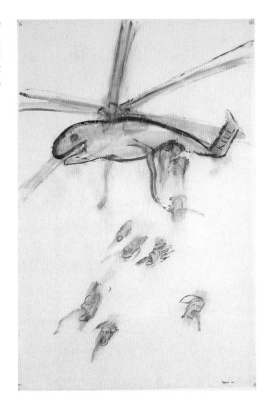

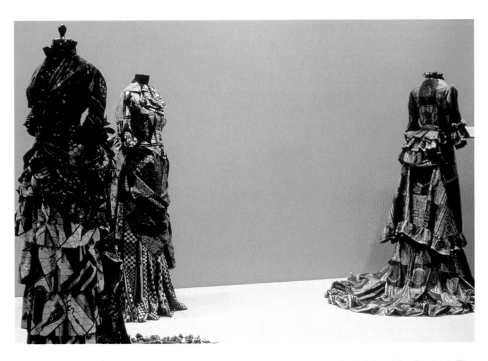

Plate XXV   Yinka Shonibare *How Does a Girl Like You, Get to Be a Girl Like You?* 1995 The mannequins in Shonibare's fashion show are dressed in ethnic cloth the origins of which in the cultural toing and froing between uneven powers has become obscured. Courtesy of the artist and Stephen Friedman Gallery.

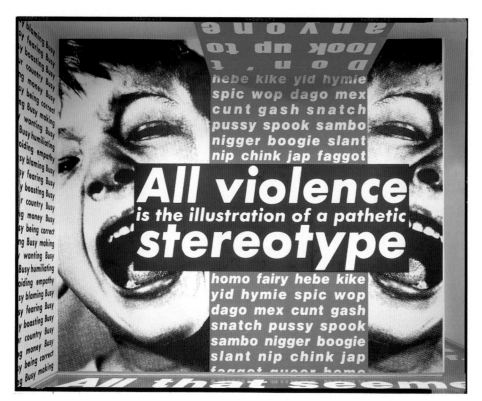

Plate XXVI   Barbara Kruger *Untitled (All Violence is the Illustration of a Pathetic Stereotype)*
1991 In this installation Kruger's audience is engulfed by the physicality of the art work. The floors, wall and ceiling are covered with images and text which mirror the colour and typography of tabloid newspapers. At the same time the viewer is confronted with the crude slang terms which contribute to the creation of stereotypes. Courtesy of the Mary Boone Gallery, New York.

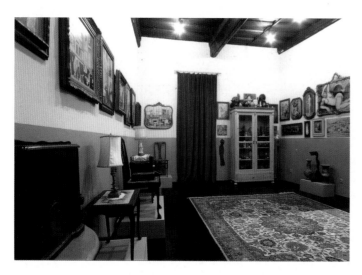

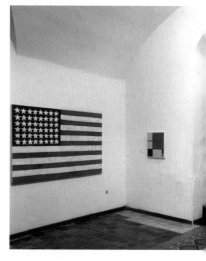

Plate XXVIII   Marina Grzinic (curator) *Fiction Reconstructed – The Last Futurist Show* **2001**
including Malevich's exhibition from 1915 and the New York *Armory Show* from 1913. In these reconstructed (in the absence of original works) the structures that supported notions of authenticity. Courtesy of Marina

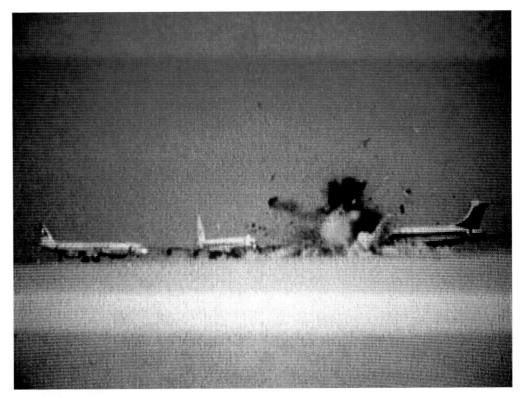

Plate XXVII Johan Grimonprez *Dial H-I-S-T-O-R-Y* 1995–7 Grimonprez's early video work often critiqued Western ethnocentrism. In works such as *Dial H-I-S-T-O-R-Y* however, he turned his attention to the shaping of contemporary reality through technology. Courtesy of Flatland Gallery, Utrecht.

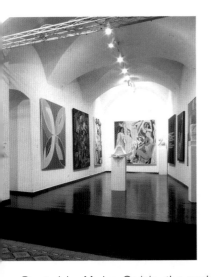
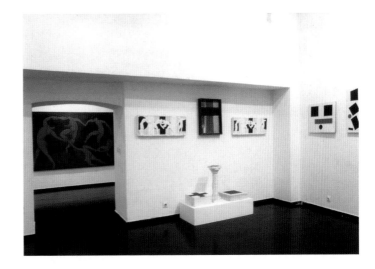

Curated by Marina Grzinic, the works consisted of distinct reconstructions of collections and exhibitions, works, the status of the authentic within avant-garde culture is questioned by forcing the viewer to contemplate Grzinic. Gallery Skuc, Ljubljana and Gallery for Contemporary Art, Celje.

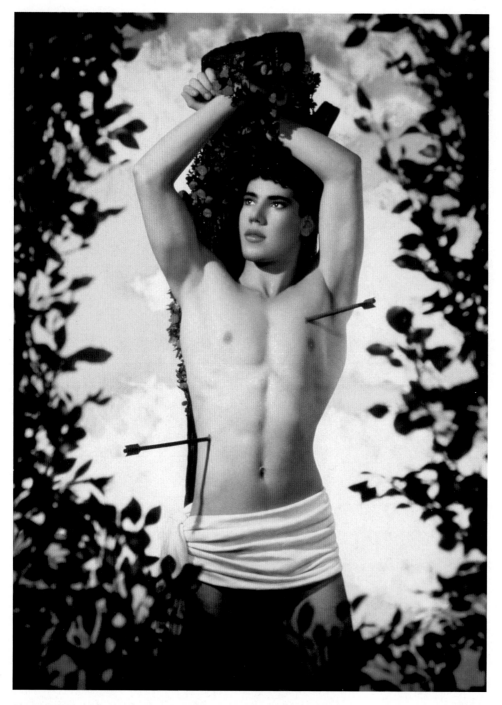

Plate XXIX   Pierre et Gilles *Saint Sebastian* **1987** Saint Sebastian, the unofficial patron saint of homosexuals, was a third-century martyr who was actually killed by being bludgeoned with a rock; however, artists generally depict the (unsuccessful) attempt to martyr him when Roman soldiers tied him to a tree and shot him with arrows. Courtesy Galerie Jérôme de Noirmont, Paris © Pierre et Gilles.

Kaprow, using the language of modernism and avant-garde culture, suggests that Pollock's heroic stand had been futile. What is important here is that the historic moment of abstract expressionism was brief, shifting swiftly from an adversarial culture to a sedimented modernism. Even before Pollock's death, as we saw at the beginning of this chapter, Rauschenberg had erased de Kooning's drawing and Pollock's most significant contributions, as identified by Greenberg, had already been made. Greenbergian formalism evolved to promote the younger abstractionists (colour-field painters) Morris Louis, Kenneth Noland and Jules Olitski. Ironically, by the early 1960s the work of the earlier generation of abstract painters gained institutional acceptance, becoming an orthodox climax to the story of modern art.

Postmodernism and abstract expressionism

Adolph Gottlieb predicted that abstract expressionism would reign for a thousand years (Rodman 1961: 87) and, given that the language of abstract expressionism was imbued with transcendentalism and universalism, there seemed little reason to doubt this. Subsequent parodies and pastiches of abstract expressionist works have not necessarily undermined the strength of the modernist project. In 1997 Vik Muniz produced *Action Photo (After Hans Namuth)*, one in a series of cibachrome photographs of soft toffee dripped to represent the image of Pollock throwing paint in the Hans Namuth film and photographs from the 1950s. Muniz parodies the painter's technique by simulating his gestures, dripping chocolate syrup on to paper and then photographing the result. For Muniz this is a subversively political act which calls into question the traditional readings of Pollock and, by extension, of other abstract works. Muniz's *Action Photo* simultaneously critiques all of modernism's sacred cows: like Rauschenberg's erasure of the de Kooning drawing, it is both homage and reproach, but, like Sherrie Levine's appropriation of Edward Weston, it uses a photographic process. The photograph, mechanically reproducible, is a challenge to the authentic act of painting. The substitution of toffee for paint is an ironic reference to both the preciosity of paint and the act of painting itself.

The nature of creativity and the status of abstraction in modern art and modernism, particularly its American manifestation, have become contested arenas. Elitism is the usual charge against works represented as white, male and middle class. This chapter's emphasis on men, at the expense of women, is in part a reflection of abstract expressionism's machismo. There were influential women artists and theoreticians such as Elaine de Kooning and Lee Krasner, but their status as artists' wives has militated against their inclusion in the pantheon of great artists. For instance, Krasner's work was widely regarded as 'domesticated Pollock' – a less authentic and tamer mode of self-expression. Feminist critiques of abstract expressionism, like Muniz's irreverent gesture in toffee, have tended to critique by mocking the gestures of action painting and the primacy given to paint. Therefore, like Shikego Kubota (as we will see in Chapter 8), many women artists turned to performance art or to new technologies as a way out of the perceived gender bias of abstract expressionism.

The avant-garde's failure to resist institutionalisation and its easy co-option into politics, ironically through a process of depoliticisation, have undermined the original radicalism of the artistic enterprise. Postmodernism has, however, opened up the terrain, thus allowing a reappraisal. Richard Pousette-Dart, once a casualty of the narrow ranks of abstract expressionist artists deemed worthwhile, has been one beneficiary of the recuperative effects of postmodern re-evaluations. In part, his earlier 'dismissal' was due to the rejection of notions of the spiritual in a secular world. Pousette-Dart's 'search for the sacred' had seemed anachronistic at best. Many abstract expressionists, however, were influenced by notions of magic and ritual, and by modern-man discourse through the anthropological works of writers like Margaret Mead and Ruth Benedict. More recently, an increasing emphasis on the psychological and social changes brought about by the Second World War has also informed writing on the period. As we saw in Chapter 3, a move towards a kind of modern spirituality has been a preoccupation of many artists, from the Romantics to the expressionists, and even those involved in the machine aesthetic saw the endeavour as more than the glorification of speed and technology. Pousette-Dart and others working in post-war art believed that spirituality could offer more than a means of merely personal redemption:

> For Pousette-Dart the implicit need for healing and regeneration is . . . historical as well as personal; the quest for the sacred is also characteristic of war culture in modern times, and that culture undoubtedly had a catalytic effect on the search for respiritualization manifested in the work of Pousette-Dart and others.
>
> (Polcari 1997: 62)

For Pousette-Dart this meant a 'return' to the primitive, which was accessed through Jungian notions of archetypes and the unconscious (see Plate X). Believing his work to be transcendental, Pousette-Dart uses symbolic forms invoking ritual as a way in to a spiritual world. Drawing heavily on a knowledge of Native American symbolism, totemic and shamanistic, of medieval stained glass and imagined Gothic emblems, Pousette-Dart 'imagined' a world of transformation and regeneration through the creative act. Pousette-Dart reworked the modernist idea of nature, which was 'a mystical identification with the soil as cosmic force' (Polcari 1997: 67).

Ben Shahn and the *Lucky Dragon*

> It is impossible to contemplate the Bomb. At the Down Town Galleries one can.
>
> (O'Doherty 1961: 40)

Another artist to be recovered from the narrow canon of modernist art history is Ben Shahn. Unlike the example of Pousette-Dart, however, we want to make a different point about exclusions by returning to the artists who worked during the 1930s to look at one post-war career of the quintessential New Dealer. During the late 1940s Shahn featured in *Look* magazine's poll, had been represented in 'Advancing American Art' and was, according to Michael Kimmelman, 'the most popular artist in America in the 1950s' (Kimmelman 1998: E 35). In reviewing the 1998 exhibition *Common Man: Mythic Vision. The Paintings of Ben Shahn* at the Jewish Museum in New York, Kimmelman wrote:

I emphasise his popularity because we easily forget how popular Shahn was. With the Pollock and Rothko retrospectives now at the Modern and Whitney, the Shahn exhibition is a useful reminder that it was he more than they who dominated the country's public consciousness at mid-century.

(Kimmelman 1998: E 35)

Orthodox modernists have dismissed Shahn as a 1930s social realist with unreconstructed illustrative and narrative tendencies. It is often assumed that artists who had been successful in the 1930s either turned towards abstraction or ceased to have a career after the war.

Ben Shahn, although usually 'relegated' to the role of political artist, continued working in the 1950s and 1960s on the themes of social injustice characteristic of his earlier work. Where Shahn is acknowledged as a 'truly modern' post-war artist, it is usually because art historians perceive a shift away from the social to a more 'personal' vision. In fact Shahn's greatest institutional successes came not in the 1930s but in the 1940s and 1950s, with major 'one-man' shows at MoMA in 1947 and critical acclaim at the Venice Biennale in 1954. His retrospective at MoMA included his political posters designed for labour organisations and peace programmes. Shahn's inclusion at MoMA was not without its moments of tension. His Congress of Industrial Organisation – Political Action Committee (CIO–PAC) posters were the subject of controversy at MoMA and at the Venice Biennale, but were shown nonetheless, although with access severely restricted. 'Retrogressive' realism was still his preferred working method and, heretically for modernist critics, his works had often first appeared as illustrations in popular magazines and were derived from photographs (he had been a photographer with the Farm Security Administration (FSA) in the 1930s).

During the late 1950s and early 1960s Shahn produced the *Lucky Dragon* series, consisting of twenty-six paintings. The *Lucky Dragon* series was based on an incident involving the exposure of a Japanese fishing crew to radiation. On 1 March 1954 the US detonated its first thermonuclear bomb at Bikini Atoll in the South Pacific. The crew of the *Lucky Dragon* (*No. 5 Fukuryu Maru*) were unwittingly exposed to the testing, Kuboyama, the radio operator, died as a result, and the Japanese fishing industry was brought to a halt. The political fallout was so great that Secretary of State John Foster Dulles, who negotiated the final Peace Treaty with Japan in 1951, worried that it might 'rip apart the essential elements of American national security policy'. He hypothesised that America and her allies would 'conclude that alliances and atomic weapons were not complementary instruments for the preservation of national security and world peace' (Dingman 1990: 187). The negative international response to the testing and the sudden realisation of the destructive potential of the H-Bomb (the *New York Times* ran front-page articles showing diagrammatically what would happen should Manhattan be the epicentre of a blast) contributed to the general despair. The work of Ralph Lapp, an atomic physicist sent to Japan to monitor the condition of the fishermen, was at least in part responsible for the peace movements of the 1960s and 'laid the foundations for the Nuclear Test Ban Treaty of 1963' (Dingman 1990: 207).

Shahn's response to this crisis utilises the formal language of modernism – loose brushwork – and combines it with social commentary in an accessible illustrative style. Shahn was not alone in questioning abstract expressionism's ability to respond to the modern world in all its complexity – asking must 'all our pity and anger be reduced to a few tastefully arranged straight lines?' (Shahn, *New York Times*, January 1953).

Shahn's work originally appeared in *Harper's Magazine* in 1957 and 1958, as illustrations to Lapp's *Lucky Dragon* articles and then in Richard Hudson's book *Kuboyama and the Saga of the Lucky Dragon*. Shahn's support of the plight of the Japanese fishermen, who saw themselves as victims, for the second time, of American nuclear bombing, came at an anxious time in both art and world politics. With American political involvement in Indo-China leading to the Vietnam War, the Russians launched their first Sputnik satellite in 1957, with consequent outbreaks of patriotic fervour. Reaction to Shahn's work is therefore instructive. Late in 1961, the Down Town Gallery in New York showed the *Lucky Dragon* series. The exhibition attracted record attendances – more than 7,000 visitors in the first two weeks, setting an attendance record at the gallery. Reviews were outstandingly positive, although Jack Kroll, writing in the influential *Art News* in 1961, argued that Shahn had illustrated the victims to no real effect, noting the cartoon-like presence of the dragon, used 'to symbolise the malignity of the holocaust'. Kroll sensed that the 'real tragedy of these paintings is that something has gone, not out of Shahn, but out of us and our time. These people are innocent in a way for which we have as yet found no plastic symbology' (Shahn, *New York Times*, January 1953).

There are echoes here of earlier comments by Rothko, who had said: 'it was with the utmost reluctance that I found the [human] figure could not serve my purposes . . . but a time came when none of us could use the figure without mutilating it' (quoted by Dore Ashton, *New York Times*, 31 October 1958). Shahn, in his lecture series *The Shape of Content* given at Harvard University in 1957, did not separate content from form – for him they were inseparable. Of Clive Bell's mantra 'the representative element in a work of art may or may not be harmful, but it is always irrelevant', Shahn retorted that it was 'a credo, that might well have been erased by time, but which instead has grown to almost tidal proportions and which constitutes the Procrustean bed into which all art must either be stretched or shrunk' (Shahn 1957: 26). For Shahn, and many like him, abstraction inadequately met the needs of the age but was still a standard by which 'other' art was measured. Contrary to the kind of formalist readings that Greenberg provided, it was possible to read into abstract art the unstable 'spirit of the age'. For instance, the art historian Henry McBride read Pollock's drip paintings in terms of their relationship to war, stating that 'the effect it makes is that of a flat, war shattered city, possibly Hiroshima, as seen from a great height in moonlight' (quoted in Kroll 1961: 20). It is to be doubted that this metaphorical reading of Pollock's work was more than speculative, but it does demonstrate just how broad the response to postwar anxieties was and, moreover, how open to interpretation abstract art could be.

The 'reemergence' of realism and protest art: a resurgent avant-garde

Although formalist theories separated aesthetics from traditional 'realist' practices, placing aesthetics within the abstract realm, there was, as we have seen, in the example of Shahn a considerable continuity of realist, political art from the 1940s to the 1960s.

The nascent conflicts rumbling in Indo-China in what was to become the Vietnam War resulted in a more widespread recovery of differing forms of realism for artists previously committed to abstraction, pop and conceptual art. A culture of opposition to aspects of US culture had existed post-war, whether that was to be found in abstract expressionist's withdrawal from the world or in the continuing commitment to uncovering social inequalities that still motivated many artists usually designated Depression or New Deal artists. The war in Vietnam, however, compelled many artists to rework their art to accommodate overt forms of political commentary. For instance, Jasper Johns, whose work had the American flag as a central motif, produced a lithograph titled *Moratorium* in 1969. The painting of the American flag, with black stripes on top of an orange and green field, contained one white bullet hole. The arrangement of colours produces a red, white and blue after-image. Faith Ringgold also used the American flag to call the US government to account in the 1960s. In works such as *God Bless America* (1964), *The Flag is Bleeding* (1967) and *Flag for the Moon: die nigger* (1967–9) Ringgold obscures symbols and language, making it hard to decipher meaning, and in so doing draws attention to the covert power relations that masquerade as democracy. Other artists used printmaking to make visible acts of war, as in the Uruguayan printmaker Antonio Frasconi's *Viet Nam!* (1967), a book-object woodcut measuring 29 inches × 23 inches, that combines multiple prints of bombers releasing their cargo over heavily worked graphite areas representing the fields of Vietnam. Nancy Spero's 1967 series of fragile paintings on rice paper in the *War Series* (see Plate XXIV) grew out of apprehension about the atomic bomb and here the Vietnam War.

It is worth noting that the radicalism of the 1960s has often been used as a pinnacle in a series of culmination points in history; this usually sustains a modernist myth of breakthroughs and regressions. Such a strategy can easily absorb counter-culture works in order to prove the rule of the established canon of art and do nothing to undermine its presumptions. Although the art of the 1930s is severed from the modernism of the 1950s (physically separated in some galleries even today), inclusion can also be problematic. Works included from the edges of modernism that challenge the established canon, such as Shahn's or Lawrence's, always run the risk of being displayed in a way that does nothing to contradict the dominant culture. However, not withstanding the high-profile activities of the AWC's and the Guerrilla Art Action Group's (GAAA) interventions into museum spaces, artists unwilling to work in abstraction continued their working practices from the 1930s into the 1960s and in some cases beyond. For instance, Jacob Lawrence, whose work we encountered earlier (p. 175), pursued a figurative practice into the late twentieth century. He made use of sequential narratives similar to cartoons, as well as emphasising the *historical* in art, familiar strategies during the 1930s and in popular culture. As with many other artists, the end of the 1930s did not significantly alter his practice, as storytelling was a crucial element for him that formalist abstraction did not accommodate. In order to tell the historical narratives of the African American diaspora and black community aspirations, Lawrence's works often contain explanatory text in their titles, a strategy, as we saw, widely used during the 1930s. Lawrence preferred to take from modernism what he regarded as appropriate: formal devices rooted in cubism and expressionism. He used such devices as a vehicle with which to communicate his subjects to a contemporary audience. Although he was clearly concerned with formal values in art, formalism as such was not adequate for Lawrence's purpose; in fact for him formalism remained something to be resisted or subverted through a continuing use of narrative. Moreover, working in hybrid forms, Lawrence could integrate folk and African motifs into high art. Lawrence's racially conscious art rejected Greenberg's insistence that story-telling and narrative painting 'had become nothing more than ghosts and "stooges" of literature' (Greenberg 1990: 63).

Any sense that the radicalism of the 1960s brought about absolute equity between social groups and abstraction and realism needs to be tempered by the knowledge of an exhibition which took place at the Whitney Museum of American Art in 1971. In response to protest by the Black Emergency Cultural Coalition about the lack of exhibitions of black artists the Whitney organised a survey exhibition: *Contemporary Black Artists in America*. It is the presentation of realism and abstraction that concerns us here. Abstraction's claim to universal values was used as a curatorial device and realism was relegated to a small gallery. In response to the aesthetic apartheid several artists withdrew from the exhibition. Although currently the ahistoric exhibition with its thematic schema (see Chapter 7) has gone some way to ameliorating a heavily circumscribed history, the presentation of social-realist art and abstract expressionism is still problematic.

To sum up, the division between abstraction and realism has been hotly contested and advocacy for both positions has been ideologically motivated. A history intent on high points, breakthroughs and culminations has left us with a history that has separated aesthetics from the art of the 1930s and by the same token separated politics from the art of the 1950s. As we have seen, the history is less tidy than the binary opposition would suggest. Although there have been productive artistic clashes between the two polarised positions, we should be alert to the continuities between artists' politics and practices that this period of extremes produced.

The artist and the museum: muse or nemesis?

> I want art that does something more than sit on its ass in a museum.
>
> (Claus Oldenberg, in Harrison and Wood 2003: 744)

In 1938, at the fourth international surrealist exhibition, held at the Galérie Beaux-Arts in Paris, 1,200 dusty burlap coal bags stuffed with newspapers were suspended from the ceiling.[1] The gallery was dark, and what light there was came from glowing braziers. Torchlight was required to search out and view the assorted surrealist art works after travelling through a hallway lined with sixteen female mannequins (all dressed by different surrealist artists, only one of whom was female), clothed in ways designed to reveal suppressed fetishes (see Figure 7.1). Formally titled *Le Baillon vert à bouche de pensée*, a play on the fact that '*pensée*' means both 'purple flower' and 'thought', André Masson's *Masson mannéquin* was displayed with other models about 2 metres apart in a narrow corridor, forcing the exhibition visitor into close physical proximity with it. As well as a black velvet band covering the mouth and a birdcage enclosure over the head, Masson's mannequin's genitalia were covered with a G-string made up of a mirror surrounded by tiger's eyes, which had the effect of forcing viewers to contemplate their own gaze. Man Ray showed his mannequin with large tears running down her face and soap bubbles foaming out of the hair. Here, dismembered dolls, puppets and mannequins served as objects of transference, objects of subliminal motivations and desires.

The installation revelled in obscurantism, in 'not seeing' (*cherchez la femme*, closed eyes and blindness are familiar leitmotifs of surrealism). The treatment of the female muse, however, is less important for our purposes in this chapter than is the surrealists' pleasure in displays that destabilised conventions of creativity, production and display. In many senses, the surrealist display stands as a metaphor for the paradoxes and contradictions that surround the practices of display in the twentieth and twenty-first centuries.

The project of questioning the 'art' object's relationship to the gallery centred around several assumptions: first, that there is something worth displaying, second, that there is a specific context for display and, third, that the 'installation' disorients expectations of the display, particularly by its acknowledgement that display can also be an act of

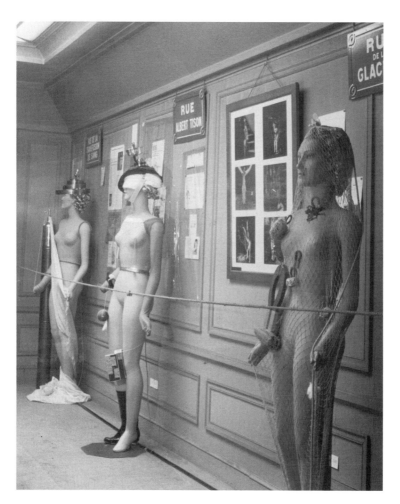

Figure 7.1 *Exposition Surréaliste,* **Paris, 1938.** Photograph by Josef Breitenbach. Post-humous reproduction from original glass negative. © The Josef Breitenbach Trust, New York. Courtesy of the Joseph Breitenbach Archive, Center for Creative Photography, The University of Arizona. The corridor of mannequins led to the installation *1200 Coal Sacks* on the ceiling. It operated at the level of the surrealist trope of *déreglement*; that is, disorientation by reversing expectations and norms as well as bringing the darkened ceiling perilously close to the visitor's head. The floor was covered with a layer of sand and dead leaves as part of the exhibition's aspirations to make viewing of art works an uncomfortable, rather than contemplative, experience.

concealment. The surrealists' strategy of deracinating bags of coal and shop fittings high-lighted the myth that masks art's autonomy, exposing art as merely a designated cultural category, in this case chosen by the artists. Art, it seemed, was not a neutral category of identifiable quality – the preserve of disinterested scholarship and curatorial practices. The surrealist intervention, however, while iconoclastic on one level, was ultimately validated by the weight of institutional apparatus – the Galérie Beaux-Arts was a presti-gious venue. The surrealist exhibition was an ambiguous gesture that at once laid bare and yet was complicit in the fiction of the art gallery and its romance with the artist.

The move from the private collections of the eighteenth century to the public spaces of museums and galleries in the nineteenth century was not a seamless transition. It can be seen as part of a hegemonic process of regulation in which the 'improving' societies were voluntarily attended by the complicit labouring classes. Universal entry to museums, initially conceived of as a possible threat to public order through the pernicious over-indulgence of the masses, was quickly, through the manifest visible order and restraint of display, co-opted into the orthodoxies of the state apparatus. On 22 February 1856 the *Guardian* reported on a parliamentary debate on Sunday opening (to take place after morning service) at the British Museum and the National Gallery, observing that

> the working classes themselves considered that their admission to these institutions would improve their social condition, tend to draw them away from more debasing and demoralising pursuits, and would not in any way interfere with [the] religious rites or devotional exercises.
>
> (Anonymous 2003: 7)

Moreover, the writer surmised that given entry into the gallery and museum away from the courts, alleys and public houses of the metropolis the working classes would 'in the end have their moral and social condition improved, and be led to attend also upon a place of worship' (Anonymous 2003: 7). The improving aspects of both devotional activities are made explicit.[4]

Entry to the sanctified spaces of the secularised temples, however, was a dubious privilege – the experience of works of art was framed within high-Victorian discourses of class and gender. The workers' societies tutored appropriate forms of behaviour for entry to the galleries, to both see and become, through self-regulation, part of the spectacle, a more consciously regulated process than that of Bourdieu's 'habitus'. An unholy alliance of education, discipline and art was formulated at the formation of the National Gallery in 1824 (a model disseminated throughout the world) that was in part a regulatory practice by which the productive working-class visitor was socialised into Victorian notions of citizenship. Within this context what was important was not what was exhibited so much as what the gallery represented and the mechanisms by which social control and regulation were imposed. The linking of education programmes to the art gallery is still very much part of the remit of many galleries, but its function now is, arguably, largely subordinate to the aesthetics of display, although citizenship and culture are regularly heard of in each other's company. The language of regulation is less overt currently than it was in the nineteenth century, but the acquisition of taste and cultural refinement is still the underlying reason for museum-visiting.

The etymological roots of 'museum' are derived from the Hellenistic term for a 'place of the Muses', nine sister goddesses personifying such cultural forms as music, astronomy, dance and so on. Museums were, from their inception, as much about memory[5] and its power to inspire as they were about learning. However, museums were often found to have an alienating effect on 'the masses', in part because the physical geography of the Victorian gallery celebrated nineteenth-century private capitalism. Victorian collections were usually housed in purpose-built temples such as the Walker Art Gallery in Liverpool, the Art Institute of Chicago and the Art Gallery of New South Wales in Sydney, all classical, temple-fronted buildings with classical porticos and rotundas, and all monumental in scale. Many museums are situated with a cluster of other enlighten-ment buildings, the library and law courts, evincing civic pride and an association with reason and order. Most civic buildings (except the notably Gothic Houses of Parliament and many town halls) incorporate facsimiles of the Parthenon frieze, decorative caryatids and classical columns as signifiers of power, order and restraint. The awed Victorian visitor needed to be initiated into the spaces of the gallery.

Colin Trodd identifies the present National Gallery building at its inception (1853) as the articulated space of two possible discourses, one of connoisseurship and the other of hygiene. The gallery, he argues, acts as the site of a retreat from the urban, a sanctuary and a place of contemplation. But, more insidiously, the hallowed space of the National Gallery is one in which the working-class body, 'filthy' and with a 'most disagreeable smell', could be regulated into another social order. Within nineteenth-century discourses there was a binary opposition between the social world rudely represented by the working-class body and the cultural world entered via the aesthetic experience. For many writers on art, the 'aesthetic' signified the highest form of consciousness, its very uselessness enabling it to transcend mere corporeal existence. Paraphrasing the oratory of the mid-nineteenth century, Trodd states:

> From the ethereal enchantment of empyrean air to the epic excrete of 'foreign' bodies, we witness the way in which the city enters the language of cultural discourse and the space of the cultural institution via the collective form of the crowd.
>
> (Trodd 1994: 43)

This is an important point. Although the public gallery was nearly always an urban phenomenon, it was regarded as an elevated space which existed in a realm beyond that of industrialisation. So, paradoxically, galleries and museums came to conceal what they represented – namely, the power structures embedded in nineteenth-century patriarchal and colonial values and discourses of class.

Foucault's influential works from the early 1960s onwards, *Madness and Civilisation* (first published in English in 1964), *The Archaeology of Knowledge* (1969), and *Discipline and Punish: the birth of the prison* (1977), inform much postmodern museum discourse. His contribution to modern theory has been to use historical enquiry, what he called the 'archaeology of knowledge' to discover under what conditions and discontinuities categories of 'deviancy' such as homosexuality, criminality or insanity are produced. His explorations of the incarceration of *categories* of people designated 'insane' and 'criminal' have been utilised by cultural theorists and artists to uncover how meaning is formed and sustained within institutional practices. The Tate Gallery at Millbank, London, now Tate Britain, for instance, was built in 1893, on the site of a prison, Millbank Penitentiary. Contemporary accounts in diaries, newspapers and the like were quick to point out the 'improving' link between the two.

The replacement of one house of correction by another form of correction, the morally improving art gallery, is a Foucauldian gift. Enlightenment following punish-ment and the elimination of crime through beauty and cultural refinement, as indicated above, were well-established tropes of nineteenth-century thought. Moreover, the ordering of narratives and the regulatory periodisation of history offered a kind of systematic rationale that the enlightened Victorian felt would contribute the same prin-ciples to the disorderly lower classes. Foucault's method, however, if unimaginatively applied, does sound rather like conspiracy theory or, paradoxically, given Foucault's view of history, an attempt to correct the injustices of the past.

Nevertheless, Foucault's archaeology of epistemes – that is to say, the excavation of layers of meaning which constitute knowledge (*espisteme*) – and the adoption of the idea of discourses (practices) have opened up the museological field. His methodological inquiry into the structure of knowledge and its relation to power, particularly the institutions of state power, has proved a fruitful area for the museologist. It is to be doubted that all of his criticisms of the Enlightenment, of which the museum is a symbol, can be sustained. However, by focusing on society's exclusions, most notably the mad, the criminal and the sick, he maintained that it is possible to find out what counted as truth and what did not. Foucault's contribution to museology, therefore, is to argue that there is no *history*; rather, there are legitimised and excluded *histories*. It is important to remember, however, that even legitimised histories share much common ground with excluded histories.

As we have seen, postmodern discourse around the social regulation of the body, in relation to the physical geography of the museum, and the questioning of the universality of white middle-class masculine values can reveal other histories. The recent accelerated growth in the numbers of culturally diverse galleries and museums is a visible manifestation of the will to re-present previously marginalised or suppressed histories – such as Aboriginal, Japanese American, African American and Plains' Indian. As we will see, the retrieval of these histories by contemporary museums and art galleries has been an important, but not always successful, act of redress.

The modern museum and the politics of a universal art

The oxymoronic Museum of Modern Art has tended largely to leave behind the classical exterior and silk-wallpapered interiors of the nineteenth-century gallery, abandoning decoration in favour of the tasteful 'white cube' developed initially in the US within the streamlined aesthetic of the 1920s and 1930s. 'New' galleries such as the Musée d'Orsay in Paris and the second generation of Tate Galleries in Liverpool and at Bankside in London and even in St Ives, Cornwall, are often part of urban or rural regeneration packages, sited in disused post-industrial buildings, obsolete railway stations, warehouses and power stations. The Tate Modern at Bankside in London, for instance, was a redundant power station designed by Gilbert Scott that was only operational for a short time. Its acquisition of a light box on the roof and a millennium bridge to connect the wealth of the city of London to the relative poverty of the south side of the River Thames is paradigmatic of the new museum's role as cultural social worker and financial regenerator. The benefits of the gentrification on local communities that follows an increase in 'cultural capital' is still being assessed.

The idiosyncratic nature of the buildings, however, is sanctioned *internally* by remarkable similarities of display across the institutions. The presentation of modern art in puritanically regulated white-walled rooms with strategically placed spotlights and humidity monitors is a familiar part of any visit to the modern art gallery across the globe. But how did this design of the spaces become a universal given, bypassing local and specific cultures to take its place on the international stage? In what ways does the design of the modern gallery space 'colour' our experience of its contents? What are the postmodern 'politics of display'?

Museums and art galleries are the spaces in which histories and the fixtures and fittings of meaning are installed. Once upon a time the permanent collection was the dominant sign of power, often representing a vanquished culture or the 'trophies of empire'. The museum validated the fiction of a linear historical narrative by ordering the art of a previous epoch into convenient periods and national styles. A postcolonial age, impatient with the past, has renamed former 'colonial institutes' to 'museum' forms more appropriate to a new age, as in the Tropenmuseum (formerly known as the Colonial Institute) in Amsterdam and the Museum of Mankind in London, which was recreated as the African Galleries in the British Museum, or has created galleries with titles that announce the problematics of inclusive histories, like the Yiribana Gallery at the Art Gallery of New South Wales in Australia.

The creation of new museums has been accompanied by a reconceptualisation of their role. During the nineteenth century museums played an active part in the formation of a unitary notion of shared values that would make up nationhood. If we return to Yinka Shonibare's wrapping of nineteenth-century statues on a gallery façade that purports to be Tate Britain we can see that the notion of a single sense of Britishness is undermined by reminders of the legacy of the past and the intercultural present. The National Museum of Australia in Canberra has adopted a model that sees its role as central to the formation of one nation but that recognises that there are competing and sometimes irreconcilable histories. Established in 1980, the new museum finally opened in 2001 after a difficult twenty-year gestation period. It chooses to cherish the right of indigenous peoples to self-determination, and therefore indigenous peoples speak for and display their own histories and cultural aspirations. The gallery attempts to negotiate histories and has no pretensions to political neutrality. In Australia,

> museum practice was shifting towards exploration of how different groups within the nation engage with each other through common arenas of social action such as land, politics and historiography. This approach emphasizes the way in which all social groups participate in shaping the nation-state, and places the onus on national museums to give 'voice' to many different perspectives and experiences within a connecting historical or cultural context, while still communicating something of the varying social locations from which these voices speak. This is the process of negotiation, rather than merely inclusion.
>
> (McIntyre and Wehner 2001: xvi)

This process of negotiation, however, can also be seen against an agenda of civic reform not dissimilar to the reforming agendas of the Victorians. It has been argued that 'inclusive' strategies most commonly witnessed in community-led initiatives in galleries and museums actually produce the idea of a culturally diverse community not just representations of it. Witcomb maintains that the processes of access and equity are also about accepting and understanding culturally diverse societies, but that this is both 'descriptive and proscriptive'. The aim is not just to achieve equal representation in museums. It is also to instruct the community on the value of cultural diversity (Witcomb 2003: 82).

However, the process of negotiating history can be problematic when cultures face a gulf of misunderstandings about what counts as historical evidence. The use of oral history, widely used by many indigenous peoples, is particularly problematic for historians wedded to the notion of empirical fact and historical truths. An 'interpretative pluralism' has been suggested as a way forward for cultures operating within a fractured history, Graeme Davison suggesting

> Rather than suppressing difference by imposing a single authorial voice, or brokering an institutional consensus, ... begin with the assumption that the imagined community we call nation is by its very nature plural and in flux. ... play host to several interpretations of the national past.
>
> (Carroll et al. 2003: 8)

The debates around the frontier conflicts in Australia during the years of white settlement dogged exhibitions at the National Museum of Australia in 2003–4 as charges of black-armband history impede the progress to 'fully examine [the nation's] own past' (Carroll et al. 2003: 14). (See, in particular, Macintyre and Clark 2003.)

In sharp contrast to the museum, the modern art gallery, without the same obvious obligations to present identity-forming national collections or to serve the redemptive function of many nineteenth-century philanthropic collections, seemed, at least until the early years of the twentieth century, to provide an ideology-free space. These galleries were not, or at least not overtly, implicated in the same discourses of anthropology, colonialism and social engineering as had been their predecessors. But from their inception, in part because of their rejection of the official academies, modern art galleries have not been an ideology-free space, a sanctuary from the world.

The Museum of Modern Art (MoMA), New York[6]

As we saw in Chapter 1, artists' attempts to evade the regularising and depoliticising tendencies of museum practices have provided us with some interesting artistic alternatives. In 1960 Jean Tinguely's *Homage to New York*, a 'self-consuming artefact', was assembled in the gardens of MoMA in New York, part of Tinguely's repertoire of random robots or Metamatics. Tinguely's kinetic work was made up of sculpture, sound and painting. Its auto-destructive elements contributed to his project of producing functionless art as a reproach to a culture dominated by the relentless rationality of technology and the permanence of the museum. Tinguely's sculpture involved the construction and destruction of a machine, its components including eighty bicycle wheels, motor parts, a piano, a go-kart, battery and tubes. In the event, the machine failed to destroy itself as intended; instead it ignited and had to be extinguished by the New York Fire Department. In a radio debate in 1982, Tinguely said:

> I wanted something ephemeral, that would pass; like a falling star and, most importantly, be impossible for museums to re-absorb. I didn't want it to be 'museumized'. The work had to pass by, make people dream and talk, and that would be all, next day nothing would be left, everything would go back to the garbage cans. It has a certain complex seduction that made it destroy itself – it is a machine that committed suicide. A very beautiful idea, I must say.
>
> (Tinguely, quoted in Hulten 1987: 14)

The setting for the machine's self-immolation – the gardens of MoMA, the model for all modern museums of art – ironically is what validates the work. Had it been realised outside the museum's gardens, the work's incendiary potential might have gained notoriety in terms of arson rather than art. For many years MoMA was the museum to which the avant-garde had aspired; and although Tinguely's reluctance to be 'museumized' led him to create an ephemeral art work, paradoxically his anti-institutional stance needed to be validated by MoMA.

The Museum of Modern Art in New York, the first museum to devote itself exclusively to modern art, was founded in 1929, the year in which the stock market crashed and the US entered the Great Depression. It has been the most influential modern art museum, not just in terms of design and display but in the definition of the art that would be considered modern. It is unsurprising, then, that it, and its first director, Alfred H. Barr Jnr, have been the focus of so much anti-modernist venom. Dubbed by Emily Genauer 'the fur-lined museum',[7] it was conceived by 'the Ladies', three wealthy art collectors: Mrs John D. Rockefeller Jnr, Miss Lillie P. Bliss and Mrs Cornelius J. Sullivan. In part this silver-spoon birth has contributed to MoMA's association with power, money and politics. Its close proximity to fashionable Fifth Avenue has contributed to its status as a 'tasteful' preoccupation for 'ladies who lunch'. The Guggenheim Gallery on Fifth Avenue in New York, famously designed by Frank Lloyd Wright as a conspicuously 'modern' whitewashed spiral in which to view art on a continuous platform, has a similar pedigree. Under the direction of Hilla Rebay, it functioned as a repository for 'non-objective' art, although any charges of 'hobbyism' need to be tempered by an acknowledgement of Rebay's critical writings on abstract art.

Alfred H. Barr Jnr was aged only twenty-seven when appointed as the director of MoMA. His and MoMA's avowed mission was to distinguish 'quality from mediocrity' in art. His early enthusiasm for the machine aesthetic, De Stijl, the Bauhaus and Russian constructivism is evidenced in his fervour for and somewhat puritanical conception of the museum as a 'machine to show pictures in' (Pointon 1994: 198). Barr's 1930s and 1940s schemes showing the ideal museum as a torpedo (Figure 6.7) are emblematic of MoMA's thrusting zeal. They show the museum as a machine of the future, penetratively streamlined. The schematic design delineated modern art's evolution from its European beginnings to its apotheosis in the 1920s in the United States and Mexico. The ideal collection was to consist of 'modern' works. When they became 'tired' or just not modern enough (this fate was envisaged as a numerical certainty), art works could go to a retirement home at the nineteenth-century 'temple of art', the Metropolitan Museum on Fifth Avenue. This policy, however, proved difficult to implement. Pensionable status or the designation 'classic' did not suit works like Picasso's *Les Demoiselles d'Avignon* (1907). The pivotal role of *Les Demoiselles d'Avignon* in establishing the genesis of modern art's 'trajectory' militated against its retirement. By the late 1940s the policy of transfer was abandoned and MoMA holdings began to resemble those of other art-collecting institutions.

MoMA differed from its European counterparts in openly embracing the machinery of capitalism and in recognising the importance of efficiency and marketing, making these attributes visible in the design and display of the gallery spaces. The façade of the building and its entrance hall resemble those of a department store (see Figure 7.3). Unlike the Victorian temple, with its vast spaces designed to awe the visitor, MoMA's

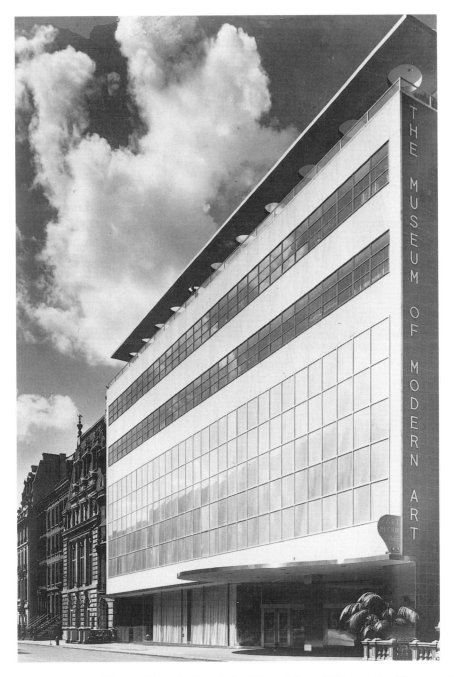

Figure 7.3 Architects Philip L. Goodwin, Edward Durrell Stone, the Museum of Modern Art, New York, 1939. Photo © 2003 The Museum of Modern Art, NY/Scala, Florence. The museum's first purpose-built home. Goodwin and Stone's 1939 building set the standard for subsequent modern art galleries for over fifty years. Unequivocally modern, the flat, glass-fronted building is indistinguishable from a shop-front façade. Its lack of a significant entrance with portico, steps and columns marked it out from its classical progenitors. Barr's early visits to the Bauhaus influenced the design of the new premises on New York's 53rd Street.

spaces, beyond the entrance hall, are relatively small and intimate. This is an important point: contemplation seems to benefit from a degree of privacy, low ceilings and small units – rather apartment-like and quite different from the civic ambition expressed in the morally elevating Victorian edifice.

If we return to an earlier epoch, the difference in the forms of display and therefore the underlying structures that supported them is visibly marked. For instance, in the seventeenth century, David Teniers the Younger, in works like *The Archduke Leopold Wilhelm in His Gallery in Brussels* (Figure 7.4), painted galleries in which the displayed works seem to have operated as floor-to-ceiling decoration. Allegorical subjects hang cheek by jowl with genre scenes, religious and mythological subjects and portraits of the great and good.

Diversity and chronology aside, it is the relationship of the spectator to the works that distinguishes the modern museum from its antecedents. When Théodore Géricault's *Raft of the Medusa* (1819) was hoisted up in the gallery, Géricault was reputedly dismayed at the height, as his heroic life-sized figures were reduced to mere mannequins.

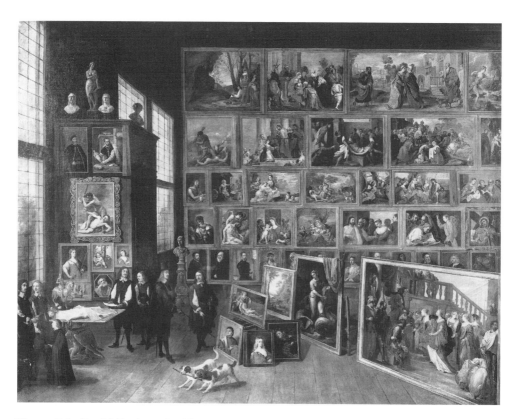

Figure 7.4   David Teniers the Younger, *The Archduke Leopold Wilhelm in His Gallery in Brussels*, before 1690. Courtesy of Kunsthistorisches Museum, Vienna. This seventeenth-century work is a showcase for the visible consumption of wealth and power. It pre-dates the modern curator/historian's tendency to create a chronology or exhibit within schools; instead works hang together with little space to contemplate individual works.

The modern museum carefully regulates the visitor. Works are usually placed at eye level, positioned to facilitate their individual contemplation. Communion with the work, it seems, requires at once a sense of other-worldliness combined with the department store's display for consumption so clearly lacking in museums of earlier epochs. The art on show in the modern museum is usually displayed with a minimum of attention to matters of context; works are usually isolated from anything that might interfere with or detract from their status as autonomous 'art' objects.

There is one aspect of MoMA's genealogy that we have to revisit, that of gender. It has been argued that the white cube of the modernist gallery space is resolutely masculine. 'The Ladies' of MoMA, although powerful, represented the regrettable face of art collecting – hobbyism. The austere Barr, who, in forming the collection, was 'guided primarily by his superb taste and connoisseurship, and his art-historical knowledge' (Sandler and Newman 1986: 9), created in the white cube a space devoid of 'troubling femininity' and of an overt sensuality.

'Aura' and the sacred space of the 'white cube'

> A painting has always had an excellent chance to be viewed by one person or a few. The simultaneous contemplation of paintings by a large public, such as developed in the 19th century, is an early symptom of the crisis which was by no means occasioned exclusively by photography but rather in a relatively independent manner by the appeal of art works to the masses.
>
> (Benjamin 1970: 236)

Walter Benjamin's influential essay 'The Work of Art in the Age of Mechanical Reproduction' (first published in 1939 and reprinted in Benjamin 1970) identified the notion of 'aura' as a major factor in our appreciation of a painting. 'Aura' was the term Benjamin used to describe the uniqueness of the single art object, occasioned by its unreproducibility. Mechanical reproduction (by which Benjamin, writing in the 1930s, meant principally photography, film and lithography), however, had the potential to undermine the uniqueness of the art object. He wrote:

> The uniqueness of a work of art is inseparable from its being imbedded in the fabric of tradition. . . . We know that the earlier art works originated in the service of a ritual – first the magical, then the religious kind. It is significant that the existence of the work of art with reference to its aura is never entirely separated from its ritual function. In other words, the unique value of the 'authentic' work of art has its basis in ritual, the location of its original in-use value. This ritualistic basis, however remote, is still recognisable as secularised ritual even in the most profane forms of the cult of beauty.
>
> (Benjamin 1970: 236)

Benjamin's argument is that the museum or art gallery legitimises the uniqueness of a relic or work of art. The work of art obtains its ritualistic significance at the level of a secular spirituality. To a Marxist such as Benjamin, this form of mystification could be endorsed only by the uniqueness of the art object. Benjamin believed that new technologies, especially film and photography, could help to create an authentic mass culture in opposition to the elitism of 'auratic' art. In this respect he can be considered the founding father of cultural studies in that his essays, such as 'The Work of Art in the Age of Mechanical Reproduction' and 'Author as Producer' (1934; see Benjamin 2003), did much to uncover the underlying elitism of fine-art practices and looked at the effects of modernism on mass culture.

The uniqueness of the art object, however, was never entirely eradicated by mechanical reproduction, and individual art works still change hands for enormous sums of money in spite of the accessibility for purchase of calendar reproductions or a Monet on an ashtray. But Benjamin's essay did establish the sacral status of the art work in a secular age. The white cube, under this rubric, becomes a secular shrine, an ersatz temple for the ritual of viewing.

The Western notion of individuality is a prerequisite of the 'aura', predicated on the basis of unitary selfhood in which one individual expresses him- or herself to another. The artist qua artist, as distinct from the artisan supported by personal patronage or the guilds, was now drawn into a web of novelty and innovation. The new art gallery, through its 'disinterested' display, embraced, albeit covertly, the art work as commodity. Subsequently the ambitious artist found it difficult to avoid the expediency of individuality and the rhetoric of originality. Moreover, the modern museum sustained the humanist myth of individual genius, with 'one-man' shows, monographs about and interviews with the artist. In its presentation of a coherent, authoritative, although usually depoliticised, account of modern art, the modern museum utilised the idea and language of the 'aura' of the art work.

Artists as curators and ahistorical exhibitions

> Fiction enables us to grasp reality and at the same time that which is veiled by reality.
>
> (Crimp 1995: 200)

Most modern galleries group works according to type and style, a curatorial method driven by chronology and periodisation. MoMA in particular has been criticised on the grounds that its displays 'lead the witness', that is, conduct the visitor on a vicarious triumphalist tour towards American abstract expressionism, extending the logic of Barr's 1936 schema (see Chapter 1). There have been interventions into what are considered by some to be 'false narratives'; that is to say, the galleries construct histories consistent with the ideologies that they represent. The kind of historical narrative that was adopted by individual modern museums was supported by periodisation – that is, the 'truths' of the history-as-chronology approach, consisting of dates, movements, styles and geographic origins. These have been regarded by postmodernist thinkers as 'false narratives' because they offer at best only a partial account of the human past.

Postmodernism's revelations, deconstructions and fictions have been cogently explored by the Belgian artist Marcel Broodthaers (1924–76). In *Les Animaux de la*

who is represented by the museum collection and, in an overt reference to the Cultural Revolution of China, what price we pay for populism.

Some displays have presented 'other' cultures as timeless, rendering their contemporary culture ahistoric. For instance, many displays of African cultures are reduced to the presentation of primitive masks and so-called tribal artefacts which are usually displayed without historic context. There have, however, recently been moves to locate Africa in the contemporary world by using artists as a signifier of modernity. The subterranean African Gallery (2000) at the British Museum, with its corporate tag, Sainsbury, has four international contemporary artists at the beginning of the display: Magdalene Odundo, Sokari Douglas Camp, Chant Avedissan and Kester Maputo. At the entrance to the gallery international artists born or working in African countries (Kenyan, Nigeria, Eygpt and Mozambique respectively) Magdalene Odundo *Ceramic Object* (2000) and Sokari Douglas Camp's (1995) *Big Masquerade with Boat and Household on His Head*, Chant Avedissan's textile work (1989–90) *Appliquéd Cotton Wall-Hanging* and Kester Maputo's (2001) *Throne of Weapons* make the links between Africa's past and its contemporary present.

Restitution, repatriation and technological alternatives

There has been another inevitable revision in museum practices: the return of cultural materials to their original owners. In 1999, Glasgow's Kelvin Grove Museum returned a Ghost Dance ceremonial robe, displayed in the museum, to the Lakota people. The shirt was acquired in 1892, and its return to the Lakota community on the Cheyenne River Reservation was the focus of much public debate. We know from the Accessions Register that the shirt, which was supposed to render its wearer invincible, had been taken from a warrior killed in the massacre at Wounded Knee in 1890. The debate around the future of the robe prompted a reinterpretation of the shirt as it was moved out of the ethnographic collection and accompanied by a three-screen video that recovered the previously untold histories of the Lakota people. The video significantly contributed to creating new meanings, bypassing some of the stereotyped images that had accompanied the original displays. Through the video the shirt is recontextualised in order to invest in the actual historic, spiritual and symbolic function of the robe. The video, a hybrid form as much art as cultural anthropology, now occupies a position in the gallery in place of the former object. It is just one example of an increasing use of technology rather than object-based collections, often resulting in new art videos. In part this is an indication of the breaking down of boundaries between different domains of culture, but paradoxically, given the debates around restitution, also of an increased belief in the sanctity of the original and a belief that any claim to authenticity is illusory. Martin Heiddegger (1889–1976) had laid claim to the power of the authentic art work and as well as the site for *truth* he saw it as the site of resistance from the alienating effects of dehumanising technology. While the place of the object is still secure in many museums, the use of technology, rather than being limited, opens up new possibilities. Culture seems poised between reifying objects in the name of individual identities on the one hand and yet wedded to new technologies as a way of bypassing centralised culture motivated by the artist's intention to explore the poly-vocality possible through new media and multi-model forms of display. There is a further issue that the return of the Ghost Dance shirt highlights: the provenance of artworks and artefacts. It we are to avoid moving, as Okwui Enwezor suggests, 'from the position of the colonial and bypass the post-colonial into the neo-colonial . . . [t]he provenance of the work has to be dealt with. We can see that very clearly with the looted art of the Nazis. There's a measure of ethical behaviour that institutions are called upon to exercise' (Enwezor 2003: 97).

Given the degree of ambivelence to the collection and display of art and artefact articulated by many artists and critics it is unsurprising to find many artists operating outside the regulatory controls of academies and museums – a posture itself a legacy of modernism's hostility to bourgoies norms, which we have repeatedly encountered.

Alternatives to the museum

While working within the gallery and museum has been a productive collaboration for artists and galleries alike, some artists have preferred to operate outside the gallery system altogether. Alienation from the gallery system has its origins in the exiled artists, poets and musicians performing collaboratively in Zurich while around them Europe engaged in the 'war to end all wars' (the First World War, 1914–18). The Cabaret Voltaire, an extension of Marinetti's legendary Italian futurist evenings, was founded and directed by Hugo Ball and Emmy Hennings. It was an anarchic extension of the concept of *Gesamtkunstwerk*, the total art work, often a reference to Wagnerian opera or theatre. The Cabaret became the focus of Zurich Dada's anti-war, anti-nationalist writers and artists, such as Tristan Tzara, Hans Arp, and Marcel Janco and Richard Huelsenbeck. At the Cabaret Voltaire the categories of culture, painting, print, music, poetry, dance, and so on were not separated into departments. The Cabaret opened with hastily collected art works made by performers and artists, but eventually the Gallérie Dada would show Janco, Kandinsky, Klee, posters by Italian futurists, 'negro art' and Picasso.

These international non-hierarchical collaborators worked across what would later become institutionalised as *disciplines*. They were involved in film, through Hans Richter, dance, philosophy and puppetry, as well as painting and printmaking, and their performances. Richard Huelsenbeck, writing in 1920, summed up the times:

> In that period, as we danced, sang and recited night after night in the Cabaret Voltaire, abstract art was for us tantamount to absolute honor. Naturalism was a psychological penetration of the motives of the bourgeois, in whom we saw our mortal enemy.
>
> (Huelsenbeck 1968: 378)

Huelsenbeck delineated the revolutionary precepts of Dada as anti-nature, evoking the abstract sculptor Alexander Archipenko (1887–1964), for whom 'any imitation of nature, however concealed, was a lie' (Huelsenbeck 1968: 378). For the Dada, truth was found in forms of abstraction, but it was not separate from the world or displayed uncritically in a vacuum as was its subsequent fate later in the century.

If the events and cabarets of Dada constituted acts of resistance to the museum and bourgeois culture in general there were other possibilities. We should bear in mind what André Malraux has defined as the 'museum without walls', the recurring issue of reproduction. Malraux's 'super-museum' was created by the 'homogenising' effects of the photographic image, which rendered disparate objects, such as the classical sculpture and the painting, the same:

> Any work of art that can be photographed can take its place in Malraux's super-museum. But photography not only secures the admittance of objects, fragments of objects, details, etc., to the museum: it is also the organising device: it reduces the now even vaster heterogeneity to a single perfect similitude.
>
> (Crimp 1995: 50)

Early examples of other museums without walls can be found in Duchamp's portable museums: the box in a suitcase which contained selected objects such as photographs and three-dimensional miniatures arranged in compartments. Duchamp's portable museums contained tiny versions of earlier works, prompting Walter Arensberg to comment that Duchamp had invented a new kind of autobiography, 'a kind of auto-biography in a performance of marionettes. You have become the puppeteer of your past' (Arensberg, quoted in Tomkins 1996: 316). At first collaborating with the American surrealist Joseph Cornell, Duchamp reproduced multiple versions of his portable museums with the intention of undermining notions both of exclusivity and of authenticity. His first boxes were contained inside a leather suitcase and referred to as *Boîte-en-valise* (*Box in a Suitcase*). There are twenty versions of the portable museum, which contain a miniature 'catalogue', consisting of sixty-nine items, images or replicas of Duchamp's work, including *The Large Glass*, *Nude Descending a Staircase* and a three-dimensional miniature of *Fountain*. Ironically, these boxes are currently much sought after, expensively acquired acquisitions displayed by orthodox museums, contrary to Cornell's and Duchamp's 'outsider' agendas.

Fluxus

There have been many interventions into the triad of museum, artist and original ('auratic') work. Inspired by Dada and in particular the work of Kurt Schwitters (1887–1948), the 1960s 'movement' Fluxus, although having the literal meaning 'to purge', programmatically resisted attempts to define itself. Like many other modern art movements it had no ambitions to be an '-ism', although 'concretism' is the other term applied to Fluxus. With an anti-high-art agenda informed by the commodity culture of post-war American affluence, its protagonists led the assault on institution-alised modernism. 'Quality' was designated under the categories of 'amusement' and 'fun' rather than the austere aesthetic of curators such as Barr. Fluxus was anti-individualist, anti-museum and anti-European high culture, attitudes summed up by Yoko Ono's *Painting to Be Walked On*, which required the literal act of trampling irreverently over the canvas.

Action Against Cultural Imperialism (*Henry Flint*) *Picket Stockhausen Concert!* (1964), a manifesto broadside designed by the founder member of Fluxus George Maciunas, was part of the culture of resistance. Through the collective creation of games, leaflets, films and performances (and, paradoxically, now the subject of intense interest and collecting), Fluxus both unsettled the auratic art object and bypassed the museum. Works produced by Fluxus would often be started by one artist but completed by others, thus subverting the traditional role of the artist under modernism (although not in Renaissance workshops) as the sole creative agent. Works like George Brecht's *Games and Puzzles/Name Kit* (1965–77) included multiple ready-made boxes that resembled earlier surrealist games. The reproduced boxes and games were attempts to remove the uniqueness of the art work and, by distributing them through mail order, to provide an alternative to the museum context. Yoko Ono's performance *A Grapefruit in the World of Park* (1961) was delivered on the street. Her particular contribution was to disrupt the notion of licence through the dissolution of the individual author/artist's signature. Ono's combinations of Zen Buddhism and haiku works were 'instruction art works' which came into being when someone acted on the instruction of the artist; for instance, 'drill a small, almost invisible hole in the centre of a canvas and see the room through it' (Ono 1995: 29). At the time of writing, Fluxus have a dedicated space in Tate Modern in London.

Art for the museum space

Attempts to undermine the art gallery, although interesting, have been largely unsuccessful. The white cube of the modern museum has acquired the status of the 'natural habitat' for the display of art works. The context afforded by the white cube, as we have seen, differs from that of the traditional museum and gallery. Older institutions often held works that previously had belonged somewhere else, most notoriously the Elgin Marbles, principally sections of the Parthenon frieze that were taken to the British Museum for 'safe keeping' in 1801–2. Religious works originally placed or built into the structure of sacred places have also been removed, deracinated and displayed out of context, thus altering the function and meaning of the work.

The Kantian notion of a 'disinterested aesthetic' has been used to legitimise this removal by its employment in support of the argument that the work of art is autonomous and can be appreciated without recourse to its original function. This approach has its merits, as we have seen: it allows for widely diverse works to be displayed without necessitating recourse to political or religious justifications. However, a reading which takes into account only the formal elements of a work of art is problematic. For example, it was the selective removal of the politics of European modernism from the art works displayed that has made MoMA and its curatorial agenda problematic. Too often art works were decontextualised and depoliticised in favour of a version of European and American modernism that seemed divorced from everyday contingencies. Christoph Grunenberg has commented:

> The austere gallery spaces with their pristine white walls epitomised MoMA's ambition for purity and neutrality, historical accuracy and objectivity: modernism became history. MoMA's politics of presentation replaced political engagement with formalist aesthetics, anarchy with rationalization, internationalism with individualism, diversity with absolute purity, and fragmentation with aesthetic autonomy.
>
> (Grunenberg, in Pointon 1994: 193)

The modern art museum adds another set of conundrums to the problem of deracination. Not all art in galleries has arrived through relocation. Many artists create specifically for the modern gallery because therein are to be found the scale and resources capable of sustaining such works. Barbara Kruger's 1991 installation '*Untitled*' (*All Violence is the Illustration of a Pathetic Stereotype*) (see Plate XXVI) at the Mary Boone Gallery in New York uses the space to physically engulf the viewer. The art work actually *is* the walls, rather than being displayed on the walls. Using the typography and uncompromising red, white and black of early tabloid newspaper culture, the work confronts the viewer with images and text that 'shout' the language of stereotypes: fairy, pussy, spook and so on. MoMA may have established the pattern of display and consumption, but many of the newer galleries have departed from the provision of intimate spaces to become sites of a different viewing experience which sets up a critical space between the object and the viewer's own corporeality.

In 2003 Anish Kapoor's *Marsyas*, a reference to Titian's *Flaying of Marsyas*, was installed in the Turbine Hall of Tate Modern, London. Reputedly the largest work of art in the world, in spite of the artist's insistence that size does not matter, the sheer scale of the work overwhelms the visitor. Kapoor's work is the latest in a line of art works that eschew quiet contemplation in favour of a more sensory and spectacular experience at a time when museums too are moving towards spectacle rather than classical restraint or minimalist chic. The Guggenheim Museum in Bilbao, Spain, designed by Frank Gehry in 1997, forswore the austerity of the white cube for flamboyance, spectacle and colossal scale. The Guggenheim Museum, subject to controversy, was built in the Basque region of Northern Spain as part of an economic revival package. It was the first major work brought to fruition by digitally reworking Gehry's sketch and then operationalising through electronic computation the construction of the building. Inside the gallery Richard Serra's 13-feet high *Snake* (1997), made of hot-rolled sheets of steel, meanders across over 100 feet of floor, towering over visitors. By the same token, the unsettling, slightly tilted sculpture *Torqued Ellipses* (1996–7) displayed at the DIA Foundation, also made from sheets of rolled steel, monopolised the vast industrial space. The audience is required to confront the scale of these works by walking between and into the structures, which tilt inwards and tower overhead.

Iwona Blazwick identifies a new sense of the gallery experience, stating:

> [T]he industrial spaces converted by Saatchi in London, the Crex Collection in Switzerland, the DIA Foundation in New York, or the hospital building converted into the Reina Sofia in Madrid, are galleries where the visitor experiences objects in a physical way. Their immense scale, the hard edged utilitarian aesthetic of their architecture, and the way objects are arranged . . . make the experience of viewing an exhibition a sensory one.
>
> (Blazwick, quoted in Papadakis 1991: 35)

The sensory experience had an increasingly high profile in both the production and the experience of art in the last decade of the twentieth century. The shift away from the tyranny of ocular centricity to more embodied forms of experience went in tandem with a move away from a belief in the separation between the intellect and what is primarily experienced through the body, via touch or smell for instance; theories of Cartesian dualism that we encountered earlier in Chapter 5. Merleau-Ponty's influential theory of the phenomenological body, the active body rather than the passive, has been crucial in this respect. Rather than view the body as a unified intellect, Ponty posited a subjective body and gave primacy to subjective perception; the implications are that we make meaning of the world through our lived experience of it, rather than through innate ideas that pre-date our experiences. (See, in particular, Merleau-Ponty 1962.)

In the monumental spaces of these converted industrial buildings, the critical space between the viewer and the object is not just an aesthetic of the eye; it is closer to Edmund Burke's notion of the sublime, which combined feelings of fear with awe. As the Victorian working-class museum visitor was awed by the beauty of the buildings and the works of art, so the contemporary visitor to the modern museum is often awed by the sublime scale of its exhibits. As is the case with Richard Serra's massive steel structures, the close physical proximity of the works is fused with a frisson of fear as well as awe.

Before we leave the actual museum building, there is one further observation to make on the architectural significance of the new museum: the franchising of the museum or gallery's iconic status as a signifier of international cultural prestige. The proliferation of Tates in Britain and the clamour to gain, for instance, a Guggenheim logo (Berlin, Bilbao, Las Vegas and perhaps Tokyo) with a significant international architect attached, are part of a growing industry and part of a perceived need by cities

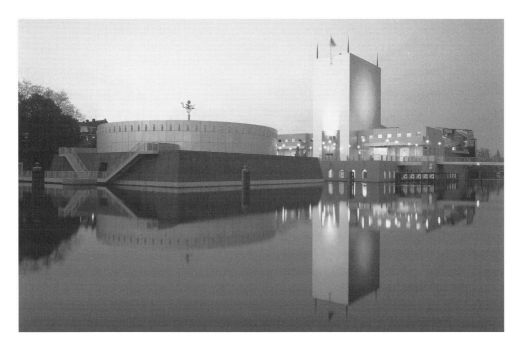

Figure 7.6 Architects Alessandro & Francesco Mendini, Philippe Starck, Michele de Lucchi & Coop Himmelblau, Groninger Museum. Courtesy of the museum. Photographer Ralph Richter. Situated in front of the railway station, the museum forsakes earlier notions of purity and simplicity in favour of a nautical theme. Part of the museum is submerged in a structure that alludes to a ship: mirroring the funnel, moreover, the interior is multicoloured.

across the globe to remarket themselves as an international outlet for culture, leaving behind a parochial past. Moreover, in what has been termed McGuggenheim, collaborations between museums to boost collective marketing and trade in pictures have resulted in a proliferation of global branding. To put a city on the tourist circuit at the same time as constructing or reconstructing local identities, a designer logo, a Philippe Starck or a Norman Foster, is called upon (see Figure 7.6). Moreover, our original premise that the museum's interior conforms to the straight puritanical geometry of the white cube is slowly being eroded by an unseemly flamboyance on both interior and exterior.

There are currently competing tensions between local identities and globalisation and the urge to attract the tourist economy, with iconic buildings as markers of international status. The balance between the needs of local and specific cultures and the pressure of internationalism is not easy to negotiate, even with the help of international artists.

Technology and the museum

As the historical frameworks for displaying both art works and artefacts in museums come under a critical gaze, the status of the authentic art work experienced through immediate and close contact has also come under threat from new media, particularly those afforded by electronic technologies. As we saw in Chapter 5, new technologies offer the experience of art works that are electronically generated; but they offer also the opportunity to experience 'virtually' material culture without ever setting foot inside the museum space. This possibility has gone some way to removing the privileges that have accrued to the 'original' object and opened objects again to the social and political meanings often bypassed in museum displays. The new technologies also offer a way past the centralised forms of power held by the museum to new decentred peripheral networks and so to a new emphasis in the museum on social interactivity.

Although often displayed in galleries, art that utilises newer technologies such as CD-ROM and web sites *does* offer alternatives to the museum, but whether this amounts to a democratising of art is another matter. Putting a camera in everyone's hand was never a guarantee of visual democracy: as Marxists demonstrated some time ago, it is the means of production, rather than production itself, that controls the implementation of technology in our culture. Nonetheless museums such as the Canadian Museum of Civilisation have reconfigured the historic basis of the relationship between audience and object to invest in the information age, with art works transmitted by electronic media rather than displayed in a collections-based museum. (For a fuller account, see MacDonald 1992.) The iconic glass structure of Urbis in Manchester has also stretched the boundaries of what constitutes a museum and, crucially, a collection. The building and contents have a resolutely young and international agenda. At least initially, it was conceived as a museum without a permanent collection. In some respects it is a virtual museum heavily dependent on interactive media which gives access to a global culture.

Any utopian prospect for new technologies needs to be tempered with the knowledge of the umbilical cord between capitalism and new technologies, as can be seen in the contemporary theme park, which has adapted the seemingly commerce-free space of the museum. History can be represented through the theme park in a painless and sanitised way almost indistinguishable from fiction. Ethnographic tourism dictates a form of re-presentation that incorporates 'living museums', in which redundant coal miners are employed to re-enact their own industrial history. Again, the 'living museum' can present live performances of dance and music as part of the 'experience' of authentic Polynesian life, for instance. Increasingly, in a global village the portrayal of other cultures is conditioned by tourist expectations and the commodification of culture.

The United States Holocaust Memorial Museum in Washington and the Beit Hashoah Museum of Tolerance in Los Angeles are paradigmatic of the problems raised by the distancing capacities of new technologies, seen most notoriously in the first Gulf War (1991), during which American bombings were allegedly timed to coincide with prime-time television broadcasts. Viewed at a safe distance, the Holocaust too can be just part of a 'virtual' experience. The issue of technological identification with the experience of an actual Jewish person during the Holocaust was part of the museum experience at Beit Hashoah, where visitors were issued with a computer-generated identity card which matched them with a person involved in the Holocaust. The card was put through a computer at the end of the visit. At that point a biography of the person was given. The barcoded card gave access to technologised images of mass murder and the 'total' concentration camp experience, an interactive experience intended to create a greater degree of empathy with the victims of persecution. The United States Holocaust Memorial Museum in Washington has a less technological experience based on the same identification with an actual person through an identity card. These museums raise many questions about the need for a place of critical reflection within such an emotional climate that cannot be easily answered (see, specifically, Andrea Witcomb 2003). What concerns us here is the artist's response to the anachronistic use of technology in such a highly charged reconstruction of the past. Alan Schechner's *Bar Code to Concentration Camp Morph* (1994) (one of a series of stills taken from the computer animation *Taste of a Generation*) (see Figure 7.7) takes issue with the experience of hyperreality by making explicit the links between capitalism and the museum experience via the barcode and the photographic images of the Holocaust, a process akin to what Andree Liss (1998) termed *Trespassing through Shadows* when writing on the relationship between memory, photography and the Holocaust, and the potential abuses and transformations in which even documentary photography can be complicit (see http://www.dottycommies.com/).

Schechner's imagery and his critique of what is fast becoming a Holocaust industry proved an artistic intervention too far in 2002 when the exhibition *Mirroring Evil: Nazi Imagery/Recent Art*, curated by Norman L. Kleeblatt, opened at the Jewish Museum in New York. Several of the artists exhibiting critically explored the relationship between popular culture, the fashion industry, technology and the Third Reich (see Chapter 1). In spite of the artists resolutely anti-fascist credentials there were calls to close the exhibition and artists received personal threats. This was less to do with the critique of capitalist society and its culpability in relation to cultural industry and the Holocaust itself than the display of images of the Nazi within the Jewish Museum. Opponents of the exhibition were doubtless aware that, in constraining freedom of expression in the name of a museum committed to anti-Fascist politics and bearing witness to the Holocaust, censorship was difficult to evoke.

The relationship between knowledge and technology has been amply critiqued by the French deconstructionists and is now a familiar theme in contemporary art practice. Johan Grimonprez's *Dial H-I-S-T-O-R-Y* (1995–7) (Plate XXVII) is a video film of almost an hour's duration which questions history and the media presentation of 'events' by initially confronting the position of the writer. The soundtrack is a fictional narrative drawn from Don DeLillo's novels *White Noise* and *Mao II*. The mixture of fiction, documentary evidence in the shape of newsreel footage, the testimony of 'experts', cartoons, movie footage, digital imaging and reconstruction with the manipulative effect of background muzak coalesces to bring into question the neutrality of histories and media representations (in this case a definitive 'chronological' history of plane hijackings). Media fictions merge with facts, and what counts as evidence becomes contradictory and even meaningless. The film collapses the polar opposition of fiction and documentary and questions our confidence in the visual image and reportage as the site of anything we ordinarily call 'truth'.

Grimonprez's earlier work, a collaboration with Herman Asselbergh, placed the viewer (spectator) effectively in the role of curator. In *Beware! In Playing the Phantom You Become One*, a video work on the history of television, the viewer could intervene in the art work, which again was a collection of facts and fictions, documentary and cartoons, experimental cinema and video extracts. The opportunity to incorporate one's own video gems into the work extended the possibilities for the spectator to undertake curatorial work. Asselbergh stated: 'Just as in life, the spectator visitor of this site creates a personal hypertext' (quoted in Joly 1997: 80).

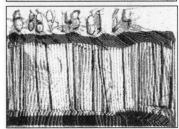
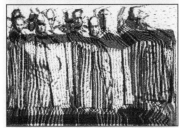
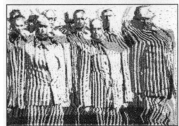
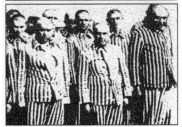

Figure 7.7 Alan Schechner, *Bar Code to Concentration Camp Morph*, 1994. Courtesy of the artist. In this work Schechner morphs the bar code of consumer culture into the uniforms of concentration camp victims, making explicit the promotion of ideologies through consumerist management.

The work of art in the electronic age

Baudrillard has made us aware, through what he terms 'image proliferation', that we live in a world saturated with images, but that our capacity for communication is not necessarily commensurate with what is required to enable worthwhile exchanges: we have fewer important things to communicate. Although Baudrillard's view of the relationship obtaining between the passive consumer of mass culture and the omnipresent television screen is problematic, what he makes clear in 'The Work of Art in the Electronic Age' (1998) is that Walter Benjamin's utopian vision, articulated in 1939 in 'The Work of Art in the Age of Mechanical Reproduction', which dispensed with art's traditional aura of 'sacredness forever', has been replaced with a nihilisitic vision. We are saturated with images, but electronic media seems nevertheless to hold out an emancipatory prospect (see Chapter 5). Many have argued that the art world's ideologies of individuality, originality and creativity have remained in place in spite of the electronic works of artists such as Bill Viola, Trinh T. Minh Hah and Gary Hill. Jonathan Harris has argued that powerful institutions and dealers 'seemingly may take hold of any raw materials [they find], and accounts of the decline or even death of auratic art begin to sound like wishful thinking' (Harris 1997: 41). The fact remains that, in a period of obsession with virtual reality and on-line communication, visiting art galleries to see an 'actual' art work has never been more popular. Surveys of galleries and museums point to a massive increase in attendance figures, showing the 'art fix' to be integral to many a tourist's itinerary.

New technologies offer the possibility of viewing the museum, by means of the CD-ROM and web sites, as a virtual gallery. The traditional curatorial system can be bypassed and viewers can create their own museums, collect their own works and install them in their own homes – an electronic museum without walls. However, as we have seen in the work of Grimonprez and Alan Schechner, the use of new technologies guarantees nothing except its own mutability. This raises the spectre of the virtual museum's short lifespan. If the permanent collection recalls a mausoleum, then the virtual museum is a case of short-term memory. Its built-in obsolescence is guaranteed by the technologically 'progressive' impulses of monopoly capitalism. Paradoxically, however, new technologies offer the conceit of 'total recall', whereby everything ever stored on computers (even an item binned from the hard disk) is recoverable.

In an age of mass reproduction, with the manipulation of images available at the touch of a remote control, cyberspace, on-line museums and virtual reality raise issues about our understanding of and relationship to the past. Technology itself, as we saw in Chapter 5, has no ideological infrastructure; its role is 'determined' by the dominant social factors. In the 1970s Raymond Williams observed, in relation to television, that technology reproduces the existing social order. It is currently relevant to ask if the Internet, email and even the mobile phone camera have contributed to political or social change. Or have the new technologies, eschewing the idealist past of Internet culture merely become a serpentine arm of corporate culture? In terms of the modern museum, and more particularly the technologised museum, it is uncertain what impact technology will have on the mission statements of the future and how it will contribute to an increasingly corporate museum culture. Linked to the leisure industry, the fortunes of the modern museum – its modes of display and its objects of desire – are riven by competing agendas. Museums and art galleries have perhaps never been more popular than they are at present, yet never have they been more vulnerable. Utopian perhaps, but new technologies still hold out the prospect of a reordering of hierarchies, a questioning of the relationship between popular culture and high art and a challenge to institutional authority. Increasingly, art works enter the public sphere without formally being housed in a gallery. The 'museum without walls' to be found in cyberspace effectively signals the erosion of the institutional structures, restraints and power relations of the old museums of modern art. They can, however, succeed only in a climate of continual questioning of what a critical digital culture might be. The place of artists in this may be crucial; Peter Lunenfield (2002) has argued that the video installations of Jane and Louise Wilson and Sam Taylor-Wood go some way to presenting an alternative form of interaction with narrative and history.

As many art historians have observed, the development of the museum is co-extensive with modernism. However, the links between modernity and the museum extend beyond the evolution of the modern museum; museums are implicated in both the evolution and sustenance of modernism. Although modernism may have become simultaneously a term with overtones both of nostalgia and of approbation, it is still true to say that modernism is tremendously successful, especially when it is endorsed by major museums. For instance, the unparalleled success on both sides of the Atlantic, between 1998 and 1999, of the Claude Monet exhibition *Monet in the Twentieth Century*, which at the height of its popularity was open to the public around the clock, demonstrates modernism's popular acclaim and its marketability. However, when viewed within the postmodern environment, modern art and its museums are in the equivocal position of having all the vestiges of institutional authority without the homogenising remit of continuity with their past: their status is provisional.

Nevertheless, viewed optimistically, the calling to account of museums under the aegis of state of the arts' debates allows for diverse strategies and eclectic practices: artists are no longer in thrall to the proscriptions of modernism, and museums have had to adapt to this, permitting the possibility of re-presenting themselves. As we are seeing, art institutions are infinitely adaptable, not only in adjusting to the demands of a postcolonial age, but in reconfiguring their spaces to absorb that which was previously excluded. In spite of postmodernism's apparently open and equalising remit, much contemporary art within Western culture appears to be 'more of the same' modernism. The difference is that proponents of postmodernism recognise that, unlike that of their modernist predecessors, their relationship with the past can never again be one of heroic rupture and revolution. Contemporary art, in sharp contrast to its modernist counterpart's futuristic ambitions, often seems condemned to revisit the past – but, ironically, only insofar as that past is mediated by the experience of museums.

In recent years it has been possible to identify a recurrent theme in contemporary culture: artists' preoccupation with revisiting and critiquing the museum or collection, some examples of which we encountered earlier in this chapter. Three recent examples will conclude this chapter.

In 2003 Goshka Macuga's *Picture Room*, exhibited at Gasworks Gallery, London, reconstructed John Soane's famous eighteenth-century picture gallery housed in the

Soane Museum, in London's Lincoln's Inn Fields. But instead of its fabled collection of William Hogarth (1697–1764) paintings and Giovanni Piranesi (1720–78) drawings the reconstruction housed over thirty collaborating contemporary artists' work. The facsimile work follows other recent interventions into the collection, such as the curator Hans Ulrich Obrist's *Retrace Your Steps: remember tomorrow, artists at the Soane* in 1999/2000.

It is not just the structure of the museums as buildings and social organisations that has occupied contemporary artists, but also the weight of the historic or seminal exhibitions that have contributed to the received chronology for modernism. Marina Grzinic's 2001 curatorial project *Fiction Reconstructed* (see Plate XXVIII) pays homage to three legendary exhibitions and collections: *The Last Futurist Exhibition* by Kasimir Malevich, held in St Petersberg in 1915; *The International Exhibition of Modern Art* (*The Armory Show*) in New York in 1913 (see Chapter 6); and a collection owned by the Gertrude and Leo Stein that dates from around the turn of the twentieth century. The third of Grzinic's curatorial projects, *Salon de Fleurus*, has been described as behaving like a virus of modern art (McDonald 2002: 187). The title is a reference to the Steins' address in Paris. *Salon de Fleurus: a fiction reconstructed* (McDonald 2002: 186), places reproductions of the Steins' collection, which consisted of paintings and sculptures of the early avant-garde, in a reconstruction of their legendary salon. It has been argued that the salon was the precursor to the modern art gallery. And so the reconstruction of the salon in New York seems to echo the modernist history of art's migration from Paris to New York. The project is more than a challenge to the idea of originality and authenticity that we have encountered before; it replicates the frameworks of modernism by uncovering the system that underpins modernism (the Steins were after all collectors). After visiting the New York salon it was possible to buy the paintings or furniture on display, they are merely replaced with another copy. There is another significant aspect to *Salon de Fleurus* that bears some comparison with what is referred to as a virus, a term now associated with electronic media. *Salon de Fleurus* is not unique; other *Salon de Fleurus* exhibitions were opened at the same time to replicate the procedures and distribution mechanisms and networks of modern art.

Identity politics in photography and performance art

Genius is nothing but an extraordinary manifestation of the body.

(Cravan 1981: 7)

You value him [Jackson Pollock] because he had made such a radical gesture with the invention of drip painting; the result didn't matter as much as the gesture. Then you valued him because the gesture meant so much, in terms of the relationship between the painter's body and the canvas, the decentring of the self, the final abandonment of the Albertian window,[1] and why not?

(de Duve 1996: 44)

The body is the new art medium of this [twentieth] century.

(Wilson 1997: 2)

Our fascination with the artist's physical appearance, especially when linked to his or her creativity, has been encouraged by artists – many of whom have permitted themselves to be filmed or photographed at work. In the hypnotic footage of Picasso, Kandinsky and Matisse in the act of painting, or the 1950 film by Hans Namuth of Jackson Pollock at work (see Figure 8.1), the creative process is as engaging as the actual art work itself. This fascination with process raised an interesting set of questions for the American art critic Harold Rosenberg, writing in the 1950s, the most pressing of which concerned the very 'essence' of a work of art. Rosenberg's theory of what he called 'action painting' (in relation to the painterly paintings of Jackson Pollock and Willem de Kooning) hinged on the belief that the instinctive and spontaneous action of painting is the truest expression of an artist's individuality. As we saw in Chapter 6, Rosenberg was transfixed by the idea that the process of making the work of art is more important than the extant work of art: 'In this act timing is decisive; the object itself is a mere souvenir of the occasion' (Rosenberg 1982: 23). The 'mere souvenir' was normally an arrangement of shapes, colour, texture, but it had scant regard for content in the sense that it depicted recognisable objects in the world. This process enabled an action painter to eliminate all reference to anything other than 'his' (and it usually meant *his*) own unique, uninhibited and unreflective gestures. Rosenberg therefore concluded that the work of art actually resided in the 'act' of painting itself, although this never militated against the commercial value of the 'souvenir'; he regarded the painter as an actor and the picture as an event. So in Jackson Pollock's dramatic confrontation with the canvas – 'an arena in which to act' – the creative moment is more important than the actual work of art. Pollock's particular brand of gestural abstraction, with its emphasis on bodily action, extended the repertoire of artistic processes. This is not to say that painting was not a bodily act before Jackson Pollock (obviously the body was a necessary tool), but the particular existential claims made on behalf of action painting implicated the body in all such energetic 'encounters with the canvas' (Rosenberg 1968: 569).

Pollock's technique and the procedures of action painters in general are often cited as forerunners of what came to be called performance art. Rosenberg's construction of the painter as actor and the painting as event (what he called 'act-painting') was motivated by a search for a more direct form of expression. Rosenberg believed that if act-painting was given primacy rather than product, then to approach the canvas with nothing in mind became an act of resistance, which, at least in the 1950s, meant challenging orthodoxies, and therefore the act itself through gesture could be seen as

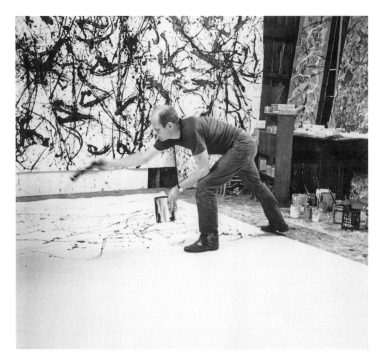

Figure 8.1 Hans Namuth, *Jackson Pollock* © Hans Namuth Ltd, 1990. Hans Namuth (1915–90) took more than 500 photographs of Jackson Pollock in his studio between July and October 1950. The portraits and accompanying films were widely reproduced in art periodicals but also in celebrity magazines, and were instrumental in bringing Jackson Pollock to a broader public and also illustrating the methods of action painting. However, there is some evidence that Pollock was disturbed by the films, which revealed, in slow motion, the performative aspects of his work.

a social or political act. This chapter looks at some of the other ways in which artists have used their bodies in the production of art. From performance art to artists using digital photography, we consider the use of the body not simply as 'art' but as a site of political and social discourse.

Autobiography and authenticity

Action painting certainly privileges the unique signature style of the artist – even though, as in the case of Pollock, its effects may seem accidental and uncontrolled. By privileging the unique signature style of the modern artist, modernism also privileges the notion of the artist as a conveyor of personal 'truths'. The confessional mode, in which the artist or writer assumes a quasi-autobiographical intimacy with the audience, is a feature of post-war art and film – especially in the United States. The self-referential and angst-ridden expressionistic mode of painters such as Pollock and Norman Lewis, and of writers such as Norman Mailer and Erica Jong, could be seen as part of what was called the 'culture of narcissism' (a culture parodied in many of Woody Allen's films).[2]

Autobiography has a privileged status in the hierarchy of discourses produced in the modern Western world, and if we extend the definition of the genre to include other forms of self-writing such as memoirs, diaries and journals, then autobiography can be seen as a key component of the West's literary heritage. The notion of the author as sole authority, solely responsible for his or her writing, is important to our consumption of autobiography because modernism has made it possible to be highly personal and yet, at the same time, to convey a 'truth' that is communal. Autobiography allows the interior expression of personal self-writing to become the exterior collective story of a communal group with a vested interest in sharing desires, aspirations and histories. So Wordsworth's *Prelude*, Jean-Jacques Rousseau's *Confessions* and Gertrude Stein's *The Autobiography of Alice B. Toklas* communicate under various autobiographical guises to a like-minded community.[3]

Finally, the art of autobiography is contingent on a particular set of notions of *self*. There has first to be a consensus about what constitutes a self before one self can represent itself to another. In telling one's unique story one has to have common ground, a common sense of self, with others before the story can be consumed. We have to believe that the 'I' doing the speaking is not dissimilar to the 'we' doing the reading. This is one reason why the West finds it so hard to deal with art from other cultures and tends to understand that art in terms of its own knowledge – for instance regarding the Aboriginal art of Australia as though it were akin to abstract expressionism.

The autobiography, whether communicated in art or in literature, is a form of myth-making which casts the self-writer as the hero or heroine. This may extend to writing which is about another subject, as in the case of Rosenberg, who cast de Kooning in the starring role in 'the mythic act' of action painting. However, autobiographies do not always have to be genuine or to have been actually lived. Unlike an earlier generation of artists, who believed that the authenticity of lived experience conveyed all sorts of universal truths, in much of the art we will consider in this chapter the artist's ability to establish a point of view or a narrative which is believable is far more important than conveying absolute truth. This belief sits well with contemporary critical theory, where the suggestion that truth is relative rather than absolute has been amply explored, for instance in 'Myth Today' (1957; see Barthes 1993), where Roland Barthes questions the relationship between 'ideology' and 'truth'.

In *Seedbed* (1971), at the Sonnabend Gallery, New York, spectators were invited to walk across a ramp beneath which the performance artist Vito Acconci was reportedly masturbating while his grunts were amplified around the space;[4] in the 1970s the Vienna *Aktionist* Rudolf Schwarzkogler exhibited pictures of a bloody bandaged stump, claiming to have cut off his penis (he had not, although some books have erroneously insisted that he did); in the 1960s the French artist Yves Klein collaged a photograph to show himself jumping off a high wall (which he had not). These 'suggestions' are interesting precisely because the artist's body is temporarily designated as the site of 'truth' – not necessarily true in the sense of 'actual' but true in the sense of being 'capable' of truth within the confines of a consensus of agreement about what, historically at least, constitutes art.

Other examples of artistic 'untruth' include the Australian performance photography collaborators Farrell and Parkin, who deliberately play upon linked ideas of sex, pain and death, in what look like reconstructions of torture chambers (see Figure 8.2). In their exhibition *Black Room* (1992–3) they use their own bodies in order to tell 'untruths'. Specifically, they have researched eighteenth-century bandaging techniques and use prosthetics to play upon visual ambiguities that confound the viewer. The works excavate, in the archaeological sense, lost forms of knowledge – such as alchemy and forms of healing. Crucially, the viewer interprets the past in the light of the present, often misreading the works as sadomasochistic, and not as a history of early medicine. For instance, *Untitled Image #1* shows a 'tranquillising chair' designed by Benjamin Rush in 1810. The chair was designed to restrain and blindfold distraught patients in order to restabilise them by removing sensory experiences. However, to the contemporary viewer *Untitled Image #1* evokes images of the electric chair or an instrument of torture. Because we do not possess the visual references to read Farrell and Parkin's work correctly, the images force us to re-evaluate the status of what we currently call knowledge.

Queer art

The question of 'truth' in art practice is a difficult one. On the one hand, the authenticity of lived experience is highly important in validating modern art. For instance, from the pseudo-confessional paintings of David Hockney in the 1960s to the queer politics of the 1980s and 1990s, the importance of openly acknowledging one's sexuality ('coming out') is one example of the way in which authenticity is a hallmark of 'truth' in modern art. Having said that, it is not always possible to be truthful through art. Hockney's *Third Love Painting* (1960) (Figure 8.3) combines text, poetry and graffiti in a self-referential and semi-autobiographical work of art, but because the painting was made at a time when homosexuality was illegal in Britain it could not be explicit in its themes. Hockney said that the painting was an act of propaganda for homosexuality which he felt 'should be done' because it was 'part of me'. However much Hockney felt that *Third Love Painting* 'should be done', the painting is of necessity highly coded and not immediately accessible to those culturally deprived of gay markers and references.[5]

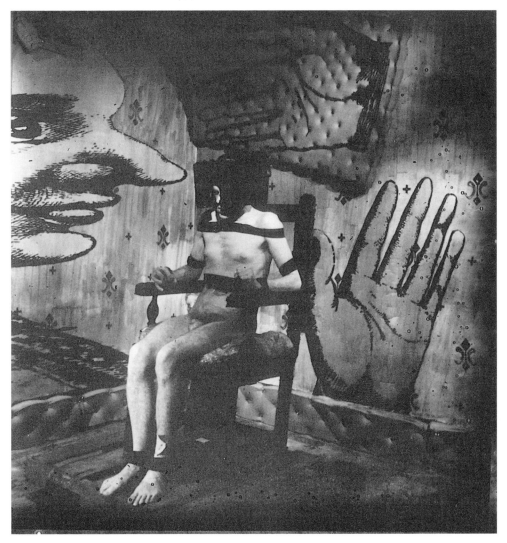

Figure 8.2 Farrell and Parkin, *Untitled Image #1, from 'Black Room'*, 1992–3. Courtesy of the artists and MY Art Prospects, New York. The performance pieces were staged with sets that were subsequently destroyed, leaving the photographs as the only evidence. The photographs are very large with high resolution which is ultra-detailed and stands in opposition to the untruth of the staged imagery.

Hockney's oblique works of the early 1960s contrast markedly with the work of artists working in much more uncompromising terms in tandem with the lifting of restrictions on homosexuality in the late 1960s.[6] For instance, Bruce Naumann's explicit neon-lit outlines of homosexual group sex show by how much the overt has superseded the covert. Any survey books about gay art, for example, will have content that might be called explicit. To some extent it could be claimed that the representation of same-sex relations is so important to queer art simply because frank statements of homosexuality have been outlawed for so long.

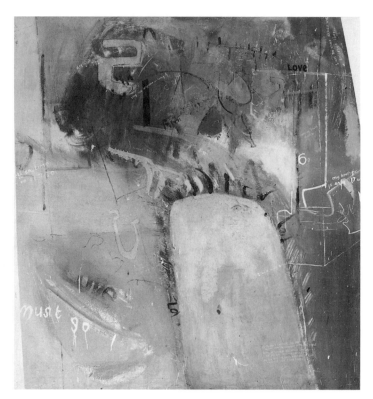

Figure 8.3 David Hockney, *Third Love Painting*, 1960. Courtesy of the artist. © David Hockney. Photo © Tate, London, 2003. The painting contains several coded references to homosexual culture. The pink phallic shape at the centre of the painting is overscored with graffiti and text. The graffiti replicates exhortations that could be found in public lavatories, in this case those specifically found at Earl's Court tube station. The text comes from Walt Whitman's poem 'When I Heard at the Close of the Day' (1860), which contains more decorous invocations to love.

However, does the acknowledgement of queer culture and the production of images which have an openly queer content constitute a category of art production – queer art? And, if so, is the distinction any more useful than other categories such as women's art or ethnic art? As with other groupings within art made on the basis of the personal or political relations of the artist, the designation queer art begs the question: What is queer art? Is it anything painted by a man or woman who happens to be gay or lesbian or is queer art something more specific than that, in the sense of being the representation (or suggestion) of same-sex relations? For instance, there are many artists, such as Monica Sjoo or Lenore Chinn, who depict same-sex relations in their art. There are also artists who work in a camp idiom that could be read as a feature of some aspects of gay culture. For instance, Pierre et Gilles ape the combined styles of fashion, pop and advertising in a trademark style of portraiture which could be called high camp and therefore suggestive of its special place within gay culture (see Plate XXIX). However, there are numerous gay artists in modern art – Robert Rauschenberg, Andy Warhol, Francis Bacon, to name but a few – whose work is not primarily to represent gay relations. Is everything they make as artists – regardless of content – therefore 'queer art'? Since elsewhere in this book we have been rather sceptical of essences as a way of explaining works of art, to discuss queer art as something rooted in metaphysical questions about essences would be an uncharacteristic instance of special pleading.

So if we argue that there is no question of being able to make a single distinction, queer art, then we can only conclude that there is a category of gay or lesbian artists who make art. To this end we have to examine queer art as a form of identity endorsement which seeks to operate as a corrective to norms within the dominant heterosexual culture. Judith Butler regards the categorising of identity as a series of 'necessary errors', and many groups, especially those concerned with minority rights and queer theory, are ambivalent about sexual identities.[7] Clearly numbers of individuals do regard their sexual orientation as crucial in their perception of who they are and how they form social and political relations. Sexuality is, then, at the very least, a component of personal identity. The current popularity of performative accounts of identity categories may go some way to explaining how identities play a crucial role in our psychological make-up. Performative accounts of identity argue that the repetition of practices makes norms. So sexual identities have a social significance that, say, mere likes and dislikes do not have. Sexual identities make a difference to how you are treated in society and, much more crucially, how society thinks you should be treated.

One way in which gay activists have been campaigning in the past twenty years has been on the issue of government policy towards the AIDS epidemic. Whilst acknow-ledging that AIDS has long since been a global problem affecting heterosexuals, children and African men and women in particular, the campaigning for AIDS charities, lobby-ing of public health services and the battles with drugs companies have been largely in the orbit of gay pressure groups. Some have argued that AIDS has slipped out of the centre of gay activism to be replaced by issues such as gay and lesbian marriages or the position of gays in the army, but Douglas Crimp (2002) argues that the AIDS epidemic should be a determining force in queer politics. In terms of the kind of art that has been produced in response to HIV and AIDS, then, there are many examples of personal or autobiographical performance, for example the work of Ron Athey (see p. 25), but it is arguably the idea of shared autobiography or collective experience that has produced the most consciousness-raising work. The *AIDS Memorial Quilt*, a project conceived and organised by Cleve Jones in 1985, is perhaps the most ambitious work to come out of the AIDS epidemic in the US. Like Maya Lin's *Vietnam Veterans' Memorial* (see Chapter 3), with which it is often compared, the quilt names individuals, only this time they are the casualties of the AIDS epidemic. Each person to die of an AIDS-related illness is commemorated by lovers, friends and family on a grave-sized sheet (3 feet × 6 feet). The individuals are commemorated either by writing the name of the deceased or by creat-ing a tribute out of their possessions or associated objects. Each unique panel is then connected to another panel to form a huge patchwork.

In some senses the quilt could be said to embody the idea of a return to community. The patchwork quilt is a quintessentially American art form, especially connected to communal and folk art. Therefore it has a certain poetic resonance that the *AIDS Memorial Quilt* should resort to a 'lost' art form and create identity among people whose only connection is the cause of their death. The *AIDS Memorial Quilt* was first exhib-ited in Washington, DC, in 1987 when there were around 2,000 names. At the last count there were 44,000 panels (only a fraction of the global figure of AIDS-related deaths) remembering individuals who have died of AIDS. However, the quilt is often displayed in smaller sections (because of its great size) to be viewed not just as the sum of its parts but also as a set of personalised tributes. The sewing together of different individuals, each with their own personal histories, into an enormous patchwork of collective history endows the work with the power of consciousness-raising, makes it a tool of education, a focal point of political action and a model of community organisation.

Performance art

The advent of what became known as performance art in the 1960s and 1970s gave a further dimension to Rosenberg's suggestion that an art work should strive to be a 'unique signature'. Normally, performance art involves a body or bodies localised in time and place for the purpose of a live event, which may or may not be documented. In performance art the art work is inseparable from the process of enactment. For example, *Breaking Test (Zerreissprobe)* (see Figure 8.4) is a 'work of art' by the Vienna *Aktionist*, or performance artist, Günter Brus in which the artist urinated, defecated, masturbated and slashed himself with a razor blade. We are offered an 'art work' that resides wholly in the artist's body located in time and space – in this case, Vienna in 1970. There is no other art work, no resulting paintings, no artefacts, only 'documentary' photographs of the live event. The 'actions' of the performance, like those of the action painter for Rosenberg, are essential to the work of art, but in this case they do not give rise to any 'incidental' work which may be bought or sold after the event.[8] Unlike conventional painting or sculpture, performance art identifies the work of art as the performed event. The event – and therefore the work of art – may last a few moments or a few days; it may involve one artist or several; it may include music, poetry and dance, or it may be silent; it may or may not invite audience participation. Performance art is often said to be the only art form which guarantees the actual presence of the artist. There are, however, numerous exceptions to that rule; for example, the German artist Rebecca Horn often choreographs models to enact her ideas rather than 'performing' herself.

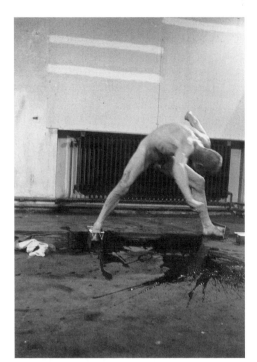

Figure 8.4 Günter Brus, *Breaking Test (Zerreissprobe)*, Aktionsraum 1, Munich, 1970. Courtesy of the artist and Galerie Heike Curtze, Vienna. Brus described his actions in this performance piece thus: 'The actor is aggressive against himself and against surrounding objects, as a result of which appropriate actions are set free: self-injury, rattling sounds in his throat, strangulation, flogging' <http://www.bmezine.com/news/softtoy/005>. The performance is choreographed to determine 'breaking point', at which moment the self-immolation ceases.

In 1967 Michael Fried published an article in *Art Forum*, 'Art and Objecthood', attacking the sculptors Robert Morris and Donald Judd for the theatricality of minimalist art (see Fried 2003). His reasoning was that the experience of minimalist sculpture in the gallery imposed certain restrictions on the viewer (namely that the viewer was required to take time and view the pieces from several angles) that rendered the experience of viewing the same as the experience of going to the theatre. Unlike the instantaneous apprehension of an abstract painting (especially, he argued, one by Kenneth Noland), the full apprehension of a minimal sculpture was time and movement dependent.

An art work which dispenses with all the paraphernalia traditionally associated with art-making – paint, brushes, frames, chisels, marble, art galleries – should really be seen in the context of the so-called 'dematerialisation of the art object' in the 1960s (see Lippard 1997). Sometimes called conceptual art, this movement within post-war Western art was often a deliberate strategy on the part of artists to expose the covert symbiotic relations between art institutions and the art market, and also to evade the institutionalism that seemed to have neutralised earlier avant-garde art movements. In theory, the 'dematerialised' art object – in performance art, conceptual art and land or earth art – undermined the authority of the gallery, the auction house and the dealer precisely because such art (grounded in concept rather than product) had no real currency in the twentieth-century operations of the art market. For example, it was supposed to be difficult to make a commodity of either the performance artist's body or the 'suggestion' made by an item of conceptual art.[9] However, the art market exists to preserve the sanctity of the commodified art work and it has been remarkably resilient in finding ways to incorporate conceptual art. The performance artist therefore parodies the 'art object' (the thing in itself), rendering its commodification futile since the work can only exist once the performance is over in the guise of documentary 'evidence' – photographs, memorabilia and film or video. Yet the will to art objecthood is strong and the art market will always find a way to barter; so incidental memorabilia – especially in the form of headline-grabbing publicity – is eminently marketable. As Lucy Lippard pointed out in 1967, the performance artist is no more exempt from economic and ideological 'exploitation' by the art market than the next painter or sculptor (Lippard 1997). Conversely, performance artists themselves can exploit the publicity value of what they do.

This somewhat romanticised view of performance art as a unilaterally defiant declaration by the artist about what constitutes a work of art points to the continuing presence of the modernist construction of the 'artist as hero'. It rests on the premise that the artist – in the sense of the unitary self which we encountered in Chapter 2 – is a figure who is expected to subvert classifications and transgress boundaries, just as those unitary selves who have made the canon of modern art were engaged in redrawing the boundaries. As we saw in Chapter 1, it is the function of a self-annointed avant-garde to do this. This type of avant-garde activity stems from a set of strategies designed to conflate the artist and the artwork that emerged at the end of the First World War. The underlying spirit of performance art and the challenge it presented to the institutional infrastructures of art have their roots firmly in the international events staged under the aegis of Dada cabaret and futurist evenings of the 1910s. It is tempting to see performance art as an extension of fine-art practice, or as merely a reductive offshoot of avant-garde theatre, or as the two combined under the rubric of 'happenings' and 'Fluxus'. We have seen how, through Dada and Duchamp, the art work could be whatever the artist said it was. Indeed, when asked 'What is art?', Kurt Schwitters replied: 'Everything the artist spits out is art'. To follow his logic, forty years on, through to the age of the dematerialised art object, it became only a small imaginative leap to accept that the artist's body, a thing in itself, can be the 'ready-made' in the orbit of the art work.

The subjective body

> [T]he old metaphysical opposition of inside versus outside, soul versus body, is the very basis of expressionism . . . however decentered in relation to society (Marx), the unconscious (Freud), language (Saussure), science and technology, the self remains sovereign in art.
>
> (Foster 1985a: 75)

The history of the study of the body is a relatively new area of inquiry, arising from a convergence of histories such as medicine, food and hygiene, gender and sexuality. Contemporary social anthropologists such as Ted Polhemus, Mary Douglas and Bryan S. Turner foreground the body in their work, making the body (as opposed to previous discourses of class) the axis around which all sociological analyses turn. Of course, the body has seldom been absent from the visual arts. In Western art the body is prominent, though it is absent from several non-Western cultural forms. However, the use of the term 'the body', as opposed to 'the nude', is a relatively recent phenomenon in the history of art.[10] The changing discourses around the body require a different set of critical tools and a vocabulary imported from social anthropology and philosophy rather than formalist aesthetics. To talk in terms of beauty and aesthetic value in relation to performance art is completely to misread the work: performance art demands a broader lexicon.

For performance art, the placing of the body at centre-stage in art from the 1960s in particular has had a profound effect on notions of artistic expression. We saw in Chapter 2 how artists' search for new and authentic experiences led some to turn in on themselves to make perceived 'inner experience' the basis of their art works. Here we revisit the process of subjectification in which social networks, political systems and cultural codes conspire to shape the subject, in order to examine how discourses of identity, histories of the subject and cultural inscriptions of the body all converge.

The artist's body, for example in Günter Brus's sadomasochistic interpretation of action painting, may be both the subject and the object of the work of art. The body becomes, literally and simultaneously, the medium and the tool. Brus's gestures with bodily fluids are analogous to Pollock's fluid skeins of paint,[11] only in Brus's case the connection between the body and the gesture is explicit – a cypher for the 'return of the repressed'. Taken from Freudian psychoanalytical theory, the return of the repressed signals the resurfacing of unwelcome emotions, thoughts and sensations to the conscious mind, although often indirectly. Brus's overarching themes of self-mutilation and self-destruction were not only corporeal expressions of Teutonic angst but part of the rhetoric of being free, in a Freudian sense. The psychoanalytic idea that sadism, aggression, greed, obscenity (all acted out in *Breaking Test* (*Zerreissprobe*)) and other primal human drives are 'buried' or repressed in every one of us implies that to express them is to be liberated and free. The idea of freedom is further rooted in the Romantic belief that the 'essence' of a work of art can overcome its material form. So, whereas Pollock, according to Rosenberg, is a subject producing the object, in the case of Brus the performing subject is also the object of the art work.

Returning to our claim that the artist's appearance in the creative act has long been of great interest to modern art, for artists actually to reconfigure their appearance or to surrender their bodies to another's control is to foreground notions of subjectivity. Take, for example, the French artist Orlan, who has enjoyed a good deal of media attention as a result of shocking cosmetic surgery by which her face and body have been spectacularly remodelled. Recalling what was said about artists' publicity-seeking tactics as commodification in recent years, Orlan's work does graphically illustrate the kind of question that accompanies this literal understanding of the body as work of art. Orlan is gradually creating a total work of art out of her body, which, she says, she intends to leave to a museum rather than to medical research when she dies. The operations she instigates are the equivalent of Rosenberg's concept of act-painting. Orlan's performances are utterly reliant on the presence of the audience. They are watched live via satellite and filmed for subsequent showing in galleries and museums. In contrast to Rosenberg's belief in the gesture being paramount, in Orlan's work it is in part in the act of watching the performed event but also in part in Orlan's reconfigured physical body that the work of art exists. While the heroic encounters with the canvas by the first generation of abstract expressionists took place in private, the work of performance artists often requires the presence of the audience – in extreme cases audience participation, as we will see when we consider the work of Marina Abramovic.

In Chapters 2 and 4 we saw that the exact nature of the subject–object division has long been a philosophical problem, but that the usual formula is to describe the subject as that which acts and the object as that which is acted upon. For instance, in the relationship between artist and model, we saw how the objectification of the female nude is contained within the discourse of subjectivity which identifies the subject as masculine and the object as feminine and presents this relationship as 'natural'. An extension of the terms 'subject' and 'object' gives the terms 'subjective' and 'objective'. To be 'objective' usually means to be impartial, rational and in command of the relevant information, while to be 'subjective' is to be involved, engaged and to stake one's claims on the basis of personal conviction. The claim to objectivity is often the hallmark of empirical history, but that any individual subject (a writer, an artist, an art historian) can ever be truly objective is a questionable proposition.

Poststructuralist thinkers such as Julia Kristeva and Michel Foucault have dealt with the notion of subjectivity as though it were a link between individuals and the ideological power structures around them. In poststructuralist writing, ideas such as 'learning to live with the contradictions' acknowledge the difficulties of any easy distinctions. The subject – that is, the acting person writing history or making art – is always constituted in and by 'language' and therefore, the French Marxist philosopher Louis Althusser (1971) argues, is in the grip of an ideology which precludes objectivity altogether. As Edward Said put it: 'Of what philosophical use is it to be an individual if one's mind and language, the structure of one's primary classifications of reality, are functions of a transpersonal mind so organised as to make individual subjectivity just one function among others?' (Said 1975: 293). The concept of individuality within Western monopoly capitalism's commodity culture is sacrosanct – the myth of the individual subject as the basis of all buying power; that is to say, the consumer makes choices based on personal preference. Said's critique of the individual is, therefore, deeply subversive when capitalism is contingent on a consensual notion of individuality shaped in terms of ownership. It follows, therefore, that paintings and works of art function in the marketplace only because their 'unique signature style' guarantees their authenticity and exclusivity. When push comes to shove, we can all paint like Pollock but it is in the interests of monopoly capitalism that there is only one Pollock. By the same token, the market takes an equally dim view of fakes and forgeries; after all, if it looks like a Van Gogh, why does it matter if it is not a Van Gogh? A non-capitalist culture, such as China during the Cultural Revolution, briefly created artist co-operatives that produced collective works of art that bypassed all the notions of subjectivity and the unique signature style outlined above.

The modernist ideal in which the artist's idiosyncratic gestures are unquestioningly received by the viewer is the basis of a notion of genius in Western culture. So it *does* matter that some of Van Gogh's paintings are now believed to have been painted by an aquaintance, Claude Émile Shuffenecker.[12] The 'authenticity' of the work includes, though is not exhausted by, the fact that it guarantees the presence of the artist. But, like Marxist social theory, poststructuralist theories of the artist tend to be dismissive of the concept of genius in terms of its potential to overcome the social constraints that shape identity. They argue that this model of the active artist and the passive viewer is unsustainable. Of course, in the 1970s, when poststructuralists began to advance such arguments, art practice had already begun to shift and to question established ideas of genius and creativity.

The body politic

> I do not need to visualize the word in order to know and pronounce it. It is enough that I possess its articulatory and acoustic style as one of the modulations, one of the possible uses of my body. I reach back for the word as my hand reaches towards the part of my body that is being pricked; the word has a certain location in my linguistic world, and is part of my equipment. I have only one means of representing it, which is uttering it.
>
> (Merleau-Ponty 1989: 180)

The period since the 1960s – whether or not we give it the title *postmodern* (and, as we have seen, the distinction between modern and postmodern is a slippery one) – has offered a radical critique of established structures of sexuality, race and gender and has revealed the political bias of what was paraded as natural and neutral under modernism. Postmodernism calls into question codes, structures and societal relationships – and with them the very structures by which we come to understand the world and our position within it.[13] What is important here is the notion of the individual subject and how that subject represents his or her position within society. Given that unmediated self-expression and subjective experience are reportedly defunct under postmodernism, it is ironic that the phrase 'express yourself' is more than ever a rallying cry for the disenfranchised and the marginalised. In an uncertain world, following our individualistic instincts seems to be one of the few ways left to validate our place in the overall scheme of things.

Postmodernism may have deprived the West of some of its staple ideas (for instance the idea of a unitary or core self) and unmasked the experience of *being* that we call 'identity' as an illusion, but it does not preclude the possibility that many individuals or groups do indeed feel that they have 'identities'. Although dismissed as a productive fiction, the trappings of individualism, especially the expressive significance of bodily activity, seem to be intact. That is not to say that we do not all have individual identities but that any idea that those identities are rooted in a pre-existing self has been undermined on several fronts. For example, scientific advances in genetic engineering and biotechnology offer the possibility of a predetermined blueprint for human life. Laying aside the proof that everything we think of as unique about ourselves is ultimately always socially instituted, there remains the sense that individuals do have a unique way of doing and saying particular things. Forgetting all the things that mark our activities as common, we are left with the realisation, however contentious, that the body is not a passive object seized by social practices but an active living entity, a being who learns from the social but then expresses what is learned in what are perceived to be unique gestures. Just as it is unsatisfying to view the body as the instrument of a non-material free will, so too it is misleading to conceive of it as the passive tool of social forces. The traditional dichotomy of free will versus determinism will not suffice as a model for the expressive body.

The expressive body becomes political when it meets other bodies, since at the point where one body ends and another one starts there are borders, and borders inevitably generate dispute. According to Judith Butler,

> If the body is not a 'being' but a variable boundary, a surface whose permeability is politically regulated, a signifying practice within a cultural field of gender hierarchy and compulsory heterosexuality, then what language is left for understanding this corporeal enactment, gender, that constitutes its 'interior' signification on its surface?
>
> (Butler 1990: 139)

The claim that the female body (and indeed other bodies) is politically and socially inscribed is symptomatic of the ways in which the physical body has been reconfigured in cultural and philosophical discourse since the 1960s. As Judith Butler argues above, the body is a political rather than biological site fixed within certain linguistic conventions (the body politic). In particular, the notion that the body is a metaphor for social and political models of behaviour is crucial to understanding the claims of much performance art. Mary Douglas wrote that 'the body is a model that can stand for any bounded system. Its boundaries can represent any boundaries which are threatened or precarious' (Douglas 1984: 115).

The artist Marina Abramovic explores the most precarious manifestation of the boundaries that can obtain between bodies – when bodies come under threat from other bodies. In her earliest work, for example *Rhythm O* (1974, Naples) (see Figure 8.5), Abramovic allowed herself to be physically and verbally abused by an audience for a period of six hours. Instruments of torture were laid out on a table as in a surgical operating theatre, and Abramovic permitted herself to be stripped and slashed. She explained the work, equating physical suffering with the emancipatory politics of self-expression: 'you have to nearly break your body before you can free the mind' (quoted in McEvilley 1983: 52). In a performance recorded on video, entitled *Art Is Beautiful. Artists Must Be Beautiful*, the artist brushes her hair in ever more vigorous strokes until she scratches her face with the hairbrush. Of course, there is ample precedent in many cultures for the idea that physical pain is a means of self-realisation (for instance in most religions where male denial of the body is a means to higher spiritual states) and that the mind is a prisoner of the body unless the body is physically undermined. It is not really surprising that women have been generally excluded from access to this form of spiritual attainment since women have historically been seen as in thrall to their bodies to the detriment of

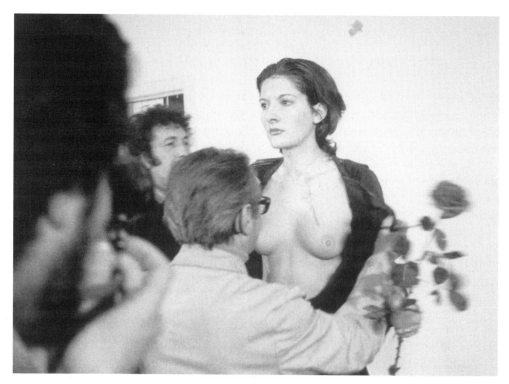

Figure 8.5 Marina Abramovic, *Rhythm 0*, 1974. © DACS, 2004. Digital image courtesy of the artist. The artist prepared the performance by laying out seventy-two items on a table, which included scissors, an axe and a loaded gun. The invitation to the audience to use the items on the performer ceased when some members became too aggressive and had to be stopped by other audience members. There are some black and white photographs that survive from the piece and Abramovic has subsequently published these in an edition of her performances, entitled *Artist Body: performances 1969–1998* (Charta, 1998).

their intellectual and spiritual development. Centuries of patriarchy have shaped and maintained a myth of woman as closer to nature, a martyr to her hormones and prone to hysteria.[14] As Diana Fuss puts it, 'on the one hand, woman is asserted to have an essence which defines her as woman and yet, on the other hand, woman is relegated to the status of matter and can have no essence' (Fuss 1989: 72).

We will return to this culturally complex designation of woman shortly, after first considering another question for the body politic raised by Abramovic's performance. Although such works as *Rhythm O* or Brus's *Breaking Test (Zerreissprobe)* (see Figure 8.4) are 'art' by declaration (since someone not sanctioned by the label 'artist' performing similar acts would be in danger of being declared obscene or insane), there is a consensus to 'suspend disbelief' around Abramovic's actions – to designate the processes of sadomasochism and self-immolation not simply as 'art' but as a gesture by the individual which is of collective interest and capable of collective representation. By definition, this is what the body politic is.

It can be inferred from the examples given thus far that many works of performance art are provocative – the result of a particular notion of spectacle and display in which expressive bodies enact their message. As we have already seen, in the past performance art has been criticised as being 'mere' theatre because it dramatises the relationship between object (in this case the artist's body) and beholder. Perhaps it is because the performance artist is generally in direct contact with the viewer (that is, unmediated by a canvas) that the message of the event can be uncompromisingly direct. 'Protest art' – as some forms of performance art were termed in the dissenting climate of the late 1960s – which sometimes mimed but more often re-enacted sadomasochistic acts, drew upon Bertolt Brecht's notion that the audience–performer relationship should be an uncomfortable one since this would reduce the gulf between the two (as we saw in Chapter 1). In 1972 the English performance artist Stuart Brisley lay in a stagnant bath in a darkened room for two weeks and invited an audience to watch the squalid spectacle, which he intended as a metaphor for the alienation of the individual. Entitled *And for Today . . . Nothing*, this was an act of symbolic self-punishment which signified Brisley's feelings about human alienation and the depoliticisation of the individual. For this performance Brisley lay in a bathtub full to the brim of water and floating detritus. Surrounding his allotted space within the gallery by rotting offal, Brisley created an oasis of squalor which caused problems for fellow exhibitors. The performative social commentary spoke up for 'the down and out' and in the spirit of other such performances was conceived as an unmarketable artistic gesture, although years later limited edition prints of the performances were made available. In 1972, however, Brisley's work demonstrated the move from body to body politic, the invocation of the body for the purposes of broader social comment or political demonstration.

Many performed events – and particularly those by women performance artists – were designed to unsettle the audience, just as surrealist film had aimed to do thirty years earlier, in the 1940s. Martha Rosler had been rallied into theatrical action by Michael Fried's 'starchy defence' of high modernism, which attacked art for being 'theatrical'. Rosler argued the opposite of Fried and maintained that art had to be in the same space as the viewer – a form of theatre (Rosler, quoted in Wood et al. 1993: 161). Rosler's video *Semiotics of the Kitchen* (1975) is relatively short, just over 6 minutes long, but in those few minutes Rosler moves from a muted demonstration of kitchen utensils to a more erratic handling of implements, explained in a voice of mounting excitement which contributes to a sense of unease in the viewer. Parodying the familiar format of a cookery demonstration, Rosler stands behind a kitchen counter with an array of standard cooking implements laid out before her. She picks up a grater, a knife, naming them and demonstrating their uses in turn. As she moves from one utensil to the next, the tone of her voice gets increasingly frustrated and the items are handled with increasing violence. Performance art's dependence on the vulnerable body has seen a large number of performances enacted in the nude and many which give recourse to sensationalist tactics. Some see the phenomena as a Brechtian intervention to disabuse the audience of its cosy middle-class sensibilities; others, however, have argued that the performance artist's banalisation of sex and bodily waste is a strategy not so much for shocking or offending middle-class sensibilities but for 'getting back to the body' (Brookes 1991: 144), precisely because in contemporary Western culture we do not generally expose our bodily functions to public scrutiny. As a metaphor for dissent or alienation, the annexed body, standing naked or being physically abused on a stage or in a gallery, rests partially on a notion of the 'abject'. Julia Kristeva's definition of the abject is that which 'does not respect borders, positions, rules' (1982: 4), and includes excrement, bodily emissions and death itself.

Whether just as a strategy for 'getting back to the body' or as exorcisms of the abject, the breaking of bodily taboos is a large part of the repertoire of performance artists. Bill Viola's *The Messenger* (1996), projected on to the Great West Door in Durham Cathedral, is a secular image of a male body floating underwater, coming to the surface and gasping for a deep breath. *The Messenger* reflects Viola's recurring motif of mortality. Viola also videotaped the birth of his child and the death of his mother in *The Nantes Triptych* (1992). Hannah Wilke recorded the last eighteen months of her life, documenting her illness in a series of photographs entitled *Intra-Venus* (1991–3). Bob Flanagan recorded his illness and death from cystic fibrosis on 4 January 1996 in a film entitled *Sick: the life and death of Bob Flanagan, supermasochist* (USA, 1997). The anatomist Gunther von Hagens has toured Europe with his collection of preserved flayed human bodies in the controversial but highly attended exhibition *Bodyworld*. Of course, there are many examples of the abject, especially the corruption of flesh, in the history of Christian art, where it served to highlight the mortality of the flesh and the transcendence of the soul. These secular images of death, although we might invest them with a 'spiritual significance', tend to reinforce the limitations of existence in and through the body. Apologists for the abject thus propose that we should not deny the visceral aspects of existence or distance ourselves from bodily functions. As Kristeva would have it, '[t]he abject is perverse because it neither gives up nor assumes a prohibition, a rule, or law, but turns them aside, misleads, corrupts; uses them, takes advantage of them, to better deny them' (Kristeva 1982: 15).

What Kristeva is saying is that the abject is a force for disrupting 'identity, system, order' and really a way of theorising one of the functions of the subconscious rather than a self-standing phenomenon. Her idea has been taken up by a number of artists who, if not exactly interested in psychoanalytical categories, are certainly interested in transgressing notions of what it is and is not permissible to display or to perform. Many artists have used the abject to make art, either by utilising actual bodily substances to make their art or by demonstrating visceral concerns. For example, Mark Boyle exhibited his

Bodily Fluids and Functions With Aldis Projection in 1966 and Piero Manzoni bottled his breath and canned his faeces in 1960. However, the new meanings given to bodily fluids in the 1980s with the onset of AIDS make other people's blood, saliva and sperm not only abject but also potentially life-threatening. For instance, the Los Angeles-based artist Ron Athey is HIV-positive and the use of hypodermic syringes, needles, razors and the artist's blood in his performances articulates his own experiences as a former drug-user. But his performances also, in Kristeva's terms, turn aside prohibitions and corrupt rules. One final thought at this point perhaps should be to acknowledge the appetite for images of people in pain. In her recent book *Regarding the Pain of Others* Susan Sontag has remarked that 'the appetite for pictures showing bodies in pain is as keen, almost, as the desire for ones that show bodies naked' (Sontag 2003: 36).

The phenomenal body

> Signifying must not be understood on the order of an immaterial mind that controls the body as a captain steers a ship. A person is his or her body. Once it is signified to someone that such and such an action is to be carried out, he therewith performs the bodily action that constitutes the signified one. For it is the same person signified who, *in being his body*, carries out bodily activity. There is no need for him to seize, occupy, or activate his body in order for bodily activity to occur ... an instrumental body does not imply that the body is an instrument.
>
> (Schatzki 1996: 45)

The emergence in the second half of the twentieth century of the notion of the 'body politic' testifies to a changing set of ideas about what the body may signify. Our way of thinking about the body changed in the post-war period largely as the result of two types of discourse – social anthropology and French philosophy. What these discourses have in common is their contention that the physical body is an object we 'perceive' rather than one which we 'possess'. For example, in the nineteenth century anthropology measured black people using quasi-scientific methods so as to order and classify 'species' as a justification for colonial rule. However, the social anthropology of the 1970s argued that 'the human body is always treated as an image of society' (Polhemus 1978: 21) and that the physiological properties of the body are subordinated to their ideological position within any given society.

James Luna's 1990 *Artifact Piece* combines performance and mixed media to question the representation of Native Americans and American Indians and the display of related artefacts in North American museums in order to show that not all bodies are equal. James Luna first performed *Artifact Piece* in the Museum of Man in San Diego in 1987. Lying on a bed of sand in a museum display case in a room full of Native American artefacts, Luna mimics all the conventions of display. The glass case is fronted with statuary labels that direct the viewer's gaze and provide factual reassurances about the items on display. However, the labels surrounding Luna point to scars on the artist's body and attribute them to excessive drinking. The museum-going public is used to looking at artefacts (textiles, woodcarvings, etc.) and even at dead bodies from ethnic

turn' (Eagleton 1983: 131). The notion of selfhood in the West continues to possess one such meaning. As we have seen, the construction of the artist as self and the viewer as self is a formalist one, where art is autonomous and comprised of discrete objects. Under this model of artist and art work, the individual is consciously and directly expressing his or her self to another self in the medium of paint, dance, poetry, music or performance. Expression in this sense is, according to Hegelian philosophy, where 'idea' achieves 'form'. It relies upon the continuing understanding that the intellectual and contingent worlds are separate and that expression is a temporary meeting of the two.

In terms of the phenomenal body, nothing is meaningful until it has been experienced by the body in and through the mind. Set against orthodox Western notions of unitary selfhood, the complex negotiations between mind and body in the understanding of self-hood are highly problematical. Writers often identify the separation of mind and body as beginning in the seventeenth century with René Descartes, who differentiated between 'matter' (*res extensa*, which is divisible – malleable) and 'mind' or 'soul' (*res cogitans*, which is indivisible – immutable). The performance artist Stelarc frequently cites Cartesian models of thinking in his work. As we will see shortly, Stelarc's desire to detach himself from his bodily functions by making 'the body' the spectacle of medical and scientific intervention or curiosity draws a sharp distinction between mind and matter.

Pre-Enlightenment theories, typified by Descartes, were gradually supplanted by constructions of rational man (formulated outside superstition) in the eighteenth century. Religious beliefs were overlayed by science to invent a rational self capable of disinterested thought. Freud, many believe, destabilised the notion of a rational self and disinterested thought at the end of the nineteenth and beginning of the twentieth centuries by identifying influences which were beyond conscious control – namely, the unconscious. For his former pupil, Jacques Lacan, and deconstructionists such as Jacques Derrida the self is a fiction – an illusion of storytelling.

Ferdinand de Saussure's theory of linguistics problematised language, arguing that the old certainties that the subject employs language to pursue his or her own purposes should in fact be reversed in favour of a model in which the subject is actually spoken by language – the autobiographer is not the speaker of a neutral language but the unwitting carrier of a loaded language. Social anthropology and the systematic inves-tigation of non-Western cultures have demonstrated that a sense of self is by no means universal and is always contained within language.

Yasumasa Morimura, through a process of reconfiguring the self into a kind of 'tech-notransvestite', uses digital technology to produce multiple selves.[15] For Morimura, currently interested in growth hormones and cosmetic surgery, the reconfiguring of the unitary self is not a negative act but opens up the possibility of freedom. He says: 'if it were possible to liberate ourselves from the bodies and characters we were given and to choose a favourite combination ourselves, expressions like "true face" would eventually become superfluous. And of course we would have no need for words like "self"' (Morimura, quoted in Weiermair 1996: 236). Morimura's *A Bar at the Folies-Bergère* (1991) reworks Manet's painting of the same name. Morimura's naked body is superimposed into the place formerly occupied by Manet's barmaid. However, and in a departure from earlier practice, Morimura changes the pose of the original occupant by crossing his arms. This change in posture leaves behind the severed arms of the first barmaid still fixed to the edges of the bar at the Folies-Bergères. In Manet's original the body of the woman Suzanne behind the bar can be seen as another commodity, amid the sale of alcohol. But Morimura superimposes his androgynous face and body on to Suzanne, thus blocking access to the customary readings of the painting. His unconvincing impersonation of Suzanne does not fool the viewer for long and the work appears not as palimpsest – a manuscript on which an earlier text has been effaced – but as an appropriation, whereby the all-too-apparent borrowing of a seminal work of modern art diminishes the privileges of the original. As Kaori Chino argues, Morimura confronts 'the violent masculine gaze' that is normally levelled at women and, she says, 'laughs it away' (Chino 2000: 252–65). Elsewhere the artist appropriates famous works of art by adding multiple versions of his own face (Burne-Jones's *Angels Descending a Staircase*, Rembrandt's *Anatomy Lesson of Dr Tulp* and Manet's *Olympia*, in which he appears as both Olympia and the maidservant). Morimura's serial replication of digitised selves attacks the West's notion of the unitary self by confronting it with sexually and racially ambiguous 'otherness'. His cultural intervention into Western universals plays on stereotypes that are dependent on the notion of unitary selfhood.

Modern art, with a handful of notable exceptions such as Picasso, purged allegory along with content and literary narrative. However, postmodernism's well-publicised 'returns', and especially its rehabilitation of the figurative within a narrative, have raised the profile of discredited styles and practices. The 'fabricated photography' of Cindy Sherman, although principally important in terms of role play and female identity, also resurrects historical imagery without ever entirely copying from historical examples. This kind of narrative is especially used in investigations of self and how the self is constructed, and role play is its favoured device.

Postmodern writers tend towards the view that there is no such thing as the unitary self. Under postmodernism the search for unitary selfhood is itself a shifting enterprise. This is not to say that there is no longer a dominant liberal humanist notion of unitary self or that all notions of unitary selfhood have suddenly been replaced by a postmodern heterogeneous model. On the contrary, the postmodern account of selfhood has been challenged by Terry Eagleton, for instance, as an 'ignorant and dogmatic travesty' which overlooks or oversimplifies the variable positioning of philosophical thinking (Eagleton 1996: 79). Nonetheless, we have seen how artists such as Morimura have played with the pieces left behind by the postmodern juggernaut.

'Decentred subject' is a phrase often used in relation to modern notions of the self. To understand the implications for current performance art practices of the 'decentred subject' the latter has to be seen as part of the project to undermine the notion of a fixed centre of any description – fixed centre of identity, of consciousness, of history. Freud's 'discovery' of the unconscious removed the certainty that there is a rational and conscious mind at the centre of being and Jacques Lacan's formulation of the 'mirror stage' has undermined it further. Reductively put, the 'mirror stage' is that stage in a child's development when, between six and eighteen months of age, the child develops the capacity to recognise his or her image and follow his or her movements in a mirror. The real conceptual leap for the child, however, is the awareness that accompanies this discovery, that there is a gap between self and self-image. Lacan also argued that women are born to a condition of 'lack'. The infant, according to Lacan, is not a human subject, but becomes one gradually through a subjectively illusory sense of autonomy. The infant gradually takes on a sexed identity, but at that moment female infants come to realise their lack of a phallus – not in the Freudian sense of lack, which leads to 'penis envy', but lack of a symbolic phallus, which stands for patriarchy. Infant girls are therefore unable to assume a place in the symbolic order of sovereign power. Although Lacan's ideas have been hotly debated, many feminist critics have seized upon his account of the moment of 'decentring' of self in the mirror phase and of the realisation of 'lack' as the mechanisms by which the individual subject is separated or alienated from larger cultural structures.

Écriture féminine: from essentialism to poststructuralism

> Linnaeus[16] what would you say,
> how define such wanton play?
> vaginal towers
> with male skirt,
> gender bending water sport?
>
> Come sit on me, my mandrill's arse
> cast priapic,
> former fold,
> suck my penis envy farce
> like old Vénus de Lespugue
>
> (Helen Chadwick, *Piss Posy*)

Nearly half of all the performance works in the 1970s were given by women. It is hardly surprising that those defined as 'other' should have been particularly concerned with questions of identity and selfhood. The female performance artist brought with her a complex, if occasionally repetitive, repertoire of experiences around which she negotiated the autobiographical intimacies of self. This coincided with the emergence of the women's movement and the wholesale reappraisal of art's objects and subjects. In 1971 the American art historian Linda Nochlin published an essay whose title asked the question 'Why Have There Been No Great Women Artists?' (see Nochlin 1989), and a year earlier Germaine Greer published *The Female Eunuch* (1970). While Nochlin's essay listed all the external constraints that had prevented women from becoming 'great' artists (most of them relating to lack of access to the institutions of art), Greer emphasised the internal constraints by which women have been 'bred' to undervalue themselves, referring to what she called 'damaged egos'. With hindsight, we can now see that both explanations were symptomatic of an unfolding history of ideas about women – from the psychoanalytical positioning of women as 'other' to the linguistic formations of a male-centred lexicon, to Marxist-feminist revelations about gender – all of which had a particular impact on women's performance art.

One feminist concern on which opinion is divided is the question of whether an art practice which is inherently female actually exists. The same question was first asked of literary practice, and to much the same effect, with women writers such as Virginia Woolf describing how they felt inhibited by the legacy of a language that is overpoweringly male and wondering what it would be like to write a female sentence. In much the same way, women artists either work within the framework of existing art practice or seek a separate one. Feminist writers such as Hélène Cixous have put forward the idea of an *écriture féminine*, which is exclusively associated with the female transgression of established forms of language, grammatical structures and meanings. Cixous believes that

> women must write through their bodies, they must invent the impregnable language that will wreck partitions, classes, and rhetorics, regulations and codes, they must submerge, cut through, get beyond the ultimate reserve-discourse, including the one that laughs at the very idea of pronouncing the word 'silence'.
>
> (Cixous 1981: 256)

This coercive language – women 'must' obey the call to a feminised separatism – is not always seen as being in the best interests of feminism. On the contrary, the idea of the 'pure essence' of the female (as expressed in an inherently female art practice) overcoming the institutional and/or gender conditioning described by Nochlin and Greer has raised eyebrows among anti-essentialists. Much feminism has been about deconstructing the idea of 'man' as a natural and normal category against which all human experience can be judged. The problem is that the proposed category of 'woman' seems also to overlook the experiences of black women, working-class women, lesbians and non-European women. Ideas about identity as the sum of socio-economic circumstances are so prevalent in contemporary critical theory that the notion of a more supranatural identity (essentialism) is untenable to many. Can women transcend conditions of time and place and just *be* women? These are questions that often concern, obliquely or directly, the female performance artist.

In the context of androcentric art practice, the popularity of performance art among women in the 1970s was part of the search for a feminised art practice. Painting and sculpture were often seen as male media; even the paintbrush has been described as ultimately phallic. When Shigeko Kubota performed her *Vagina Painting* in 1965, attaching to her knickers a paintbrush that had been dipped in red paint and squatting over a piece of paper, she parodied the associations of the paintbrush-as-phallus as used by action painters in the 1950s and Piero Manzoni's signature on the model in *Living Sculpture* (1961). On the one hand, Kubota appears literally to pre-empt Cixous's call for women to 'write through their bodies'; but, on the other hand, this kind of feminist aesthetic was subsequently revised in the 1980s on the grounds of 'biological reductivism'. But the project of 'making visible' that which traditionally was concealed – especially by drawing attention to female genitalia – was a necessary part of the genesis of the feminist project. Radical feminism of the 1960s and 1970s was very much associated with 'gynocentric' strategies. This first generation of feminism – sometimes called 'essentialist' feminism – was superseded in the 1980s and 1990s by second-generation 'poststructuralist' feminism.

Language- and text-based performance is important to much contemporary feminist art. The radical questioning of gender roles has by no means been abandoned and the body is still an important site of emancipatory politics. Helen Chadwick exhibited *Piss Flowers* (Figure 8.7), a set of twelve shiny white-enamelled bronzes arranged on the gallery floor. Each bronze is in the shape of a five-petal flower with a stamen in the middle, but was actually cast from plaster moulds made from 'piss holes' in the snow created by the artist and her male partner David Notarius. The fact that 'piss' is the origin of the form that the work takes is obviously important or else the artist would not acknowledge the fact in her title. Some critics have aestheticised the piece, commenting on the sensuous qualities of the bronzes; others read the work as a feminist subversion of the male habit of urinating to create territorial markings.[17] However, the artist described *Piss Flowers* as 'a metaphysical conceit for the union of two people expressing themselves bodily', and elsewhere it has been argued that the artist is interested in metaphysical questions of mind and body and how a work of art may unite the two. This might seem like a grand claim for pissing in the snow, but it has been argued that *Piss Flowers* are 'concrete realisations of the artist's body melting into the world outside' (Curtis 1993: 11).

Critiquing Jacques Lacan's theory that women are born to a condition of 'lack', Helen Chadwick's *Piss Flowers* can be seen as an inversion – the erect central stamen of the flower (Linnaeus's male sex organ) was made from Chadwick's urine, the flowery petals around it (Linnaeus's female sex organ) were created by the male collaborator's sprinkling of his urine. Chadwick's inversion of both Linnaeus's classification of plant species and Lacan's theory of lack parodies the virility of the creative male act by referencing one of the most basic of human activities. However, in critiquing the impartiality

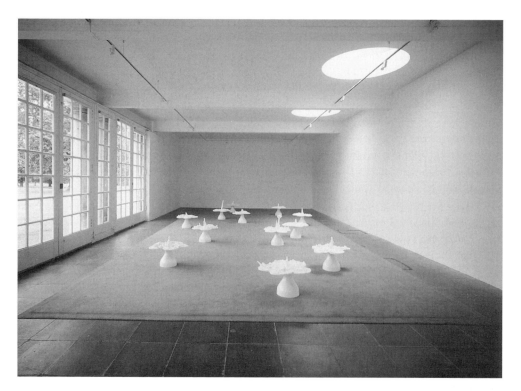

Figure 8.7 Helen Chadwick, installation shot of *Piss Flowers* at the Serpentine Gallery, London. Courtesy of the Estate of Helen Chadwick and the Zelda Cheatle Gallery. In the *Independent* newspaper Chadwick described production of the work she had begun in Canada with her partner David Notarius: 'we heaped up piles of snow and first I would piss into it and then he would piss around my mark. I made casts of the indentations which were eventually exhibited as bronze sculptures'. She regarded the creation of the Piss Flowers as a 'unique form of lovemaking'.

of science (in this case botanical classification), Chadwick also suggests the permeability of boundaries – that urine is part of the body until it is expelled, to be bounded by the body and then unbounded by the body.

Identity and 'identity politics'

The question 'what constitutes identity?' has, like notions of the self and the body, shifted in recent years. It used to be assumed that identity is a bedrock that binds us together – art works speak to 'us' and there is a universality in 'our' appreciation of them. However, the status of identity as a piece of absolute self-knowledge residing firmly in the conscious or rational mind has been questioned by Freud, Jung and Lacan. Although there are differences in approach, the abiding lesson seems to be that, since the subject is constituted in and by language, so too is identity.

We saw in Chapter 4 how notions of the 'other' put forward by Edward Said and Simone de Beauvoir have been used to differentiate the unequal relations between dominant and marginalised groups, although, increasingly in a postmodern world, it has been argued that we are all 'others'. For our purposes in this chapter, the 'other' is considered to be non-self – that is, 'not me'. To differentiate another's body in terms of its colour, sex, physical properties or sexuality is to confirm one's own identity. In terms of dominant discourses, the treatment of the 'other' is not always openly hostile: marginalisation can take a number of forms. What Gramsci (1971) defined as hegemonic control has been successful because it insinuates itself as natural and beneficial to the needs of both dominant and subservient groups. Thus hegemony may be endorsed from below by a confidence in its mutual benefits; for example, after the Second World War women vacated their 'unnatural' workplaces – shipyards, munitions factories and farms – and returned to their 'natural' workplace in the home. Hegemony operates only through complicit coercion, so that women, in the case of post-war reconstruction, continued to justify male economic privileges.[18]

Exposing these forms of control and empowering 'the other' through an exploration of identity has been very much a project of artists working from a position which they establish as 'other'. Keith Piper's *Surveillances: tagging the other* (1992) is a video showing the head and shoulders of a young black man in profile surrounded by a computer-generated box and the words 'subject' and 'reject'. The piece refers to the way in which young black men are visualised in terms of criminal stereotypes (or as potential criminals) in police photo-fits. Piper mediates representation in order to define 'identity politics' – in the sense that identity can be offered by communities formed on the basis of race, class, gender or sexual preference. That our belief in our own free agency should coincide with others' perceptions of their own free agency is the very basis of identity politics. For instance, although originally intended as shaming insults, the terms 'queer' and 'dyke' have been positively reclaimed by the gay and lesbian communities to neutralise their derogatory connotations.

While Piper exposes media stereotypes, Mary Duffy comments on the body fascism which has rendered disability and invisibility as one and the same thing. *Cutting the Ties That Bind* (1987) consists of eight panels which, when read from left to right, reveal the artist's body unravelling from a winding sheet. What starts as a 'timeless', disembodied, shrouded figure is eventually revealed to be an ambiguous image, rooted at once in the classical Greek ideal of a fragmented torso and in the less than idealistic construction of images of disability in current cultural practices. In *Stories of a Body* (1987) the artist, as both subject and object, questions attempts to normalise her body through medical technology. Our visual culture is one which does not extend the same cultural privileges to disabled bodies: the history of Western art immortalises ideals – famous people, beautiful women, magnificent horses, heroic bodies. It largely ignores old age, physical disability and disease except to use them to impart salutary lessons. The 'emancipated' image of Mary Duffy striding away from 'the ties that bind' is one which uses the conventions of autobiography (self-writing) to re-present and make visible the specificity of individual experience of the body. Characterised by Rosemarie Garland Thomson (1997: 1) as a 'stare and tell' method of performance, Duffy's accompanying narrative directly confronts the audience's prejudices and preconceptions ('you have words to describe me that I find frightening' (unscripted performance)) and forces them to reflect on their assumptions about disabilities. Duffy's performances are Brechtian in that they confront the audience. Lulling them first into a false sense of security by posing as a Venus de Milo, Duffy then uses performance and narrative to challenge the audience. She draws upon personal history that includes examples of prejudice, tactlessness and inappropriate medical intervention to demonstrate her current self-assurance and pride in her body.

The obsolete body

Thus far we have seen the body (usually the artist's body) playing a crucial role in the communication of the art work. From pure self-expression to the body politic, the placing of the body at centre-stage is a constant. However, some artists have questioned these overdeveloped notions of the self and identity as residing wholly in one's own body. For instance, the work of the Australian artist Stelarc, while firmly rooted in body art, predicts the eventual obsolescence of the body. Stelarc's body art has taken on several aspects since the 1970s: suspending himself from meat hooks through his back over selected sites; inserting an endoscope into his stomach in an act of bio-tourism; covering his body with electrodes to shock his muscles into movement. Stelarc refers to his art in the third person: he refers not to '*my* body' but to '*the* body' – for instance 'I suspended *the* body over a street in New York', 'I inserted an endoscope inside *the* body', and so on (see Schimmel 1998: 324–6). Stelarc's studied denial of first-person experience sits uncomfortably with his performances, which surely cause great physical discomfort to the artist. His performances assiduously predict the obsolescence of the body; he stands for the nihilistic belief that our assumption that we will continue to experience the world primarily through our bodies will diminish in the face of our increasingly technologised environment. Stelarc's performances in the 1990s used a 'stimulation system' to deliver up to 60 volts to electrodes strategically fixed on primary muscle sites. A touch-screen interface (sometimes controlled by Internet users who send instructions down the line) choreographs the artist's movements during the performance. He usually stands next to a 'robot', a giant yellow crane with a rotating 'eye' or video camera which scans the stage around Stelarc. Operated remotely or online by Internet users, the stimulation system causes Stelarc's muscles to contract and '*the* body' to move.

Stelarc's combining of his body with state-of-the-art technology has led some to compare him to a cyborg (although this is difficult to square with the more mechanised and sleek images of cyborgs in popular culture). As we saw in Chapter 5, the cyborg (a hybrid of human and machine) is a powerful metaphor in the twentieth and twenty-first centuries. In particular, the cyborg in postmodern culture has assumed a metaphorical state equivalent to that described under the rubric of 'decentred subject'. According to Donna Haraway's 'Manifesto for Cyborgs' (1991 first published in 1985), not only is a cyborg a metaphor for postmodern notions of identity as 'decentred' and 'hybridised', but it 'denaturalises' received ideas about whole or unitary selfhood. Haraway asks a basic but profound question: 'Why should our bodies end at our skin?' She argues that since new technologies have made it possible for us to think of ourselves as entities – a bundle of neurons that may be taken apart, combined with other entities or reconfigured altogether – we should be positive about its possibilities. Haraway is basically optimistic that new technologies will offer a truly decentred experience of selfhood and that this is of great value. She points to the fact that when the self was conceived to be unitary it was much easier to identify deviations from the norm and to judge them accordingly. With a 'split and contradictory self' there is a greater tolerance for diversity and deviation from the norm. Moreover, this idea of the self offers the possibility that, in theory at least, split halves can combine.

New technologies, then, have provided opportunities for individuals to exist beyond their skins. Since Sherry Turkle wrote of the computer as a 'second self' the prospect of 'reconstructing our identities on the other side of the looking glass' (Turkle 1995: 177) has seemed increasingly possible, especially through avatars. Avatars are artificial selves – electronically generated entities that 'exist' usually in online chat environments. The Internet user creates a (fictitious) digital alter ego to inhabit a simulated environment in cyberspace. Avatars, or digital alter egos, can assume any identity the user wishes, and as such they are currently generating a great deal of interest in debates about de-centred selfhood. The struggle to retain identity in a postmodern world, a world that is supposed to be somehow less 'real' for its inhabitants than was the modern world, makes the avatar a compelling metaphor for millennial culture. Opinion is divided on the potential of avatars.[19] For instance, it is estimated that there are eleven different genders of avatar on the Internet at the present time. However, the suggestion that life online will offer a different experience of self from that available via corporeal existence is somewhat premature.

Other ways of thinking about selfhood have been suggested by the science of biotechnology. The discovery of DNA, the engineering of animal cells and the advent of the Human Genome Project to find the blueprint for life have contributed to the notion of a 'post-human' society. The artists who comprise Gene Genies Worldwide have begun a long-term project, the *Creative Gene Harvest Archive* (see Figure 8.8), which (they say on their web site) aims 'to harvest, store, and utilize the genetic codes for creativity from some of society's most exemplary and creative individuals in order to design and imbue personalities with these same traits' <http://www.genegenies.com>. The *Creative Gene Harvest Archive* displays the genetic samples donated by individuals who lead in their respective fields. The hair from geneticists James Watson (who co-discovered DNA), Marie-Claire King (who located the gene for breast cancer) and Ian Wilmot (who cloned 'Dolly' the sheep) are displayed in glass vials alongside the hair

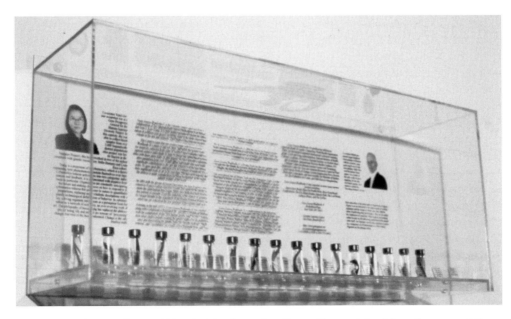

Figure 8.8 Genes Genies Worldwide, *Creative Gene Harvest Archive*. Courtesy of Gene Genies Worldwide. The two 'bio-designers' behind Gene Genies Worldwide, Tran T. Kim Trang and Karl S. Mihail, describe the *Creative Gene Harvest Archive* as 'the eighth wonder of the world'. Essentially, the project is an ongoing archive of the world's most scientifically and artistically gifted individuals. Each selected individual is represented by a sample of their hair (containing their DNA) and displayed in a neatly arranged row of vials in a plexiglass cabinet. More information can be found at <http://www.genegenies.com>.

of authors, artists and architects, including Damien Hirst, Stephen Hawking and I.M. Pei. Although the project could be seen as the creation of another DNA sample bank, the work raises (whether by design or in innocence) questions about genetic privacy, genetic property and the accountability of biotechnology which concern many organisations and individuals at the present time.

In this chapter we have seen how subjective experience, in the period we call postmodern, has been deprived of many of its privileges. As Craig Owens writes:

> For modern man, everything that exists does so only in and through representation. To claim this is also to claim that the world exists only in and through a *subject* who believes that he is producing the world through producing its representation.
>
> (Owens 1990: 67)

Avatars, cyborgs and the decentring of the self have questioned the notion of free agency: the idea that 'we' – a set of unitary selves – exercise determination if not outright control over our desires and destinies and that we create our own meanings. As the examples discussed here of performance art and photography of the body reflect, a Romantic self-absorption and preoccupation with subjective experience are by no means defunct in contemporary art practice, but the whole process of representing the self in and through the body has been made sociologically, politically and philosophically accountable.

Afterword

The relationship between the discipline we refer to as art history and the industry we call the art world is difficult to pin down. On the one hand it has been argued that art history is a parasitic practice because it seems to depend upon the industry of artists. On the other hand it has been argued that without the scholarly apparatus provided by art history the work of artists lacks legitimacy. What is commonly called the art world is less a community of people involved in the creative industries and more a co-existing network of museums, galleries, festival organisers, publishers, academics, dealers, collectors, archivists, libraries and artists not necessarily working in symbiosis. It is worth reflecting on the way in which the symbiotically linked practices of art and art history have significantly changed in the last half-century.

To take an example, *Documenta*, the world's biggest contemporary art show, a quin-quennial round-up of contemporary art with aspirations to being cutting edge in terms of work, curatorship and modes of display, was inaugurated in 1955. It was the brain-child of the painter Arnold Bode and is held approximately every four or five years in Kassel in Germany for 100 days. You may remember that Joseph Beuys's environmental project *7,000 Oaks* was initiated there (see Chapter 3). Shows such as *Documenta* are nor-mally presided over by an international jury, and *Documenta* has become the artistic equivalent of the Oscars. The title of the second show in 1959 was simply *Art after 1945*. The last *Documenta*, *Documenta 11* however, marked a departure from previous shows in several respects. First, its director, the Nigerian-born Okwui Enwezor, founding editor of *Nka: Journal of Contemporary African Art*, was not a European and some of his co-curators represented cultures normally on the fringe of avant-garde activity. Moreover, rather than be limited to the 100-day format, the curators staged what were termed 'plat-forms' across four continents. Each consisted of an artists' forum, film symposia and so on, redrawing the show's existing boundaries. The theme too marked a radical depar-ture from the norm, in political terms raising such issues as transnational justice, democ-racy and cultural translation. The exhibition covered incipient practices from cultures not normally legitimated by the international art fest: China, India and Nigeria. In this respect, New Delhian Ravi Agarwal's photographic exhibition showed the plight of India's landless and poor, victims of the international toxic waste trade. Moreover, under the overarching banner of globalisation, like *Documenta X*'s '100 days – 100 guests', 'talk' was as important as display, with the show's interdisciplinary format embracing philosophy, architecture, and film to make *dialogue* an integral part of the fair.

Enwezor's political agenda is explicit; he states:

My interest in curating came first through an attempt to interrogate the highly restricted spaces of contemporary art production. These spaces were restricted by the art market on the one hand, and on the other hand by a method of historical writing, dominated by Western academic perspectives that sought to preserve long-standing prejudices. Forms of contemporary production that were seen to have no place within the history of Western self-understanding were too often dismissed or simply ignored.

(Enwezor 2003: 92)

It was through visiting exhibitions that Enwezor became aware of the *framework* of radical art that was 'discriminatory, exclusionary and oftentimes downright arrogant about art and ideas it had little understanding or knowledge of' (Enwezor 2003: 92). Moreover, in curating *Documenta* Enwezor was committed to an interdisciplinary exhibition, forging new subject alliances, working across different cultural domains, a far cry from *Art after 1945* in 1959. Works are created specifically for *Documenta* a significant shift from being a showcase for existing works. What concerns us here is the chameleon-like quality of the works themselves in 2002. During the exhibition, installations became workshops or performance arenas and the whole Expo' took on a theatrical, multimedia atmosphere. Moreover, if it is not stretching a point, the structure of the show resembles contemporary theorists' enthusiasm for a rhizome structure made fashionable by the theorists Gilles Deleuze and Felix Guattari (1987). Like the bulbs from which the rhizome structure takes its name and form, an informal structure was used at the Expo' to evoke a system of thought and social interactions that have no central stem or original point but, rather, exist as an informal network. The rhizomatic structure is therefore a collection of local, multidimensional descriptions with no fixed points. It is doubtful, however, whether the complete overturning of the structures of the art world took place. Although there were many artists representing cultures and practices from the periphery, such as *The Nunavut (Our Land) Series* (1994–5), a work filmed as episodes from an Inuit soap opera set in 1945 that followed the fortunes of an Igloolik family, the star system of both artist and *Über*-curator was still very much in evidence. Nonetheless, the art show did attempt to disrupt what Enwezor referred to as 'the contradictory heritage of grand conclusions' (Enwezor 2003: 43) by abandoning the periphery/centre dichotomy to offer a different art circuit.

The changes at *Documenta* have been mirrored in other showcases for contemporary art, the international biennales. In the *Venice Biennale 1895–1968: from salon to goldfish bowl*, Lawrence Alloway charted the changes that took place as the discreet charm of the art salon gave way to the political battles conspicuously fought at the level of national cultural performance during the Cold War period. Post-Second World War, National Pavilions, the organising structure for the *Venice Biennale*, were prone to demonstrations of ideological superiority as well as showcasing a stylistic binary opposition: for example, socialist realism, the preferred aesthetic of the Soviet and Communist countries, was pitted against an expressive modernist art claiming the high moral ground for 'free' Western cultures. The *Venice Biennale*, although not the only international show, has dominated media interest and maintained an almost exclusive right to serious consideration as a platform for the best of contemporary art. This exclusivity was very much in evidence as a rash of new biennales from outsider groups from Havana (1984) and Liverpool (1999, 2002, 2004) to Johannesburg (1995–7) caused journalists to stretch their punning and metaphors to accommodate the peripheries' aspirations to biennalehood. Although often modelled on the progenitor in Venice, the newer biennales are significantly different; many do not deny the local in favour of internationalism but seek to reconcile the local with the international, to invest in a local-internationalism. However, before we applaud the inclusiveness of the new art worlds it is noteworthy that most of the British artists selected for 2002's *Documenta* and 2003 *Venice Biennale* can be located via dealers with London postcodes. At a more parochial level, women artists do have an increasingly higher profile; for instance, Catherine Yass represented Britain at the *Tenth India Triennale* with her series of portraits of the Indian film industry, *Star*. And for the media-friendly Turner Prize, held annually at Tate Britain in London, in 1997 all four shortlisted artists were women. However, since the competition's inception in 1984 just two of the nineteen winners have been women: Rachel Whiteread in 1993 and Gillian Wearing in 1997. Furthermore, as was the case in Johannesburg, the arrival of the cultural apparatus that surrounds art biennial, triennial and quinquennial stood in stark contrast to the political and social reality of living in post-apartheid South Africa.

The theme of the *Sydney Biennale* in 2002 was *(The World May Be) Fantastic*, the curator Richard Grayson revealing that it would focus on 'practices that use fictions, narratives, invented methodologies, hypotheses, subjective belief systems, modellings, fake and experiments . . . on the fantastic, partial, various, suggestive, ambitious, subjective, wobbly and eccentric to normal orbit' (McDonald 2002: 11). There is a link between Grayson's fragmentary register and Enwezor's criticism of the frameworks of Western art. For Grayson it is crucial that the biennale reflect on 'quotidian cultures and dominant belief systems, [and suggest] that they are not inevitable, but are mutable, contingent, developing, hallucinatory, slippery and various' (Grayson 2002: 11).

It is a commonplace observation that the world has changed, but it is worth emphasising just how different the international exhibitions are and yet how much of the same ground they tread. There are, however, two major developments that concern us here: art as spectacle and the impact of the new media which mediate our consumption of modern art. New media, film and video dominated 2002's *Documenta* – its globalisation theme being realised in part through new technologies, with their conceit of the collapse of space and time. International shows are between a rock and a hard place in this respect. While technology has come to be synonymous with globalisation, exemplified by the ubiquitous banks of computers and a supporting cast of screens and projectors at most art exhibitions, technology can also be used as a gesture to counter globalisation. The 'free' circulation of information is a prime requisite for globalisation but it is only available to those with the hardware and power to utilise it. Technology can make explicit the difference between those within the networks of power and those without. Technology, as we discussed in Chapter 5, is not neutral but is context dependent, its universal aspirations of connectedness fraudulent. Technology can authenticate difference as well as transcend boundaries.

Spectacle is not unrelated to the issue of technology. The international shows can be seen as part of what the French situationist Guy Debord (1994) termed the 'society of the spectacle'. In brief, the term refers to a way of viewing the spectacle, a process of seeing at a distance. This way of viewing the world ignores our complicity in the objectifying gaze. According to Debord, within capitalist societies everything has become a spectacle mediated by the superficial image, a condition where reality is cast into doubt and everything enters a world of appearances and commodification. Not for the first time in this introduction to modern art are we confronted by the tensions of life under capitalism, with both dystopian visions of the society of the spectacle (Debord) and the utopian promise of greater democratisation and the popularisation of culture, the collapse of the high-art/low-art divide through the levelling potential of technology.

In 2003 the *Fiftieth International Art Exhibition* at the *Venice Biennale*, which represents sixty-four nations, directed by Francesco Bonami, was called *Dreams and Conflicts: the dictatorship of the viewer*. It is worth reflecting on the earlier themes of the *Venice Biennale*: in 1954 it was *surrealism* with no aspiration to transcultural representations or deference to interpretation by an audience. The organising principle of the Fiftieth Exhibition is of no start or finish, no apex or hierarchy. According to their web site, the organisers of the biennale propose that 'the viewer-reader of this map will . . . be able to build upon each of the singular contemporary artistic experiences . . . no beginning and no end but the various locales with different visions and concepts used to tackle a contemporaneous voyage' <http://www.labiennale.org/en/visualarts/exhibition>. This particular contemporaneous voyage includes some specific transcultural commentaries that demonstrate the contingent and ephemeral existence of our experience of cultural identities. Modern states are bound together by what Eric Hobsbawm has termed 'invented tradition' (Hobsbawm and Ranger 1983: 1). A showcase for the nation-state, the 2003 *Venice Biennale* visualised the reworkings of the 'invented tradition' to present plural identities (rather than hyphenated or hybrid identities). Chris Ofili, Manchester born and of Nigerian ancestry, a former Tate Gallery Turner Prize winner, represented Britain. His five huge canvases supported by the trademark piles of elephant dung depicted a fantasy jungle-like world, at once recalling the child's picturebook of the colonial period and an imaginative world far from the reality of the lived experience of Africa. The paintings also utilise the red, black and green of the pan-African flag. Ofili's incursion into black history and diaspora chimed with the US pavilion, where Fred Wilson's *Speak of Me as I Am* made explicit the distance travelled by black peoples. The pavilion is supported by classical columns of black slaves. Inside the artist charted the history of African immigration to Venice, a journey visible in many Renaissance paintings. It is the entrance to the exhibition that points to the conflict alluded to earlier, between the international art market and the lived experience of diasporic peoples. Here, Wilson places a Senegalese street peddler selling handbags laid out on a white sheet, an overlooked and yet familiar sight in many of the world's large cities. Wilson's work makes an important point that could be usefully extended as a metaphor for the neo-liberal globalisation aspirations of curators and art markets. The restructuring of the world order is not easily accomplished and art's part in a process predicated on the principle of the unrestricted circulation of art, money, people and so on is not without its casualties. The charge of elitism laid against modernism is still largely intact.

Art history has underwritten every single one of these various biennales and art shows. Without the catalogues, scholarly web sites, periodical reviews in lifestyle magazines, plenary sessions, academic conferencing and informed curatorial agendas each biennale, triennial or *Documenta* would be exposed on a number of fronts. The regulatory bodies of arts organisations, panels and committees monitor, audit, prioritise for funding and censor the work of artists, and often work in tandem with art-historical procedures: art historians will often be on selection committees, provide critical essays or referee. Once work is selected for exhibition, funding and distribution art history again intervenes to review, curate and add gravitas to contemporary art.

Glossary of key terms

The following are broad definitions of terms or phrases contained within this book. However, some of the terms have a narrower application; these are defined in the specific sense of their usage in particular chapters.

abject Julia Kristeva's book *Powers of Horror: an essay on abjection* (1982) drew upon psychoanalysis to describe the precarious boundaries between inside and outside the body. The abject is that which the body excretes, and therefore is no longer part of the body yet remains implicated in the construction of the body. Kristeva's interest lay not in the abject so much as in the theory of abjection that manipulates and subverts boundaries, conventions and laws.

abstract Generally polarised against figurative art or naturalism, though one should guard against hard and fast distinctions since all art works are abstracted in some way. Abstract art generally refers to art that either does not represent things from the visible three-dimensional world or only partially suggests things.

abstract expressionism Although in use from the 1920s onwards, abstract expressionism came to describe the work of painters based mainly in New York in the 1940s and 1950s. Broadly speaking, their work is characterised by formal experimentations with media (generally paint) and the evolution of unique signature styles.

academies of art First formed in Europe in the sixteenth century to professionalise training for students in the fine arts. By the eighteenth century academies' institutional apparatus had enforced *classical* models of painting and sculpture, and this regime remained in place until the end of the nineteenth century. The authority of the academies was challenged by an artistic *avant-garde*.

aesthete At its most extreme a way of life that advocated art for art's sake, strangely at odds with nineteenth-century utilitarian art practice. The opposite of an aesthete was a philistine. Coming out of the Aesthetic Movement, it was by definition class based, living life as art, the pleasures of the privileged few.

aesthetic Imported from philosophy, aesthetics is concerned with the principles of taste according to which judgements about what constitutes 'beauty' are made, though art-historical discourse tends to refer rather to 'the aesthetic'. The debate around the construction of the aesthetic has, on one side, Immanuel Kant (1724–1804) and his twentieth-century acolytes Clive Bell and Roger Fry supporting the notion of a universal 'disinterested' aesthetic, immune to the contingencies of the day; on the other are the more recent theorists who have argued that the aesthetic is relative to and ultimately informed by local conditions. More recent scholarship insists that the context in which the art object was produced and that in which it is subsequently viewed (including the class, race and gender of the viewer) invariably impinges upon our appreciation of the art object's merit.

alienation   The feeling of estrangement from society or powerlessness in a given situation is characterised as alienation, although there are specific concepts of alienation within modernism. First, for Marxism alienation is a core concept to describe the distancing of the worker from the product of his or her labour under capitalism. In Romantic constructions of the artist alienation is a condition of nonconformity, a process of self- or societal exclusion that marks the artist as separate from non-artists and other more conformist artists.

alienation effect (*Verfremdungseffekt*)   This was a strategy to expose theatrical illusions by repeatedly reminding the audience that the drama they were watching was contrived; for example, scenery and props are unnaturalistic, and acting styles are exaggerated or self-referential. The alienation effect disrupts the conventional expectations of theatre-goers, who would normally 'suspend disbelief' in order to become emotionally involved rather than distanced by the scenery and acting.

art brut   Term coined by Jean Dubuffet to describe one form of 'outsider' art – that is to say, art produced by the mentally ill, the untutored, children. Typically it involves naive and unsophisticated techniques of colour and composition, although the effects tend to be more 'brutal' (in the sense of raw and crude) than expressionistic.

aura   This term gained currency within art-historical debates because of its use by Walter Benjamin. His influential essay 'Art in the Age of Mechanical Reproduction' (1937 see Benjamin 1970), argued that the aura is an attribute that we give to original works of art to distinguish them from reproductions. It is a special property of the original work of art, in respect of which we invest the work with an almost sacral presence that supposedly transcends its material fact.

autonomy   'Art's autonomy' frequently features as shorthand to assert art's freedom from cultural, political and social structures and strictures. Early in the twentieth century, notions of autonomy (especially in the sense of 'art for art's sake') fuelled debate around the direction that art should take. By the mid-1950s, through the dominance of formalist critics like Clement Greenberg, a victory for autonomy seemed assured. Since the 1960s, however, the Greenbergian notion of autonomy has been attacked for its assumption that art is radically free from social contingencies and cultural shifts.

avant-gardism   Seen by some theorists as a prerequisite condition of modernity, avant-gardism is closely linked to ideas of bohemianism, alienation and counter-culture. The term described the jettisoning by nineteenth-century artists of conventional practices (especially academic conformity) in art, music and literature. Although still a moot point, avant-gardism is often seen (for example by theorists such as Peter Burger) as having two irreconcilable strands: the political and the apolitical. The alleged death of the avant-garde as early as the 1970s can be seen in the light of increasing pluralism and a lack of consensus about that to which the avant-garde stands in opposition.

Bauhaus An influential German school of art and design located in Weimar, Dessau and Berlin between 1919 and 1933. The Bauhaus sought to unite the fine and applied arts in a utopian coalition of technology and art. Endorsing a loosely *constructivist* approach to art and design, the enforced closure of the Bauhaus by the National Socialists in 1933 failed to prevent its highly influential teachings on art and design becoming widespread after the Second World War.

bohemianism A taste for the unconventional; bohemian describes those who conform to unorthodox (according to the standards of the day) manners. Artists and writers have been associated with the term since the nineteenth century, when their lifestyles were viewed as outside bourgeois social and moral codes of behaviour.

bourgeois culture Although synonymous with the middle classes, in the first half of the nineteenth century 'bourgeoisie' designated (according to Karl Marx) a revolutionary force responsible for social upheavals in France. In the second half of the nineteenth century the bourgeoisie themselves became the establishment, and their attendant ideologies predominated. This antecedent has defined bourgeois culture as one which is essentially conventional, unadventurous and supportive of the status quo, though the often disparaging usage of the term suggests an acquisitive materialism.

camp At a time when mass culture all too readily parodies itself, it is difficult to make any enduring definitions of camp. Twenty years ago Susan Sontag said camp 'can be serious about the frivolous, frivolous about the serious' (1966: 276). Since then queer theorists have taken issue with many of the claims for camp (especially with those who confuse camp and kitsch). Nothing is inherently camp, it only becomes camp by association; so faux, retro, and pastiche cultural expressions (anything produced by Aaron Spelling, ABBA, the Village People) may be open to a process of arbitration that designates it as camp in the appropriate literature.

canon A collective noun used by art historians to identify works and artists considered to be of major significance to the development of particular forms. For an artist to be given canonical status was once seen as an issue of quality but is now seen as the result of a combination of factors – the art market, institutional validation rather than any intrinsic worth. The canon is not fixed and may be revised in the light of critical ratification.

chance A strategy associated with surrealism to bypass premeditated end results. It was considered to be a way of evoking the irrational since the techniques employed in the pursuit of chance results (frottage, decalcomania, etc.) were not subject to the controls of the conscious mind.

classical Once a formal designation of Greek and Roman artefacts, classical art came to be associated with the *academies*, which taught students to improve upon nature, idealising the subjects of the human figure and the landscape according to certain preconceptions about composition – proportion, harmony and colour. Neo-classicism was the prevailing standard of excellence in the nineteenth century in opposition to which the *avant-garde* defined itself.

Cold War   A term coined in 1947 to describe hostilities, real and imagined, between the United States and the USSR. This was a war conducted largely through political and economic wrangling and the spread of propaganda on both sides, including government support of 'culture' as a weapon. The collapse of Communism, symbolised by the dismantling of the Berlin Wall, effectively saw an end to much Cold War rhetoric.

collage/décollage   Collage is the act of attaching materials to a surface, and décollage is the act of unsticking or peeling away. While always a feature of popular and domestic craft, collage gained *high-art* status through the work of the cubists after 1912 and the artists connected with the *Dada* movement, in particular Hannah Hoch and Kurt Schwitters.

commodity   The slogan 'born to shop' may very well prove to be a defining one in the new millennium. It is a marker of the purchasable status awarded to all products, including works of art. However, since the mid-nineteenth century works of art have been subject to the forces of market values and have acquired investment status.

conceptual art   In part a reaction to the commodity status of the art object, conceptual art deliberately produced works that were irrelevant to the art market. Generally avoiding traditional fine art practice (easel paintings or conventional sculptures), conceptual art often explores ideas, often rooted in leftist and feminist political thought, rather than product. These ideas are often articulated in sound, language, the body, the gallery space, and in the 1960s they confounded the expectations of the art market and the gallery-going public.

connoisseur   Authority deriving from an ability to judge the merits of a work of art on the basis of taste justifies the epithet connoisseur. Since the 1960s authority through taste alone has been superseded, in art-historical terms, by *Marxist*, *feminist* and *postcolonialist* scholars, who base their judgements on more tangible criteria.

constructivism   This term has come to describe the work of painters, designers and architects in revolutionary Russia during the first two decades of the twentieth century. Constructivists usually worked in an *abstract* idiom to an impersonal and common revolutionary agenda. Its utopian associations, fuelled by an enthusiasm for socialism, technology and the machine, were developed by the Bauhaus after 1923.

culture   A term which so proliferates as both suffix and prefix (youth culture, mass culture, television culture, culture shock, culture vulture) that in *postmodern* societies culture is inclusive of much more than what even today passes as art. Art history has both benefited and lost out from the academic romancing of cultural studies: on the one hand, the inclusion of popular culture, comics and film has opened up the discipline; on the other, it has caused a crisis of confidence about the identification, for purposes of study, of art's appropriate subjects.

Dada   The name selected for a loose confederation of artists (including Hugo Ball, Emmy Hennings, Marcel Duchamp, Francis Picabia, Hans Arp, Man Ray, John Heartfield and Kurt Schwitters), musicians, poets and performers working in Zurich, New York, Berlin, Cologne, Paris and Hanover between 1916 and 1921. Appalled by the destruction left after the First World War, Dada responded by challenging notions of rationality and *bourgeois* values through *performance*, soundworks, *readymades* and *collage*.

décollage   See **collage**.

deconstruction   Jacques Derrida's influential book *Of Grammatology* (first published in 1967) highlighted the contradictions between the conscious intentions of the writer and the meanings supplied by the text (he was writing specifically about literary texts). The application of deconstruction to art history tends towards an analysis of the complex 'play of meanings' in visual images.

degenerate art (entartete Kunst)   The name given to the exhibition organised by the Nazis in 1937 in Munich and used to describe the art of key modernists. Equating modern art practice with cultural (and frequently Jewish) bolshevism, Hitler and Goebbels attempted to discredit many established modern artists by exhibiting their works alongside work produced by children, 'primitives' and inmates of lunatic asylums. It was seen as degenerate in the sense that the work was an atavism and it was juxtaposed with the official state-sponsored art (National Socialism) exhibited at the nearby Haus der Deutsche Kunst.

dematerialisation of the art object   Lucy Lippard's influential book *Six Years: the dematerialisation of the art object from 1966 to 1972* (first published in 1973) first coined the phrase to describe a phase in art history in which the traditional art object 'dematerialised' (for Lippard this was between 1966 and 1972). As part of the *conceptual art* movement, the dematerialisation of art works was part of a strategy to remove the artist from much fine-art practice by embracing cross-disciplinary activities (sound, poetry, performance and film) and distancing the artist from the crude capitalist culture that surrounded the successful artist. The attainment of an entirely uncommodified art work was arguable since the art market swiftly found ways to incorporate the activities of those dematerialising their art within existing institutions and structures.

discourse   According to Michel Foucault, discourses generate knowledge about particular groups, objects or ideas (as well as being specific to those groups – hence medical discourse, legal discourse, etc.). A dominant discourse is the product of dominant social and institutional formations, which may be why discourse is sometimes confused with *ideology*.

earthworks/land art   The practice of creating large, outdoor works of art in the environment greatly extended the scope and influence of sculpture in the 1960s (see Ros Krauss's *Sculpture in an Expanded Field*). Generally, but not exclusively, allied to an interest in ecology and green politics, land or earth artists concentrate on creating 'interventions' in the landscape (arranging stones, temporarily wrapping landscape features or building biodegradable structures). Many land artists work within communities or on communal projects, and these are often to create structures that are temporary. The projects are nearly always documented, resulting in some form of gallery exhibitions of portions of the project.

Enlightenment   An eighteenth-century philosophical (in the broadest sense) movement, also called the 'Age of Reason', characterised by the tendency to order the world through systematic categories of knowledge. The Enlightenment was epitomised by the production of the world's first encyclopaedia. The Enlightenment project is associated with humanistic scepticism, political reform and a thoroughgoing belief in the efficacy of science and the centrality of man (as opposed to God). The reforming zeal of Enlightenment thinkers deeply influenced the French and American Revolutions, and underscored the shift from aristocratic to *bourgeois culture*.

epistemology   The theory of the method of or grounds for knowledge which distinguishes between what it is possible and what it is impossible to know as well as the reliability of knowledge.

ethnography   Strictly speaking, this term designates the study of cultures from the inside. However, within Western art history the term has a more specific application, since so much modernism was driven by a desire to simulate the *primitive*. Paradoxically, African masks and Aboriginal 'paintings' have traditionally been displayed in cabinets in museums rather than on the walls and pedestals of art galleries alongside modernist approximations.

Existentialism   Existentialism is an important element in post-war thought. Although its philosophical roots can be traced back to mid-nineteenth-century Europe and Søren Kierkegaard (1813–55) and later Martin Heidegger (1889–1976), its influence on American painting is most usually situated in post-war France and the writings of Jean-Paul Sartre and Simone de Beauvoir. Existentialism emphasised the need to take responsibility for one's own existence but acknowledged the unpredictable and anxiety-producing state that a rejection of any sense of determinism might produce. In the context of post-war uncertainty it is relatively easy to relate existentialism to abstract expressionism.

expressionism   This term has come to signify paintings, sculpture, dance, theatre and film which emphasise mood and exaggerate feeling. Although the roots of expression theory are wrapped up in psychoanalytical theory and philosophy, expressionism is often located in the work of early German modernists – such as Käthe Kollwitz and Ernst Ludwig Kirchner – whose unconventional techniques (exaggerated outlines and unnaturalistic colours) were highly influenced by notions of *primitivism*. Hal Foster's influential essay 'The Expressive Fallacy' (1985c) has uncovered some of the myths of expression theory.

feminism/post-feminism   Well-documented 'interventions' in mainstream art and art history have exposed a system of patriarchy which has long controlled the institutions of art. Feminism introduced more rigorous methodologies as a way of uncovering *gender* bias in relation to images and writing about images. The term post-feminism acknowledges that the debate has moved on; post-feminists have revised earlier positions and introduced a greater plurality of references.

fin-de-siècle   French term used widely across Europe to describe 'the end of the (nineteenth) century'. The end of the century was characterised by anxieties about the momentous social and political changes, which included the moves for the emancipation of women, the enfranchisement of working men and the decline of the aristocracy in a climate of increasing secularisation and erosion of older certainties. In art and literature morbid preoccupations with death, disease and errant female sexuality are characteristic of the *fin-de-siècle*.

Fluxus A loose confederation of international writers, musicians and artists first visible in New York in 1960 but with centres across Europe and Japan. Incorporating much conceptual and performance art as well as experimental music, Fluxus attacked many of the institutions and orthodoxies of the art world, specifically notions of *originality* and authenticity. Fluxus contributed to the *dematerialisation of the art object* through strategies such as mass-producing works of art in the style of games and boxes, *performance* and 'instruction art works' which defied formal modernist notions of authorship.

formalism The critical practice of privileging an art work's formal qualities (colour, composition, technique, etc.) over its content (subject matter and socio-historical context). Its key twentieth-century exponents include the Bloomsbury writers Clive Bell and Roger Fry, and the American modernist critic Clement Greenberg. In recent years formalism has been challenged on the grounds that criticism should be more responsive to a wider range of contexts.

futurism Filippo Marinetti launched the movement in Italy with the first futurist manifesto in 1909 (Marinetti 2003). The futurist programme rejected earlier Italian movements, particularly the *Renaissance*, in favour of a celebration of the machine age, speed, the automobile and cities. The movement covered all the arts, from painting and sculpture to performance, music and dance, and fashion design.

gaze The acknowledgement that looking is socially and culturally regulated has given rise to theories of the gaze. The understanding that across different cultures there are codes of looking (i.e. that determine who can be looked at, for how long and at what parts of the body individuals may look) has led to a re-evaluation of the power relations implicit in looking. Thus today it is possible to talk about the 'gay gaze' or the 'female gaze'.

gender The understanding that there is a difference between biological sex (male or female) and the social constructions of men and women is at the root of gender studies. Commencing with *feminism* in the 1960s, gender has since extended to studies of *masculinity*. More recent gender studies emphasise the performative aspects of gender; that is, then argue that gender is not to be understood so much as something we are as something we do.

happening The term, coined by Allan Kaprow in 1959, is applicable to art which at some stage of its production incorporated a *live* element of performance. Starting in New York the phenomena of happenings became an international one by the early 1960s. Happenings are mostly performed in galleries (in front of an invited audience) and include the neo-*Dada* strategies of action painting, *collage* and assemblage.

hegemony In its original application, hegemony meant 'lordship', but it came to be used to signify the dominance of one group or culture over another. In Marxist criticism it has a more precise application: hegemony designates the complex socio-economic and political control exerted by the dominant social class over less powerful groups. The pattern of hegemonic control is often invisible because it is 'naturalised' into existing practices and is a subtle form of coercion which appears to serve mutual interests.

high art   The antithesis of all modes of expression to which the words mass or *popular* normally apply, high art is perceived by proponents of the former as elitist; or, one might say, if popular art forms connect the tastes, opinions, activities and habits of the majority, high art assumes the interest of a minority. So, painting and sculpture, to the extent that they issue in unique art objects, are definitively elitist activities. The accommodation within much modern art practice of populist modes and styles has contributed to a gathering scepticism about – even, in some circles, disdain for – high art's endeavours.

humanism   *Renaissance* humanism was the conviction that the individual was of paramount importance in the shaping of his or her own world. Believing that the human realm was explicable without having recourse to notions of the divine, humanist thinkers such as Descartes placed man at the centre of things. *Postmodern* critics have pointed out that humanist values posit a false unity that belies the specific determinants of class, race, *gender* and *sexual* orientation.

ideal   The representation of perfection, according to prevailing notions of excellency in form and conception, seeks to embody an ideal which exceeds the physical properties of the actual thing represented (generally a nude body or a landscape).

identity   One use of the word 'identity' is to describe one's sense of self as being a specific person. Another is to describe people's sense of belonging to a group – usually based on class, race, *gender* or *sexuality*, but also age, subcultural groups, etc. For example, the term 'identity politics' is used when describing groups who feel that they have been oppressed on the basis of their class, race, sexual orientation.

ideology   Broadly speaking, an ideology is the set of values, practices or beliefs which underpin a particular society or group. Ideologies marginalise alternative or conflicting systems of belief that run counter to their ideas. These counter-cultures (peoples, systems or sets of values dispossessed by a dominant ideology) are often referred to as 'others'.

illusion   The links between art and illusion have become complex in the twentieth century, since modernist art frequently employs anti-illusionistic devices which confound the viewer's visual expectation of a facsimile of nature. *Modernism* has given artists creative licence to explore *abstract* alternatives which have more to do with individuated *self-expression* than shared visual perception.

imperialism   The conquest and subsequent rule of land and peoples by a more powerful nation-state. The heyday of imperialism extended from the late nineteenth century up until the First World War, when, for example, powerful European countries ruled over the various territories that had been colonised. Imperialism is interpreted by *Marxists* as an outlet for economic trade and political gain, although often justified in terms of 'civilising' a 'lesser developed' group. Latterly imperialism has included global strategies, such as the McDonaldisation and Disneyfication, that employ more subtle economic practices.

impressionism   In the 1990s the subject of blockbuster exhibitions, it is difficult from a contemporary vantage-point to see impressionism as revolutionary art and the first *avant-garde*. But from the 1860s onwards the impressionists challenged the authority of the *academic* system and paved the way for twentieth-century *modernism*. As a style, impressionism used looser brushwork and a lighter palette to depict modern life.

individualism/individuality   A central tenet of *bourgeois* ideology is that each person 'owns' his or her destiny. *Postmodernist* writers have argued that individuals' lives are determined by their social relations and that true individualism is a fiction. *Poststructuralists* argue that we are determined and maintained in and by language (you are what you communicate).

installation   A term to describe art works which are usually commissioned, generally site-specific and often temporary. An installation occupies a site (sometimes in a gallery, but theoretically in any agreed spot) and can take its physical dimensions, materials and occasionally its thematic cue from its surroundings.

intentionality   While the new art history has undermined some of the confidence in artists' intentions as a way of extracting meaning from a work of art, the notion of intentionality has surfaced to question the artist's place in his or her works of art. The artist's intention, as the indelible trace of the artist's mind or purpose in the work of art, can still be discussed within art history but only by means of the qualifying and critically accountable term 'intentionality'.

kitsch   Clement Greenberg's essay 'Avant-Garde and Kitsch' (first published in 1939) established the necessity of defending *high art* against mass bad taste, or kitsch. Kitsch in this sense means something that copies quality but falls short in terms of taste and conception. It is a measure of a major contemporary cultural shift that the reverse strategy of employing 'low' art forms in contemporary practice has such currency. The appropriation of mass culture into high art is evidence of a collapse of consensual values.

land art   See **earthworks**.

live art   This encompasses all time-based genre, including *performance*, and is often a platform for those dealing with *identity*. Experimental film and video, while strictly speaking recorded rather than live, often fall under the aegis of live art agencies.

Manifesto: towards a free revolutionary art   (1938) Meyer Schapiro, whose articles in *Marxist Quarterly and Dissent: a quarterly of socialist opinion* were major contributions to contemporary debates on art and politics, helped broker the alliance that made up the manifesto. The collaborative manifesto by Trotsky, Rivera and Breton offered a way out of art practices dependent on the predetermined Communist Party aesthetics of socialist realism. The manifesto proposed an independent art, ('complete freedom for art') which has subsequently been reduced to mean abstract expressionism. However, during the period many artists committed to political action through their art also took their cue from the statement 'we believe that the supreme task of art in our epoch is to take part actively and consciously in the preparation of the revolution' (Breton et al. 1968).

Marxism/post-Marxism   Since 1989 and the collapse of the Soviet Union, Marxism as a political discourse, so characteristic of art-historical studies in the 1960s and

1970s, has been less influential. Its totalising tendencies have rendered it ill equipped to deal with the fragmented, *pluralistic* and heterogeneous 1990s. Nonetheless, some of the central tenets of Marxist art history – for instance that art does not possess any intrinsic, immutable values and that art is, to a greater or lesser degree, contingent upon social, economic and political conditions – have become enshrined in most art-historical discourses.

masculinity   While *feminism* has spawned a whole area of women's studies since the 1960s, masculinity has been a more recent object of attention. Drawing from feminist blueprints of *gender* theory, masculinity is also predicated on the crucial distinction between being born male and being socialised as a male. Models of masculinity, arising from personal, social, sexual and political circumstances, seek to account for the social construction of the male and the way that this impacts on *cultural* forms, such as making or viewing art.

mimesis   The representation of images based upon imitation is rooted in post-*Renaissance* art theory and became a benchmark for notions of artistic skill. However, mimesis alone should not be regarded as the motor for pre-*modern* art since much *academic* art production was motored by fixed standards of the *ideal*.

minimalism   A deliberate reaction, dating from the 1960s, against the idiosyncratic gestural qualities of *abstract expressionist* painting. Characteristically, in art minimalism employed sheet metal, perspex and house bricks to make regular geometric constructions, sometimes on a grand scale, for art galleries and *earthworks*. In music minimalist works are characterised by a relentless repetition of sounds or even total silence.

modern period   Within the remit of this book, the modern period is taken to be synonymous with the urban industrial and the post-industrial age. The term 'modern' has had a currency for art historians ever since Baudelaire's 'The Painter of Modern Life' (first published in 1863) described the work of those who were actively engaged with the subjects of modern city life. However, 'the modern painters' as defined by John Ruskin in the 1840s and 1850s constituted merely the category for contemporary artists.

modernisation   See **modernity**.

modernism   The term has a long and varied usage as a designation of a *period*, a style and a theoretical stance. Broadly speaking, the inception of modernism can be dated to the 1840s, where it described the efforts of artists, musicians, architects, designers and poets to break with the predominant codes and conventions of cultural production. Typically modernist art was concerned with the 'new' – using unconventional materials, novel means of construction and experimentation with new ways of depicting the subject.

modernity/modernisation   In his book *All That Is Solid Melts into Air: the experience of modernity* (1983) Marshall Berman distinguishes between *modernism*, modernity and modernisation. According to Berman, modernisation describes processes of economic, social and technological advance based on innovations associated with capitalism, whereas modernity is the transformed condition or state brought about by capitalism in the nineteenth and twentieth centuries in Europe and North America.

naturalism Often used in opposition to both the idealising tendencies of *classicism* and the 'unnaturalistic' distortions of *modernism*; the term is synonymous with *realism*, the term 'naturalism' defies precise definition. Naturalism itself is a shifting category which has changed over the centuries and across cultures. In Western art history the term has come to mean an imitation of perceived reality.

neo-plasticism A term invented by Mondrian (in Dutch '*die neiuwe beelding*') to describe his method of colour and composition, which became the benchmark for De Stijl artists. Neo-plasticism is the restrictive practice of only painting in primary colours (plus black, white and grey) and using only horizontal and vertical lines. Philosophically, Mondrian's ideas derive from Calvinism and theosophy.

new art history The theoretically rigorous and 'politically correct' approach to the discipline, especially where certain issues of class, race and *gender* are concerned. As its name implies, the new art history was a reaction to the 'old art history'. Targeting *connoisseurial* and *formalist* as well as certain *Marxist* art histories, 1980s practitioners of the new art history introduced what they believed to be a more accountable approach to the discipline.

New Deal The American stock market crash in 1929 was followed by a decade of economic and social depression. The New Deal was a domestic policy delivered by President Franklin D. Roosevelt to rescue the American economy. The New Deal programmes established a degree of state intervention unprecedented in America. In particular, government-sponsored Federal Art Programs employed artists on community-based projects, reconfiguring the role of the artist as socially responsible rather than as an individual outsider.

ontology The theory and study of existence, closely bound up with metaphysics, relates to being or the essence of things. Ontology distinguishes between different ways of existing; for example, there are different kinds of existence for, say, weather systems, human bodies or mental states.

orientalism Edward Said's influential books *Orientalism* (1995) and *Culture and Imperialism* (1993) exposed the dynamics of the power relations at play in the Western perception of the Orient. Crucially, Said explored the ways in which the power relations between *cultures* are reinforced through their visual and literary productions. The implications have been far-reaching, forcing art historians to question misconceptions based on long-held stereotypes of Orientals.

other The 'other' is non-self. It describes peoples and systems marginalised by prevailing dominant ideologies (such as Euro-centrism, patriarchy, etc.). The precise term – 'other' – stems from the writings of the French theorist and feminist Simone de Beauvoir, whose book *The Second Sex* (1949) pointed out the patriarchal sense of woman as other. Since then Edward Said has used 'other' to describe anyone dispossessed by a dominant cultural force (usually white, Western, middle-class, heterosexual males). Moreover, the dominant force presumes the task of representation whilst the 'other' is usually represented. So the basic condition of 'otherness' is 'to be spoken of' rather than 'to speak'.

performance art In the visual arts, a form of *live art* which uses the artist's body or bodies delegated by the artist to enact a work of art.

periodisation   The retrospective division of the historical past into periods has given us terms such as mediaeval, *Renaissance* and *modern*. Periods are often described on the basis of stylistic shifts, which in the broadest sense mark a change in the dominant art practice. The concept of periodisation may vary from one discipline to the next and there is not always parity between, say, music, literature and art history. In contemporary art history periodisation is normally characterised as problematic on the grounds that is a Euro-centred way of presenting history replete with value judgements that distort the specificity of time and place.

photography   Photography – that is the fixing of the first photographic image – is usually dated to 1839. Although the claim to be the originator of the technique is split between Fox Talbot in England and Daguerre in France, others were experimenting with fixing images of concentrated light during the same period. An interest in the image borne on light has been known since Aristotle (384–322) and formed the basis of experiments in *camera obscura* for over a millennium.

plein-air painting   *Plein-air* (open-air) painting is often cited as the invention of French *impressionists*, although there is ample evidence to support the claim that artists were painting out of doors long before Monet took to painting excursions. The practice of painting *plein-air* is often seen as one of the conditions of *modernity*, through which artists could record their individual and personal experience of nature at a particular time and place directly and spontaneously, without recourse to studio reconstructions after the moment had passed. The widespread practice of *plein-air* painting is often attributed to the commercial availability of artist's pigments in ready-mixed tubes of colour, and to the preference for smaller, more portable, easel-sized canvases, which also reflects the shift in patronage to the *bourgeoisie*, requiring more domestic-scale paintings.

pluralism   One of the most problematic aspects of *postmodernism* is pluralism; as an attitude which maintains (nominally, at least) that all points of view, all styles of art, all cultural forms, are open and equal, it would seem to offer but another *utopian* prospect. However, pluralism is ultimately relative and, at its most pessimistic, can be seen as a dissolution of the *modernist* confidence that quality is an identifiable datum.

politics of representation   As a gauge of the changing relationship between language and art, the politics of representation acknowledges the values inherent in seeing and representing. The politics of representation attacks notions of 'disinterested' representation, exposing the power relations implicit in the act of looking and how art has legitimised certain forms of surveillance.

popular culture   The collapse of the division between *high art* and popular culture has been a hallmark of *postmodernism*. Previously beyond the preserve of art history, popular culture (comics, television, pulp fiction, popular music) has now joined the list of respectable objects of academic study.

postcolonialism   A considerable shift has taken place in global power relations between the former colonial powers – British rule in India or French rule in North Africa – and their 'subjects'. Postcolonial theories have had an impact on *culture* in two ways: first, giving voice to the recipients of the legacy of colonialism; and, second, rereading art works in the light of previous power relations.

post-feminism   See **feminism**.

post-human   A term to describe the human condition in the light of new developments in genetic engineering whereby DNA can be manipulated to alter the basic blueprint of individual life. The possession of biotechnological knowledge has led many writers to question the consequences of the genetic revolution for humanity.

post-impressionism   The term retrospectively applied to artists whose time and styles of working followed those of the *impressionists*. While having few things in common, works by post-impressionists are identifiable by their formal rejection of the *naturalism* of impressionism.

post-Marxism   See **Marxism**.

postmodernism   An overused catch-all for anything playful, humorous, ironic, knowing, appropriative, *pluralistic* and code-breaking in our *culture*. The downside of postmodernism's lack of fixed principles acid standards is a melancholic schizophrenia, in which the lack of boundaries becomes itself restrictive and even repressive. The current general apprehension about the future, endemic in millennial Western cultures, is offset by the emancipatory prospects a postmodernism vision offers to counter-cultures (simultaneously depriving them of that status).

poststructuralism   Although often erroneously used as a synonym for *postmodernism*, the term 'poststructuralism' has more precise applications. The works of Jacques Derrida, Julia Kristeva, Jacques Lacan, Jean-François Lyotard and Michel Foucault collectively debunk older notions of absolutes, essences and legitimised power structures, replacing them with contingencies and the decentred subject, and exposing all forms of cultural behaviour as linguistic constructions.

Pre-Raphaelite Brotherhood   A group of painters who styled themselves 'the pre-Raphaelites' in London in 1848. Their radical intention to operate in opposition to academic conventions surely gives them *modernist* credentials, although they will not be found in many books on modernism! They were a self-styled group with a title, they produced manifestos of sorts, some of them were scandalously *bohemian* and anticipated much of what came to be standard behaviour for modern art movements. The pre-Raphaelites actively sought to distance themselves from the present, first in their choice of subject matter (which was often mediaeval or mythical) and, second, in terms of their techniques of painting, which were unnecessarily laborious (for *academic* success anyway).

primitivism   Once the preserve of anthropology, primitivism entered the lexicon of art history as a problematic term in the 1960s. Although the term had a long usage as a label for anything that was non-European, folkish or childlike, primitivism came to have political ramifications within *postcolonial* cultures. While *modernists* benefited from the stylistic innovations gleaned from primitive models, their a historic appropriation of, for instance, 'other' cultural artefacts never extended to a radical review of the power relations between *imperialist* cultures and their subject peoples.

productivism   A short-lived Russian art movement (1920–2) which sought to apply the principles of *avant-garde constructivism* to functional design and utilitarian projects.

psychoanalytic theory of art   The theory that the psychological state of the artist – open, repressed – can be uncovered in the work of art has a long precedence; for example, Sigmund Freud's interpretation of Leonardo da Vinci's *Virgin and Child With Saint Anne* reads unresolved tensions in the artist's relation to his two 'mothers'. While a much-used method of inquiry (for example in T.J. Clark's *Farewell to an Idea*), psychoanalytic theories applied to the visual arts are necessarily speculative and frustratingly elliptical.

queer theory Queer theory theorises on behalf of all groups outside heterosexual culture, including lesbian, gay, bisexual and transgender groups. Some lesbians and gay men began reappropriating the previously derogatory term 'queer' in the early 1990s to define an oppositional and agitational set of beliefs and practices (queer theory) that are the intellectual expression of queer politics. Queer theory uses *post-structuralist* strategies to articulate not just the mechanics of oppression and discrimination but the construction of images and the politics of representation. Queer theory challenges the neutrality of heterosexual culture to insist that the subject position of the artist or viewer resides to some extent in their *sexuality*.

ready-mades The staple diet of twentieth-century art and almost a prerequisite of *postmodernism*. From Marcel Duchamp's urinals and bottle racks to Damien Hirst's farmyard life-forms, the use of ready-mades is a constant and accelerating feature of twentieth-century art practice. The significance of ready-mades in the bifurcated history of *modernism* is that they dispensed altogether with the notion of a fine-art practice that was skill-based and attacked notions of *self-expression*, hierarchy and taste by using objects from the 'real' world as 'art'.

realism Almost all twentieth-century art lays claim to a notion of realism, whether social, psychological, political or optical. Hyperrealism, superrealism and virtual reality all testify to the continuing currency and elusiveness of the term. At its simplest it is inextricable from the notion of resemblance to actual life, in which artists' depictions are 'true to life' or use technical means to approximate closely the way things 'really' appear. Realism is bedevilled by any simple understanding of lived experience, whether actual or virtual.

Renaissance The belief that a revival of *classical* models in art and literature had started in the fourteenth and fifteenth centuries conditioned every aspect of dominant Western *academic* art practice. Within *modernism*, therefore, the Renaissance was the moment of inception of the dogmatic, classicising and rule-bound conventions of Western art. The rejection of orthodoxies within modernism required a dismantling of this tradition. Modernism has at once, however, both romanced and rejected the Renaissance, although not always in equal measure.

Romanticism Often erroneously opposed to bloodless *classicism* as its passionate counterpart. The works of Beethoven, the paintings of Géricault and Delacroix and the poetry of Lord Byron are axiomatically Romantic. Storm-tossed landscapes, violent human encounters between isolated subjects and exotic locations are the stock in trade of the Romantic imagination.

self-expression This modern notion underlines the *individuality* of the artist as a self endowed with a unique ability to represent feelings or ideas through art. *Modernism* is predicated on essentialist notions of *expression* as a capacity unrestricted by cultural constructions and accessible only to the gifted few.

semiotics   The science of signs that dates from the start of the twentieth century and informs a great deal of the art history from the second half of the twentieth century. Unlike iconography (in which meanings are fixed by their historical specificity), semiotics studies verbal, oral and visual sign systems, which may not be fixed and indeed are liable to float (floating signifier). A semiotician may consider a wide variety of signs so that, effectively, a comic book could be considered according to the same principles as a *Renaissance* altarpiece.

sexuality   In most of the texts sexuality is simply the way that individuals express their sexual preferences, but this has become more complex and terms such as 'heterosexual' and 'homosexual' tend to have been redefined as straight, gay, lesbian, queer, bisexual, in order to take account of the various ways of practising human sexuality.

situationists/situationism   An anarchic but politically unaffiliated confederation of artists and intellectuals who first outlined their views in the magazine *Internationale Situationniste* in 1958. Situationism evades any single definition since it refers to a programme of 'construction situations', and its adherents advocated a 'revolution of everyday life' which extended to all forms of intellectual activity. It was, therefore, process rather than product which was significant. Famously, the situations were responsible for much of the graffiti and many of the slogans that featured in the student-led demonstrations of 1968.

socialist realism   Unlike its close namesake social realism, socialist realism is marked by optimism and *utopianism*. The official doctrine in the 1930s in revolutionary Russia favoured all the art works that were at once accessible to a mass audience and a celebration of the audience itself. Replete with images of labour in the collective fields and co-operative factories of the new Russia, socialist realism favoured *naturalism* over the earlier revolutionary *constructivism*.

subjectivity   Together with its *modernist* polarity objectivity, subjectivity haunts the pages of *modern* literature. While objectivity lays claim to some kind of disinterested neutrality, subjectivity demands interested partiality. Modernism's espousal of the essential individual permits a *Romantic* involvement with the work of art on the basis of feeling and imagination.

the sublime   The *Romantics* used the notion of sublimity when faced with overpowering natural forces, an experience which, in the eighteenth century, was associated with oceans, steep cliffs, volcanoes and raging torrents. The *Enlightenment* philosopher and statesman Edmund Burke's designation of the sublime, for example, was the simultaneous apprehension of terror and beauty in the face of natural forces, or even of the collective anger expressed in the French Revolution. Within *postmodernism* the sublime has become associated with experiences mediated by new technologies.

surrealism   Led by the writer André Breton, surrealism was an anti-establishment, anti-*bourgeois*, international art movement that grew out of the political disenchantment of *Dada* and culminated in the first 'Surrealist Manifesto' of 1924 (Breton 2003). By defamiliarising and 'making strange' the object, the surrealists typically confounded the viewer by juxtaposing objects, images, words and sounds in an irrational manner. In thrall to the *psychoanalytic theories* of Freud and Jung, the surrealists attempted to account for the irrationality of *modernity* by uncovering civilisation's *unconscious* motivations and desires.

symbolist art   Beginning as a French literary movement, symbolism spilled over into painting across Europe and North America during the *fin-de-siècle*. Although the artists who could be called symbolists range widely in artistic practice, they could be loosely said to share an ambiguous approach to *naturalism* in painting and a preference for representing inner experience, mood and emotion rather than naturalistic depictions of the material world. Their subject matter is often drawn from mythology and religion and emphasises fantasy and the imagination.

technological determinism   The argument that technology is not a neutral force for good but one that is driven by social forces was advanced by Raymond Williams (1979) with specific reference to communication technologies. The argument against technological determinism runs that just because we are capable of doing something it does not automatically follow that we ought to do it. For example, just because we can clone a human being it does not mean that we should. The uses to which we put technology often shape its future development.

teleology   Usually a pejorative term in art history to criticise the retrospective strategies of writers involved in *periodisation* and *canon*-making. Teleology is to write, in this case, an art history that is consistent with notions of progress that belong to the time of writing and to impose those values on history. For example, Alfred Barr, writing in 1936, presented *avant-garde* art as a series of breakthroughs leading towards full abstraction by 1936.

the unconscious   Under Freud the unconscious was conceptualised as a pre-rational space, the repository of repressed feelings, fears and memories which struggle to surface. The therapeutic method devised by Freud for treating patients claimed to be able to access the unconscious and release repressed emotions. For *postmodernists* the unconscious is a constructed category that is formed rather than fixed. The unconscious in Freudian theory should not be confused with other constructions of the unconscious, such as Jungian notions of 'collective unconscious' as an archive of human memory.

universal   The totalising tendencies of Western culture rest on the possibility of universal laws and grand narratives. The assumption that Western values are universal was predicated on our inability to 'know the other' and a capacity for marginalising alternative or counter-culture experiences. Under this rubric beauty and truth were assumed to be unchanging givens – a priori categories beyond the realms of contingencies such as cultural constructions, *gender*, class and race.

utopian   The unrealised project of *modernism*, in all its manifestations, was undoubtedly utopian, in the sense that it held sacred a vision of a better world for all. Modernism's democratic allegiance to progressive socialism motivated a number of experimental approaches to art which both embraced and rejected technology.

Key figures and events

Abramovic, Marina (b.1946) Yugoslavian artist who lives and works in Amsterdam. Abramovic was a pioneer of performance art whose work explores the limits of mental and physical endurance. *Rhythm O* was one in a series of performances, collectively entitled *Rhythms*, made between 1973 and 1974.

Adorno, Theodor W. (1903–69) German philosopher and musicologist whose principle contribution to the philosophy of art is to question whether art or an artefact is significantly different from any other cultural product. Adorno argues against any timeless category for art or any special pleading, maintaining that art is not an absolute given but a changeable, culturally constructed category.

Althusser, Louis (1918–90) French philosopher of structuralist Marxism. His most significant work lay in his definition of ideology as a system of representations that maintain state power; that is, ideology is a false perception of the real world which protects us from the harsh facts of capitalism.

The 1913 Armory Show Popularly known as the *Armory Show*, the *International Exhibition of Modern Art* took place at the armory of the National Guard's 69th Regiment in New York. It is usually credited with bringing modern European art to a provincial US audience. Although there is plenty of evidence of American artists being familiar with European modernism, Marcel Duchamp's *Nude Descending a Staircase, No. 2* (1912) did cause a stir. *The Armory Show* also marked the entry of cubism into the lexicon of a broader range of American artists.

Ball, Hugo (1886–1927) German painter and poet who founded the journal and night-club Cabaret Voltaire and who with Emmy Hennings (1885–1948), his collaborator and wife, orchestrated the anarchic performances of Zurich Dada, which included puppetry and poetry.

Banham, Reyner (1922–88) Writer on architecture and design whose pro-technological stance put the machine aesthetic at the centre of writings about modernism. His book *Theory and Design in the First Machine Age* (1996), first published in 1960, charts the history of the machine aesthetic in the twentieth century.

Barr, Alfred H., Jnr (1902–81) Although subsequently the personification of all that was wrong with institutional modernism and formalism in art criticism, during the 1950s Barr was a tireless champion of modernism and an advocate of freedom of artistic expression when support for artists with a left-wing past was deemed anti-American. His ambition to define quality in modern art has led inevitably to charges of elitism and pitted him and MoMA against the New Left in the United States.

Barthes, Roland (1915–80) French social and literary theorist whose writings on semiotics serve as a blueprint for much of the new art history. His works include *Mythologies* (1993), first published in 1957, and *Image–Music–Text* (1977). The article on 'The Death of the Author' has been particularly influential in shifting the attention of the work of art on to the community of readers, who consume the object at different times, with different agendas and different positions.

Baudelaire, Charles-Pierre (1821–1867) Baudelaire's centrality in modernist thinking is through his essay 'On the Heroism of Modern Life' (1846) and book *The Painter of Modern Life* (1863). For Baudelaire and the urban artists of modernity, beauty was not found in mythological subjects but in the ordinary and everyday, and in the sexual frisson of Parisian low-life.

Beauvoir, Simone de (1908–86) French existential theorist whose book *The Second Sex* (1949) sought to uncover the operations of patriarchy that naturalised women's (and others') subordinate position in relation to the centrality of Western men. She reminded us that 'one is not born a woman: one becomes one' (de Beauvoir 1949: 000).

Bell, Clive (1881–1964) A contemporary of Roger Fry and engaged in much the same project, Bell sought a new and innovative system for viewing modern art. Given that the old standards of judgements which were applied to classical art could not operate with modernism's shift from technical skill in the representation of classical subjects to subjective brushwork and everyday subject matter, Bell devised the notion of 'significant form'. The phrase has become shorthand for a formalist dogma. Bell's ostensibly inclusive doctrine maintained that all that was needed to appreciate a work of art (even an unfamiliar one) was sensibility and an appreciation of the formal elements of, say, a painting, divorced from any relationship to ideology or subject matter. The experience of the art work proceeded as an aesthetic experience: a stirring of the emotions caused by a pleasing arrangement of lines and colours. For Bell the experience of the art work is a deeply subjective one devoid of political inferences.

Bennett, Gordon (b.1955) A Brisbane artist whose paintings, in particular the 1998 *The Nine Richochets* (*Fall Down Black Fella, Jump Up White Fella*), most typically critique the quoting of Aboriginal art by contemporary Australian artists.

Bernard, Émile (1868–1941) The concept of truth in painting would have occupied the spiritually inclined symbolist Bernard, who was interested in the Platonic and Plotinian notion of anamnesis: the doctrine of the memory of a pre-natal state in which the soul exists and gains its ideas.

Bloch, Lucienne (b.1909) In sharp contrast to the received history of abstract expressionism which seemed to be dominated by masculine creativity, during the New Deal many women artists and photographers such as Bloch, Marion Greenwood, and

Dorothea Lange and Margaret Bourke-White enjoyed high-profile careers across a range of artistic fields.

Bonnard, Pierre (1867–1947) A French painter of decorative, highly coloured interiors closely associated with Maurice Denis and the work of the Nabis (see Chapter 2). Bonnard's paintings were influenced by the two-dimensional graphic quality of Japanese prints, and so often emphasised pattern over depth.

Bouguereau, Adolphe William (1825–1905) Now seen as all that was wrong with academic painting, including the charge of overt sentimentality and a reliance on Renaissance techniques, Bouguereau's reputation suffered under the widespread rejection of mimetic techniques and idealised compositions that marked the early work of realist and impressionist paintings.

Bourke-White, Margaret (1904–71) Perhaps best known for her photographs of human casualties of the Great Depression, produced independently of the FSA, Bourke-White also created photographs of factories and machinery during the 1920s that celebrated the machine aesthetic.

Brancusi, Constantin (1876–1957) The Romanian sculptor's increasingly simplified forms were based on the natural world, typically birds or fish, subjects that were repeated throughout his life. His other major subject was the endless column created around modular units. He often harnessed his admiration for primitive arts by imitating the 'crude' direct carving techniques of some African sculpture.

Breton, André (1896–1966) The self-appointed 'Pope of Surrealism', who had visited Freud in Vienna in 1921, although the two differed in their attitudes to hysteria: Freud thought that it was a form of neurosis which should be cured and Breton that it should be cultivated.

Brisley, Stuart (b.1933) British artist, performance artist and professor of art at the Slade School of Art. Brisley's feats of endurance as a performance artist were well known in the 1970s but more latterly he has worked with found objects and detritus, which he installs into gallery spaces. Referring to himself as 'a curator of shit', Brisley continues to test the aesthetic and olfactory senses of the art-loving public.

Broodthaers, Marcel (1924–76) Investing in a repertoire of familiar and found objects such as mussels, eagles, broken eggshells and printed materials, the Belgian poet-turned-artist Broodthaers worked across a wide range of media. His iconic interventions into the aspirations of art and its co-dependent museum practices had an anarchic, arbitrary foundation that contributed to the artist's own iconic status.

Brus, Günter (b.1938) Austrian performance artist and founder member of Aktionismus. Aktionismus attacked taboos and vented repressed emotions throughout the 1970s in a series of shocking and sexually explicit performances. Günter Brus, acknowledging his own 'cesspool aesthetics', was responsible for particularly gorey and scatological performance pieces, which put him constantly at odds with the Austrian authorities.

Burke, Edmund (1729–97) A major figure of the Enlightenment, the Irish philosopher and statesman's influential book *A Philosophical Enquiry into the Origin of Our Ideas of the Sublime and the Beautiful* was published in 1757.

Burn, Ian (1939–93) A member of New York's *Art and Language*, Burn eventually returned to his native Australia and transformed his conceptual art into political activism, working on a range of trade union and community group projects which utilised more democratic forms of media: posters and campaigning brochures. Burn regarded this as a move away from art practice to an engagement with a more active form of political action than that of making art.

Carrington, Leonora (b.1917) British artist and writer currently working in Mexico City. Carrington's colourful life includes fleeing from the Nazis with her lover Max Ernst and being temporarily institutionalised following a nervous breakdown, before settling in Mexico in 1942. She was associated with the British Surrealist movement and evolved a personal iconography based on occult and spiritual subjects.

Chadwick, Helen (1953–96) British artist who once described her own work as 'gorgeously repulsive, exquisitely fun and dangerously beautiful' (quoted in Curtis 1993: 12).

Cixous, Hélène (b.1937) French theorist and pioneer of a distinctive feminist set of readings for literature. 'The Laugh of the Medusa' (1981, first published in 1975) outlined the ways in which women's voices had been silenced in the history of patriarchy and described the possibility of a feminine writing.

Colquhoun, Ithell (1906–88) Painter and writer on occult matters. She was associated with the British Surrealist movement before 1940 and was a close friend of André Breton. Her books include *The Sword of Wisdom* (1975) and *The Goose of Hermogenes* (1961). Colquhoun invented *parsemage* (or powdering), a Surrealist technique whereby chalk dust is sprinkled on to water and skimmed off by a piece of card or paper.

Cornell, Joseph (1903–72) Producing assemblages of found objects, usually built into complex box-like structures resembling miniature theatres, the American sculptor mixed nostalgic images of popular icons with natural and industrially produced found objects such as train tickets, postage stamps and so on. Cornell was loosely associated with the surrealist movement although without recourse to their overtly sexual or sadistic imagery.

Courbet, Gustave (1819–77) Typically associated with realism, Courbet is often granted status as the founding father of the modern movement. Leaving aside the endeavour to find a genealogy for modernism, and Courbet's self-proclaimed position of no ideals and no religion, which adorned his writing paper, with Courbet we have the quintessential modernist artist in rebellion both artistically and politically. Moreover, he had left-wing credentials: he fought on the side of the communards during the Paris Commune of 1870 and suffered exile as a consequence. Exile (in its many forms) was almost a prerequisite of avant-gardism for over a century.

Cunningham, Merce (b.1919) American dancer and choreographer whose work has been performed by most of the major ballet companies in the world. His distinctive style of choreography dispenses with linear narrative and assumes the same concerns as an abstract artist; that is, that form (movement, gesture, sound and staging) is expressive in its own right.

Danto, Arthur (b.1924) Although at odds with much postmodern thinking, Danto's views, expounded in works such as *Beyond the Brillo Box: the visual arts in post-historical* *perspective* (1992) and *Encounters and Reflections: art in the historical present* (1990), offer an interesting perspective on, in particular, the art of the 1960s.

David, Jacques-Louis (1748–1825) French neo-classical painter whose pro-Bonaparte high Republicanism led him to endow the mythological scenes that were the bread and butter of academic painters with contemporary relevance.

Davis, Stuart (1892–1964) Editor of the politically radical *Art Front* and active in the politics of the American Artists' Congress. He argued for a range of approaches to art, stating

> There is a need for an art of social comment, and for an art of domestic naturalism, and for an art of generalized spatial equations – abstract art. The social need for any one of these does not negate the need for the others.
>
> (Davis, in O'Connor 1973: 000)

Moreover, in Art Front he demanded an end to the aura attached to artists, maintaining that they be treated like other workers, with insurance and union pay scales.

Degas, Edgar (1834–1917) French painter and sculptor whose works, unlike those of his Impressionist peers, represent in the main indoor scenes – ballet dancers, laundresses, circus performers and women bathing. His own form of modernism lay in his unconventional cropping of these subjects and the snapshot quality of the scenes he conveys, famously described by the artist himself as 'through the keyhole'.

Delaunay, Robert (1885–1941) and **Sonia Delaunay** (1885–1979) Husband and wife artists who founded Orphism, a branch of cubism, in 1912. Orphism expounded a particular form of painting through colour as form, that is to say, 'colour is both form and subject' (Delaunay and Delaunay 1978: 23). The Delaunays' writings on colour have been edited as *The New Art of Colour: the writings of Robert and Sonia Delaunay* (1978).

Demuth, Charles (1883–1941) Demuth was an exponent of precisionism and part of the Duchamp-inspired move to celebrate the machinery and buildings if not the mechanised assembly-line labouring processes, of the factory. Although they sometimes overlooked the dehumanising effects of technology, US artists found in the buildings of factories, mills and industrial sites a specifically modern American subject matter.

Denis, Maurice (1870–1943) French Nabi painter and theoretician whose reminder that 'a painting – before it is a battlehorse, a nude woman, or some anecdote – is essentially a flat surface covered with colours assembled in a certain order' (Denis 1968a: 94) is often quoted as a standard to formalist theory. Many of his post-Nabi works are devotional images and include designs for tapestries and stained-glass windows.

Derrida, Jacques (b.1930) French philosopher principally associated with linguistic theory and the anti-authoritarian stance of deconstruction. His theories undermine structural linguistics by arguing that meaning is constantly evolving and therefore all attempts at totalising systems are doomed to failure. In the questioning of authority Derrida destabilised binary oppositions – for our purposes, those that pit the primitive against the civilised.

Descartes, René (1596–1650) French-born scientist, mathematician and philosopher who is best remembered for formulating the modern form of the mind–body problem. In Cartesian terms the existence of characteristic 'properties' is supported by meta-physical 'substances', so the crux of this question for Descartes was how the 'substances' of mind and matter are brought together to constitute a person.

Dove, Arthur Garfield (1880–1946) Dove exhibited in the legendary Armory Show, popularly credited with bringing modern art to the USA. If modernist art history was looking for a 'first' abstractionist Dove would be a likely candidate. His early works, called 'extractions' were among the earliest abstract works in the Western world, allegedly pre-Kandinsky.

Driggs, Elsie (1898–1992) American artist associated with the precisionist movement. Like many women artists, her long career as an artist is cut in half by years of family commitments.

Dubuffet, Jean (1901–85) French artist and exponent of *art brut*. Dubuffet was highly influenced by Hans Prinzhorn's book *Artistry of the Mentally Ill* (first published in 1922), which outlined a theory of the restorative powers of personal expression through art. Prinzhorn's collection of art by psychiatric patients was used by the Nazis in the Degenerate Art Exhibition of 1937 to make quite the opposite point to Prinzhorn's own idea that unbridled instinct was a sign of spiritual strength.

Duchamp, Marcel (1887–1968) French artist, although largely known through his work in the USA. His dynamic painting of a figure in motion, *Nude Descending a Staircase No. 2* (1912) caused a sensation at the New York Armory Show of 1913. By 1913, however, he had all but abandoned painting and introduced the 'ready-made' into art vocabulary, eventually pressing into service the urinal, bottle rack, bicycle wheel and 50cc of Paris air.

Duffy, Mary (b.1961) Irish performance artist and poet. Born before the Thalidomide drug was taken off the market, Mary Duffy's body experienced the effects of the drug which include malformations to the upper limbs. Her work as an advocate for disability rights includes live performance, photography and poems. She is also a researcher in media broadcasting and she continues to initiate educational and training projects to promote disability awareness.

Duncan, Carol US writer coming out of the New Left of the late 1950s and 1960s whose political activism, particularly in the civil rights and anti-war movements, was rooted in the Marxist notion of alienation. Duncan has written widely on the political and artistic implications of corporate power in US museums.

Eakins, Thomas (1844–1916) American painter whose scientific interest in human anatomy led him to insist that the students at the Pennsylvania Academy of Fine Arts (where he was a teacher until 1886) should study from the nude. He was reportedly forced to resign his position after permitting a mixed class to draw from a male nude model.

Eisenstein, Sergei (1898–1948) The Russian avant-garde filmmaker who, with films such as *October* (1927–8) and *Battleship Potemkin* (1925), used montage, editing and cutting to create specific ideological meanings. He also used typage – that is, non-actors chosen for the type they could represent – to recreate on film significant events leading up to the Russian Revolution of 1917 without resorting to a discredited star system. His later work, such as *Alexander Nevsky* (1938), while still celebrating Russian revolutionary achievements, was less artistically experimental, as the strictures of socialist realism buried the cosmopolitan experiments of the avant-garde.

Epstein, Jacob (1880–1959) American-born sculptor who lived and worked in Britain and became a naturalised British citizen. Epstein worked on several public and private commissions and had a distinctive style for making portrait busts. The various preparatory stages of *The Rock Drill* show that Epstein's attitude to the piece changed radically. In its early conception it could be read as a heroic and optimistic rendition of the figure, but later reworking of the figure led to readings of the piece as a profoundly pessimistic pronouncement on technology.

Evergood, Philip (1901–73) Evergood's fusion of surrealism/realism and left-wing politics resulted in accessible figurative paintings with a clear emancipatory message. Committed to the politics of labour organizations, Evergood did not abandon his form of realism for a fully realised abstraction in the post-war period but continued to produce work that espoused left-wing causes against the tide of post-war liberalism and conformity of formalist aesthetics.

Farm Security Administration (FSA) The photographs of the FSA probably constructed the dominant image of the Depression era. The FSA was formed in 1937 and incorporated the Information Division of the Resettlement Administration, responsible for supporting sharecroppers and tenant farmers, who were particularly hard hit by the Depression, often becoming enforced migrants. Photographers such as Russell Lee, Dorothea Lange and Walker Evans documented, in particular, the victims of the Dust Bowl that parts of the rural Southwest became. The photographs, widely and cheaply available, were used both as a testament to the lives of ordinary Americans and as a graphic vehicle to affect social change.

Farrell, Rose (b.1949) and **George Parkin** (b.1949) Australian performance artists and photographers who have been exhibiting together since the 1980s. Typically they construct large tableaux using both live actors and papier-mâché figures, then take photographic records of the pieces which are exhibited in large-scale prints.

Foucault, Michel (1926–84) French philosopher whose academic title, Professor in the History of Systems of Thought, best sums up his research. His work was principally concerned with the patterns of power, systems of knowledge and constructions of self in society. The particular systems of thought that he studied included the police, prisons, gay rights, the care of the mentally ill, medicine and social welfare.

Freud, Sigmund (1856–1939) Czech-born doctor who, from his clinic in Vienna, founded the set of theories that are the basis of psychoanalysis. Freud devised a therapeutic method of psychoanalysis which accessed the experiences repressed (held in the unconscious) to treat patients. This formulation of the unconscious as a site which only trained Freudian psychoanalysts can reach has subsequently been challenged from many quarters.

Fried, Michael (b.1939) Usually associated with formalism and support for the American colour-field painters of the late 1950s and early 1960s, Fried ascribed to an art capable of generating 'authentic' aesthetic experience in the viewer and therefore is heir to some of Greenberg's theories. Fried imported the term theatrically into art criticism to describe pejoratively works that and viewers who failed to comply to his proscription for an authentic experience of a work of art. This was acquired through a state of what he termed 'presentness', which required a suspension of the art's 'object-hood' and the spectator's temporal state. See, specifically, Fried's 'Art and Objecthood' originally published in *Artforum* Summer 1967 (Fried 2003).

Frith, William Powell (1819–1909) A painter popularly cited as an example of all that was wrong with academic painting in England. Roger Fry remarked that prints of paintings such as his *Derby Day* (1858) or *Paddington Station* (1862) were useful for whiling away time in waiting rooms but were not 'real' art.

Fry, Roger (1866–1934) A prodigious writer and lecturer in the early decades of the twentieth century, the British critic's publications, such as *Vision and Design* (1920) and *Transformations* (1926) reached a wide and popular audience. He introduced French modernism and the term 'post-impressionism' to an often hostile British audience in 1910 and 1912 when he organised the *First* and *Second Post-Impressionist Exhibitions*, held at the Grafton Galleries in London.

Fusco, Coco (b.1960) Cuban-born artist, writer and curator. Fusco's publications include *English Is Broken Here* (1995); her performances include *Better Yet When Dead* (1998); and her videos include *Havana Postmodern: the new Cuban art* and *Pochonovela*.

Gablik, Suzi (b.1934) An artist, art critic and teacher whose disillusionment with modernism wedded to a scepticism about notions of 'progress in art' has given rise to several influential books. Her latest book, *Living the Magical Life*, argues that 'life is more like an ecosystem than a linear equation . . . nothing exists separately from the rest. And synchronicities are the nodal points, magic moments where seemingly unrelated events are woven together to form a single, undivided world fabric' (Gablik 2002: 7).

Gauguin, Paul (1848–1903) Self-taught French post-impressionist artist who spent most of his professional life in self-imposed exile, first in Brittany and then in Tahiti. As part of the Pont-Aven School, Gauguin evolved a style of painting called synthesism, which advocated the imagination above description and led to a series of idealised, colourful and graphic images of Breton peasant life.

Gautier, Théophile (1811–1872) French novelist, dramatist and critic who reviewed all aspects of art production from theatre, literature and the visual arts. He was involved with the Romantic movement in art and literature and had begun his career with the intention of becoming a painter.

Géricault, Théodore (1791–1824) The French painter Géricault's short life and limited exhibiting do nothing to convey the depth of his influence on the later Romantic movement in France. His brand of realism, heroic working-class subjects and interest in insane and marginal figures proved influential to a later generation.

Gilbert, Alfred (1854–1934) English sculptor, most famously of the Shaftesbury Memorial Fountain, better known as *Eros*, at Piccadilly Circus in London. Gilbert was responsible for several royal tombs.

Gill, Simryn (b.1959) Gill was born in Singapore and works in Sydney, Australia. Her work is particularly concerned with the cultures of postcolonial places.

Goldsworthy, Andy (b.1956) Goldsworthy is a British environmental artist whose works are often made of mutable materials that biodegrade into the environment or disappear, such as ice melting and sand being transformed by the action of waves.

Gombrich, Ernst (1909–2001) Written in 1950, the Austrian-born British art historian's *The Story of Art*, a populist art history classic, is still in print and has been translated into over twenty languages. Although questions have been raised about the lack of female and non-Western artists and its periodisation strategies, it remains a standard text on the history of art. In a later work of 1960, *Art and Illusion*, Gombrich investigated the role of psychology in not only the creation but the reception of art works.

Goncharova, Natalia Sergeevna (1881–1962) Goncharova worked across all of the major movements of early European modernism. As a member of the Russian avant-garde that made its way to Paris in the second decade of the twentieth century, she often drew on the rich visual art traditions of Russian folk and peasant culture and infused them with modernist experimentation. She worked with her fellow Russian Serge Diaghilev during the 1920s designing sets and costumes for the Ballet Russe, as well as experimenting with abstract painting.

Gormley, Anthony (b.1950) British sculptor whose work with or about local communities has produced some high-profile works, such as the 1995 commission for Gateshead Metropolitan Borough Council *The Angel of the North*. Standing a colossal 20 metres high, the anthropomorphic structure has a 'wing-span' of 175 feet; its 'roots' and mechanical restraining devices are in the mine workings situated below. Standing at the entrance to Tyneside, it was made in a local foundry.

Graham, Dan (b.1942) American installation artist and writer. Graham began using film and video in the 1970s to explore notions of time and space in relationship to spectatorship. Much of his work manipulates the viewer's perception by displacing time and space through mirrors, live video broadcast and time-delay recording. He is the author of *Video–Architecture–Television* (1980).

Graham, Martha (1894–1991) Graham often worked with sets designed by the abstract expressionist sculptor Isamu Noguchi, and her notebooks (1973) read as a chronicle of avant-garde activity in post-war New York. However, in earlier work such as *El Penitente* (1940), a passion play set in Mexico, a broader set of social concerns can be detected prior to the more introspective, Jungian-inspired works of the mid-1940s onwards.

Gramsci, Antonio (1891–1937) Italian Marxist, political theorist and activist responsible for the high profile accorded in contemporary theory to the notion of 'cultural hegemony'; that is to say, he denaturalised the common-sense notions derived from a middle-class world-view that are used to undermine working-class values. Moreover, he argued that hegemony operates through the complicity of the oppressed group. See, in particular, Antonio Gramsci (1971).

Greenberg, Clement (1909–94) Although considered by many to be the most influential theoriser and advocate for mid-twentieth-century US modernism, Greenberg's legacy is a contested one. His polemical essays and biting art criticism, which sought to define quality in art through the experience of the work alone, separate from any effect it might have in the world, helped establish abstract expressionism as the dominant art practice in the 1950s. In the process Greenberg relegated most other forms of 'realism' as a failure of nerve, reserved for those who, as he put it, refused to go to the limits. The insistence on painterly issues contributed to his redundancy as a critic with the advent of pop and conceptual art in the 1960s, which failed to meet his unforgiving criteria.

Greyworld British-based art collective involved in projects for art in public spaces. Their work typically includes sound and uses self-generative systems. In the FACT (Film, Art and Creative Technology) building in Liverpool, Greyworld have installed a sound system that is triggered by visitors to the new state-of-the-art centre. Their web site <http://www.greyworld.org> gives details of recent projects and sound pieces.

Gropius, Walter (1883–1969) German architect, industrial designer and first director of the Bauhaus. Under Gropius the Bauhaus espoused social change through architecture, design and an art based on function, mass production and adherence to a universal geometric style of clean lines and clarity of construction.

Guernica (Pablo Picasso 1937) *Guernica* was shown by the Republican Spanish government in the 1937, International Exhibition in Paris. The power of art to represent ideological differences was played out against a backdrop of mounting national tensions, with the Spanish government already struggling against the fascist Nazi-backed General Franco at home. The work provided a blueprint for artists trying to reconcile modernist art with a political practice.

Haraway, Donna (b.1944) Academic, writer and theorist in the history of science and consciousness. Her 'Manifesto for Cyborgs' was first published in 1985 and, together with subsequent books, has contributed to a theory of the body in the technological age. Collectively her work explores the interfaces between machines and organic life in terms of larger issues such as the politics of race and gender.

Hatoum, Mona (b.1952) Video, installation and performance artist born in Beirut and living and working in London since 1975.

Haussmann, Baron Georges Eugène (1809–91) The term Haussmannisation, broadly used to describe large-scale town-planning projects, was derived from Haussmann's radical modernisation of Paris. The human casualties of Haussmann's replacement of medieval Paris by sweeping boulevards and covered arcades proved a productive inspiration for writers and artists.

Hegel, Georg Wilhelm (1770–1831) German philosopher who outlined a theory for the production of works of art in general by identifying large-scale cyclical developments in the history of human culture.

Hepworth, Barbara (1903–75) Usually associated with St Ives, in Cornwall, Hepworth's simplified sculptural forms placed her within the English avant-garde centred around the Seven and Five Society (7 and 5), which by 1935 had become the Seven and Five Abstract Group, broadcasting their refined form of artistic extremism. During the 1930s, Unit One, of which she was a founder member, was also committed to a refined abstraction.

Hiller, Susan (b.1942) American artist who works in London. Her work often questions the function of memory and ritual using a range of media, including drawing and video installation. She explores the underbelly of cultural ritual via the unconscious in works such as *The Muse in the Museum* (1999).

Hirst, Damien (b.1965) Hirst's use of formaldehyde, taxidermy and glass vitrines bears witness to the compelling but ambiguous art of collecting, display and looking. With titles such as *The Physical Impossibility of Death in the Mind of Someone Living* (1991) (a tiger shark in a glass tank of formaldehyde), we are confronted with the kind of questions visits to a museum raise but seldom answer.

Hockney, David (b.1937) British artist associated with the pop art movement in the 1960s and who has subsequently worked in California. During the 1960s, while still resident in Britain, Hockney's work wedded personal autobiography to a range of avant-garde techniques, from art brut to pop art.

Horn, Rebecca (b.1944) German installation artist whose early work used theatrical performances to explore issues around the body and sensation. Subsequent work has also included sculptural installations and feature-length films.

Irigaray, Luce (b.1930) Belgian-born feminist philosopher whose crucial theoretical contributions include *The Speculum of the Other Woman* (first published in 1974) and *The Sex Which Is Not One* (1975). Her radical deconstruction of patriarchal hegemony through psychoanalytical readings of the symbolic order provided a damning critique of the phallocentric cultural, economic and political structures of post war society.

Janco, Marcel (1895–1984) The Romanian artist and architect is best known for the short period that he spent with Dada. As well as painting the evening performances at the Cabaret Voltaire, Janco also designed sets and costumes and grotesque masks for the performances.

Jerichau-Baumann, Elisabeth (1819–81) Danish artist who kept a studio in Rome. Armed with letters of introduction from the Prince of Wales she was given access to the royal harem at Smyrna and permitted to paint the royal wives (Clayton 1876, vol 2: 98–107). She also travelled widely in the East and some of her reminiscences were published.

Jung, Carl Gustav (1875–1961) Swiss psychologist whose influential work on the 'collective unconscious' differed from Freud's notion of the unconscious in that Jung conceptualised the unconscious as a repository of archetypes. His work on dreams and psychopathological symptoms convinced him that humankind inherited an archive of mythic forms and symbols which could be evidenced across cultures and throughout history.

Kahlo, Frida (1907–54) Kahlo was a member of the Communist Party and married to the mural painter and political activist Diego Rivera. She was a self-taught painter without formal training whose paintings, as well as including imagery of her own physical suffering, often included traditional references to Mexican folk traditions.

Kandinsky, Wassily (1866–1944) Russian-born artist working in Germany, first as a founder of der Blaue Reiter (1909–14) and later as a teacher at the Bauhaus. His pamphlet *Concerning the Spiritual in Art* (1977), first published 1911/12, put into print his own spiritual epiphany and described his aim of granting painting a degree of autonomy by freeing it from subject matter rooted in the material world.

Kant, Immanuel (1724–1804) It is Kant's 1790 *Kritik der Urteilskraf* (Critique of Judgement) (Kant 1952), part of which specifically deals with issues of aesthetic judgement, that plays an important part in modernist theory. Kant recognised the subjectivity involved in making judgements about artwork but he allowed this subjectivity as long as it was disinterested; that is to say, the object was of no practical significance, it was the beauty of the object's appearance that was in question. Pursuing Kant's logic it follows that a judgement of pure disinterestedness, through the free play of the imagination, must have a universal validity.

Kant, Immanuel and Greenbergian formalism Kant reasoned that if a judgement could be purely aesthetic and therefore free of personal subjectivity it would have a universal validity. A genuinely aesthetic experience, therefore, was concerned with appearance alone and for Greenberg became an issue of defining quality by reference to the surface of paintings rather than the content. The 'intuition of quality' was arrived at through the experience of the work alone. The disinterested autonomous aesthetic, according to Kant was experienced through the free play of the imagination, and this was widely interpreted as an expression of freedom. There was a further important concept in Kant's work that was ignored by Greenberg. Rather than issues of taste being interpreted as a bloodless pursuit of art appreciation, Kant also insisted on a spiritual dimension to art works. Through the innate disposition of Kant's artist as genius, art works were able to communicate with an audience in a sensory and spiritual way that eschewed spoken language as a means of understanding.

Kesey, Ken (1935–2001) Author of *One Flew Over the Cuckoo's Nest* (1962) and early enthusiast for the drug LSD. Ken Kesey and the Merry Pranksters periodically took to the road and crossed the United States of America in a bus decorated in psychedelic Day-Glo colours. His early exploits with the Merry Pranksters are retold in Tom Wolfe's *The Electric Kool-Aid Acid Test* (1967).

Kirchner, Ernst Ludwig (1880–1938) Founder member of Die Brücke and German expressionist artist.

de Kooning, Willem (1904–97) American painter associated with the Abstract Expressionist movement. Completing his art training in his native Netherlands, de Kooning moved to the US at the age of twenty-two. He began work on the first of a series of *Women* paintings in 1938. The series that dates from the 1950s has been regarded as provocative for its allegedly angry brushwork and unsympathetic characterisations (although de Kooning always maintained that these were supposed to be humorous). Robert Hughes called him 'probably the most libidinal painter America ever had'. Although considered revolutionary, his brand of action painting only intermittently entirely forsook the staples of Western art's humanist tradition, which had the figure and landscape at its core.

Koons, Jeff (b.1955) The American Koons' trademark kitsch sculptures include a ceramic statue with a golden glaze of Michael Jackson and Bubbles (1988), Jackson's chimp, which plays with the glamour and ostentatious bad taste of celebrity culture using a kind of casino or fairground baroque to remind us of the tastefulness of high art.

Kosuth, Joseph (b.1945) A one-time member of the conceptual artist group Art and Language, Kosuth's work often critiques cultural institutions through text-based interventions.

Kristeva, Julia (b.1941) Bulgarian-born French writer who placed the body at the centre of her theories of human science and outlined a notion of abjection as a way of understanding oppression. In 1996 her book *The Sense and Nonsense of Revolt* (Kristeva 2000) proposed that creativity was the result of psychic revolt – that is, a rejection of authority in all its forms.

Kruger, Barbara (b.1945) Much of Kruger's work involves text and image. She maintains that she is suspicious about any claims to truth, and certainly suspicious about language as a claim to truth. She states:

> What I think I was saying was that there's a meaning implicit in the image itself, but its literally mute. When an image is stilled or there's an image without a word, there's a sort of withholding, which is about coolness or muteness. The use of language over the picture, the declarativeness of that, was totally uncool, as opposed to the cool of withholding of the image'
>
> (Kruger, quoted in Raney 2003: 116–17)

Kruschev, Nikita and de-Stalinisation: Joseph Stalin (1879–1953) whose style of leadership became synonymous with the cult of the personality, succeeded Lenin as the leader of the Soviet Union in 1924. Responsible for enforced collectivisation of agriculture and the coercive measures of a police state, his policies were denounced in 1956 by Kruschev.

Kupka, František (1871–1957) Czechoslovakian artist working in Paris. His interest in spiritualism and occultism framed much of his art practice and his treatise on abstract art, Creation in the Plastic Arts (1923, see Kupka 1997), outlined his belief in a purely spiritual art. Kupka was particularly interested in correspondences between painting and music and signed himself 'colour symphonist' in his letters. He was also a founder member of the group Abstraction-Création in 1931.

Lacan, Jacques (1901–81) French psychoanalyst who transformed Freudian theory on the basis of structuralist linguistics. Lacan conceptualised the unconscious as a system of linguistic signifiers rather than the Freudian notion of the unconscious as a repository of instincts and drives. Lacan's writings, *Écrits*, are notoriously difficult but have been influential on literary theorists, art historians and philosophers, who have applied his ideas to various disciplines.

Lawrence, Jacob (1917–2000) The young Jacob Lawrence taught at the WPA-sponsored Harlem Art Workshop during the 1930s. The African American Lawrence's work was shown at New York's Downtown Gallery, which championed American 'realist' artists such as Ben Shahn, Stuart Davis and Lawrence during the 1940s. His work was also purchased by MoMA, although his experience was atypical of artists associated with the Left, who continued to work in a 'realist' mode post-war.

Le Corbusier (Charles Édouard Jeanneret) (1887–1965) Swiss-born painter, although perhaps better known as an influential and pioneering modern architect. Le Corbusier met Amédée Ozenfant in 1916 and the pair formulated a series of attacks on the style of late cubism that was dominating Paris in the period.

Leary, Timothy (1920–96) American writer and pro-drugs activist who formed an LSD advocacy group, the League of Spiritual Discovery. Leary spent his later years exploring cyberculture and the possibilities of virtual reality.

Léger, Fernand (1881–1955) French artist whose early cubist style yielded to a more idiosyncratic one following the First World War. In line with his socialist outlook Léger evolved a distinctive style of painting which rendered men and women as cylindrical figures, their contours outlined in heavy black paint, in order to express his sense of their common purpose rather than emphasise their individualism.

Lenin, Vladimir Ilyich (1870–1924) Russian leader of the Bolshevik Revolution who sought to overthrow state capitalism and establish a dictatorship of the proletariat secured by a raising of class-consciousness and the hegemony of the Communist Party.

Levine, Sherrie (b.1947) American artist Sherrie Levine's central concern during the 1980s was the destabilising of the central tropes of modernism: authenticity, originality and authorship. Making references to canonical works of art, a process known as Appropriation Art, Levine reworks typically male 'masterpieces' as ironic starting points for female creativity. In 1991 she serially reproduced urinals in bronze placed on plinths called *Fountains, after Duchamp.*

Lévi-Strauss, Claude (b.1908) French anthropologist best known for developing 'structural anthropology' in relation to histories of cultural development. His books include *The Raw and the Cooked* (1969), *The Savage Mind* (1972) and *Structural Anthropology and Totemism* (1977), and blend his passion for Marxism, psychoanalysis and myth to show that there are no simple distinctions between 'savage' and 'civilised'.

Lin, Maya Ying (b.1959) The young Asian American Lin was still a postgraduate student when she won the commission for the monument. She commented: 'the Vietnam Veterans' Memorial is not an object inserted into the earth, but a work formed from the act of cutting open the earth and polishing the earth's surface' (Lin 1996: 535).

Lippard, Lucy (b.1947) American academic and cultural critic. Her book *Six Years: the dematerialisation of the art object from 1966 to 1972*, first published in 1973, chronicled the development of conceptual art between 1966 and 1972. She has since written numerous books, her latest entitled *On the Beaten Track: tourism, art and place* (1999).

Lissitzky, El (1890–1941) Russian painter, topographer, architect and designer who was involved with all the main constructivist movements of the 1910s and 1920s and whose work was influential on the Bauhaus design programme and the De Stijl movement. His wife, Sophie Lissitzky-Kuppers, edited his writings into a book, *El Lissitzky: life, letters, text* (1992).

Live Art Development Agency (LADA) supports the development of artists and organizations involved in Live Art and offers a range of resources including a library of over 500 videos documenting the work of British Performance Artists. There is also a comprehensive library on live art practice at <http://www.liveartlondon.demon.co.uk>.

Loos, Adolf (1870–1933) Czech-born architect who practised in Vienna. His buildings are typically stark, box-like structures with none of the ornament or detailing customary, for example, in the early twentieth-century construction of windows, doors and entablature. Loos's severe conception of design went hand in hand with his utopian belief that 'the evolution of culture marches with the elimination of ornament from useful objects'.

Luna, James (b.1950) An installation, video and performance artist of Mexican and Luiseno Indian origin whose work draws upon Native American and American Indian art forms and popular culture, including surf music. The content of his work often parodies Western perceptions of Native American culture by turning personal autobiography against the viewer.

Maciunas, George (1931–78) The American founder of Fluxus and responsible for some of the anarchic happenings of the 1960s, including the events at Wiesbaden in Germany in the 1960s, the first recorded Fluxus happening.

Mackensen, Fritz (1866–1953) German figure painter who trained at the Academy in Düsseldorf. Mackensen was the first of the artists associated with the Worpswede colony to visit the area and began bringing his artist friends (already formed into a student protest group in Düsseldorf) with him throughout the 1880s.

McLuhan, Marshall (1911–80) Canadian critic, academic and 'guru' of media culture. McLuhan's belief in technological determinism ('we shape our tools and they in turn shape us') led to a series of books which question the operations of communications in the age of electronic media. His books include *The Mechanical Bride* (1951), *The Gutenberg Galaxy* (1962), *The Medium is the Massage* (1967b) and *The Global Village* (1988).

Magritte, René François Ghislain (1898–1967) A Belgian artist whose surrealist strategy of following the dictates of the unreasoning unconscious resulted in works that juxtaposed often paradoxical or bizarre images, often with sexual overtones.

Malevich, Kasimir (1878–1935) Working as an artist and teacher at a time of intense revolution followed by periods of intense reaction, the Russian, Kasimir Malevich's essays such as 'Non-Objective Art and Suprematism', first published in 1919, sought to explain the philosophical ambitions that lay behind suprematism. He argued that 'the artist must transform the colour masses and create an artistic system, but he must not paint pictures of fragrant roses since all this would be dead representation pointing back to life' (Malevich 2003: 292).

Malraux, André (1901–76) The French art historian, author and resistance leader during the Second World War published *The Imaginary Museum* (1947) in the immediate post-war period, although it was written during the war. Malraux's work was a plea for a reconceptualisation of the museum space, in part an imaginary museum: a virtual museum without boundaries.

Man Ray (1890–1976) American artist known as much for his innovative rayogram photography and surrealist films as his painting, sculpture and graphic work. He founded New York Dada with Duchamp and Francis Picabia. In 1926 he made the film Anemic Cinema with Duchamp.

Manzoni, Piero (1933–63) Italian artist who worked with the body, sometimes others' bodies but also the products of his own body. The resulting art works include *Artist's Breath* (1960) and *Artist's Shit* (1961).

Marinetti, Filippo Tommaso (1876–1944) The erstwhile symbolist poet published 'The Foundation and Manifesto of Futurism' in 1909 in the Parisian daily *Le Figaro*. In a marked renunciation of symbolism Marinetti declared in favour of the speed of the car and noise of machines:

> We affirm that the world's magnificence has been enriched by a new beauty: the beauty of speed. A racing car whose hood is adorned with great pipes, like serpents of explosive breath – a roaring car that seems to ride on grapeshot is more explosive than the Victory of Samothrace.
>
> (Marinetti 2003: 147)

Masson, André (1896–1987) The French surrealist painter, educated in Belgium, was an enthusiastic exponent of explorations into the unconscious, often through the process of automatism. His works were marked by images of extreme violence, often with sexual connotations.

Mayakovsky, Vladimir (1893–1930) Russian poet and sloganeer. In the 1920s Mayakovsky provided copy for Rodchenko's advertisements for the state-owned companies of Russia. Mayakovsky's text supported Bolshevik state ideology by selling the product through communist proselytising, for example Trekhgornoe beer 'drives out hypocrisy and moonshine'.

Merleau-Ponty, Maurice (1908–61) French philosopher and Professor of Child Psychology and Pedagogy at the Sorbonne in Paris. Merleau-Ponty's *Phenomenology of Perception* (1945) identified perception as the source of all knowledge and the experience of being a body as the basis of all perceptual consciousness. Intentions are inseparable from bodily expression since the body makes sensations and feelings incarnate.

Modersohn-Becker, Paula (1876–1907) She joined the artist's colony at Worpswede in 1897, where she was married to the artist Otto Modersohn. Her *Letters and Journals* were first published in 1917 and contain a vivid account of her artistic concerns.

Modigliani, Amedeo (1884–1920) Italian painter and sculptor who came to Paris in 1906 and, like many other modernists, was influenced by the African art on display in the Trocadero and in artists' collections. His short life was marked by drug-taking, excessive drinking, womanising and a tubercular condition.

Modotti, Tina (1896–1924) The commitment to formal values found in Modotti's work is a legacy of the formalist photographer Edward Weston, who also worked in Mexico and made a significant number of nude studies of Modotti that initially eclipsed Modotti's photographic career. However, Modotti's imagery is often suffused with oblique political commentary.

Moholy-Nagy, László (1895–1946) Hungarian artist, photographer and teacher at the Bauhaus, where he taught his own pseudo-scientific brand of abstraction and experimental media on the preliminary course for all incoming students.

Mondrian, Piet Cornelius (1872–1944) Sharing with Kandinsky a belief in the spiritual dimension of art, although from the different perspective of theosophy, Mondrian's ambition was to achieve a universal harmony in his primary-coloured paintings: red, yellow and blue. Working in black-and-white grid-like formations filled with 'pure' colours, Mondrian's arrangements of shapes aspired to a universally accessible abstraction. Although he clearly had a unique signature style, Mondrian attempted to exorcise any sense of individualism from his paintings.

Monet, Claude (1840–1926) The French painter Monet is credited with initiating Impressionism as a technique and through his painting *Impression Sunrise* (1874) unwittingly giving the movement a style label. A veteran of the Paris Commune, Monet worked on natural subjects in a range of loosely structured works using broad-brush work with scant attention to detail.

Morimura, Yasumasa (b.1951) Japanese artist and photographer. Morimura has produced a series of self-portraits based on famous paintings (Manet's *Olympia*, Leonardo's *Mona Lisa*) in which he digitally manipulates the image to put his own body into the place of an existing figure. His repeated female impersonations hark back to a tradition within Japanese kabuki theatre and in recent works he poses as popular female icons such as Marilyn Monroe, Liza Minelli and Madonna.

Mukhina, Vera Ignatievna (1889–1953) Mukhina, like many of her contemporaries, worked across media, graphics, stage and textiles as well as sculpture and painting. In 1941 and 1943 she won the Stalin Prize for official portraits of the party officials Khizhnyak and Yusupov.

Mulvey, Laura (b.1941) British critic whose influential work on film spectatorship has been taken up by feminists and theoreticians of the gaze. Using Lacanian psychoanalysis, Mulvey's study of mainstream cinema points to a dichotomy between the male and female gaze which has subsequently been contested in a number of fields.

Naumann, Bruce (b.1941) American West Coast artist involved in funk art in the 1970s, which took pornography as one of its neo-Dada shock tactics. Naumann works across photography and installation, including holographs, video and neon-signage.

Newman, Barnett (1905–70) Championed by Clement Greenberg, this Polish-born American painter developed a mystical abstraction rooted in themes taken from classical mythology or Jewish theology. His leitmotif was of a zip-like strip that intersected austere, meticulously applied minimal paintings in a restricted colour range.

Odundo, Magdalene (1950) Although working in ceramics, Kenyan-born Adundo's work confounds classification systems, as the functional pot is more valued in her home culture than the highly prized functionless object of Western fine-art value systems.

Oldenburg, Claus (b.1929) This Swedish-born American sculptor is most often associated with pop art in its revolt against the perceived high-art ambitions of abstract expressionism. His 'soft' sculptures drew on the imagery of consumer culture.

Ono, Yoko (b.1933) and **John Lennon** (1940–80) The Japanese-born conceptual artist and British musician met in 1966 and began to collaborate on art and music projects, including the album *Two Virgins* (1968), which controversially featured the couple frontally naked on the front cover and naked from behind on the rear.

Orlan (b.1947) French performance artist who is best known for her surgical performances. Since the early 1990s she has been working on a project entitled *The Reincarnation of Saint Orlan*, in which her face has been repeatedly remodelled in order to question notions of beauty; as she says, 'my body has become a site of public debate that poses crucial questions for our time'.

Orozco, José Clemente (1883–1949) Orozco's mural works carried out in public buildings often drew on mythical and pre-conquest/pre-Colombian sources fused with contemporary political commentary on fascism and capitalism. His stylistic devices of rough caricature were gleaned from his early work as an illustrator for radical newspapers.

Ozenfant, Amédée (1886–1966) French artist and theorist who co-wrote 'Après le cubisme' with Le Corbusier in 1918 and produced the review *L'Esprit nouveau* between 1920 and 1925. Le Corbusier and Ozenfant accused the cubists of turning to mere decoration and launched their own alternative machine aesthetic based on the easily reproducible formulae of purism.

Parkin, George *see* Farrell, Rose

Picabia, Francis (1879–1959) French painter and poet associated with the cubist and Dada movements. He is sometimes thought to have pipped Kandinsky to the post by painting an abstract picture in the year before Kandinsky reportedly did. However, the question 'who invented abstract art' is a vexed one, and others, including Arthur Dove, Kupka and Vrubel, could also claim the initiative.

Pierre et Gilles (founded 1976) French artists who have been working together since 1976. Their trademark hand-coloured photographs are frequently portraits of celebrities rendered in a decorative manner. With the aid of theatrical lighting and exaggerated Technicolor, Pierre et Gilles's portraits include camp icons such as Jean-Paul Gautier, Kylie Minogue and Boy George.

Piper, Keith (b.1960) British artist who has worked across a variety of media and most recently in digital and multimedia arts. As a black male, his work explores the politics of representation in terms of young black men's experiences in postcolonial Britain.

Piper's on-line studio can be found at <http://www.iniva.org>. Keith Piper was a member of Digital Diaspora, an organisation which saw a connection between new technology and culturally diverse notions of identity.

Pissarro, Camille (1830–1903) An outsider in France through his Jewishness and Creole background, Pissaro's political affiliation to the Anarchic Syndicalists spoke of his aspirations for a traditional peasant existence. His later works were dominated by cityscapes that replaced his earlier evocations of a simple rural life.

Plant, Sadie (b.1964) British writer and academic. Her influential book, *Zeros + Ones: digital women and the new technoculture*, first published in 1992, argues that women laid the foundations of modern technology.

Pollock, Jackson (1912–56) The archetypal American abstract expressionist artist whose later all-over abstractions came to represent the ultimate form of self-expression during the late 1940s and early 1950s.

Popova, Liubov Sergeevna (1889–1924) In tandem with the idea of a useful art and a rejection of bourgeois values of art as relaxation and contemplation, the Russian Popova was an exponent of productivism, conceptually committed to art that had a socially serviceable basis in industrial production. Giving up easel painting for theatre design in the revolutionary theatre of the playwright Meyerhold, Popova produced costumes and set designs for plays such as *The Magnanimous Cuckold* in 1922.

Pousette-Dart, Richard (1916–92) American artist and one of the founders of the New York School of Abstract Expressionism. Pousette-Dart's belief in the spiritual nature set him apart from mainstream abstract expressionism. He was included in exhibitions at the Peggy Guggenheim Art of this Century Gallery in 1944, a venue famous for nurturing the nascent abstract expressionist group. His work drew on symbolic forms, often reworking ancient Native American symbols. Pousette-Dart's aspirations were to create a new visual language that could encompass a 'transcendental language of form, spirit, harmony [which] means one universal presence' (Sims and Polcari 1997: 13). He left the city in 1951 in order to work in solitude and quiet in the rural countryside of upstate New York, where he continued to paint until his death. His interest in the metaphysical was articulated in two much quoted statements about art: 'art is a cosmic prayer' and 'abstract art is a transcendental language'.

Protest groups The Art Workers' Coalition (AWC) (1969), the Guerrilla Art Action Group (GAAA) (1969–76), Black Emergency Cultural Coalition and Artists and Writers Protest bear testament to the wave of political activity that swept through the art world during the 1960s.

Rauschenberg, Robert (b.1925) Like many of his generation, Rauschenberg was a student at the legendary Black Mountain College in North Carolina, which was run along Bauhaus principles. Many of his art works are assemblages or collages made up of 'real' objects, in line with his edict that paintings should relate to both art and life. He declared: 'a pair of socks is no less suitable to make a painting with than wood, nails, turpentine, oil and fabric' (Rauschenberg, in Stiles and Selz 1996: 321).

Rebay, Hilla (1890–1967) An early enthusiast of 'non-objective' painting, who was instrumental in the formation of the Solomon R. Guggenheim Museum in New York.

She also promoted the careers of European modernists Kandinsky, Mondrian, Chagall and Delaunay in the United States during the Second World War. (See Lukach 1983.)

Renoir, Pierre Auguste (1841–1919) Often described as a decorative painter, Renoir's early training in painting porcelain contributed to his art practices. He is mostly associated with scenes of everyday French life and impressionist art, although he experimented with different techniques throughout his life.

Rilke, Rainer Maria (1875–1926) Czech-born German writer and poet who briefly joined the artists' colony at Worpswede in 1903. He firmly believed in the co-existence of material and spiritual realms but his poetry tends towards melancholy and loss. He wrote a monograph on the Worpswede artists in 1903.

Ringgold, Faith (b.1930) Ringgold is an African American artist active in black and feminist politics since the 1960s protest movements. Ringgold has been influential in bringing to mainstream art the politics, imagery and media of African American cultural heritage.

Rivera, Diego (1886–1957) Mexican social-realist mural painter, book illustrator and political writer who, like his close, if quarrelsome, collaborator, Siqueiros, held technology in high regard and celebrated it in murals such as the *Detroit Industry* mural of 1932–3. It is his rejection of Parisian modernism that concerns us here, as he sought an art form accessible to the Mexican people and the masses in general. Like Siqueiros and Orozco, a pre-Colombian history and an emancipatory politics informed his imagery. He travelled in Russia, was a sometime member of the Communist Party and helped secure sanctuary in Mexico for the exiled Russian political leader Leon Trotsky.

Rodchenko, Aleksandr Mikhailovich (1891–1956) Working across a range of media, from photography to poster design and constructivist painting, Rodchenko put his art in the service of revolution, at one time abandoning easel painting altogether to champion Productivism.

Rodin, Auguste (1840–1917) Although the expressive surfaces of Rodin's sculptures put him at odds with the smooth finish of academic sculpture, he in turn was pitted against the vogue for direct carving that was so important to later modernist artists.

Rosenberg, Harold (1906–78) American author, critic and advocate of abstract expressionism. It was Rosenberg who coined the term 'action painting' in his article for *ARTnews* in 1952. In it he argued that the spontaneous gesture of the action painter was more important than the finished product: 'act as art'. 'The American Action Painters' (Rosenberg 1985) became an unofficial manifesto for the movement.

Rosler, Martha (b.1943) American writer, photographer, performance and video artist who was part of the new left in the 1960s as a political activist and artist. Since the mid-1960s Rosler's work has scrutinized women's experience in society, the role of the mass media and the operations of urban structures to deconstruct cultural and social relations.

Rothko, Mark (1903–70) Russian-born American painter who, by the late 1940s created large-scale abstract canvasses using a limited colour range. The subject matter was also limited, mostly to luminous floating triangles.

Rousseau, Théodore (1812–1867) French landscape painter who settled in the village of Barbizon on the edge of the forest of Fontainebleau in the 1840s. Rousseau painted in opposition to academic practices several years before the Impressionists made plein-air landscapes a badge of avant-gardism.

Ruskin, John (1819–1900) The Victorian critic Ruskin championed Joseph William Mallord Turner (1775–1851) and the Pre-Raphaelite Brotherhood (founded in 1848) in the series Modern Painters. Ruskin's lyrical descriptions of paintings and his enthusiasm for art with moral and practical purpose pitted him against the 'art for art's sake' ethos of the late-Victorian Aesthetic Movement.

Russolo, Luigi (1885–1947) Italian painter, composer and noise artist. His manifesto 'The Art of Noises' was compiled in 1913 and extolled the virtues of accidental sounds and cacophonous street noises. He made a classification of noise based on the aural qualities of each and these included roars, gurgles, explosions and howls made by animal, vegetable or mineral.

Ryder, Albert Pinkham (1847–1917) The local hero of the Armory Show through his early rejection of detailed illustrations of the world of appearances, Ryder is considered the only American precedent for modernism. Ryder was the painterly equivalent of the poetic transcendentalists Ralph Waldo Emerson and Henry David Thoreau, who were concerned to find 'truth' through feelings and intuition rather than through the auspices of logic.

Sachs, Tom (b.1966) American artist working in New York in a field the artist terms 'cultural prosthetics'.

Said, Edward (1935–2003) American critic and writer born in Jerusalem and a passionate spokesperson for the Palestinian cause. Said's books include *Beginnings: intention and the method* (1975), *Orientalism* (1978) and *Culture and Imperialism* (1993).

Salon des Refusés (Salon of the Rejected) A one-time exhibition held in Paris in 1863 is a seminal moment in modernist art history through its rejection of official academicism. Although the gesture was more striking for its panache than any subsequent reform of the official academy, many avant-garde artists, such as Manet and Whistler, had their work displayed and ridiculed there.

Sant'Elia, Antonio (1888–1916) Italian futurist architect, more on paper than in practice, since his death in the First World War prematurely cut short his career. There is some debate about whether it was Sant'Elia who actually wrote *The Manifesto of Futurist Architecture* in 1914; the manifesto accorded with Sant'Elia's ideas about buildings that should resemble machines and cities that should be rebuilt by each new generation.

Saussure, Ferdinand de (1857–1913) Swiss linguist and founder of structural linguistics and semiology whose work has been influential for Lacan and the poststructuralists. His most important work, the *Course in General Linguistics* (1915), outlined a scientific model for linguistics which distinguished speech (*la parole*) from grammatical rules (*la* *langue*). Furthermore, Saussure differentiated between the phonetic component of language (the signifier) and the semantic (the signified), which contributed to his overall theory that linguistics is part of a social system of signs.

Schapiro, Meyer (1904–96) Schapiro, a Marxist art historian, is an important advocate for abstract expressionism not least because he did not feel compelled to denigrate the 'social' art of the 1930s in order to promote it. Moreover, he saw in abstract expressionism a political and artistic commitment that countered the formalism of Clement Greenberg. For Schapiro the process of painting, in the handmade and the spontaneous, was an act of resistance in an increasingly alienating, technologised culture. Abstract expressionism's very lack of overt social content or commentary, familiar in the New Deal work of the 1930s, could be interpreted as a political act in opening up an ideologically free space for individual expression.

Schechner, Alan (b.1962) British artist currently working in the US. His often interactive works look at the relationship between technological determinism and power relations in contemporary culture, as well as exploring the exploitation of the past.

Schlemmer, Oskar (1888–1943) German artist who led the Bauhaus sculpture and theatre workshops in the 1920s. Schlemmer's life-drawing classes encouraged students to see the body in terms of its function and to analyse movement through highly stylised representations of the human form. He also choreographed student performances at the Bauhaus, including the well-known Triadic Ballet.

Schwitters, Kurt (1887–1948) German collagist and sound poet involved with the Hanover and Berlin Dada movement. His own form of Dada activity, *Merz*, was to juxtapose ephemera, *objets trouvés* in two-dimensional collage arrangements and later three-dimensional installations, *Merzbau*. His work was highly influential in neo-Dada movements of the 1960s and 1970s.

Serra, Richard (b.1939) Often working in steel with a patina of rust as it ages, Serra's works are minimalist in conception. Sometimes occupying public spaces such as squares, simple shapes are rendered awesome by the American sculptor's use of scale and materials that create a contradictory sense of stable unease. *Tilted Arc*, which bisected Federal Plaza in Lower Manhattan, proved too intrusive and menacing for the workers who used the Plaza and it was removed in 1985 after a protracted and hostile debate.

Seurat, Georges Pierre (1859–91) French painter who is usually grouped with the post-Impressionists on the grounds that he continued the Impressionist experiments with colour and light. His distinctive way of rendering the motif in the combination of small dots of colour (pointillism) reflected the experimental aspects of his study of art and his scientific interest in colour theory.

Shahn, Ben (1898–1969) Shahn's work found widespread popularity in Europe following the Venice Biennale of 1954, where, along with de Kooning, he represented American painting. His fusion of modernism and realism did incorporate a more personal iconography post-war but rarely deviated from his political commitment to a form of liberal humanism that in his painting had the figure at its core.

Sheeler, Charles (1883–1965) American precisionist painter and photographer. He was commissioned by the Ford Motor Company in 1927 to photograph the River Rouge plant, and the series of celebratory images of stamping presses, foundries and chimney stacks was subsequently published. The photographs are striking for their sumptuous presentation of the machine and for their deliberate effacement of the workers who operated the plant.

Shonibare, Yinka (b.1962) Shonibare's work often plays with the cultural borrowing that exists between a colonial power such as Britain and a colonised culture through the metaphor of fashion and fabric. For instance, in 2000 he questioned notions of Britishness by wrapping the statue of Britannia that tops Tate Britain with 'ethnic' cloth, covering the supposed timelessness of the original Greek classic drape. He typically paints on to the powerful patterning of African fabric in preference to unprimed canvas.

Simmel, Georg (1858–1918) The German sociologist was critical of aesthetic idealism, preferring to situate art into broader networks of social exchange that resulted in ambiguities in the aesthetic response; pointing away from aesthetic autonomy to a social aesthetics.

Siqueiros, David A. (1896–1974) A veteran of the Mexican Revolution (1910) and the Spanish Civil War (1937–9) and a political inmate of numerous prisons, Siqueiros produced murals that combined radical politics, Mexican identity and an enthusiasm for new technologies, which he used to create innovative ways of making art.

Smithson, Robert (1938–73) Artist, filmmaker, writer and one of the pioneers of earthworks or land art. Best known perhaps for his monumental 1970 *Spiral Jetty*, a spiral of basalt rock and salt crystals 1,500 feet in length and approximately 15 feet in width in the Great Salt Lake in Utah, Smithson was also an articulate advocate for what he termed 'earthworks', named after Brian Aldiss' ecological disaster novel of the same name. Initially artworks made from the stuff of nature and shown in galleries, the earthworks eventually became site-specific locations. He is an important theorist, *The Writings of Robert Smithson* was first published in 1979.

Sokari, Douglas Camp (b.1958) Nigerian-born artist who lives and works in Paris and London and whose typically welded, kinetic works in a figurative mode depict scenes from her Nigerian experiences: *School Run* and *Church Ede*. The works in the African Gallery explore the masquerade tradition of the Kalabari.

Sontag, Susan (b.1933) American cultural theorist and writer, whose *On Photography* (1987) while not as rigorous as later theoreticians' work on photography, questioned received wisdom in relation to the use of photography as a neutral technology.

Spence, Jo (1934–92) British artist and pioneer of performance-based photography which draws upon psychoanalytical theory and therapeutic autobiography. Her works are often a form of catharsis in which she exorcises gender and class politics to expose the body fascism of media images of women that narrow the range of acceptable imagery of and for women.

Spero, Nancy (b.1926) Spero was a founder member of Women Artists in Revolution (WAR) in 1969 which grew out of the Art Workers' Coalition and was part of the ad-hoc committee of women artists. Among other political activities, Spero picketed the Whitney Museum of American Art in protest at the lack of women artists represented in the collection.

Sprinkle, Annie (b.1954) American performance artist who began by working in the pornography industry and turned her performances to the service of the avant-garde in the body of work she began in the mid-1980s and called 'post-porn modernism'.

Stelarc (b.1946) Cypriot-born Australian artist. Since the 1960s his work has explored the body through performance, electronic manipulation, enhancements and surgical procedures. His latest project proposes grafting a laboratory-grown ear on to his body. The artist's authorised web site is at <http://www.stelarc.va.com.au>.

Stieglitz, Alfred (1864–1946) American photographer who was an early pioneer of photographic modernism promoted through his own Photo-Session Gallery (later *291*), which also supported New York Dada. Stieglitz also edited influential magazines such as *Camera Work* (1903–17) that discussed avant-garde culture.

Tatlin, Vladimir Evgrafovich (1885–1953) Tatlin's revolutionary constructivism initially found favour with the Soviet authorities. His modernist innovations, which included a radical reworking of cubism, were eventually deemed unsuitable for revolutionary purposes.

Taylor, Frederick Winslow (1856–1915) Supporting industry's adoption of a rational efficiency model, Taylor, the pioneer of 'time and motion' studies, helped regulate workers engaged in assembly-line procedures (most famously in Henry Ford's motor-car factories) through the adoption of repetitive, time-saving motions.

Teniers, David, the Younger (1582–1649) The Flemish painter Teniers was appointed Court painter to Archduke Leopold Wilhelm of Austria. In counter-distinction to the modernist impulse to originality, part of Teniers' job included the copying of pictures held in the royal collection.

Thoreau, Henry David (1817–1862) American author whose most famous book, *Walden* (1854) was based on his stay in a cabin in the woods at Walden Pond between 1846 and 1848. As a transcendentalist poet, Thoreau sought the essence of reality beyond appearances and the emancipation of the individual rather than social reform.

van Doesburg, Theo (1883–1931) Dutch artist and architect associated with De Stijl and editor of the magazine *De Stijl* (1917–28). As a teacher and writer on art, van Doesburg espoused the machine as a tool of social liberation and formulated an art practice that matched the rational, functional and democratic rhetoric of the machine aesthetic.

Varo, Remedios (1908–63) Spanish-born artist who settled in Mexico City in 1942, where she became firm friends with Leonora Carrington. Varo's own iconography was inspired by her occult interests and often shows fantastic landscapes and buildings populated by bird-women.

Veblen, Thorstein (1857–1929) American sociologist and economist who coined the term 'conspicuous consumption'. His most famous work is *The Theory of the Leisure Class* (1899).

Virilio, Paul (b.1932) French writer and critic who is characteristically sceptical about the effects of new technologies. He argues that instantaneous access to information and globalisation (the global village becomes a 'global ghetto') has contributed to a loss of democracy and curbed the rights of the individual.

Wall Street Crash Wall Street is shorthand for the machinery of US capitalism, although geographically it is a street in the financial district of Manhattan, New York. In 1929 newspaper photographs of stockbrokers faced with financial ruin jumping from high-rise buildings as the stock market fell fixed in the public's memory the dawning of the Depression era.

Warhol, Andy (1930–87) As famous for the coterie of musicians, starlets and filmmakers that inhabited his Factory in New York as for his art output, Warhol is the quintessential pop artist, typically revelling in brash, kitsch images of movie stars and consumer products. In his 1962 work *Black and White Disaster*, part of the deaths and disasters series, Warhol did key into a more serious side to contemporary life in the USA.

Weber, Max (1881–1961) Russian-born American artist and writer. His cubist experiments before 1920 brought together the work of artists such as Picasso with the work of futurism. Interior of the Fourth Dimension fuses cubo-futurism with his particular belief in the idea of sacred geometry.

Weston, Edward (1886–1958) A celebrated formalist of American photography. Weston's images of nudes and landscapes blurred the boundaries between abstraction and realism. It was his image of his young son posed in reminiscence of a Greek male torso that made his work such a compelling subject for an appropriation artist such as Levine. In focusing on her act of thievery Levine draws attention to Weston's own appropriation of Ancient Greek culture, at the same time as questioning notions of authenticity, the centrality of the male nude to early Western culture, and control through copyright.

Whistler, James Abbott McNeill (1834–1903) American-born artist working principally in Britain. His published writing in 1890, *The Gentle Art of Making Enemies*, confirmed his radical, anti-establishment credentials, setting him firmly within avant-garde culture. His paintings lack of 'finish' provoked Ruskin's outburst on charlotry. Whistler won a subsequent libel action but was bankrupted in the process.

Whiteread, Rachel (b.1963) Whiteread became the first female winner of the Turner Prize in 1993 during the period of *House*'s demise. Her work, although often taking concrete form, is concerned with inner reality rather than external appearance, although actual traces of the presence of people often remain through the direct casting technique. She casts negative forms, often concentrating on the spaces between things rather than the object itself; that is, the spaces between chair legs rather than the chair itself.

Whitman, Walt (1819–92) Whitman is the most American of poets in his quest for a vernacular form of poetry that would rid the US of its dependency on European poetic precedents. His life's work in progress was *Leaves of Grass*. Within it the poem 'Song of Myself' celebrates his vision of the universality of US democracy and the transcendent self. Whitman's role in defining American identity has been appropriated by very different ideological positions in US culture – for our purpose, everyman for the 1930s and the transcendent self for the 1950s.

Williams, Raymond (1921–88) An influential Welsh cultural theorist working principally in literary theory, who pointed to the underbelly of class politics in relation to the production of cultural values, exposing the elitism of avant-garde culture. Key works such as *Culture* (1981), *Culture and Society* (1958) and *Keywords* (1988) collectively unravelled the supposed neutrality of language and laid bare the class politics that buttressed much of modernism.

Wilson, Fred (b.1954) Wilson represented the USA in the Fiftieth Venice Biennale in 2003. His interventions into over twenty museum collections involved research into the origins of collections which resulted in the repositioning or relabelling of works, or the introduction of 'alien' pieces in order to create new meanings. In 1999 he relabelled the eighteenth-century maritime paintings at the Liverpool Maritime Museum to draw attention to the gendered language surrounding shipping. His re-presentation of objects is designed to disrupt exclusive histories in order to 'discover' exclusions and 'other' histories.

Wittgenstein, Ludwig (1889–1951) An important touchstone for postmodern theorists, in works such as Culture and Value (*Vermischte Bermerkungen*) (1980) Wittgenstein, rather than developing theories and structures of increasing complexity, sought a way of achieving philosophical clarity and transparency in opposition to a society based on scientific progress.

Works Progress Administration/Federal Art Project (WPA/FAP) The guiding light of the project, Holger Cahill, saw it through the philosophy of John Dewey, declaring that the project 'proceeded on the principle that it is not the solitary genius but a sound general movement which maintains art as a vital functioning of any scheme'. He sought integration across all the arts rather than giving fine art a privileged position, continuing:

> The importance of integration between the fine arts and the practical arts has been recognized from the first by the Federal Arts Project, as an objective desirable in itself and as a means of drawing together major aesthetic forces in this country'.

> (Cahill, quoted in O'Connor 1973: 18)

Worringer, Wilhelm (1881–1965) German theorist whose influential Abstraction and Empathy was first published in 1908 but was not translated into English until 1953. His own conception of abstraction is coloured by his involvement with the work of German expressionists (Worringer is sometimes credited with inventing the term 'expressionist') and, in particular, with Kandinsky. Worringer does not mean abstraction as distinct from figurative art but abstraction as an artistic impulse separate and distinct from mere copying. Thus the viewer's empathy is only engaged if the work possesses the requisite impulses.

Xu Bing (b.1955) Born in Chongqing, China, Xu Bing now lives and works in New York. His work explores the relationship between visual and written languages.

Notes

1 What, when and where was modernism?

1 The question 'What Was Modernism?' was asked by Harry Levin in the title of an essay first published in 1960. The chapter title, 'When Was Modernism?', refers to Raymond Williams's essay (1989b) of the same name.

2 *Batman: The Killing Joke* (© 1986; published by Titan Books, 1988).

3 The new system of composition sometimes referred to as dodecaphony was developed in 1921. The system utilised twelve notes of the chromatic scale, in which, potentially at least, each note was of equal importance.

4 Jules Michelet and Jacob Burckhardt in the second half of the nineteenth century are usually subsequently credited with 'inventing' periodisation, building on Enlightenment thought.

5 See, for instance, the works of Ernst Gombrich, David Britt, H.W. Jansen. The (1997) Tate Gallery series Movements in Modern Art includes editions on minimalism (Batchelor 1997b), realism (Malpas 1997), conceptual art (Wood 1997) and modernism (Harrison 1997).

6 Catriona Miller claims, as do many others, that 'it was the mechanised murder of the Western front which consigned the old nineteenth century order to oblivion. . . . But the artistic death knell had been sounded some ten years earlier' (Miller 1996: 159). She cites fauvism (1905) and cubism (1907) as the 'two vital sparks which kick started modernism into existence' (Miller 1996: 159). These two seminal dates – 1905 and 1907 – refer to two art-historical events: in 1905 the fauves, a group of artists, including Derain, Matisse and Vlaminck, exhibited their work at the Salon d'Automne and in 1907 Picasso painted the proto-cubist work *Les Demoiselles d'Avignon*.

7 There is only one mention of Duchamp in Charles Harrison's book *Modernism: movements in modern art* (1997).

8 Notable writers such as Victor Hugo and Émile Zola wrote in defence of Manet's works and against Napoleon III.

9 This in spite of the political allegiances of Fry and company, who came largely from a socialist background, which included, for some, working with the Workers' Educational Association (WEA).

10 A group of people who work together stitching a design through layers of cloth to make, typically, bed covers.

2 Retreats from the urban

1 In Chapter 1 we noted how the pre-Raphaelites fulfilled many of the conditions of modernity much earlier than had the French impressionists usually credited with 'inventing' modernism.

2 This idea that painting could achieve a state of 'pure art' has precedence in philosophy and had been most famously reinstated by the English proto-aesthete Walter Pater when he prescribed (in another debt to Hegel) that 'all art constantly aspires to the conditions of music' (1873: 106). His (albeit embryonic) idea of a work of art that is capable of overcoming its materiality to become pure art was to gain momentum, especially among artists searching for the spiritual through art.

3 This belief that humans would eventually evolve into a much more cerebral life form, outgrowing the body, recurs in twentieth-century science fiction, which features highly evolved life-forms with out-sized brains and little or no body.

4 There is an issue over exactly what Duchamp's connection to alchemy was. J.F. Moffitt's book *Alchemist of the Avant-Garde: the case of Marcel Duchamp* (2003) traces the influence of occultism and alchemy on Duchamp. And, although Duchamp puts on record his interest in alchemy, some see it as nothing more than a flirtation on his part. Duchamp is characteristically ambivalent and himself refutes any practising interest in the subject (see Tomkins 1996: 456–7).

5 This connection between the 'regressive' tendency of modern art (namely abstraction) and the 'primitive' obviously pre-dates Hitler's notion of 'degenerate art'.

6 In the US there was a thriving artist colony at Provincetown in Massachussets.

7 Secessionist groups in Northern Europe emerged in opposition to the prevailing academic strictures that appeared to limit avant-garde art practices, such as impressionistic styles of painting and themes of modern life.

3 Monuments, modernism and the public space

1 Most of the histories of modernism were written after 1950 at a time when the teleological approach instituted by Alfred H. Barr was further endorsed, for instance in John Rewald's *History of Impressionism* (1973).

2 See *The End of History and the Last Man* (Fukuyama 1992).

3 The subtitle reads 'Alexander the Third', though it is referred to by Rosalind Krauss (1977: 7) as 'Nicholas the Second'.

4 What is now called St Petersburg was called Petrograd after the Bolshevik Revolution, and later Leningrad.

5 Clement Greenberg did promote the work of the sculptor David Smith. Smith was a significant advocate for American sculpture. A useful essay in this respect is from 1952, 'Aesthetics, the Artist and the Audience' (David Smith 2003).

6 'Flatness' found its sculptural equivalent and often epic scale in 1960s minimalism, in particular in the 'primary structures' of Donald Judd and Carl Andre.

7 Benjamin 1979: 487.

8 Le Corbusier's 1920s plan to rebuild the centre of Paris allocated more space to some of the city's monuments.

9 Whiteread's work is notorious for simultaneously winning the prestigious Turner Prize at the Tate and the K Foundation's prize for the worst piece of art that year in 1993.

10 Modern artists often sought newer materials with which to record modernity, and so stone became a casualty of modernism, its very permanence an impediment. Lewis Mumford noted that 'stone gives a false sense of continuity, and a deceptive assurance of life' (quoted in Young 1993: 20).

11 See, particularly, Martha Rosler, '*Untitled*', from 'Bringing the War Home: House Beautiful' (1969–71).

12 Baudrillard means that once a print of a celluloid film is copied and circulated for screening it has no original. Of course, these days we view videos of films on our television screens, while organisations such as the British Film Institute (BFI) are currently trying to retrieve any surviving 'original' prints of celluloid film.

4 The nude in modernity and postmodernity

1 The life class, a fixture of all art schools, has had a problematic history. Most academies and art schools denied female students access to the life room. Unusually, the Pennsylvania Academy of Art permitted women to attend life classes (to draw female models from 1868 and male models from 1877), but by and large entry to the life classes of Europe and North America gradually began at the turn of the century. It was customary for male models to wear loin cloths covering their genitals when posing for women artists.

2 The identity of Modigliani's models in generally unknown, but he painted over twenty such images of nudes in the three years before his death. His one-man show in 1917 was closed when the police declared the works on display obscene. Decades later, at the other end of the century, the United States Postal Service complained about the Modigliani image circulating in the postal system on the back of postcards sold at the Guggenheim Museum.

3 This is a moot point in relation to nineteenth- and twentieth-century art-historical scholarship. Many well-known art historians have been homosexual but unable openly to acknowledge their subject position (see Chapter 8).

4 Manzoni signed both male and female models and called them 'living sculptures', although it is his female models that are most frequently reproduced in books. He also provided the signed models with 'certificates of authenticity' to underwrite their status as art works and, moreover, designated two plinths as 'magic bases', which meant that as long as the model was on either plinth it was officially a work of art.

5 Laura Mulvey's work on spectatorship (1989) was preceded by that of John Berger (1969, 1972), who raised the question of the gendering of spectatorship.

6 Sara Baartman, originally from the Khoisan people of the Cape Colony, was displayed in London and Paris in the early nineteenth century. The displays generally took the form of Sara walking naked along a raised dais so that her genitals and buttocks could be better inspected. After her premature death her remains were put on display at the Musée de l'Homme in Paris but were repatriated in

2002 after a long campaign. A documentary film, *The Life and Times of Sara Baartman* (directed by Zola Maseko), was released in 1998.

7 In 1989 in the US Senator Jesse Helms mounted a campaign to stop state funding through the National Endowment for the Arts (NEA) to finance exhibitions of work by Robert Mapplethorpe, Annie Sprinkle and André Serrano.

8 The American lawyer Catherine MacKinnon and the writer Andrea Dworkin have always been anti-porn. They have moved for legislation in the US to define pornography as 'the graphic sexually explicit subordination of women through pictures or words' (see Catherine MacKinnon 1993; Dworkin 1981).

5 From the machine aesthetic to technoculture

1 The historic reluctance or disinclination of the Museum of Modern Art in New York to display sound art, theatre or costume design has led to criticism in the past. The history of art, it has been observed, is often the history of what is on display in museums and art galleries.

2 Severini and Picasso, for example, had 'classical periods' in the 1920s. Although Picasso's ability to work simultaneously in different styles, including monumental classical figures, helped him to hang on to his radical credentials in a period of conservatism.

3 Tatlin was probably poking fun at artists such as Kasimir Malevich. Tatlin and Malevich were famously at odds in the early years of the Russian avant-garde. Tatlin thought of himself as a technician or 'inventor' and Malevich believed himself to be a mystical 'creator'.

4 Weimar was the town in Germany which gave its name to the Weimar Period (1917–33), the period of Republican government that ended when Hitler became Chancellor.

5 This is especially the case with the mystic Johannes Itten. Itten was replaced by the Hungarian constructivist László Moholy-Nagy as master of the foundation course.

6 To leap ahead of chronology for a moment, we are reportedly now in a *post-photographic* era where digital photography, in theory, tests the veracity of analogue photography. The so-called digital revolution means that a photograph, a frame of a film or a piece of sound can all be digitised, enhanced and manipulated. The notion of post-photography is predicated on the notion that photography is a 'transparent' technology, though photographers early on in the century were aware, as was Rodchenko, that analogue photographs were never simple reflections of the world because they were framed and edited by photographers.

7 The division of the avant-garde into two, introduced in Chapter 1, is in evidence here at the time of the Russian Revolution. There has been a tendency among historians in the West to see this period in the history of the Russian avant-garde in terms of Cold War politics; that is, to see the revolutionary enthusiasm of these artists as politically naive. Their anti-bourgeois imperative to defy the Romantic individualism of early modernism and to work in the mode of mass production conjured up the spectre of artists being used as political pawns.

8 *Modern Times*, the classic satire of American capitalism, begins in a factory where all the workers are watched over by foremen and a company president monitors their activities via a television monitor in a palatial office. Bullied by the foreman to keep up with the relentless pace set by efficiency models for production, Chaplin, a metaphorical small cog in the factory machine, suffers a momentary breakdown and literally becomes a cog in the machine.

9 The technological imperative has been questioned by Victor Papanek, whose book *Design for the Real World* criticised accident-prone automobiles, injury-inflicting domestic items and the 'Kleenex culture' of disposability (Papanek 1977: 77ff.).

10 Martha Rosler is suspicious of McLuhan's soundbite effects on early video art: 'the idea of simultaneity and a return to an Eden of sensory immediacy gave hippies and critics of the alienated and repressed one-dimensionality of industrial society a rosy, psychedelic, wet dream' (Rosler 1996: 274).

11 However, the 'postmodern sublime' is understood in relation to critiques of the aesthetic. Whereas beauty in a given work of art is apprehended via the form that the work of art assumes, the sublime is generally formless or 'unpresentable' (Lyotard 1982). For the French philosopher Jean-François Lyotard (1924–98) the sublime is simply 'the unpresentable', so this can include 'ideas' as well as experiences: 'nobody has ever *seen* a society. Nobody has ever *seen* a beginning. An end. Nobody has ever *seen* a world' (Lyotard 1989: 23). Lyotard argues that it is our powerlessness to represent such things that is sublime.

12 According to Michael Benedikt, cyberspace 'does not exist' (1991: 3).

13 At time of writing one company is anticipating the production of cybersmells.

14 The ultimate is 'virtual warfare', as Paul Virilio has remarked. The First Gulf War (1991–2) was in two respects the first electronic war: at the level of both arms' production and the transmission of the war via live satellite link-ups.

15 Contemporary anthropologists and scientists have observed that memory is constructed through social forces, so that the learning of dates, for instance, is culturally specific.

16 *Blake's* 7, episode 3: 'Cygnus Alpha Time Squad', by Terry Nation.

6 Modernism and realism in US art

1 The modernist argument maintains that only the immediate past is important. The 'historic', artistic past, they argued, was re-worked by Manet to such an extent that it need not be revisited.

2 The captions were removed from many FSA documentary photographs in the 1940s and 1950s, which were then re-presented to evoke purely aesthetic responses.

3 Stuart Davis, in 'Abstract Painting Today' (1973), lamented the loss of experimental work and acknowledged that the WPA programmes sometimes had conservative agendas. However, there is plenty of evidence to suggest that a wide range of work was produced during this period.

4 The article was originally published, for 'tactical' reasons, under the name of Diego Rivera, not Trotsky (Chipp 1968: 457).

5 The Truman Doctrine was the name given to a policy which established a commitment to policing the planet that maintained democracy and where necessary rolled back Communism in the name of freedom.
6 See Harris (n.d.) for a fuller account of the Left's retreat during the late 1930s and the 1940s.
7 Schlesinger's *The Vital Center* (1949) was a highly influential tract that established a set of liberal business values for its generation.
8 Clement Greenberg's 1948 essay 'The Decline of Cubism' promoted the idea of a weakened School of Paris and the opportunity for culture to be revived in the USA.
9 Clyfford Still wrote of the restriction placed upon him by the picture frame, which he likened to a 'Euclidian prison' needing to be annihilated (interview with Ti-Grace Sharpless, published in the 1963 catalogue *Clyfford Still*, Philadelphia Institute of Contemporary Art, University of Pennsylvania, Pennsylvania).
10 Frederick Turner's 'thesis' *The Significance of the Frontier in American History* (1893), delivered at the Chicago World's Fair, held that American democracy developed in line with the movement westwards, bypassing conventional wisdom, which held that American democracy was dependent upon German and English models.
11 William Boddy estimated that

> in the 1957–8 season, four of television's five most popular programmes were Westerns and the following season, despite wide-spread predictions of saturation, Westerns represented nine of TV's top eleven shows – the 570 hours of TV. Westerns in the 1958–9 season were estimated to be the equivalent of 400 Hollywood features a year.
>
> (Boddy 1998: 119)

12 This is the title of a 1947 article by Barnett Newman (see Newman 1968a: 551).
13 Stephen Polcari's *Abstract Expressionism and the Modern Experience* (1991) principally uses iconography as a tool for analysing abstract expressionism.
14 Florence Rubenfeld reflected: 'Pollock's funeral was barely over when Janis sold for $10,000 a de Kooning he had been unable to move a month earlier for half that amount' (1998: 210).

7 The artist and the museum: muse or nemesis?

1 For a full account of this exhibition, see Lewis Kachur, *Displaying the Marvelous* (MIT Press, 2001).
2 *Seen/Unseen Exhibition* catalogue (*1994*) Bluecoat Gallery, Liverpool, p. 10.
3 It is outside the scope of an introductory text such as this to pursue the Freudian interpretation; however, Susan Pearce (1998) is interesting in this respect.
4 The National Curriculum for Art (England) still maintains that a sense of spiritual and moral growth is related to the acquisition of taste.
5 The Muses were the daughters of Zeus and Mnemosyne (memory).
6 For a fuller account of the formation of the Tate Gallery at Millbank, see Taylor 1994.

7 This was also a reference to Meret Oppenheim's surrealist sculpture *Fur Breakfast* (1936) that was being exhibited at the time.

8 Meijers writes in relation particularly to Harald Szeeman's *A-Historische Klanken* (*Ahistorical Sounds*), Museum Boymans-van Beuningen, Rotterdam, 1988, and Peter Greenway's *The Physical Self*, Museum Boymans-van Beuningen, Rotterdam, 1991–2.

8 Identity politics in photography and performance art

1 Leon Battista Alberti the Renaissance architect, artist and author of *On Painting* (1436), was the first writer to describe single-point perspective as the rational system by which artists should describe the world in painting.

2 In *The Culture of Narcissism* (1979) Christopher Lasch, American historian and social critic of modern culture, identifies an unhealthy preoccupation with the self.

3 However, our trust in autobiography has been undermined in recent years by notions such as the 'unreliable narrator' and the possibility that such accounts will be self-justifying and include gaps and omissions.

4 The claim was that he was masturbating for six hours a day, twice a week.

5 Recently released (July 2001) British Foreign & Commonwealth Office papers reveal that Hockney's illustrations to the poems of C.P. Cavafy were withdrawn from a touring British Council exhibition in 1968 for being 'filthy'.

6 Legislation to regulate homosexuality differs from country to country and, in the US, from state to state. In Britain in 1967 the Sexual Offences Act decriminalised private sexual acts between consenting males over the age of twenty-one years. Homosexuality was not decriminalised in South Australia until 1975 and New South Wales until 1984.

7 Some aspects of queer theory have been pilloried for uncritical celebration of all forms of sexual diversity and some lesbian groups continue to work against their unwilling co-option into a genre dominated by gay men.

8 Nowadays it is commonplace for video footage of performances to be commercially available after the event.

9 Today physical evidence of the activities of performance artists is systematically collected and collated. For example, the Live Art Development Agency (LADA) supports the development of artists and organisations involved in live art and offers a range of resources, including a library of over 500 videos documenting the work of British performance artists. There is also a comprehensive library on live art practice, www.liveartlondon.demon.co.uk.

10 Works such as Kenneth Clark's *The Nude* (written in 1956) have been replaced by books such as Marcia Pointon's (1990) *Naked Authority: the body in Western painting*, where the term 'the body' heralds a more anthropological content.

11 Steven Naifeh and Gregory Whitesmith connect Pollock's drip paintings with his much-publicised habit of urinating in inappropriate places. They see Pollock's art as some kind of transference of indiscreet urination: 'for all his problems with impotence and bedwetting, Jackson could "control the flow" in the studio. Creative potency, like sexual potency, came down to a peeing contest' (Naifeh and Whitesmith 1989: 541).

12 Shuffenecker is now believed to be the author of one version of *Sunflowers*, sold for a record £22.5 million to a Japanese insurance firm.

13 However, as Terry Eagleton has cogently argued, the casualty within postmodernism's political radicalism has been class: 'social class tends to crop up in postmodern theory as one item in the triptych of class, race and gender' (Eagleton 1996: 56–7). The history of visual representations of class is currently conspicuous by its absence.

14 'Hysteria' was the term given to a malady, to which women were believed to be subject, that was characterised by irrational behaviour. The diagnosis of hysteria acquired a psychoanalytical credibility with the work of Sigmund Freud. The term comes from the Greek for 'womb', and the word 'hysterectomy' describes the surgical removal of the womb, which was also a 'cure' for hysteria and irrationality.

15 This digital technology is commercially available, and as such is an obvious example of the fusion of art and commodity – for instance T-shirts with the wearer's head digitally reproduced over famous paintings.

16 Carolus Linnaeus's *Systema naturae* (1735) stated that all living things in the world were created by God. The original of each species of plant was classified by its sex organs – that is, seed, stamen, pistil.

17 For example, Duchamp's urinal (1917), Warhol's 'oxidation' paintings were made by urinating on to a copper-oxide-coated canvas, Serrano's *Piss Christ* (1989), Gilbert and George's *Friendship Pissing* (1989). Annie Sprinkle is a notable exception, with her public performances of urination.

18 In fact, so established had women become as part of the workforce during the Second World War that post-war reconstruction was impossible without women fulfilling two roles – a series of 'Twilight Acts' encouraged women to rejoin the workforce 'after hours' to supplement the labour force but still to remain 'feminine' wives and mothers during the day.

19 Michael Gibbs berates online avatars for their lack of imagination and regards them 'as boring and self-centred as anyone else' (Gibbs 1998: 53).

Bibliography

Ader, Kathleen and Marcia Pointon (eds) (1993) *The Body Imaged: the human form and visual culture since the Renaissance*, Cambridge: Cambridge University Press.

Ades, Dawn (1995) *Art and Power: Europe under the dictators, 1930–45*, London: Thames & Hudson.

Alberti, Leon Battista (1991) [1461] *On Painting*, London: Penguin.

Allen, Christopher (1997) *Art in Australia: from colonization to postmodernism*, London: Thames & Hudson.

Alloway, Lawrence (1968) *The Venice Biennale 1895–1968: from salon to goldfish bowl*, London: Faber & Faber.

Althusser, Louis (1971) *Lenin and Philosophy and Other Essays*, London: New Left Books.

—— (2003) [1971] 'Ideology and Ideological State Apparatuses, in Charles Harrison and Paul Wood (eds) *Art in Theory*, Oxford: Blackwell, pp. 929–36.

Anonymous (2003) [1856] 'From the Archives: debate on Sunday opening at the British Museum', *Guardian Review*, 11 January: 7; reported in the *Guardian*, 22 February 1856.

Appignanesi, R. and C. Garrett (1995) *Postmodernism for Beginners*, London: Icon Books.

Armstrong, Carol M. (1986) 'Edgar Degas and the Representation of the Female Body', in Susan Rubin Suleiman (ed.) *The Female Body in Western Culture: contemporary perspectives*, Cambridge, Mass.: Harvard University Press, pp. 223–42.

Arnheim, Rudolf (1974) [1954] *Art and Visual Perception: a psychology of the creative eye*, rev. edn, Berkeley, Calif.: University of California Press.

Ball, Gordon (1966) 'Triptape: An Interview with Richard Aldcroft', *Film Culture* (43), Winter: 4–5.

Banham, Reyner (1996) [1960] *Theory and Design in the First Machine Age*, Tyne and Wear: Athenaeum Press.

Bann, Stephen (ed.) (1974) *The Tradition of Constructivism*, New York: Da Capo Press.

—— (1995) 'Shrines, Curiosities and the Rhetoric of Display', in Lynne Cooke and Peter Wollen (eds) *Visual Display: culture beyond appearances*, Seattle, Wash.: Bay Press, pp. 14–29.

Barr, Alfred H. Jnr. (1975) [1936] *Cubism and Abstract Art: introduction*, New York: Secker & Warburg.

—— (1986a) [1936] 'Cubism and Abstract Art', in Irving Sandler and Amy Newman (eds) *Defining Modern Art: selected writings of Alfred H. Barr, Jr.*, New York: Harry A. Abrams, pp. 84–91.

—— (1986b) [1926] 'Russian Diary', in Irving Sandler and Amy Newman (eds) *Defining Modern Art: selected writings of Alfred H. Barr, Jr.*, New York: Harry A. Abrams, pp. 103–37.

—— (1988) [1943] *What is Modern Painting?*, 9th edn, New York: Museum of Modern Art.

Barthes, Roland (1977) [1968] *Image-Music-Text*, New York: Hill & Wang.

—— (1993) [1957] *Mythologies*, London: Vintage.

Batchelor, David (1997a) *Chromophobia*, Leeds: Centre for the Study of Sculpture, Henry Moore Institute.

—— (1997b) *Minimalism: movements in modern art*, London: Tate Gallery.

Baudelaire, Charles (1964) [1863] 'The Painter of Modern Life', *The Painter of Modern Life and Other Essays*, London: Phaidon, pp. 12–15.

—— (1965) [1846] 'On the Heroism of Modern Life', *Art in Paris 1845–1862, Salons and Other Exhibitions*, London: Phaidon, pp. 116–20.

Baudrillard, Jean (1988) *America*, London and New York: Verso.

—— (1993) *Simulations*, New York: Semiotext(e) Publications.

—— (1994) 'The System of Collecting', in John Elsner and Roger Cardinal (eds) *The Cultures of Collecting*, London: Reaktion, pp. 7–24.

Baur, John I.H. (1963) [1960] 'Beauty or the Beast? The machine in American art', in Jean Lipman (ed.) *What Is American in American Art?*, New York: McGraw-Hill, pp. 33–6.

—— (1976) *Revolution and Tradition in Modern American Art*, New York: Frederick A. Praeger.

Beauvoir, Simone de (1949) *The Second Sex*, London: Jonathan Cape.

Becker, S. Howard (1982) *Art Worlds*, Berkeley, Calif.: University of California Press, Berkeley.

Bell, Clive (1982) [1914] 'The Aesthetic Hypothesis', in Francis Frascina and Charles Harrison (eds) *Modern Art and Modernism: a critical anthology*, London: Paul Chapman, pp. 66–74.

Belting, Hans (1984) *The End of the History of Art?*, Chicago, Ill.: University of Chicago Press.

—— (2001) 'Place of Reflection or Place of Sensation', in Peter Noever/MAK (ed.) *The Discursive Museum*, Ostfildern: Hatje Cantz, pp. 72–82.

Benedikt, Michael (ed.) (1991) *In Cyber Space: first steps*, Cambridge, Mass.: MIT Press.

Benjamin, Walter (1970) *Illuminations*, London: Jonathan Cape.

—— (1979) *One-Way Street and Other Writings*, London: New Left Books.

—— (1999) *The Arcades Project*, Cambridge, Mass.: Harvard University Press.

Benthall, Jonathan (1972) 'The Body as a Medium of Expression: a manifesto', *Studio International* (184), July/August: 6–8.

Benton, Tim and Charlotte Benton, with Dennis Sharp (1975) *Form and Function: a source book for the history of architecture and design 1890–1939*, Milton Keynes: Open University Press.

Berger, John (1969) *Art and Revolution*, London: Writers' and Readers' Publishing Co-operative.

—— (1972) *Ways of Seeing*, London: BBC Books.

Bergson, Henri (1914) [1907] *Creative Evolution*, London: Macmillan.

Berman, Marshall (1983) *All That is Solid Melts into Air: the experience of modernity*, London: Verso.

Bernheimer, Charles (1989) 'Degas's Brothels: Voyeurism and Ideology', in R. Howard Bloch and Frances Ferguson (eds) *Misogyny, Misandry and Misanthropy*, Berkeley, Calif.: University of California Press, pp. 158–86.

Betterton, Rosemary (ed.) (1987) *Looking On: images of femininity in the visual arts*, London: Pandora.

Blavatsky, H.P. (1972) [1877] *Isis Unveiled*, 2 vols, Wheaton, Ill., and London: Theosophical Publishing House.

Bloch, Lucienne (1973) 'Murals for Use', in Francis V. O'Connor (ed.) *WPA. Art for the Millions. Essays from the 1930s by artists and administrators of the WPA Federal Art Project*, Boston, Mass.: New York Graphic Society, pp. 76–7.

Boddy, William (1998) 'Sixty Million Viewers Can't Be Wrong: the rise and fall of the television western', in E. Buscombe and Roberta E. Pearson (eds) *Back in the Saddle Again: new essays on the western*, London: BFI Publishing, pp. 119–40.

Bohn, Willard (1980) 'In Pursuit of the Fourth Dimension: Guillaume Apollinaire and Max Weber', *Arts* 54(10), June: 166–9.

Bonami, Francesco and Maria Luisa Frisa (eds) (2003) *Dream and Conflicts: the dictatorship of the viewer: 50th International Art Exhibition*, Padua: Graffice Peruzzo.

Borzello, Frances (1982) *The Artist's Model*, London: Junction Books.

—— (1987) *Civilising Caliban: the misuse of art 1875–1980*, London: Routledge.

Bourdieu, Pierre (1984) *Distinction: a social critique of the judgement of taste*, London: Routledge & Kegan Paul.

—— (1990) 'Structures, Habitus, Practices', in *The Logic of Practice*, Cambridge: Polity Press.

Bowie, Andrew (1995) *Aesthetics and Subjectivity: from Kant to Nietzsche*, Manchester: Manchester University Press.

Breton, André (1972) *Manifestos of Surrealism*, Ann Arbor, Mich.: University of Michigan Press

—— (1997) [1936] 'Oscar Dominquez: concerning a delcalomania with preconceived object', in Patrick Waldberg (ed.) *Surrealism*, London: Thames & Hudson, pp. 87–8.

—— (2003) [1929] 'The Second Surrealist Manifesto', in Charles Harrison and Paul Wood (eds) *Art in Theory*, Oxford: Blackwell, pp. 463–7.

Breton, André, Diego Rivera and Leon Trotsky (1968) [1938] 'Manifesto Towards a Free Revolutionary Art', in Herschel B. Chipp (ed.) *Theories of Modern Art: a sourcebook by artists and critics*, Berkeley, Calif., and London: University of California Press, pp. 483–6.

Bright, Deborah (ed.) (1998) *The Passionate Camera: photography and bodies of desire*, London: Routledge.

Brookes, Liz (1991) 'Vile Bodies', *Artscribe* (88): 144.

Brown, Matthew Cullerne and Brandon Taylor (1993) *Art of the Soviets: painting, sculpture and architecture in a one-party state, 1917–1992*, Manchester: Manchester University Press.

Bryson, Norman (1983) *Vision and Painting: the logic of the gaze*, London and New Haven, Conn.: Yale University Press.

Bunn, David (1997) *Here, There and Everywhere*, Liverpool Central Library and London: Book Works.

Bürger, Peter (1984) *Theory of the Avant-Garde*, Minneapolis, Minn.: University of Minnesota Press.

Burgin, Victor (1986) *The End of Art Theory: criticism and postmodernity*, London: Macmillan.

Burke, Edmund (2001) [1757] *Harvard Classics*, vol. 24, part 2, New York: Bartleby.

Butler, Judith (1990) *Gender Trouble: feminism and the subversion of identity*, London: Routledge.

—— (1993) *Bodies that Matter: on the discursive limits of 'sex'*, London: Routledge.

Byrne, John (1999) 'Cybersublime: representing the unrepresentable in digital art and politics', *Third Text* 47, Summer: 27–38.

Cahill, Holger (1969) [1933] *American Sources of Modern Art*, New York: Museum of Modern Art.

Carrington, Leonora (1989) [1937] *The House of Fear*, London: Virago Press.

Carroll, John, Richard Longes, Philip Jones and Patricia Vickers-Rich (2003) *Review of the National Museum of Australia: its exhibitions and public programs*, a report to the Council of the National Museum of Australia, July, Commonwealth of Australia, Canberra: National Museum of Australia.

Carter, Michael (1990) *Framing Art: introducing theory and the visual image*, Hale & Iremonger, Sydney: Transvisual Studies.

Caton, Joseph Harris (1984) *The Utopian Vision of Moholy-Nagy*, Ann Arbor, Mich.: UMI Research Press.

Caws, Mary Ann, Rudolf Kuenzli and Gwen Raaberg (eds) (1991) *Surrealism and Women*, Cambridge, Mass.: MIT Press.

Celeste-Adams, Marie (ed.) (1986) *America: art and the west*, New York: American-Australian Foundation for the Arts and the International Cultural Corporation.

Chadwick, Whitney (1991) *Women Artists and the Surrealist Movement*, London: Thames & Hudson.

Cheetham, Mark (1991) *The Rhetoric of Purity: essentialist theory and the advent of abstract painting*, Cambridge: Cambridge University Press.

Chevlowe, Susan (ed.) (1998) *Common Man, Mythic Vision: the paintings of Ben Shahn*, Princeton, NJ: Princeton University Press.

Chino, Kaori (2000) 'A Man Pretending to be a Woman: on Morimura's "actresses"', in Peg Zeglin Brand (ed.) *Beauty Matters*, Bloomington, Ind.: Indiana University Press, pp. 252–65.

Chipp, Herschel B. (ed.) (1968) *Theories of Modern Art: a sourcebook by artists and critics*, Berkeley, Calif., and London: University of California Press.

Choucha, Nadia (1991) *Surrealism and the Occult*, Oxford: Mandrake.

Cixous, Hélène (1981) [1975] 'Laugh of the Medusa', in Elaine Marks and Isabelle de Courtivron (eds) *New French Feminisms*, Brighton: Harvester Press, 245–64.

Clark, Kenneth (1980) *The Nude*, Harmondsworth: Penguin.

Clark, T.J. (1973a) *The Absolute Bourgeois: artists and politics in France, 1848–1851*, London: Thames & Hudson.

—— (1973b) *Image of the People: Gustave Courbet and the 1848 revolution*, London: Thames & Hudson.

—— (1994) 'In Defense of Abstract Expressionism', *October* (69): 23–48.

—— (1999) *Farewell to an Idea: episodes from a history of modernism*, London and New Haven, Conn.: Yale University Press.

Clayton, Ellen C. (1876) *English Female Artists*, 2 vols, London: Tinsley Brothers.

Cleto, Fabio (ed.) (1999) *Camp: queer aesthetics and the performing subject, a reader*, Edinburgh: Edinburgh University Press.

Cockcroft, Eva (1985) 'Abstract Expressionism: weapon of the Cold War', in Francis Frascina (ed.) (1985), pp. 125–33.

Colquhoun, Ithell (1949) 'The Mantic Stain', *Enquiry* 2(4), October: 15–21.

—— (1961) *Goose of Hermogenes*, London: Peter Owen.

—— (1975) *Sword of Wisdom*, London: Spearman.

Commonwealth of Australia (2003) Review of the National Museum of Australia: its exhibitions and public programs: a report to the Council of the National Museum of Australia July 2003, Commonwealth of Australia.

Contreras, Belisario (1983) *Tradition and Innovation in New Deal Art*, London: Associated University Presses.

Cooke, Lynne and Peter Wollen (eds) (1995) *Visual Display: culture beyond appearances*, Seattle, Wash.: Bay Press.

Cork, R.G. (1976) *Vorticism and Abstract Art in the First Machine Age*, 2 vols, London: Gordon Fraser.

Crane, Diana (1987) *The Transformation of the Avant-Garde: the New York art world, 1940–1985*, Chicago, Ill.: University of Chicago Press.

Cravan, Arthur (1981) [1914] 'Exhibitions of the Independents' in Robert Motherwell (ed.) *Dada Painters and Poets: an anthology*, London: G.K. Hall, pp. 3–12.

Craven, David (1989) *The New Concept of Art and Popular Culture in Nicaragua since the Revolution in 1979: an analytical essay and compendium of illustrations*, Lewiston, NY: Lampeter, E. Ellen.

—— (1999) *Abstract Expressionism as Cultural Critique: dissent during the McCarthy period*, Cambridge, Mass.: Cambridge University Press.

—— (2000) 'Abstract, Automatism and the Age of Automation', in Francis Frascina (ed.) *Pollock and After: the critical debate*, London: Paul Chapman, pp. 234–60.

Crimp, Douglas (1995) *On the Museum's Ruins*, Cambridge, Mass.: MIT Press.

—— (2002) *Melancholia and Moralism: essays on AIDS and queer politics*, Cambridge, Mass.: MIT Press.

Crow, Thomas (1996) *Modern Art in the Common Culture*, London and New Haven, Conn.: Yale University Press.

Curtis, Penelope (ed.) (1993) *Elective Affinities*, Liverpool: Tate Gallery.

Danto, Arthur C. (1997) *After the End of Art: contemporary art and the pale of history*, Princeton, NJ: Princeton University Press.

Davidson, Abraham A. (1994) *Early American Modernist Painting 1910–1935*, New York: Da Capo Press.

Davis, Mike (2002) *Dead Cities: a natural history*, New York: New Press.

Dawtrey, Liz, Toby Jackson, Mary Masterton, Pam Meecham and Paul Wood (eds) (1996) *Investigating Modern Art*, London and New Haven, Conn.: Yale University Press.

de Duve, Thierry (1993) 'Ex Situ', *Art & Design: installation art*, London: Academy Group, pp. 25–30.

—— (1996) *Kant after Duchamp*, Cambridge, Mass.: MIT Press.

Debord, Guy (1994) [1967] *Society of the Spectacle*, New York: Zone Books.

Delaunay, Robert and Sonia Delaunay (1978) *The New Art of Colour: the writings of Robert and Sonia Delaunay*, ed. by Arthur A. Cohen, London: Viking Press.

Deleuze, Gilles and Felix Guattari (1987) [1980] 'Introduction: Rhizome', in *Capitalism and Schizophrenia*, Minneapolis, Minn.: University of Minnesota Press, pp. 3–25.

Demarco, Richard (1982) 'Conversations with Artists', *Studio International* 195 (996): 000–00.

Denis, Maurice (1968a) [1890] 'Definition of Neo Traditionism', in Herschel B. Chipp (ed.) *Theories of Modern Art: a sourcebook by artists and critics*, Berkeley, Calif., and London: University of California Press, pp. 94–105.

—— (1968b) [1909] 'Subjective and Objective Deformation', in Herschel B. Chipp (ed.) *Theories of Modern Art: a sourcebook by artists and critics*, Berkeley, Calif., and London: University of California Press, pp. 105–7.

Derrida, Jacques (1976) [1967] *Of Grammatology*, Baltimore, Md.: Johns Hopkins University Press.

Dickstein, Maurice (1996) 'Depression Culture: the dream of mobility', *Partisan Review*, Winter: 65–80.

Dijkstra, Brain (1986) *Idols of Perversity: fantasies of feminine evil in fin-de-siècle culture*, Oxford: Oxford University Press.

Dingman, Roger (1990) 'Alliance in Crisis: the Lucky Dragon incident and Japanese–American relations', in Warren I. Cohen and Akira Inye (eds) *The Great Powers in East Asia 1953–1960*, New York: Columbia University Press, pp. 187–214.

Doss, Erica (1991) *Benton, Pollock and the Politics of Modernism: from regionalism to abstract expressionism*, Chicago, Ill.: University of Chicago Press.

Douglas, Mary (1984) *Purity and Danger: an analysis of the concepts of pollution and taboo*, London: Routledge.

Downs, Linda (1998) *Diego Rivera: the Detroit industry murals*, New York: W.W. Norton & Co.

Duncan, Carol (1995) *Civilizing Rituals: inside public museums*, London: Routledge.

Durden, Mark (1997) 'The Beyond and the Ridiculous', *Art Monthly* (207), June: 207–8.

Dworkin, Andrea (1981) *Pornography: men possessing women*, London: The Women's Press.

Eagleton, Terry (1983) *Literary Theory: an introduction*, Oxford: Blackwell.

—— (1990) *The Ideology of the Aesthetic*, Oxford: Blackwell.

—— (1996) *The Illusions of Postmodernism*, Oxford: Blackwell.

Elderfield, John (1994) *The Museum of Modern Art at Mid-Century: at home and abroad*, New York: Museum of Modern Art.

—— (1995) *The Museum of Modern Art at Mid-Century: continuity and change*, New York: Museum of Modern Art.

Eliot, Simon and Beverly Stern (eds) (1979) *The Age of Enlightenment: an anthology of eighteenth-century texts*, London: Ward Lock and the Open University Press.

Ellis, Havelock (1897–1928) *Studies in the Psychology of Sex*, 7 vols, Philadelphia, Pa.: F.A. Davis Company.

Elsen, Albert (1974) *Origins of Modern Sculpture: pioneers and premises*, London: Phaidon.

Elsner, John and Roger Cardinal (eds) (1994) *The Cultures of Collecting*, London: Reaktion.

Enwezor, Okwui (2003) 'Interview with Okwui Enwezor', in Karen Raney *Art in Question*, London: Continuum, pp. 91–112.

Featherstone, Mike, Mike Hepworth and Bryan S. Turner (1991) *The Body: social process and cultural theory*, London: Sage.

Feenberg, Andrew (1999) *Questioning Technology*, London: Routledge.

Ferguson, Russell and Martha Gever (eds) (1990) *Out There: marginalization and contemporary cultures*, Cambridge, Mass., and New York: MIT Press and New Museum of Contemporary Art.

Ferren, John (1968) [1958] 'Epitaph for an Avant-Garde', in Herschel B. Chipp (ed.) *Theories of Modern Art: a sourcebook by artists and critics*, Berkeley, Calif., and London: University of California Press, pp. 573–4.

Flint, R.W. (ed.) (1972) *Marinetti: selected writings*, London: Secker & Warburg.

Foster, Hal (1985a) *Recordings: art, spectacle, cultural politics*, Seattle, Wash.: Bay Press.

—— (1985b) 'The Primitive Unconscious in Modern Art', *October* (34): 45–70.

—— (1985c) 'The Expressive Fallacy', in *Recodings: art, spectacle, cultural politics*, Seattle, Wash.: Bay Press, pp. 59–77.

—— (ed.) (1990) [1983] *Postmodern Culture*, London: Pluto Press.

—— (1996) *The Return of the Real: the avant-garde at the end of the century*, Cambridge, Mass.: MIT Press.

Foucault, Michel (1970) *The Order of Things: an archaeology of the human sciences*, London: Tavistock Publications.

—— (1977) [1977] *Discipline and Punish: the birth of the prison*, Harmondsworth: Penguin.

—— (1990) [1964] *Madness and Civilisation: a history of insanity in the age of reason*, London: Routledge.

—— (1994) [1969] *The Archaeology of Knowledge*, London: Routledge.

Frascina, Francis (1982) *Manet and Modernism*, Milton Keynes: Open University Press.

—— (2000) *Pollock and After: the critical debate*, London: Paul Chapman.

Frascina, Francis and Jonathan Harris (eds) (1992) *Art in Modern Culture: an anthology of critical texts*, London: Phaidon.

Frascina, Francis and Charles Harrison (eds) (1982) *Modern Art and Modernism: a critical anthology*, London: Paul Chapman.

Freud, Sigmund (1976) *The Interpretation of Dreams*, ed. by J. Strachey and A. Richards, Harmondsworth: Penguin.

Freud, S., J. Strachey, N. Potter Gregg and W. Hoffer (1949) [1905] *Three Essays on the Theory of Sexuality*, London: Imago Publishing Co.

Fried, Michael (2003) [1967] 'Art and Objecthood', in Charles Harrison and Paul Wood (eds) *Art in Theory*, Oxford: Blackwell, pp. 835–46; original published in *Artforum*, Summer 1967.

Fry, Roger (1920) *Vision and Design*, London: Chatto & Windus.

—— (1926) *Transformations*, London: Chatto & Windus.

—— (1928) 'Introduction', *A Record of the Collections in the Lady Lever Art Gallery*, London: B.T. Batsford.

—— (1993) [1961] 'Art and Socialism', in S.P. Rosenbaum (ed.) *A Bloomsbury Group Reader*, London: Blackwell, pp. 181–204.

Fukuyama, Francis (1992) *The End of History and the Last Man*, Harmondsworth: Penguin.

Fusco, Coco (1995) *English Is Broken Here: notes on cultural fusion in the Americas*, New York: New Press.

—— (2001) *The Bodies That Were Not Ours and Other Writings*, London and New York: Routledge/inIVA.

Fuss, Diana (1989) *Essentially Speaking: feminism, nature and difference*, London and New York: Routledge.

Gablik, Suzi (1991a) [1984] *Has Modernism Failed?*, London: Thames & Hudson.

—— (1991b) *The Re-Enchantment of Art*, London: Thames & Hudson.

—— (2002) *Living the Magical Life: an oracular adventure*, Grand Rapids, Mich.: Phanes Press.

Gallagher, Catherine and Thomas Laquer (eds) (1987) *The Making of the Modern Body: sexuality and society in the nineteenth century*, London: University of California Press.

Gibbons, T.H. (1981) 'Cubism and "the Fourth Dimension" in the Context of Late 19th and Early 20th century Revival of Occult Idealism', *Journal of the Warburg and Courtauld Institutes* 44: 130–47.

Gibson, William (1984) *Neuromancer*, London: Grafton.

Giedeon, Siegfried (1948) *Mechanisation Takes Command*, Oxford: Oxford University Press.

Gilman, Sander L. (1985) 'Black Bodies, White Bodies: toward an iconography of female sexuality in late nineteenth century art, medicine and literature', in Henry Louis Gates Jnr (ed.) *'Race', Writing and Difference*, London: University of Chicago Press, pp. 223–61.

Glimcher, Marc (ed.) (1987) *Jean Dubuffet*, New York: Pace Publications.

Goldberg, Rose Lee (1990) *Performance Art*, London: Thames & Hudson.

Golding, John (2000) *Paths to the Absolute: Mondrian, Malevich, Kandinsky, Pollock, Newman, Rothko and Still*, London: Thames & Hudson.

Goldwater, A. (1938) *Primitivism in Modern Art*, Cambridge, Mass.: Harvard University Press.

Gombrich, Ernst (1950) *The Story of Art*, London: Phaidon.

—— (1960) *Art and Illusion: a study in the psychology of representation*, New York: Pantheon Books.

Goodrich, Lloyd (1967) *The Artist in America, Compiled by the Editors of* 'Art in America', an Art in America book, New York: W.W. Norton & Co.

Graham, Dan (1979) *Video-Architecture-Television*, Nova Scotia: Press of Nova Scotia College of Art and Design/New York University Press.

Graham, Martha (1973) *The Notebooks of Martha Graham*, New York: Harcourt Brace Jovanovich.

Gramsci, Antonio (1971) *Selections from the Prison Notebooks of Antonio Gramsci*, London: Lawrence & Wishart.

—— (1984) [1971] *Selections From the Cultural Writings*, ed. by D. Foracs and G. Nowell-Smith, London: Lawrence & Wishart.

Grayson, Richard (2002) 'Introductory Essay', in Ewen McDonald (ed.) *Biennale of Sydney 2002 (The World May Be) Fantastic*, Melbourne: Biennale of Sydney.

Greenberg, Clement (1948) 'The Decline of Cubism', *Partisan Review* XV(3), March: 36–9.

—— (1982) [1954] 'Master Léger', in Francis Frascina and Charles Harrison (eds) *Modern Art and Modernism: a critical anthology*, London: Paul Chapman, pp. 109–14.

—— (1985) [1939] 'Avant-Garde and Kitsch', in Francis Frascina (ed.) (1985), pp. 21–32.

—— (1986a) 'The Beginnings of Modernism', in John O'Brian (ed.) *Clement Greenberg: the collected essays and criticism*, 4 vols, Chicago, Ill.: University of Chicago Press, pp. 000–00.

—— (1986b) 'Newness in Sculpture', in John O'Brian (ed.) *Clement Greenberg: the collected essays and criticism*, 4 vols, Chicago, Ill.: University of Chicago Press, pp. 000–00.

—— (1990a) [1952] 'Art Chronicle: feeling is all (Newman)', in David Shapiro and Cecile Shapiro (eds) *Abstract Expressionism: a critical record*, Cambridge: Cambridge University Press, pp. 330–1.

—— (1990b) 'Towards a Newer Laocoon', in David Shapiro and Cecile Shapiro (eds) *Abstract Expressionism: a critical record*, Cambridge: Cambridge University Press, pp. 61–74.

—— (2003a) [1965] 'Modernist Painting 1960–1965', in Charles Harrison and Paul Wood (eds) *Art in Theory*, Oxford: Blackwell, pp. 773–9; originally published in *Art and Literature* (Lugano) 4, Spring 1965.

—— (2003b) [1940] 'Towards a Newer Laocoon', in Charles Harrison and Paul Wood (eds) *Art in Theory*, Oxford: Blackwell, pp. 562–8.

Greenberg, Reesa, Bruce W. Ferguson and Sandy Nairne (eds) (1996) *Thinking About Exhibitions*, London: Routledge.

Greer, Germaine (1970) *The Female Eunuch*, London: Flamingo.

—— (2001) [1979] *The Obstacle Race: the fortunes of women painters and their work*, London: I.B. Tauris.

Gretton, Tom (1986) 'New Lamps for Old', in A.L. Rees and F. Borzello (eds) *The New Art History*, London: Camden Press, pp. 63–74.

Guggenheim Museum (1975) *Frantisek Kupka 1871–1957: a retrospective*, New York: Solomon R. Guggenheim Museum.

Guilbaut, Serge (1983) *How New York Stole the Idea of Modern Art: abstract expressionism, freedom, and the Cold War*, Chicago, Ill.: University of Chicago Press.

—— (1985) [1980] 'The New Adventures of the Avant-Garde in America: Greenburg, Pollock, or from Trotskyism to the new liberalism of the "vital centre"', in Francis Frascina (ed.) (1985), pp. 153–166.

Habermas, Jürgen (1990) 'Modernity – An Incomplete Project', in Hal Foster (ed.) *Postmodern Culture*, London: Pluto Press, pp. 3–4.

Hadjinicolaou, Nicos (1982) [1973] 'Art and Class Struggle', in Francis Frascina and Charles Harrison (eds) *Modern Art and Modernism: a critical anthology*, London: Paul Chapman, pp. 243–8.

Hagen, Margaret (1986) *Varieties of Realism: geometries of representational art*, Cambridge: Cambridge University Press.

Hall, Doug and Sally Jo Fifer (1990) *Illuminating Video*, New York: Aperture/BAVC.

Hall, Stuart and Paul Virilio (1988) 'The Work of Art in the Electronic Age', *Block* 14: 3–14.

Hamilton, George Heard (1984) *Painting and Sculpture in Europe 1880–1940*, Harmondsworth: Penguin.

Haraway, Donna (1991a) *Simians, Cyborgs and Women: the reinvention of nature*, London: Routledge.

—— (1991b) [1985] 'A Cyborg Manifesto: science, technology and socialist-feminism in the late twentieth century', in *Simians, Cyborgs and Women: the reinvention of nature*, London: Routledge, pp. 149–81.

Harries, Dan (ed.) (2002) *The New Media Book*, London: BFI Publishing.

Harris, Jonathan (1995) *Federal Art and National Culture: the politics of identity in New Deal America*, Cambridge: Cambridge University Press.

—— (1997) 'Art Education and Cyber Ideology: beyond individualism and technological determinism', *Art Journal*, Fall: 39–45.

—— (1999) 'Seeing "Red" The American Artists' Congress and New York Art: left activism in the late 1930s', unpublished ms.

Harrison, Charles (1997) *Modernism: movements in modern art*, London: Tate Gallery.

Harrison, Charles and Paul Wood (eds) (2003) *Art in Theory*, Oxford: Blackwell.

Hartley, Keith, Henry Meyrick Hughes, Peter-Klaus Schuster and William Vaughan (eds) (1994) *The Romantic Spirit in German Art, 1790–1990*, London: Thames & Hudson.

Harvey, David (1989) *The Condition of Postmodernity*, Oxford: Blackwell.

Haskell, Barbara (1999) *The American Century: art and culture 1900–1950*, New York: Whitney Museum of American Art.

Hauptman, William (1974) 'The Suppression of Art in the McCarthy Decade', *Artforum*, October: 000.

Hawking, Stephen (1988) *A Brief History of Time: from the Big Bang to black holes*, London: Bantam.

Heartney, Eleanor (2003) 'Hilla Rebay: visionary baroness', *Art in America*, September: 112–17.

Henderson, Linda Dalrymple (1983) *The Fourth Dimension and Non-Euclidean Geometry in Modern Art*, Princeton, NJ: Princeton University Press.

Highsmith, Carol M. and Ted Landphair (1995) *Forgotten No More: the Korean War Veterans' Memorial story*, Washington, DC: Chelsea.

Hiller, Susan (ed.) (1991) *The Myth of Primitivism: perspectives on art*, London: Routledge.

Hobsbawm, Eric (1994) *The Age of Extremes: a history of the world 1914–1991*.

Hobsbawm, Eric and Terence Ranger (eds) (1983) *The Invention of Tradition*, Cambridge: Cambridge University Press.

Hollander, Anne (1993) *Seeing through Clothes*, London: University of California Press.

Holt, Nancy (ed.) (1996) *The Writings of Robert Smithson*, rev. edn, Berkeley, Calif.: University of California Press.

Home, Stewart (1991) *The Assault on Culture: utopian currents from lettrism to class war*, Stirling: AK Press.

Hooper-Greenhill, Eileen (1992) *Museums and the Shaping of Knowledge*, London: Routledge.

Huelsenbeck, Richard (1968) 'Richard Huelsenbeck, from En Avant Dada: a history of Dadaism, 1920', in Herschel B. Chipp (ed.) *Theories of Modern Art: a sourcebook by artists and critics*, Berkeley, Calif., and London: University of California Press, pp. 377–82.

Hughes, Robert (1987) [1980] 'Ten Years that Buried the Avant-Garde', in Andreas C. Papadakis (ed.) 'Post-Avant-Garde Painting in the '80s', *Art and Design*, London: Academy Group; originally published in *Sunday Times Magazine*, January 1980.

—— (1997) *American Visions: the epic history of art in America*, London: Harvill Press.

Hulten, Pontas (1987) *Jean Tinguely: a magic stronger than death*, London: Thames & Hudson.

Hunt, Ian (1997) *Library Relocations*, London: Book Works.

Huysmans, (1997) *Against the Grain*, London: Penguin.

Impey, Oliver and Arthur Macgregor (eds) (1985) *The Origins of Museums: the cabinet of curiosities in sixteenth- and seventeenth-century Europe*, Oxford: Clarendon.

Irigaray, Luce (1985a) [1975] *Speculum of the Other Woman*, Ithaca, NY: Cornell University Press.

—— (1985b) *This Sex Which Is Not One*, Ithaca, NY: Cornell University Press.

Jacobs, Michael (1985) *The Good and Simple Life: artist colonies in Europe and America*, London: Phaidon.

James, P. (1992) *Henry Moore on Sculpture*, New York: Da Capo Press.

Jameson, Fredric (1991) *Postmodernism, or the Cultural Logic of Late Capitalism*, London: Verso.

Joel, Yale (1966) 'Psychedelic Art', *Life*, 9 September: 60–9.

Johnson, Eden H. (ed.) (1982) *American Artists on Art from 1940 to 1980*, New York: Icon Editions.

Joly, Françoise (ed.) (1997) *Short Guide to Documenta X*, Kassel: Cantz.

Jones, Steven G. (1995) *Cybersociety: computer-mediated communication and community*, New York: Sage.

Jung, C.J. (1933) *The Modern Man in Search of a Soul*, London: Routledge & Kegan Paul.

—— (1980) [1933] *Psychology and Alchemy*, Princeton, NJ: Princeton University Press.

Kachur, Lewis (2001) *Displaying the Marvelous: Marcel Duchamp, Salvador Dali, and surrealist installations*, Cambridge, Mass.: MIT Press.

Kandinsky, Wassily (1977) [1911] *Concerning the Spiritual in Art*, New York: Dover.

Kant, Immanuel (1952) [1790] *The Critique of Judgement*, Oxford: Clarendon Press.

Kaplan, Janet A. (1988) *Unexpected Journeys: the art and life of Remedios Varo*, London: Virago.

Kaprow, Allen (1958) 'The Legacy of Jackson Pollock', *Art News*, October: 24–6, 55–8.

Kent, Sarah and Jacqueline Moreau (1985) *Women's Images of Men*, London: Pandora.

Kerouac, Jack (1957) *On the Road*, New York: Viking Press.

Kesey, Ken (1962) *One Flew Over the Cuckoo's Nest*, New York: Viking Press.

Kimmelman, Michael (1998) 'Trying to Separate Ben Shahn's Art from his Politics', *New York Times Weekend*, 13 November: E35.

Kleblatt, Norman (ed.) (2002) *Mirroring Evil: Nazi imagery/recent art*, New Brunswick, NJ: Rutgers University Press.

Kozloff, Max (1967) 'The "Poetics of Softness"', in Maurice Tuchman (ed.) *American Sculpture of the '60s*, New York: New York Graphic Society, pp. 000–00.

—— (1985) [1973] 'American Painting during the Cold War', in Francis Frascina (ed.) (1985), pp. 107–23.

Krauss, Rosalind (1977) *Passages in Modern Sculpture*, London: Thames & Hudson.

—— (1986) *The Originality of the Avant-Garde and Other Modernist Myths*, Cambridge, Mass., and London: MIT Press.

—— (1990) [1983] 'Sculpture in the Expanded Field', in Hal Foster (ed.) *Postmodern Culture*, London: Pluto Press, pp. 31–42.

Kristeva, Julia (1982) *Powers of Horror: an essay on abjection*, New York: Columbia University Press.

—— (2000) *The Sense and Nonsense of Revolt*, Chichester, NY: Columbia University Press.

Kroll, (1961) 'Reviews and Previews', *Art News*, November.

Krutch, Joseph W. (ed.) (1981) *Walden and Other Writings by Henry David Thoreau*, New York: Bantam Classic.

Kuhn, Thomas (1970) *The Structure of Scientific Revolutions*, 2nd edn, London: University of Chicago Press.

Kupka, František (1997) [1923] *Creation in the Plastic Arts*, Portland, Oreg.: International Specialized Book Services.

Lacan, Jacques (1977) *Ecrits: A Selection*, New York: W.W. Norton & Co.

Lapp, Ralph E. (1957) *The Voyage of the Lucky Dragon*, London: Frederick Muller, Ltd.

Lasch, Christopher (1979) *The Culture of Narcissism: American life in an age of diminishing expectations*, New York: W.W. Norton & Co.

Le Conte, Joseph (1891) *Evolution: its nature, its evidences, and its relation to religious thought*, New York: D. Appleton & Co.

Leja, Michael (1993) *Reframing Abstract Expressionism: subjectivity and painting*, New Haven, Conn., and London: Yale University Press.

Levin, Harry (1966) [1960] 'What Was Modernism?', in *Refractions: essays in comparative literature*, New York and Oxford: Oxford University Press; originally published in *Massachusetts Review*, August 1960.

Léger, Fernand (1975) [1924] 'The Machine Aesthetic: the manufactured object, the artisan and the artist', in Benton and Benton (eds), pp. 96–101.

Lévi-Strauss, Claude (1969) *Introduction to a Science of Mythology: The raw and the cooked*, London: Cape.

—— (1972) *The Savage Mind*, London: Weidenfeld.

—— (1977) *Structural Anthropology and Totemism*, Harmondsworth: Penguin.

Lewis, Reina (1996) *Gendering Orientalism: race, femininity and representation*, London: Routledge.

Lin, Maya Ying (1996) 'Untitled Statements 1983, 1993 and 1995', in Kristine Stiles and Peter Selz (eds) *Theories and Documents of Contemporary Art: a sourcebook of artist's writings*, Berkeley, Calif.: University of California Press, pp. 524–5.

Lindey, Christine (1990) *Art in the Cold War: from Vladivostock to Kalamazoo, 1945–62*, London: Herbert Press.

Lipman, Jean (ed.) (1963) *What Is American in American Art?*, New York: McGraw-Hill.

—— (1976) *Bright Stars: American painting and sculpture since 1776*, New York: E.P. Dutton & Co.

Lippard, Lucy R. (1983) *Overlay*, New York: New Press.

—— (1990) *A Different War: Vietnam in Art*, Seattle, Wash.: Watcom Museum of History and Art and Real Comet Press.

—— (1997) [1973] *Six Years: the dematerialisation of the art object from 1966 to 1972*, Berkeley, Calif., and London: University of California Press.

—— (1999) *On the Beaten Track: tourism, art and place*, London: I.B. Tauris.

Lipsey, Roger (1997) *An Art of Our Own: the spiritual in twentieth-century art*, Boston, Mass.: Shambhala.

Liss, Andree (1998) *Trespassing through Shadows: memory, photography, and the Holocaust*, Minneapolis, Minn.: University of Minnesota Press.

Lissitzky, El (1992) *El Lissitzky: life, letters, text*, ed. Sophie Lissitzky-Kuppers, London: Thames & Hudson.

Lissitzky-Kuppers, Sophie (1992) *El Lissitzky: life, letters, text*, London: Thames & Hudson.

Littleton, Taylor D. and Maltby Sykes (1989) *Advancing American Art, Painting, Politics and Cultural Confrontation at Mid-Century*, Tuscaloosa, Ala.: University of Alabama Press.

Lodder, Christina (1993) 'Lenin's Plan for Monumental Propaganda', in Matthew Cullerne Brown and Brandon Taylor (eds) *Art of the Soviets: painting, sculpture and architecture in a one-party state, 1917–1992*, Manchester: Manchester University Press, pp. 000–00.

Longhauser, Elsa (ed.) (1993) *Dan Graham: public/private*, exhibition catalogue, Philadelphia: The Galleries at Moore.

Loos, Adolf (1998) [1908] *Ornament and Crime. Selected essays*, Riverside, Calif.: Ariadne Press.

Lovink, Geert (2002) *Dark Fiber: tracking critical internet culture*, Cambridge, Mass.: MIT Press.

Lübbren, Nina (2001) *Artists' Colonies in Europe, 1870–1910*, Manchester: Manchester University Press.

Lukach, Joan M. (1983) *Hillay Rebay: in search of the spirit in art*, New York: George Braziller Inc.

Lumley, R. (1988) *The Museum Time-Machine*, London: Routledge.

Lunenfeld, Peter (2002) 'The Myths of Interactive Cinema', in Dan Harries (ed.) (2002) *The New Media Book*, London: BFI Publishing, pp. 144–57.

Lutz, Catherine A. (1990) 'Engendered Emotion: gender, power, and the rhetoric of emotional control in American discourse', in Catherine A. Lutz and Abu-Lugodh (eds) *Language and the Politics of Emotion*, Cambridge: Cambridge University Press, pp. 000–00.

Lynes, Russell (1973) *Good Old Modern: an intimate portrait of the MoMA*, New York: Athenaeum.

Lyotard, Jean-François (1982) 'Presenting the Unpresentable: the sublime', *Art Forum* XX (8): 69–74.

—— (1989) 'Complexity and the Sublime', in Lisa Appignanesi (ed.) *Postmodernism: ICA documents*, London: Free Association Books, pp. 1–17.

McDonald, Ewen (ed.) (2002) *2002 Biennale of Sydney: (the world may be fantastic)*, Sydney: Biennale of Sydney Ltd.

MacDonald, Sharon (1992) 'Change and Challenge: museums in the information society', in I. Karp, C. Mullen Kreamer and S.D. Lavine (eds) *Museums and Communities: the politics of public culture*, Washington, DC: Smithsonian Institution Press, pp. 158–81.

McEvilley, Thomas (1983) 'Marina Abramovic/Ulay Ulay/Marina Abramovic', *Artforum* 13(1), September: pp. 52–3.

McIntyre, Darryl and Kirsten Wehner (eds) (2001) *National Museums: negotiating histories*, Canberra: National Museum of Australia.

Macintyre Stuart and Anna Clark (2003) *The History Wars*, Melbourne: Melbourne University Press.

MacKinnon, Catherine (1993) *Only Words*, Cambridge, Mass.: Harvard University Press.

McLuhan, Marshall (1962) *The Gutenberg Galaxy: the making of typographic man*, London: Routledge and Kegan Paul.

—— (1967a) *The Mechanical Bride: folklore of industrial man*, London: Routledge.

—— (1967b) *The Medium is the Massage*, Harmondsworth: Penguin.

—— (1988) *The Global Village*, Oxford: Oxford University Press.

McPherson, Tara (2002) 'Self, Other and Electronic Media', in Dan Harries (ed.) *The New Media Book*, London: BFI Publishing, pp. 183–94.

Madonna and Stephen Meisel (1992) *Sex*, New York: Warner Books.

Malevich, Kasimir (2003) [1919] 'Non-Objective Art and Suprematism', in Charles Harrison and Paul Wood (eds) *Art in Theory*, Oxford: Blackwell, pp. 292–3.

Malpas, James (1997) *Realism: movements in modern art*, London: Tate Gallery.

Malraux, André (1947) *Le Musée imaginaire*, Milan: Skira.

Mansbach, Steven A. (1979) *Visions of Totality: Lazlo Moholy-Nagy, Theo Van Doesburg, and El Lissitzky*, Ann Arbor, Mich.: UMI Research Press.

Marcuse, Herbert (1968) *Negations: essays in critical theory*, London: Lane.

—— (1978) *The Aesthetic Dimension: towards a critique of Marxist aesthetics*, Boston, Mass.: Beacon Press.

Margolin, Victor (1997) *The Struggle for Utopia: Rodchenko, Lissitzky and Moholy-Nagy, 1917–1946*, Chicago, Ill., and London: University of Chicago Press.

Marinetti, Filippo Tommaso (2003) [1909] 'The Foundation and Manifesto of Futurism', in Charles Harrison and Paul Wood (eds) *Art in Theory*, Oxford: Blackwell, pp. 146–9; originally published in *Le Figaro*.

Markopoulos, Leigh (ed.) (2001) *Give and Take: 1 exhibition 2 sites*, London: Serpentine Gallery.

Meijers, Deborah J. (1996) 'The Museum and the "Ahistorical" Exhibition: the latest gimmick by the arbiters of taste, or an important cultural phenomenon?', in Reesa Greenberg, Bruce W. Ferguson and Sandy Nairne (eds) *Thinking about Exhibitions*, London: Routledge, pp. 7–20.

Merleau-Ponty, Maurice (1962) [1945] *Phenomenology of Perception*, London: Routledge & Kegan Paul.

—— (1989) [1945] *Phenomenology of Perception*, London: Routledge.

Michalski, Sergiusz (1998) *Public Monuments: art in political bondage, 1870–1997*, London: Reaktion.

Miller, Catriona (1996) 'Modernism and Modernity', in Shearer West (ed.) *Guild to Art*, London: Bloomsbury, pp. 159–74.

Mitchell, W.J.T. (ed.) (1992) *Art and the Public Sphere*, London: University of Chicago Press.

Modersohn-Becker, Paula (1998) [1917] *Letters and Journals*, Evanston, Ill.: Northwestern University Press.

Moffitt, John F. (1986) 'Marcel Duchamp: alchemist of the avant-garde', in E. Weisberger (ed.) *The Spiritual in Art: abstract painting, 1890–1985*, New York: Abbeville Press.

—— (2003) *Alchemist of the Avant-Garde: the case of Marcel Duchamp*, Albany, NY: State University of New York Press.

Moholy-Nagy, László (1975) [1922] 'Constructivism and the Proletariat', in Tim Benton and Charlotte Benton, with Dennis Sharp *Form and Function: a source book for the history of architecture and design 1890–1939*, Milton Keynes: Open University Press, pp. 95–6.

Morgan, Robin (1977) [1974] 'Theory and Practice: pornography and rape', in *Going Too Far: the personal documents of a feminist*, New York: Random House.

Mulvey, Laura (1989) *Visual and Other Pleasures*, Bloomington, Ind.: Indiana University Press.

Museum of Modern Art (1994) [1934] *Machine Art*, 60th anniversary edn, New York: Museum of Modern Art.

Naifeh, Steven and G.W. Whitesmith (1989) *Jackson Pollock: an American saga*, New York: Clarkson N. Porter Inc.

Nead, Lynda (1992) *The Female Nude: art, obscenity and sexuality*, London: Routledge.

Nelson, Robert S. and Richard Schiff (1997) *Critical Terms for Art History*, London: University of Chicago Press.

Newman, Barnett (1968a) [1947] 'The First Man Was an Artist', in Herschel B. Chipp (ed.) *Theories of Modern Art: a sourcebook by artists and critics*, Berkeley, Calif., and London: University of California Press, pp. 551–2.

—— (1968b) [1948] 'The Sublime is Now', in Herschel B. Chipp (ed.) *Theories of Modern Art: a sourcebook by artists and critics*, Berkeley, Calif., and London: University of California Press, pp. 552–3.

Nietzsche, Friedrich (1990) [1889] *Twilight of the Idols and the Anti Christ*, London: Penguin.

Nochlin, Linda (1989) [1971] 'Why Have There Been No Great Women Artists?', *Women, Art and Power and Other Essays*, London: Thames & Hudson, pp. 145–71.

—— (1991) *The Politics of Vision: essays on nineteenth-century art and society*, London: Thames & Hudson.

Noever, Peter/MAK (ed.) (2001) *The Discursive Museum*, Ostfildern: Hatje Cantz.

O'Brian, John (ed.) (1986) *Clement Greenberg: the collected essays and criticism*, 4 vols, Chicago, Ill.: University of Chicago Press.

O'Connor, Francis V. (ed.) (1973) *WPA. Art for the Millions. Essays from the 1930s by artists and administrators of the WPA Federal Art Project*, Boston, Mass.: New York Graphic Society.

O'Doherty, (1961) 'Shahn is Masterly', *New York Times*, 10 December: 40.

—— (2000) [1979] *Inside the White Cube: the ideology of the gallery space*, California: The University of California Press.

O'Neil, John (1993) 'McTopia: Eating Time', in K. Kumar and S. Bann (eds) *Utopias and the Millennium*, London: Reaktion, pp. 129–37.

Olmi, Giuseppe (1985) 'Science-Honour-Metaphor: Italian cabinets of the sixteenth and seventeenth centuries', in Oliver Impey and Arthur Macgregor (eds) *The Origins of Museums: the cabinet of curiosities in sixteenth- and seventeenth-century Europe*, Oxford: Clarendon, pp. 1–17.

—— (2001) 'Science-Honour-Metaphor: Italian cabinets of the sixteenth and seventeenth centuries', in Oliver Impey and Arthur Macgregor (2001), pp. 1–17.

Ono, Yoko (1995) *Instruction Paintings*, New York and Tokyo: Weatherhill.

Open University (1982) *Modern Art and Modernism: Manet to Pollock (Third Level Arts' Course)*, A316, Milton Keynes: Open University Press.

Ouspensky, P.D. (1922) [1911] *Tertium Organum*, New York: Alfred A. Knopf.

Owens, Craig (1990) 'The Discourse of Others: feminists and postmodernism', in Hal Foster (ed.) *Postmodern Culture*, London: Pluto Press, pp. 57–77.

Panofsky, Erwin (1987) [1955] *Meaning and the Visual Arts*, Harmondsworth: Penguin.

Papadakis, Andreas C. (ed.) (1991) *New Museology*, London: Academy Group.

Papanek, Victor (1977) *Design for the Real World*, 2nd edn, London: Paladin.

Parker, Rosika and Griselda Pollock (1989) *Old Mistresses: women, art and ideology*, London: Pandora.

Pater, Walter (1873) *The Renaissance: studies in art and poetry*, London: Macmillan.

Paz, Octavio (1987) *Essays on Mexican Art*, New York: Harcourt Brace & Co.

Peacock, Kenneth (1988) 'Instruments to Perform Color-Music: two centuries of technological experimentation', *Leonardo* 21 (4): 397–406.

Pearce, Susan (1998) *Collecting in Contemporary Practice*, London: Sage.

Penny, Simon (ed.) (1995) *Critical Issues in Electronic Media*, New York: SUNY Press.

Perry, Gillian (1979) *Paula Modersohn-Becker*, London: The Women's Press.

Philippi, Desa and Anna Howell (1991) 'Dark Continents Explored by Women', in Susan Hiller (ed.) *The Myth of Primitivism: perspectives on art*, London: Routledge, pp. 238–60.

Phillips, Harlan (1963) Transcript of Interview with Ben Shahn, Archives of American Art, Smithsonian Institution.

Phillips, Lisa (ed.) (1999) *The American Century: art and culture 1950–2000*, New York: Whitney Museum of Modern Art.

Picon, Gaëtan (1978) *The Birth of Modern Painting*, New York: Rizzoli.

Pinkham Ryder, Albert (2003) 'Paragraphs from the Studio of a Recluse', in Charles Harrison and Paul Wood (eds) *Art in Theory*, Oxford: Blackwell, pp. 62–3.

Piper, Keith (2001) 'Notes on the Mechanoid's Bloodline: looking at robots, androids and cyborgs', *Art Journal* 60(3), Fall: 96–7.

Plant, Sadie (1993) 'Beyond the Screens: film, cyberpunk and cyberfeminism' *Variant* 14: 12–17.

—— (1998) *Zeros + Ones: digital women and the new technoculture*, London: Fourth Estate.

—— (1999) *Writings on Drugs*, London: Faber & Faber.

Pogglioli, Renato (1968) *The Theory of the Avant-Garde*, Cambridge, Mass.: Harvard University Press.

Pohl, Frances K. (1989) *Ben Shahn: New Deal artist in a Cold War climate, 1947–54*, Austin, Tex.: University of Texas Press.

—— (1993) *Ben Shahn, with Ben Shahn's Writings*, San Francisco, Calif.: Pomegranate Artbooks.

Pointon, Marcia (ed.) (1989) *Pre-Raphaelites Re-Viewed*, Manchester: Manchester University Press.

—— (1990) *Naked Authority: the body in Western painting*, Cambridge: Cambridge University Press.

—— (ed.) (1994) *Art Apart: art institutions and ideology across England and North America*, Manchester: Manchester University Press.

Polcari, Steven (1990) 'Martha Graham and Abstract Expressionism' *Smithsonian Studies in American Art*, Winter: 3–27.

—— (1991) *Abstract Expressionism and the Modern Experience*, Cambridge: Cambridge University Press.

—— (1997) 'Richard Pousette-Dart: towards the historical sacred', in Lowery Stokes Sims and Stephen Polcari (eds) *Richard Pousette-Dart, 1916–1992*, New York: Metropolitan Museum of Art, pp. 60–8.

Polhemus, Ted (1978) *The Social Aspects of the Human Body*, Harmondsworth: Penguin.

Pollock, Griselda (1990) *Vision and Difference: femininity, feminism and the histories of art*, London: Routledge.

Pollock, Jackson (2003a) 'Jackson Pollock (1912–1956) Answers to a Questionnaire', in Charles Harrison and Paul Wood (eds) *Art in Theory*, Oxford: Blackwell, pp. 569–70.

—— (2003b) 'Jackson Pollock (1912–1956) Two Statements', in Charles Harrison and Paul Wood (eds) *Art in Theory*, Oxford: Blackwell, pp. 570–1.

Porter, Roy (1990) *The Enlightenment: studies in European history*, Basingstoke: Macmillan.

—— (2000) *Enlightenment: Britain and the creation of the modern world*, Harmondsworth: Penguin.

Portman, Neil (1993) *Technopoly: the surrender of culture to technology*, London: Vintage Books.

Posner, Helaine and Andrew Perchuk (1995) *Masculine Masquerade: masculinity and representation*, Cambridge, Mass.: MIT List Visual Arts Center.

Postman, Neil (1993) *Technopoly: the surrender of culture to technology*, New York: Vintage Books.

Prather, Marla (1994) *Willem de Kooning Paintings*, London and New Haven, Conn.: National Gallery of Art Washington and Yale University Press.

Prinzhorn, Hans (1972) [1922] *Artistry of the Mentally Ill*, New York: Springer-Verlag.

Raney, Karen (2003) *Art in Question*, London: Continuum.

Ratcliff, Carter (1994) 'Jackson Pollock and American Painting's Whitmanesque Episode', *Art in America*, February: 64–9.

Rauschenberg, Robert (1996) [1959] 'Untitled Statement', in Kristine Stiles and Peter Selz (eds) *Theories and Documents of Contemporary Art: a sourcebook of artist's writings*, Berkeley, Calif.: University of California Press, pp. 000–00.

Rees, A.L. and Frances Borzello (eds) (1986) *The New Art History*, London: Camden Press.

Rewald, John (1973) [1946] *History of Impressionism*, 4th edn, London: Secker & Warburg.

Rian, J. (1993) 'What's All this Body Art?', *Flash Art* XXVI (168): 51–5.

Richter, Hans (1965) *Dada: art and anti-art*, London: Thames & Hudson.

Rilke, Rainer Maria (1930) *The Notebook of Malte Laurids Brigge*, London: Hogarth Press.

—— (1991) *Letters on Cézanne*, London: Vintage.

Ringbom, Sixten (1966) 'Art in "The Epoch of the Great Spiritual". Occult elements in the early theory of abstract painting, *Journal of the Warburg and Courtauld Institutes* (29): 386–418.

Ringgold, F. (1995) *We Flew Over the Bridge: the memoirs of Faith Ringgold*, Boston, Mass.: Little, Brown & Co.

Rivera, Diego (2003) [1932] 'The Revolutionary Spirit in Modern Art', in Charles Harrison and Paul Wood (eds) *Art in Theory*, Oxford: Blackwell, pp. 000–00.

Roberts, James (1992) 'Painting as Performance', *Art in America*, May: 113–19.

Rodchenko, A. and V. Stepanova (1975) [1920] 'The Programme of the Productivist Group', in Benton and Benton (eds), pp. 91–2.

Rodman, Selden (1961) *Conversations with Artists*, New York: Capricorn.

Rorimer, Anne (2004) [2001] *New Art in the 60s and 70s: redefining reality*, London: Thames & Hudson.

Rose, Barbara (1975) *American Art since 1900: a critical history*, New York: Frederick A. Praeger.

Rosenberg, Harold (1968) 'The American Action Painters', in Herschel B. Chipp (ed.) *Theories of Modern Art: a sourcebook by artists and critics*, Berkeley, Calif., and London: University of California Press, pp. 000–00.

—— (1982) [1969] *Art Works and Packages*, Chicago, Ill.: University of Chicago Press.

—— (1990) 'The American Action Painters', in David Shapiro and Cecile Shapiro (eds) *Abstract Expressionism: a critical record*, Cambridge: Cambridge University Press, pp. 75–85.

Rosler, Martha (1996) 'Video: shedding the utopian moment', in the BLOCK Editorial Board (ed.) *The Block Reader in Visual Culture*, London: Routledge, pp. 258–78.

Rubenfeld, Florence (1998) *Clement Greenberg: a life*, New York: Scribner.

Rubin, William (ed.) (1984) *Primitivism in Twentieth-Century Art*, New York: Museum of Modern Art.

Ruskin, John (1930) [1843–60] *Modern Painters*, 5 vols, London: J.M. Dent, Everyman's Library Edition.

Russolo, Luigi (1973) 'The Art of Noises (extracts)', in Umbro Apollonio (ed.) *Futurist Manifestos*, London: Thames & Hudson, pp. 74–8.

Said, Edward (1975) *Beginnings: intention and method*, New York: Basic Books.

—— (1993) *Culture and Imperialism*, London: Chatto & Windus.

—— (1995) [1978] *Orientalism: western conceptions of the orient*, Harmondsworth: Penguin.

Sandford, Mariellen (ed.) (1995) *Happenings and Other Acts*, London: Routledge.

Sandler, Irving (1970) *The Triumph of American Painting*, New York: Praeger Inc.

—— (1993) *American Art in the Twentieth Century: painting and sculpture (1913–1993)*, London: Prestel and the Royal Academy.

Sandler, Irving and Amy Newman (eds) (1986) *Defining Modern Art: selected writings of Alfred H. Barr, Jr.*, New York: Harry A. Abrams.

Saussure, Ferdinand de (1983) [1915] *Course in General Linguistics*, London: Duckworth.

Schapiro, Meyer (0000) 'American Painters Today' [[MORE DETAILS???]].

—— (1956) 'The Younger American Painters of Today', *The Listener*, BBC London, 26 January.

—— (1957) 'The Liberating Quality of Avant-Garde Art', *Art News* 56(4), Summer: 000–00.

—— (1978) *Modern Art: 19th and 20th Centuries. Selected papers*, London: George Brazillier.

—— (2003) [1936] 'On the Social Basis of Art', in Charles Harrison and Paul Wood (eds) *Art in Theory*, Oxford: Blackwell, pp. 515–20.

Schatzki, Theodore (1996) *Social Practices: a Wittgensteinian approach to human activity and the social*, Melbourne: Cambridge University Press.

Schimmel, Paul (ed.) (1998) *Out of Actions: between performance and the object*, London: Thames & Hudson.

Schlesinger, Arthur, Jnr (1962) [1949] *The Vital Center: the politics of freedom*, Boston, Mass.: Riverside Press.

Schneider, Rebecca (1997) *The Explicit Body in Performance*, London: Routledge.

Senie, Harriet F. and Sally Webster (eds) (1992) *Critical Issues in Public Art: content, context, and controversy*, New York: HarperCollins.

Serota, Nicholas, Sandy Nairne and Adam D. Weinberg (1997) *Views from Abroad: European perspectives on American art 3, American realities*, New York: Whitney Museum of American Art.

Severini, G. (1975) [1922] 'Machinery', in Benton and Benton (eds), p. 96.

Shahn, Ben (1955) *New York Times*, 10 January.

—— (1957) *The Shape of Content*, Cambridge, Mass.: Harvard University Press.

Shapiro, David and Cecile Shapiro (1985) 'Abstract Expressionism: politics of apolitical painting', in Francis Frascina (ed.) (1985), pp. 135–51.

—— (eds) (1990) *Abstract Expressionism: a critical record*, Cambridge: Cambridge University Press.

Sharp, Willoughby (1970) 'Bodyworks', *Avalanche*, Fall: 1–10.

Shaw, Jeffrey, with Dirk Groeneveld and Gideon May (1996) 'The Legible City: an interactive installation', in Kristine Stiles and Peter Selz (eds) *Theories and Documents of Contemporary Art: a sourcebook of artist's writings*, Berkeley, Calif.: University of California Press, pp. 487–9.

Sherman, Frederic Fairchild (1963) 'The Marines of Albert P. Ryder', in Jean Lipman (ed.) *What Is American in American Art?*, New York: McGraw-Hill, pp. 80–2.

Shilling, Chris (1993) *Body and Social Theory*, London: Sage.

Showalter, Elaine (1991) *Sexual Anarchy: gender and culture at the fin de siècle*, London: Bloomsbury.

Simmel, Georg (1978) [1900] *Philosophy of Money*, London: Routledge & Kegan Paul.

Sims, Lowery Stokes and Stephen Polcari (eds) (1997) *Richard Pousette-Dart, 1916–1992*, New York: Metropolitan Museum of Art.

Skipwith, Joanna (ed.) (1997) *Rhapsodies in Black: art of the Harlem Renaissance*, London: Hayward Gallery.

Smith, Alison (1996) *The Victorian Nude: sexuality, morality and art*, Manchester: Manchester University Press.

Smith, Bernard (1992) *Australian Painting 1788–1990*, Melbourne: Oxford University Press.

—— (1998) *Modernism's History: a study in twentieth-century art and ideas*, London and New Haven, Conn.: Yale University Press.

Smith, David (2003) [1952] 'Aesthetics, the Artist and the Audience', in Charles Harrison and Paul Wood (eds) *Art in Theory*, Oxford: Blackwell, pp. 586–8.

Smithson, Robert (1979) *The Writings of Robert Smithson*, ed. by Nancy Holt, New York: New York University Press.

—— (2003) 'Cultural Confinement', in Charles Harrison and Paul Wood (eds) *Art in Theory*, Oxford: Blackwell, pp. 970–1.

Solomon-Godeau, Abigail (1999) *Male Trouble: a crisis in representation*, London and New York: Thames & Hudson.

Sontag, Susan (1966) [1964] *Against Interpretation: and other essays*, New York: Dell.

—— (1987) *On Photography*, London: Allen Lane.

—— (2003) *Regarding the Pain of Others*, London: Hamish Hamilton.

Spence, Jo (1988) *Putting Myself in the Picture: a political, personal, and photographic autobiography*, Seattle, Wash.: Real Comet Press.

Stanley, Nick (1998) *Being Ourselves for You: the global display of cultures*, London: Middlesex University Press.

Stearns, Carol Z. and Peter N. Stearns (eds) (1988) *Emotion and Social Change: toward a new psychohistory*, New York: Holmes & Meier.

Stiles, Kristine and Peter Selz (eds) (1996) *Theories and Documents of Contemporary Art: a sourcebook of artist's writings*, Berkeley, Calif.: University of California Press.

Stott, William (1973) *Documentary Expression and Thirties' America*, Oxford: Oxford University Press.

Stracey, Frances (2003) 'Surviving History: a situationist archive', in Deborah Cherry and Fintan Cullen (eds) *Art History Journal of the Association of Art Historians* 26(1), February: pp. 56–77, Oxford: Blackwell Publishing.

Suleiman, Susan Rubin (ed.) (1986) *The Female Body in Western Culture: contemporary perspectives*, Cambridge, Mass.: Harvard University Press.

Sypher, Wylie (1979) *The Loss of Self in Modern Literature and Art*, Westport, Conn.: Greenwood Press.

Sztulman, Paul (1997) 'Johan Grimonprez', in Françoise Joly (ed.) *Short Guide to Documenta X*, Kassel: Cantz, pp. 80–1.

Tagg, John (1992) *Grounds of Dispute: art history, cultural politics and the discursive field*, London: Macmillan.

Tarabukin, Nikolai (1982) [1923] 'From the Easel to the Machine', in Francis Frascina and Charles Harrison (eds) *Modern Art and Modernism: a critical anthology*, London: Paul Chapman, pp. 135–42.

Taylor, Brandon (1994) 'From Penitentiary to "Temples of Art": early metaphors of improvement at the Millbank Tate', in Marcia Pointon (ed.) *Art Apart: art institutions and ideology across England and North America*, Manchester: Manchester University Press, pp. 9–32.

Thistlewood, David (ed.) (1993) *American Abstract Expressionism*, vol. 1, Liverpool: Liverpool University Press and the Tate Gallery.

Thomas, Selma and Ann Mintz (eds) (1998) *The Virtual and the Real: media in the museum*, Washington, DC: American Association of Museums.

Thomson, Rosemarie Garland (1997) *Extraordinary Bodies: figuring physical disability in American culture and literature*, Columbia, NY: Columbia University Press.

Thoreau, Henry David (1995) [1854] *Walden*, Boston, Mass.: Houghton Mifflin Co.

Tickner, Lisa (ed.) (2003) 'A Strange Alchemy: Cornelia Parker', *Art History* 26(3): 364–91.

Timms, Edward and Peter Collier (eds) (1988) *Visions and Blueprints: avant-garde culture and radical politics in early twentieth-century Europe*, Manchester: Manchester University Press.

Tomkins, Calvin (1996) *Duchamp*, London: Chatto & Windus.

Trodd, Colin (1994) 'Culture, Class, City: the National Gallery, London, and the spaces of education, 1822–57', in Marcia Pointon (ed.) *Art Apart: art institutions and ideology across England and North America*, Manchester: Manchester University Press, pp. 33–44.

Trotsky, Leon (1970) [1923] *Leon Trotsky on Literature and Art*, ed. by P.N. Siegel, New York: Pathfinder Press.

Tucker, William (1974) *The Language of Sculpture*, London: Thames & Hudson.

Turkle, Sherry (1995) *Life on the Screen: identity in the age of the Internet*, London: Weidenfeld & Nicolson.

Turner, Bryan S. (1996) *The Body and Society*, 2nd edn, London: Sage.

Turner, Frederick J. (1893) *The Significance of the Frontier in American History*, New York: Irvington Publishers.

van Doesburg, Theo (1975) [1922] 'The Will to Style', in Tim Benton and Charlotte Benton, with Dennis Sharp *Form and Function: a source book for the history of architecture and design 1890–1939*, Milton Keynes: Open University Press, pp. 92–4.

Veblen, Thorstein (1921) *The Engineers and the Price System*, New York: B.W. Huebsch.

—— (1988) *The Theory of the Leisure Class: an economic study in the evolution of institutions*, New York: Macmillan.

Vergo, Peter (ed.) (1989) *The New Museology*, London: Reaktion.

Virilio, Paul (1995) *The Art of the Motor*, Minneapolis, Minn.: Minnesota University Press.

—— (1997) *Open Sky*, London and New York: Verso.

Walters, Margaret (1978) *The Male Nude: a new perspective*, London: Paddington Press.

Warner, Marina (1985) *Monuments and Maidens: the allegory of the female form*, London: Picador.

Waterfield, Giles (ed.) (1991) *Palaces of Art: art galleries in Britain 1790–1990*, London: Dulwich Picture Gallery.

Watson, Peter (1992) *From Manet to Manhattan: the rise of the modern art market*, London: Hutchinson.

Weber, Max (1910) 'The Fourth Dimension from a Plastic Point of View', *Camera Work* (31), July: 25.

Weiermair, Peter (1996) *Prospect Photography and Contemporary Art*, Frankfurt, Kilchberg and Zurich: Edition Stemmle.

Wells, Liz (ed.) (2002) *Photography: a critical introduction*, London: Routledge.

Wheale, Nigel (ed.) (1995) *The Postmodern Arts*, London: Routledge.

Whistler, James Abbott McNeill (1890) *The Gentle Art of Making Enemies*, London: William Heinemann.

Whitman, Walt (1986) *The Complete Poems*, Harmondsworth: Penguin.

Willet, John (1987) *The New Sobriety: art and politics in the Weimar period, 1917–33*, London: Thames & Hudson.

Williams, Raymond (1958) *Culture and Society: 1780–1950*, New York: Harper & Row.

—— (1979) *Television: technology and cultural form*, Glasgow: Fontana.

—— (1981) *Culture*, London: Fontana.

—— (1988) *Keywords*, Harmondsworth: Penguin.

—— (1989a) *The Politics of Modernism*, London: Verso.

—— (1989b) 'When was Modernism?', in Raymond Williams *The Politics of Modernism*, London: Verso, pp. 31–5.

Williamson, Judith (1996) 'Baudrillard Interview', in the BLOCK Editorial Board (ed.) *The Block Reader in Visual Culture*, London: Routledge, pp. 306–13.

Wilson, Martha (ed.) (1997) 'Performance Art: (some) theory and (selected) practice at the end of this century', *Art Journal* 56 (4): 2–83.

Witcomb, Andrea (2003) *Re-Imagining the Museum: beyond the mausoleum*, London: Routledge.

Wittgenstein, Ludwig (1980) *Culture and Value*, Oxford: Oxford University Press.

Wodiczko, Krzysztof (1996) [1986] 'Memorial Projection', in Kristine Stiles and Peter Selz (eds) *Theories and Documents of Contemporary Art: a sourcebook of artist's writings*, Berkeley, Calif.: University of California Press, pp. 424–7.

Wolfe, Tom (1967) *The Electric Kool-Aid Acid Test*, New York: Farrar, Straus & Giroux.

Wood, Paul (2002) *Conceptual Art: movements in modern art*, London: Tate Publishing.

Wood, Paul, Francis Frascina, Jonathan Harris and Charles Harrison (1993) *Modernism in Dispute: art since the forties*, Milton Keynes and New Haven, Conn.: the Open University and Yale University Press.

Worringer, Wilhelm (1963) [1908] *Abstraction and Empathy*, London: Routledge & Kegan Paul.

Young, James (1993) *The Texture of Memory: Holocaust memorials and meaning*, New Haven, Conn.: Yale University Press.

Zylinska, Joanna (ed.) (2002) *The Cyborg Experiments: the extensions of the body in the media age*, London: Continuum Press.

Index

Note: Page references in *italics* refer to figures.